D0906080

AUBURN, F.M. Antarctic law and politics. Indiana, 1982. 361p maps bibl index 81-48081. 32.50 ISBN 0-253-30749-X. CIP
The most comprehensive, contemporary source on the subject. Given the quality of the research as well as readability and style, this book should be considered the standard work. The author, an Australian law professor, has written extensively on the ice-covered continent. His discussion covers the international law of sovereignty and how it relates to the various national sector claims by exploring states in the Antarctic. A thorough examination of the 1959 Antarctic treaty (which is appended) beginning with its diplomatic origins in 1939 is provided. The treaty is further analyzed article by article. Auburn also covers jurisdictional problems of crime, offering no firm solutions, however; torts, relying heavily on the language of the treaty; property rights and standards. Ecological questions dealing with the preservation of the Antarctic krill, the location and availability of oil and gas resources and basis of exploration, and even various aspects of tourism are adequately covered. The collection of legal documents appended and the solid bibliography offer the researcher a real assist. The choice for a reference work on the topic. Recommended for four-year college and university libraries.

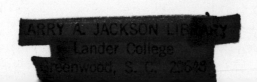

ANTARCTIC LAW AND POLITICS

F.M. AUBURN

ANTARCTIC
LAW AND
POLITICS

Indiana University Press
Bloomington

Manufactured in Great Britain

Library of Congress Cataloging in Publication Data

Auburn, F. M.
 Antarctic law and politics.

 Bibliography: p.
 Includes index.
 1. Antarctic regions—International status. I. Title.
JX4084.A5A89   341.2′9′09989   81-48081
ISBN 0-253-30749-X   AACR2
1 2 3 4 5 86 85 84 83 82

To Susie Auburn

PREFACE

With the advent of the first major Antarctic resource regime in 1980 and the ongoing negotiation of the second, it is time for a re-assessment of the Antarctic system. This study examines the framework of the Antarctic club of nations, stressing current issues. So the analysis of the provisions of the Treaty is intended to bring out matters which have concerned the Antarctic system in practice or may do so in the future. Discussion of national interests places emphasis on the South American sector, where sovereignty issues continue to be publicly displayed; the vigorous expansion of the Soviet programme; and a contrast with the efforts of the United States.

Until 1973 Antarctic politics could be seen in the static terms of scientific research and Article IV of the Antarctic Treaty, freezing claims. Since then the Treaty system has been under pressure from a number of issues. So far, the Consultative Parties have succeeded in retaining their monopoly of decision-making. Whether the organisation devised for regulating international scientific research can deal with resources in practice remains to be seen. The major challenges to the Antarctic system are yet to come. This review of its working during the first twenty years of the system will serve to suggest the extent to which it may succeed in dealing with resource and other contentious issues.

Now that the continent is becoming open to the influences of conventional problems, one faces the question of what topics are to be included in a general review of Antarctic affairs. Two matters have not been dealt with in detail. The first of these, the exploitation of icebergs for fresh water, is at present very far from practical realisation. There is no agreement as to the technology to be adopted. No one has yet towed even a small iceberg from Antarctic waters to the nearest potential customers in Australia. Until there is a clearer indication of how, when and where icebergs are to be exploited, it is somewhat premature to enter into a detailed discussion of the political and legal implications. Secondly, several proposals have been made for the long-term storage of high-level radioactive wastes in the Antarctic ice-sheet. Apart from requiring an amendment to the Treaty, the Consultative Parties affirmed their opposition to the concept by Recommendation VIII-12 in 1975, and there is no indication that officials of any government are prepared to undertake the preliminary research necessary to examine the scientific feasibility of the project.

At a late stage in the writing of this work, two significant events took place which could only be briefly mentioned. First, the establishment of the Georg von Neumayer station by West Germany in February 1981, together with the admission of that country to Consultative status, raises again several issues which have been discussed in relation to Poland. And secondly, the publication in April 1981 of the Royal Commission Report on the Air New Zealand DC-10 crash on Mount Erebus has given rise to considerable discussion. A full assessment must await the outcome of the claims.

Special thanks go to the Center for Polar and Scientific Archives and the Cold Regions Bibliography Project of the Library of Congress, the Division of Polar Programs of the National Science Foundation, the Polar Research Board of the National Academy of Sciences, and the Rockefeller Foundation. Pages 147–153 originated in an article in (1979) 28 *I.C.L.Q.* 514–22 and pages 270–7 are from 1981 *Y.B.W.A.* 252–62. These are reproduced by kind permission of the British Institute of International and Comparative Law and the *Year Book of World Affairs* respectively.

August 1981   F.M. AUBURN

CONTENTS

MAPS

ACRONYMS

ACMRR	Advisory Committee on Marine Resources Research
AJIL	*American Journal of International Law*
BIOMASS	Biological Investigations of Marine Antarctic Systems and Stocks
BYBIL	*British Yearbook of International Law*
CSAGI	Comité Spécial de l'Année Géophysique Internationale
DSDP	Deep Sea Drilling Programme
DSIR	Department of Scientific and Industrial Research (NZ)
DVDP	Dry Valley Drilling Project
EAMREA	Group of Specialists on Environmental Impact Assessment of Mineral Resource Exploration and Exploitation in the Antarctic
EEZ	Exclusive Economic Zone
FAO	Food and Agriculture Organization
ICSU	International Council of Scientific Unions
IGC	International Geophysical Co-operation
IGY	International Geophysical Year
IOC	Intergovernmental Oceanographic Commission
ISAS	International Survey of Antarctic Seabirds
IUCN	International Union for the Conservation of Nature and Natural Resources
IWC	International Whaling Commission
NEPA	National Environmental Policy Act (USA)
NIEO	New International Economic Order
NSF	National Science Foundation (USA)
NZLJ	*New Zealand Law Journal*
Rec.	Recommendation
RGDIP	*Revue Générale de Droit International Public*
RISP	Ross Ice Shelf Project
SCAR	Scientific Committee on Antarctic Research
SCOR	Special Committee on Oceanic Research
SPA	Specially Protected Area
SSSI	Site of Special Scientific Interest
TAE	Trans-Antarctic Expedition
UGO	Unmanned Geophysical Observatory
UNEP	United Nations Environment Programme
WMO	World Meteorological Organization

MAPS

Antarctica: geographical features

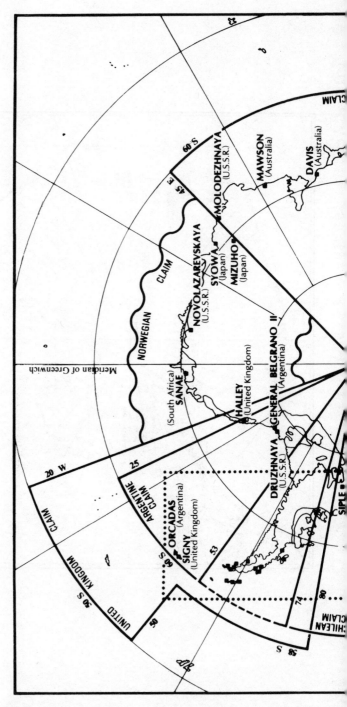

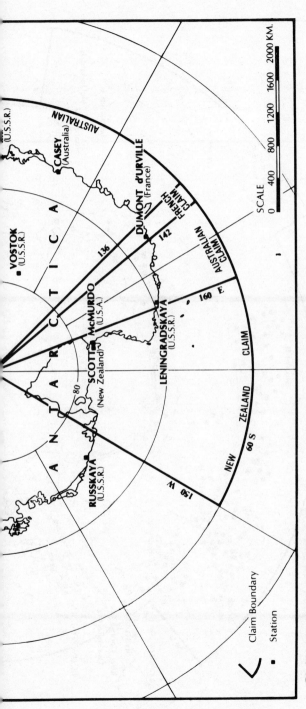

CLAIMS AND STATIONS

xvii

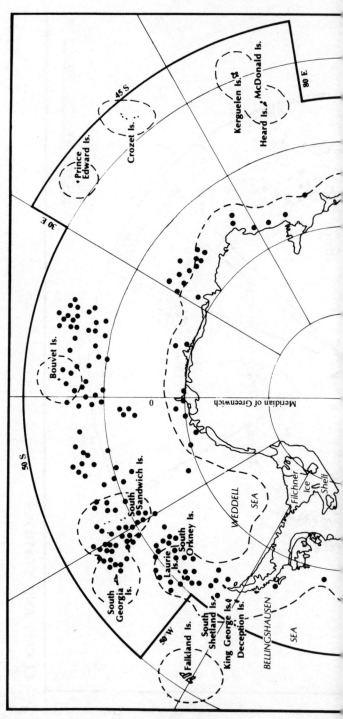

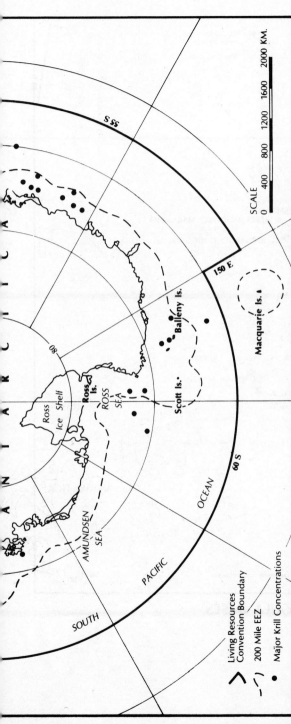

KRILL AND THE 200 MILE EXCLUSIVE ECONOMIC ZONE

Living Resources
Convention Boundary

200 Mile EEZ

• Major Krill Concentrations

SCALE

0   400   800   1200   1600   2000 KM.

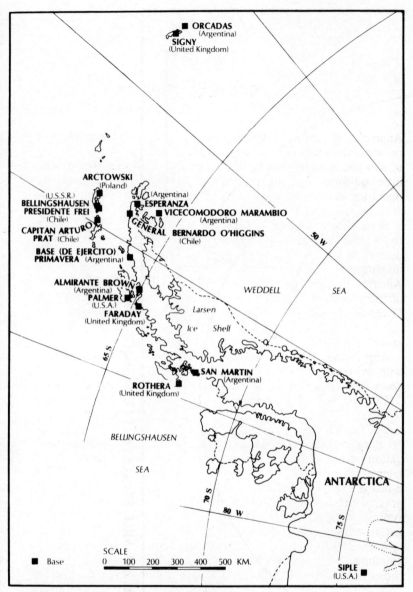

ANTARCTIC PENINSULA BASES

1
INTRODUCTION

Antarctica is unique, an entire continent of disputed territory. For twenty years activities in the area have been directed by a small group of nations, including the United States and the Soviet Union, with little outward sign of dissension. Peaceful international co-operation has continued despite the Cold War, the Cuban missile crisis and the invasion of Afghanistan.

Geography and climate have been determining factors in setting the course of Antarctic politics. Isolation from inhabited areas delayed man's exploration of the Antarctic and continue to place limitations on work there. Although the nearest continent, South America, is 1,000 km. from Antarctica, a more useful indication of distance is from major bases there to population centres. From Deception Island, off the Antarctic Peninsula, to Buenos Aires is 3,000 km.[1] McMurdo, the largest United States base, is a similar distance from Christchurch.

Approximately 95 per cent of Antarctica is covered by an ice-sheet with an average thickness of more than one mile.[2] Parts of the sheet cover the adjacent sea. The Ross Ice Shelf, with an area of at least 325,000 sq. km., is hundreds of metres thick.[3] Such shelves give rise to extremely large icebergs. Antarctic ice is composed of pure fresh water. Smaller icebergs may, in the future, be towed to arid regions for domestic and irrigation uses.[4] At present they constitute a navigation hazard and one of the major obstacles to any future petroleum exploitation offshore. In winter the continent is surrounded by a belt of sea-ice 1−3 metres thick and up to 19,000,000 sq. km in area, which is reduced to a minimum of 2,600,000 sq. km in summer.[5] Even then, icebreakers may be required to assist navigation or to rescue conventional vessels.

Antarctica has the highest average elevation of all the continents.[6] Combined with a number of other factors, such as the degree of radiation reflection from snow surfaces,[7] this makes it the coldest

1. N. Potter, *Natural Resource Potentials of the Antarctic* (1969), 5.
2. Central Office of Information, *The Antarctic* (1966), 2.
3. F.M. Auburn, *The Ross Dependency* (1972), 45.
4. A.A. Husseiny, *Iceberg Utilization* (1978).
5. Central Intelligence Agency, *Polar Regions Atlas* (1979), 38.
6. 2.5 km. (Tetra Tech, *The Antarctic Krill Resource: Prospects for Commercial Exploitation* (1978), 7).
7. J.F. Lovering and J.R.V. Prescott, *Last of Lands . . . Antarctica* (1979), 8.

region on earth. The mean temperature of the plateau of East Antarctica is − 56°C.[8] Temperatures in coastal areas are less severe, although the most favoured regions of the Antarctic Peninsula only have mean summer readings above freezing for four months.[9] Steady winds of over 100 km. per hour are not uncommon in winter.[10] Most of Antarctica − the high plateau − is the world's largest and driest desert. At the South Pole, there is precipitation (usually snow) of less than 5 cm. each year,[11] and Antarctica's only river, the Onyx, flows in summer from the melt waters of the Wright Glacier in the Ross Dependency over a course of 30 km.[12] There are no land vertebrates. It is the sole continent without trees, and all its three flowering plants are recent and marginal invaders.[13] In contrast to the land, the Southern Ocean supports large populations of a small number of species which are to a large degree dependent upon krill, a crustacean averaging 5 centimetres in length.

This distant continent, uninhabited and with few apparent resources, was the last to be discovered and explored. Cook first circumnavigated Antarctica in 1773−4. His reports attracted British and American sealers to South Georgia. By 1820 they had reached the South Shetlands. First sighting of the mainland was reported in 1820: this honour has been claimed for a Russian (Bellingshausen), an American (Palmer) and a Briton (Bransfield). In 1840 and 1841 three major discoveries were made: Wilkes (United States) found the coast which bears his name, Dumont d'Urville of France saw and claimed the Adélie coast, and Ross of Britain reached the Ice Shelf named after him and laid claim to that area.

From 1893 onwards a series of expeditions carried out the next stage of exploration. One motive was a search for new whaling areas following the depletion of the Arctic. Another was scientific research. Finally the British initiated action to support national claims. Borchgrevink's expedition of 1899 was the first to spend a winter on the continent. The South Pole was reached by Amundsen of Norway in 1911 and Scott of Britain in 1912. Whaling began from shore stations in the South American sector, and this led to the first public claim in 1908, by Great Britain. Norwegian whaling in the Ross Sea area after the First World War brought another sector claim in 1923. This territory became New Zealand's Ross Dependency. In the following year France proclaimed its sovereignty over a

8. Tetra Tech, *The Antarctic Krill Resource: Prospects for Commercial Exploitation* (1978), 9.
9. Central Intelligence Agency, *Polar Regions Atlas* (1979), 37.
10. G.A. Bertrand, 'Antarctica' (1978), 43(1) *Frontiers*, 9.
11. U.S. Naval Support Force, Antarctica, *Introduction to Antarctica* (1967), 3.
12. 'Warm weather aids Onyx River flow' (1980), 9(2), *Antarctic* 49.
13. G.A. Llano, *The Terrestrial Life of the Antarctic* (1962), 3.

sector based on Dumont's discovery. At the Imperial Conference of 1926 it was agreed that most of the then unclaimed portions of the continent belonged to the Empire by right of discovery. Norwegian pelagic whaling began in the Ross Sea, without need for a British licence, and this was coupled with exploration along the coast of Wilkes Land and beyond. In 1929 the first Byrd expedition to the Ross Sea brought the possibility of an American claim. Four years later the huge Australian Antarctic Territory was proclaimed.

A desire to protect its whaling industry, the precedent of the claims for the British Empire, and the spectre of a German territory arising from the German Neu Schwabenland expedition of 1938, convinced Norway of the need to establish its Antarctic territory in 1939. An official US expedition led by Byrd in that year was accompanied by secret assurances to the South American Republics that their common interests would be preserved. The effect was contrary to the purpose of the United States. Chile published its Antarctic territorial limits in 1941 and Argentina expressed renewed concern. During the Second World War British stations were built in the Antarctic Peninsula area, followed by those of the two South American countries. Increasing rivalry and United States attempts in 1948 to discuss a condominium or trusteeship brought a Soviet declaration in 1949 that no settlement could be reached without its participation.

By this time Antarctic expeditions had begun to change completely. Technological developments set in train a process which now makes large-scale research programmes the main focus of activity. Modern communications enable almost continuous contact between bases and the outside world. Inland stations can be entirely supported by air. Ski-equipped Lockheed Hercules planes can transport small stations across the continent.[14] Several nations operate icebreakers during the Antarctic summer to permit clear passage for conventional shipping. Land transport relies on specially adapted tracked vehicles.

The current logistic effort is a response to the decision of countries after 1959 to maintain permanent stations, together with substantial scientific research programmes. Their expense has ensured that activities have to be based on government funding. To take a few examples, the US icebreaker *Polar Star* cost $53,000,000 and the Argentinian icebreaker *Almirante Irizar* $65,000,000. For the budget year 1980 the National Science Foundation planned to spend $55,000,000 on Antarctic research and support. Accidents can cost millions of dollars. In one season, 1964–5, the United States had seven air crashes including two total losses.[15]

14. US Naval Support Force, Antarctica, *Support for Science: Antarctica* (1968), 3.
15. *Report of Operation Deep Freeze 1965*, 39.

Even governments have been affected by the expense of Antarctic operations: in 1961 Belgium closed its station for this reason. American studies to evaluate a possible solid rock air facility near McMurdo put the cost at over $100,000,000 and the much-needed project had to be shelved. Financial considerations have also been a factor in encouraging the numerous research programmes involving international co-operation such as the Ross Ice Shelf and Dry Valley Drilling Projects.

Scientific research remains the predominant human activity on the continent. From July 1957 to December 1958, twelve nations manned bases in the Antarctic as part of the International Geophysical Year. When the Soviet Union indicated that its research would continue, other countries felt impelled to take the same course. The Antarctic Treaty was therefore a maintenance of the pre-existing state of affairs. Stations became permanent. Scientific research was the only useful manifestation of interests on the continent, and its support was perpetuated by governments for reasons of sovereignty and politics. Antarctic decision-making was reached by the original twelve signatories to the Treaty at regular Consultative Meetings.

The Treaty was predicated upon the *status quo*. It did not provide a solution for the conflicting claims. As long as politicians saw Antarctica essentially as an area devoted to fundamental research, such an *ad hoc* arrangement could continue without major dissension. But within the last decade, issues not covered by the Treaty have required solution. In 1972 the Convention on the Conservation of Antarctic Seals was prepared to regulate seal harvesting. Although an industry did not develop, this agreement can be seen as an initial attempt to deal with offshore resources.

Discussion of a minerals regime by the Consultative Parties was initiated in 1969, and after the oil crisis of 1973 this issue was taken up with more vigour. Offshore oil and gas are seen as the most likely resource to be exploited under such an agreement over a time-scale of twenty years. While these negotiations went on, priority was assumed by the need to provide for growing interest in harvesting krill which is the staple food of whales and could become the world's largest fishery stock. In May 1980 the Convention for the Conservation of Antarctic Marine Living Resources was signed. This agreement, drafted by the Consultative Parties, establishes a Commission to provide conservation and regulation measures for krill and other marine resources of the Southern Ocean. Having settled a regime for krill, negotiation of the outstanding issue of a minerals regime should now proceed.

2
SOVEREIGNTY

Issues

Rules in international law for the acquisition of sovereignty over unclaimed territory were formed in the nineteenth century. They reflect the requirements and power structure of that period. The traditional test is cited in Article 35 of the Final Act of the Conference of Berlin in 1885,[1] which required establishment of authority by European powers on the coasts of Africa. This was demonstrated by the control of population. It is hardly adaptable to the vast uninhabited regions of the Antarctic continent. Material on boundary disputes will be used as an aid to the discussion of sovereignty. Theoretically one should differentiate between the existence of sovereignty and its extent but such a distinction has not been adhered to in practice.

Requirements for the establishment of sovereignty must depend on the nature of the territory concerned. Less will be required for a remote, uninhabited and inaccessible portion of the globe[2] than for a populated area in relative proximity to the claimant state. Stress is placed on actual effective control.[3] Much depends on the creation of facts.

Provided that another State cannot make out a superior claim, tribunals have often been satisfied with very little in the way of the actual exercise of sovereign rights.[4] Experience shows that a decision between two competing claims is frequently enough to establish title.[5] Even if the claim is not good, it may be 'better'.[6] This tendency is reinforced by agreements requiring a decision as between two claimants.[7] Therefore arguments which appear to have little merit in general international law require consideration. If both parties to a dispute rely on the same dubious doctrine, neither will dispute its

---

1. (1909) 3 *AJIL*, Supp. 7 at 24.
2. *Legal Status of Eastern Greenland* 1933 PCIJ Ser. A/B No. 53: 22 at 50–51.
3. R.Y. Jennings, *The Acquisition of Territory in International Law* (1963), 4.
4. *Legal Status of Eastern Greenland* 1933 PCIJ Ser. A/B No. 53, 22 at 46.
5. R.Y. Jennings, *The Acquisition of Territory in International Law* (1963), 5.
6. I.L. Head, 'Canadian Claims to Territorial Sovereignty in the Arctic Region' (1963), 9 *McGill LJ*, 200 at 217.
7. Evidence of the will of the parties that the proceedings should not be concluded by a non liquet (*Island of Palmas Case* (1928) 2 UNRIAA, 829 at 869). See further F.M. Auburn, *The Ross Dependency* (1972), 13–14.

general validity. Claims which are not absolute may have relative
validity.[8]

Claimants frequently invoke contradictory doctrines to support
their title,[9] e.g. discovery and effective occupation; sectors and
contiguity. More is demanded of a competitor than of oneself,[10] and
claimants may use arguments which are not permitted to others.
Antarctic claims are most difficult to resolve at customary international law. A further complication is the impact of the freezing of
rights by the Antarctic Treaty.

Discussion of sovereignty and national interests will be divided
into three parts. The first will examine the arguments put forward in
support of Antarctic rights and claims. In the second (see Chapter 3)
the position of particular States will be reviewed. Finally the effect of
Article IV on claims will be discussed in Chapter 4 (pp. 104ff.).

Discovery

Acts of discovery provide a major legal argument for Antarctic
claimants – except in the case of Argentina and Chile – and for
those countries (the United States and the Soviet Union) which
reserve a right to make claims in the future. This view exists despite
well-known statements that discovery alone cannot give
sovereignty,[11] even if there is an intent to occupy eventually.[12] Title
must be consummated by possession.[13]

Where reliance is placed on discovery, it is usually argued that title
accrued before a formal claim was made public. The United Kingdom asserted that Letters Patent of 1908 and 1917 formally confirmed its rights. But the British title did not originate with or depend
on these documents for it had been in existence many decades previously.[14] The purpose of this assertion is to support the inference
that competing acts of other States are deprived of legal validity
because they took place after Britain's rights had been confirmed by
law.[15] For the lawyer this advantage is at least balanced out by a

8. G. Battaglini, *La Condizione dell'Antartide nel Diritto Internazionale* (1971), 59.
9. J.-F. de Costa, 'Le problème de le souveraineté sur les régions antarctiques', thesis, University of Paris (1948), 127.
10. G. Smedal, *Acquisition of Sovereignty over Polar Regions* (1931), 12.
11. *Island of Palmas Case* (1928), 2 UNRIAA, 829 at 846.
12. R.Y. Jennings, *The Acquisition of Territory in International Law* (1963) 4.
13. Marshall C.J. in *Johnson* v. *M'Intosh* (1823), 8. Wheaton, 543 at 573.
14. Application instituting Proceedings, *Antarctica Case* (*UK* v. *Argentina*) (1955), 16.
15. The critical date argument (see National Interests/*South America*).

concomitant disadvantage: it is extremely difficult to argue that the British claim to what later became the Falkland Islands Dependencies was based on any other ground than discovery if the relevant date is taken to be many decades before 1908.

Similar conclusions apply to the other British Commonwealth territories in the Antarctic. In 1922 the Colonial Office held:[16]

The British claim to [the Ross Dependency] rests on discovery . . . the territories being at the time of discovery, and now, wholly uninhabited and never having been at any time inhabited except for a few months by scientific expeditions.

At the Imperial Conference of 1926, British title by virtue of discovery was asserted over the whole of what now constitutes the Australian Antarctic Territory.[17] When France annexed Adélie Land in 1924, its sovereignty could only be attributed to discovery by Dumont d'Urville in 1840.[18] Exclusion of the French territory from the Australian sectors in 1933 was an implicit acknowledgment of title by right of discovery.[19] Queen Maud Land was proclaimed by Norway in 1939 on the basis of discovery.[20] The United States and Soviet Union do not recognise existing claims and reserve their own rights. For the Soviet Union this means reliance on the discoveries of Bellingshausen and Lazarev in 1820.[21]

United States official policy held that discovery does not support a valid claim unless followed by actual settlement.[22] But that country's rights include assertions based on discoveries 'commencing in the early eighteen-hundreds'.[23] Government instructions to expeditions in 1939 and subsequently specifically referred to the dropping of written claims from aeroplanes and depositing such writing in cairns.[24] It may be accepted that the rights of both countries are in good part based on discovery.

There are a number of practical reasons for the rejection of dis-

16. D.P. O'Connell and A. Riordan (eds.), *Opinions on Imperial Constitutional Law* (1971), 311.
17. Summary of Proceedings, Cmnd. 2768 (1926), 33–4.
18. La Documentation Française, *L'Antarctide et les problèmes soulevés par son occupation* (28 March 1949), 6.
19. S.O. Butler, 'Owning Antarctica' (1977), 31(1) *Journal of International Affairs*, 35 at 40.
20. J.C. Puig, *La Antártida Argentina ante el Derecho* (1960), 44.
21. Note to USA (2 June 1958), M.M. Whiteman, *Digest of International Law*, Vol. 2. (1963), 1254–5.
22. Secretary of State Hughes (13 May 1924), G.H. Hackworth, *Digest of International Law*, Vol. I (1940), 399.
23. Mr. Phleger in Department of State, *The Conference on Antarctica* (1960) 3.
24. President Roosevelt's order to Admiral Byrd (25 November 1939), K.J. Bertrand, *Americans in Antarctica 1715–1948* (1971), 473.

covery as a root of title. It is notoriously difficult to decide who made particular discoveries. Mountains found by an Argentinian flight in 1955 were 'discovered' by the United States in 1956 and the United Kingdom in 1957.[25] Soviet writers insist that Bellingshausen discovered the Antarctic continent[26] but their view is contested.[27] Partisan controversy has arisen as to whether the American Palmer or the Briton Bransfield first sighted the Antarctic mainland.[28] Such arguments obviously have a bearing on current claims and asserted rights. Discoveries made by nationals of other countries have been claimed, even though it is a contradiction to speak of a second discovery.[29] A quest for first discoverers is self-defeating, Maori legend suggests that an Antarctic voyage was made by Ui-te-Rangiora.[30] Hunters decimated seal colonies very rapidly[31] and were reluctant to inform others of their discoveries.[32] Early sightings in Antarctica are often doubtful because of weather conditions. Dark shadows of icebergs give the illusion of land, and clouds have been described as islands; even Antarctic veterans have made such errors.[33] Reports of islands which could not be found later were not unusual, leading to governments granting concessions over non-existent areas.[34]

Multinational expeditions have been common in Antarctica.[35] Five different countries were represented on the *Belgica* expedition of 1898. In 1899 Borchgrevink, a Norwegian living in Australia, led a British team consisting predominantly of Norwegian nationals.[36] Norwegians were frequently sought after for expeditions of other countries[37] due to their practical experience of Arctic operations.

A particularly questionable practice in the Antarctic has been the

25. F. Ronne, *Antarctic Command* (1961), 31.
26. K.K. Markov, V.I. Bardin, V.L. Lebedev, A.I. Orlov I.A. Suetova, *The Geography of Antarctica* (1970), 10.
27. T. Armstrong, 'Bellingshausen and the Discovery of Antarctica' (1971), 15(99) *Polar Record*, 887 at 889.
28. J.F. Lovering and J.R.V. Prescott, *Last of Lands . . . Antarctica* (1979), 115.
29. M.F. Lindley, *The Acquisition and Government of Backward Territory in International Law* (1926), 135.
30. L.B. Quartermain, *South to the Pole* (1967), 6.
31. For instance, a quarter of a million seals were taken in the South Shetlands in 1820–1: W.N. Bonner, *The Fur Seal of South Georgia* (1968) 21.
32. B. Roberts, 'Chronological list of Antarctic Expeditions' (1958), 9(59) *Polar Record*, 97 at 102.
33. G.J. Dufek, *Operation Deepfreeze* (1957), 137.
34. F.M. Auburn, *The Ross Dependency* (1972), 17.
35. K.J. Bertrand in G.S. Schatz (ed.), *Science, Technology and Sovereignty in the Polar Regions* (1974), 17.
36. H. Bogen, 'Main Events in the History of Antarctic exploration' (1957), *Norsk Hvalfangst Tidende*, 218.
37. For instance, W. Sullivan, *Quest for a Continent* (1957), 81 (7 Norwegians with Byrd in 1928).

making of claims extending to the South Pole on the basis of off-shore expeditions (France)[38] or coastal ones (Australia). Dropping claims notices from aeroplanes had also led to very large assertions of sovereignty: in 1939 Ellsworth deposited over the American Highlands a claim made 'so far as this act allows'.[39] In many cases even this limitation on aerial discovery was omitted.[40]

Discovery may be relied upon as giving an inchoate title if completed by effective occupation within a reasonable period.[41] 'Reasonable' may be defined in view of all the circumstances,[42] but there is no agreement as to a precise figure. Writers have suggested twenty, twenty-five, thirty or forty years. If the inchoate title test is to be recognised after longer periods, the dormant ashes of alleged discoveries might be raked up at any time.[43] Swifter and modern means of transport should reduce the period permitted. It would seem logical to agree that one hundred years is too much to allow,[44] and a lapse of seventy or eighty years, even in the nineteenth century, may be queried.[45] Time runs from the date of discovery to that of effective occupation. Governmental proclamation of sovereignty is not decisive. In a number of instances (France, New Zealand, the Soviet Union, the United States) the period is over one hundred years, and the relevant discoveries do not comply with an objective international law standard.

As a source of title, discovery is contrary to the accepted rules and raises severe logical difficulties. No claimant today relies on this root of title alone, but seven States (the United States and the Soviet Union among them) utilise discovery. Only two, Norway and Australia, can point to a period – approximately twenty-five years – which is arguably reasonable.

Symbolic Annexation

When novelists write about exploration and the appropriation of territory, much is made of various forms of colourful ceremonial. So

38. (D. Schenk, *Kontiguität als Erwerbstitel im Völkerrecht* (1978) 50).
39. Department of Foreign Affairs (Australia), *Documents relating to Antarctica* (1976), XIV, 1.
40. Acting Secretary of State (14 December 1946), M.M. Whiteman, *Digest of International Law*, Vol. 2 (1963), 1249.
41. *Island of Palmas Case* (1928) 2 UNRIAA, 829 at 846.
42. J.B. Scott, 'Arctic Exploration and International Law' (1909), 3 *AJIL*, 928 at 939.
43. T. Twiss, *The Oregon Question Examined* (1846), 167.
44. K. Taijudo, 'Japan and the Problems of Sovereignty over the Polar Regions' (1959), 3 *Japanese Annual of International Law*, 12 at 13.
45. J.C. Puig, *La Antártida Argentina ante el Derecho* (1960), 191.

after Vincent of Mountjoy reached the Moon and claimed it for the Duchy of Grand Fenwick he was told: 'Our claim is quite firm, I think. We were there first and raised our flag first and the whole world was informed that we had arrived before the others'.[46] International lawyers have often regarded such symbolic acts as adding nothing to the inchoate title raised by discovery.[47] But the novelist's interest in these matters has a very lengthy pedigree and can be justified by numerous actual examples,[48] including the practice of both Great Britain and the United States.[49]

Doctrinal support may be found in the *Clipperton Island Case*.[50] In 1858 a naval officer on board a ship half a mile offshore acting under government instructions proclaimed French sovereignty over the island. The act, coupled with notice to the Hawaiian Government and publication in a local newspaper, was held to suffice. One can argue that this is a special case of the adaptation of the effective occupation test to a small, isolated and uninhabited Pacific atoll. But whatever explanations may be advanced, the decision falls well within the meaning of symbolic annexation. That case is not alone in regarding symbols such as flags and coats of arms as 'external signs of sovereignty'.[51] There are a number of instances of such acts in relation to Pacific islands carried out by Britain and the United States in the late nineteenth and twentieth centuries.[52]

Arctic explorers have consistently made symbolic claims. Flags were raised, crosses or cairns erected, proclamations read and records deposited.[53] Some claims covered very large areas. On 1 July 1909 at Winter Harbour, Melville Island, Captain Bernier took possession for Canada of the 'whole Arctic Archipelago between 60°W and 141°W'.[54]

Claimants to Antarctic rights invoking discovery also rely on actions of this type. Instructions from the Prime Minister of Australia to Mawson, leader of the BANZARE Expedition of 1929–31, required the planting of the British flag, where practicable, reading a proclamation of annexation, attaching two copies of the proclama-

46. L. Wibberley, *The Mouse on the Moon* (1962), 186.
47. O. Svarlien, *The Eastern Greenland Case in Historical Perspective* (1964), 56.
48. A.S. Keller, O.J. Lissitzyn and F.J. Mann, *Creation of Rights of Sovereignty through Symbolic Acts 1400–1800* (1938), passim.
49. N. Hill, *Claims to Territory in International Law and Relations* (1945), 151.
50. (1932) 2 UNRIAA 1105.
51. *Island of Palmas Case* (1928) 2 UNRIAA, 829 at 870.
52. B. Orent and P. Reinsch, 'Sovereignty over Islands in the Pacific' (1941), 35 AJIL, 443 at 450.
53. G.W. Smith in R. St.J. MacDonald (ed.), *The Arctic Frontier* (1966) 197.
54. J. Bernier, *Report on the Dominion of Canada Government Expedition to the Arctic Islands and Hudson Strait* (1910) 195.

tion to the flagstaff and the recording of the act.[55] Acheson's instructions in 1946 specifically referred to 'symbolic claims' on behalf of the United States.[56] These are only two examples of many.

It may well be said that these acts affirm the inability to pass from fiction to reality.[57] Symbolic annexation is essentially discovery coupled with a manifestation of intent to claim. It is backed by a considerable body of practice. At least insofar as it is linked with an inchoate title, some measure of validity should be attributed to these ceremonial acts.

Effective Occupation

In the nineteenth century the penetration of competing powers in Africa and North America supported the adoption of a test more stringent than that of discovery and symbolic annexation. A rapid increase in population on the Northwest coast of America led to the theory that actual occupation should be required for the acquisition of territory.[58] Occupation and settlement, more or less permanent, under sanction of a State was required.[59] Possession must be actual, continuous and useful.[60]

Authority for the international law test is frequently taken from Article 35, Chapter VI, of the Act of Berlin which concerned the Congo.[61] In the territories occupied by them upon the coasts of the African continent, signatories recognised the obligation to assure the existence of an authority sufficient for acquired rights to be respected and, in the case occurring, the liberty of commerce and of transit.[62] Objections have been taken to the general adoption of this provision in customary international law. The Congo was occupied by native tribes and not considered *res nullius*.[63] In its terms Chapter VI referred to new occupations and only applied to future instances.[64] In express words it only affected the coasts of Africa,

55. A. Grenfell Price, *The Winning of Australian Antarctica, Mawson's BANZARE Voyages 1929–1931* (1962), 22.
56. M.M. Whiteman, *Digest of International Law*, Vol. 2 (1963), 1249.
57. La Documentation Française, *L'Antarctide et les problèmes soulevés par son occupation* (28 March 1949), 6.
58. J. Simsarian, 'The Acquisition of Legal Title to Terra Nullius' (1938), 53 *Political Science Quarterly*, 111 at 127.
59. *Mortimer* v. *NY Elevated Railroad Co*. 6 NY Supp. 898 at 904 (1889).
60. *Jones* v. *US* 137 US 202 at 212 (1890).
61. (1909) 3 *AJIL* Supp., 7 at 24.
62. Art. 35.
63. M.F. Lindley, *The Acquisition and Government of Backward Territory in International Law* (1926), 32.
64. *Daour Diop* v. *French State*, Court of Appeal, French West Africa (8 February

and two signatories made formal reservations to this effect.[65] It has
therefore been held that Article 35 does not bind third parties.[66]

Despite such reasoning it is suggested that the Article embodies
customary international law.[67] So in the *Caroline Islands Case* Spain
was required to render her sovereignty effective by establishing as
quickly as possible a regular administration with sufficient force to
guarantee order and rights acquired.[68]

Three cases suggest that a less severe test may be required for distant and uninhabited regions. The *Clipperton Island Case* turned on
symbolic annexation. Although actual and not fictitious taking of
possession was put forward,[69] there was no physical occupation of
the island by France. In the *Island of Palmas Case* the Netherlands
succeeded against the United States claiming as successor to Spain in
right of the Philippines. Holland's claim was described as an
inchoate title based on a display of authority as against the American
inchoate title derived from discovery.[70] Emphasis was placed on the
continuous and peaceful display of the functions of State.[71] As there
was no evidence of such actions by Spain,[72] the Netherlands had in
fact to prove very little. As late as 1898 it was said that no steamer
had ever been to the island in living memory.[73] Dutch reliance was
largely placed on the payment of taxes and the distribution of coats
of arms and flags.[74]

For Antarctic claimants the *Eastern Greenland Case*[75] is of particular interest. There are some limiting factors which must be taken
into account. Denmark's claim was held to have been uncontested
for five hundred and fifty years.[76] Norway's case was further
weakened when the court accepted that a statement by Norway's
Foreign Minister in 1919 was an unconditional and definitive under-

1907) in A.C. Kiss, *Répertoire de la pratique française en matière de Droit International Public*, Vol. II (1966), 148–9.
65. P.D.G. Skegg, 'Some Aspects of Constitutional Law relating to the Cook Islands
1888–1901', LL.B. Hons. thesis, University of Auckland (1968), 64.
66. *Clipperton Island Case* (1932) 2 UNRIAA 1105 at 1110.
67. O. Svarlien, *The Eastern Greenland Case in Historical Perspective* (1964), 55.
68. J.B. Moore, *International Arbitrations*, Vol. V (1898), 5043. It may be noted
that the mediator's points were declared in 1885, the islands were in the Pacific,
and the parties (Spain and Germany) were signatories to the Act of Berlin.
69. (1932) 2 UNRIAA 1105 at 1110.
70. (1928) 2 UNRIAA 829 at 870.
71. p. 840.
72. p. 868.
73. p. 865.
74. Ibid.
75. (1933) PCIJ Ser. A/B, No. 53, 22.
76. Ibid., at p. 46.

taking[77] amounting to a form of estoppel. Despite these drawbacks, the case is of practical application in Antarctica. Stress was placed on the need to bear in mind the Arctic and inaccessible character of the uncolonised part of the country.[78] Such a claim involves 'the intention and will to act as sovereign, and some actual exercise or display of such authority'.[79] For several hundred years there was no contact between Denmark and Greenland, yet the Danish King's 'pretensions' were held valid because they were not disputed.[80]

Reservations may be made to these decisions. In the *Western Sahara Case*[81] the International Court of Justice was asked whether Rio de Oro and Sakiet El Hamra had been *res nullius* at the time of colonisation by Spain. Had this issue been argued by an interested party in the cases examined, it is suggested that the requirements for sovereignty would have been stricter. The matter is not purely hypothetical. The United States does not recognise existing Antarctic claims. Should a sovereignty dispute be dealt with on the merits by an international tribunal, America might decide to intervene in order to argue that the continent remained *res nullius*.

One may also point out that a case concerning a small uninhabited atoll should not apply to a continent. Recognition played a considerable part in the *Eastern Greenland Case*. The actual display of authority in that instance was largely on paper.[82] But such criticism still leaves the essential core of the decisions intact. It is now arguable that no act performed by a sovereign is wholly devoid of probative value.[83]

There is a clear trend towards a lenient standard for sparsely populated regions.[84] The borderline between attentuated conditions of effectiveness and total relinquishment of the requirement may be said to be shadowy.[85] But it is going too far to say that occupation has been effectively and gratefully jettisoned by both tribunals and

77. p. 70.
78. pp. 50–1. The requirement of occupation is less essential in relation to a 'barren tract incapable of habitation and of any but intermittent use for limited purposes' (*Rann of Kutch Arbitration* (1968) 7 ILM 633 at 681).
79. p. 46.
80. p. 48.
81. (1975) ICJ 12 at 14.
82. T. Cheng, 'The Sino-Japanese Dispute over the Tiao-yu-tai (Senkaku) Islands and the Law of Territorial Acquisition' (1974), 14 *Virginia Journal of International Law*, 221 at 235.
83. G.G. Fitzmaurice, 'The Law and Procedure of the International Court of Justice 1951–1954' (1955–6), 32 *BYBIL*, 20 at 52.
84. E.W. Johnson, 'Quick, before it melts: Toward a Resolution of the Jurisdictional Morass in Antarctica' (1976), 10 *Cornell International Law Journal*, 173 at 182.
85. H. Lauterpacht, 'Sovereignty over Submarine Areas' (1950), 27 *BYBIL*, 376 at 416.

jurists.[86] Even in disputes between two parties the more active side
should prevail. For Antarctica there will be a requirement of occupation although less will be needed than for a region of temperate
climate and substantial population.

State Acts

Considerable confusion has resulted from the attempts of claimants
to invoke every conceivable argument. Reference is made to all and
any acts of nationals relating to the territory.[87] If legal criteria are to
be relevant, it must surely be accepted that only those actions carried
out by a State or ratified by it subsequently may be advanced.

The United Kingdom's case against Argentina relies upon acts of
formal possession in the name of the Crown.[88] It is improbable that
these annexations received any form of endorsement by the British
Government in the nineteenth century,[89] and this is underlined by the
absence of any such indication in the British Memorials in the
Antarctica Cases.[90] Major early discoveries of United States citizens
were not officially endorsed at the time.[91] Even Wilkes' government-
sponsored expedition of 1838–42[92] suffered the same fate. Where
acts are carried out by private citizens, there must be an assent or
authority of the State.[93] To ensure that the act of an individual
becomes that of his country the intention of the sovereign should be
manifested in unmistakable terms.[94]

Even though unauthorised at the time, an individual's actions can
be subsequently adopted by a State.[95] For Antarctic claimants the
lapse of time between the action relied on and State approval has
been considerable. In some instances there has been no official
acceptance. The factual basis of the problem is the same as that for

86. A.L.W. Munkman, 'Adjudication and Adjustment – International Judicial
    Decision and the Settlement of Territorial and Boundary Disputes' (1972–3), 46
    BYBIL, 1 at 94.
87. A.G. Roche, *The Minquiers and Ecrehos Case* (1959), 119.
88. Application instituting Proceedings, *Antarctica Case* (*UK* v. *Argentina*) (1955),
    11–13.
89. C.H.M. Waldock, 'Disputed Sovereignty in the Falkland Islands Dependencies'
    (1948), 25 *BYBIL*, 311 at 324.
90. J.C. Puig, *La Antártida Argentina ante el Derecho* (1960) 191.
91. J.P.A. Bernhardt, 'Sovereignty in Antarctica' (1975) 5 *California Western Inter-
    national Law Journal*, 297 at 320.
92. K.J. Bertrand, *Americans in Antarctica 1775–1948* (1971), 160.
93. *Jones* v. *US* 137 US 202 at 212 (1890).
94. J.B. Scott, 'Arctic Exploration and International Law' (1909), 3 *AJIL*, 928 at
    939.
95. *Secretary of State of India* v. *Kamachee Boye Sahaba* (1859), VII Moore Ind.
    App., 476 at 540.

the perfection of inchoate title, but the legal implications are different. Unless the individual's action has been ratified, the State cannot *prima facie* rely on it as a source of title.

Such circumstances usually demand an immediate decision by the government concerned.[96] On general principles it can be argued that stability of international affairs requires a State to adopt its ·nationals' acts with due celerity. For this reason discoverers of guano islands had to notify the State Department of the facts as soon as practicable.[97] Long-delayed ratification, or its total absence, is a substantial objective defect in several claims. Approval must be unequivocal. Therefore the Congressional award of a medal to Ellsworth in 1936 cannot be seen as an official endorsement of his claim.

It could well be argued that if a government's support has been requested by the leader of an expedition and refused,[98] that government has made its choice and cannot subsequently ratify the expedition's claims. Similarly it may be said that where an individual has obtained the permission of a foreign nation, his own State's ratification of his acts is conditioned by these circumstances.[99]

Actions of individuals, however numerous and extensive, do not *per se* confer title on a State.[100] It is therefore assumed that private acts are not entitled to legal significance.[101] This is not necessarily so. In certain circumstances the presence of nationals of a given State may signify or entail occupation by that State.[102] So scientific expeditions organised by non-official institutions have been taken into account.[103] Such activities may be seen not as the foundations of sovereignty but rather as evidence of its validity.

Notification

It is suggested that although the criteria of effective occupation have been considerably relaxed, the test itself is still law. Particular emphasis is now placed on the 'intention and will to act as sovereign'.[104] One aspect of the *animus occupandi* is the extent to

96. As in *Buron* v. *Denman* (1848), 2 Ex., 167.
97. J.B. Moore, *Digest of International Law*, Vol. I (1906), 558.
98. Byrd in 1933 (E.P. Hoyt, *The Last Explorer* (1968) 265).
99. This may have been the case with Byrd and the New Zealand Government (L.B. Quartermain, *New Zealand and the Antarctic* (1971) 65).
100. G.G. Fitzmaurice, 'The Law and Procedure of the International Court of Justice 1951–1954' (1953), 30 *BYBIL*, 1 at 48.
101. *US* v. *Alaska* 422 US 184 at 190–1 (1975).
102. Judge Levi Carneiro, *Minquiers and Ecrehos Case* (1953) *ICJ*, 47 at 104.
103. *Legal Status of Eastern Greenland* (1933) *PCIJ*, Ser. A/B No. 53; 22 at 62–3.
104. Ibid., at p. 46.

which a claimant is under a duty to make its assertions public. At first glance the question would seem unnecessary. Surely a claim to territory must require some form of information available to other States?

British Commonwealth Antarctic claims were put forward as having legal validity before legislation was passed. In the case of the British Antarctic Territory (formerly part of the Falkland Islands Dependencies) it would seem that events dating back several decades before the Letters Patent of 1908 are relied on. Ellsworth in 1938 and Byrd in 1940 were given secret instructions to carry out symbolic acts which were not to be made public without the authority of the State Department.[105] To confuse the issue further, such instructions were subsequently published, but the United States did not make any specific claims in reliance upon the actions taken by its nationals.

Article 34 of the Act of Berlin[106] provided that parties henceforth taking possession of territory on the coast of Africa should accompany the act of possession with a notification to the other signatories. Such information was intended to enable others to make their own reclamations. This provision was described at the time as '*une garantie nouvelle*'.[107] Unlike Article 35, Article 34 is not considered to embody customary international law.[108] But rejection of Article 34 only means that the specific rule therein is confined to the General Act of 1885. Some other form of notification may still be needed. Strong practical arguments may be cited for such a custom. Unless there is some form of public announcement, other States have no grounds of objection to the claim.[109] Without notice from the government concerned it is impossible to tell whether a particular symbolic act by an explorer has official sanction.

Frequently governments have specifically stated that they do not endorse claims. An example is Peary's offer of the North Pole to the United States in 1909 and the President's refusal. While notification to other States has not been demanded, there must be an open display of sovereignty. Clandestine exercise of authority over an inhabited territory for a considerable length of time would seem impossible.[110] Some public act is needed.[111]

---

105. C. Hartley Grattan, *The Southwest Pacific since 1900* (1963) 613–14.
106. (1909) 3 AJIL Supp. 7 at 24.
107. A.C. Kiss, *Répertoire de la pratique française en matière de Droit International Public*, Vol. II (1966), 143.
108. *Island of Palmas Case* (1928) 2 UNRIAA, 829 at 868.
109. J. Daniel, 'Conflict of Sovereignties in the Antarctic' (1949) 3 *YBWA*, 241 at 255.
110. *Island of Palmas Case* (1928) 2 UNRIAA, 829 at 868.
111. *The Fama* (1804) 5 C. Rob. 106 at 115–16.

More difficulty is encountered in attempting to define the precise type of act to be invoked. In the *Clipperton Island Case*[112] a communication to the government of the nearest nation (Hawaii) and publication in a local journal were held to give sufficient notoriety. On the other hand legislation, of itself, may not suffice. In the *Anglo-Norwegian Fisheries Case*[113] Norway's decrees were upheld because the United Kingdom was a maritime State greatly concerned with fisheries and the freedom of the high seas in the area. As France had commented on the Norwegian Law of 1869, Britain must have known of it. Even routine enforcement of legislation may be deprived of effect if foreign governments are not aware that territorial sovereignty is being claimed.[114]

Sovereignty must be asserted openly and in some well-understood and unequivocal manner.[115] The mode of assertion may vary. Publicity appears to be essential but not sufficient of itself. There must be proof that the other States affected know, or should have known, of the existence of the claim.

Arctic Sectors

Claimants publicly defined the initial boundaries of their Antarctic territories between 1908[116] and 1943.[117] During this period there were no permanent stations on the continent. On an objective test the countries concerned would have been hard put to show that there was occupation, let alone that it had been made effective. But this was the only generally accepted means of acquisition of *res nullius*. To avoid the problem, claimants rely on a dilution of the accepted test and on the sector principle.

Sector claims were first proposed in the Arctic. Countries whose possessions went up to the Arctic should, it was argued, have a right to all lands in the waters between lines extending from their east and west extremities to the North Pole.[118] Presumably the geographical boundaries were to be an extension of the land boundary with the United States and the boundary (at that time not yet defined) between Canada and the sovereign of Eastern Greenland. There is

112. (1932) 2 UNRIAA, 1105 at 1110.
113. (1951) ICJ, 116 at 139.
114. *US* v. *Alaska* 422 US 184 at 200 (1975).
115. M.F. Lindley, *The Acquisition and Government of Backward Territory in International Law* (1926), 293.
116. British Letters Patent creating the Falkland Islands Dependencies.
117. Argentine Note to the United Kingdom (J.C. Puig, *La Antártida Argentina ante el Derecho* (1960) 112).
118. Sen. P. Poirier, Senate Debates (Canada) (20 February 1907), 271.

no doubt why this theory was put forward: both Canada and Russia feared that other powers would claim sovereignty over Arctic islands, apprehensions which were quite reasonable in the circumstances. Russia sold Alaska to the United States because it was unwilling to bear the cost of defending the colony against continued American encroachments. 'It was a question of our selling them or our seeing them [the United States] seize it'.[119] After Peary reached the North Pole in 1909, he put it at the disposal of the President.[120] A consideration in Denmark's cession of the Virgin Islands in 1916 was United States recognition of that country's interests in the whole of Greenland.[121]

Proponents of the Arctic sector theory would trace it to nine-teenth-century agreements defining Alaska's boundary.[122] These treaties are of interest from a historic point of view and also raise some of the problems of the sector principle. Concerned at the free movement of United States nationals in the fur trade, Czar Alexander I issued an *ukase* in 1821 proclaiming Russian territorial waters along the Northwest coast of America for 100 miles offshore from the Bering Straits to 51°N and closing the area to all foreigners. The United States and Britain contested this legislation at the time.[123] Both disputes were settled by treaty. Article III of the 1825 agreement with Great Britain provided a line of demarcation, which subsequently — under the Treaty of Cession of 1867 — became the Alaska-Canada boundary. Its northern limit is described in the French text as extending '*dans son prolongement jusqu'à la mer glaciale*'.[124] The western limit, between Alaska and Russia, was described in the 1867 treaty of cession as a meridian proceeding 'without limitation into the . . . Frozen Ocean'.[125] In favour of the sector theory it is suggested that both lines should be taken as intersecting at the North Pole.

Even supporters of the principle are constrained to admit that the framers of the 1825 Convention were ignorant of such implications.[126] At best the argument for a sector is weak. Parties to

119. De Stoeckl, Russian Ambassador to the United States, cited in H.I. Kushner, *Conflict on the Northwest Coast* (1975), 156.
120. G.H. Hackworth, *Digest of International Law*, Vol. V (1943), 445.
121. W. Lakhtine, 'Rights over the Arctic' (1930), 24 *AJIL*, 703 at 708.
122. H.I. Kushner, *Conflict on the Northwest Coast* (1975), 32–3.
123. In the course of argument in the *Fur Seal Arbitration* in 1893, the United States reversed its position and endorsed the ukase (J.B. Moore, *International Arbitrations*, Vol. I (1898) 821).
124. J.B. Moore, *Digest of International Law*, Vol. I (1906) 466. Rendered in English as 'in its prolongation as far as the Frozen Ocean'.
125. 57 BFSP, 454.
126. Dominions Office (31 December 1931) in D.P. O'Connell and A. Riordan

the Alaska negotiations were concerned with whaling,[127] fisheries, smuggling and naval power. Geographically it is correct that a meridian cannot be lost and hence extends all the way to the North Pole.[128] But the circumstances leading up to the treaties indicate that no attention was paid to the Arctic Ocean. From the diplomats' viewpoint, the 1825 settlement delimited the boundary between Canada and Russian America. This boundary stopped at the Arctic Ocean. The phrase '*jusqu'à*' is ambiguous and may be interpreted as either inclusive or exclusive of the frozen sea.[129] Divergences between the French and English versions of the 1867 treaty support the view that the parties were indifferent as to the precise location of the northern limits of the boundary. At the most the agreements are evidence of the state practice of three nations, one of which – the United States – clearly rejects the sector theory. Arguments based on the 1825 and 1867 treaties fail to provide precedents to justify the later sector claims.

It would appear that the source of the Arctic sector theory was Captain J.G. Bernier. On his first expedition in the ship *Arctic* in 1906–7 Bernier made many landings and took formal possession[130] at several places. For a number of years Canada had been concerned as to the title to islands in the Arctic Archipelago. A report by the Chief Astronomer had been completed in January 1904.[131] From 1898 Bernier campaigned for funds and a ship to explore the islands for Canada.[132] It would seem probable that Bernier inspired Senator Poirier's speech in 1907, which provides the first clear formulation of the sector theory.[133] Poirier referred to Bernier specifically in relation to the principle. The Senator's case was fully documented, bore signs of careful preparation and was delivered after Bernier's report on his acts of possession. One can easily be persuaded that the two men had acted in concert. Poirier's formula reflected Canada's practical concerns. A claim should cover 'lands and islands'.[134] There was no suggestion of appropriating seas or ice. Pointing to the precedent of Alaska, Poirier argued that 'when the United States

(eds.), *Opinions on Imperial Constitutional Law* (1971), 320.

127. R.J. Jensen, *The Alaska Purchase and Russian – American Relations* (1975), 48.

128. T.A. Taracouzio, *Soviets in the Arctic* (1938) 353.

129. *The Monastery of Saint Naoum* (1924), *PCIJ*, Ser. B, No. 9, 6 at 20.

130. (1975), 3(51) *Canada Weekly*, 6.

131. W.F. King, *Report Upon the Title of Canada to the Islands North of the Mainland of Canada* (1905).

132. M. Zaslow, *The Opening of the Canadian North 1870–1914* (1971), 261 *et seq.*

133. Senate Debates (Canada), (20 February 1907) 271.

134. Ibid., at p. 271.

people hold an inch by possession they claim to hold a yard'.[135] Such a partition was natural,[136] being based on proximity.

Even for the Arctic it must be stressed that there was only a theory of sectors. Both legal acceptance and practical application were at best doubtful. There could be no Arctic sectors unless they were claimed by States. Between the First and Second World Wars, Finland had an Arctic coast whose sector would have contained an island of Spitsbergen (Svalbard); but it put forward no claim. Finland's interest was dismissed on account of its sector's insignificant size.[137] But absence of a Finnish claim weakens the case for a rule of customary law in the Arctic. Nothing in the *Eastern Greenland Case* supports a Danish sector or even tacit recognition of certain elements of the theory, as has been suggested.[138] Norway specifically refused to recognise the Arctic sector principle,[139] as did the United States.[140]

There has been much debate as to whether the Soviet Union and Canada have advanced sector claims. Soviet action in the form of a decree in 1926 may be traced to the dispute over Wrangel Island,[141] situated 80 nautical miles north of Siberia and 160 miles west of the Bering Sea boundary meridian. Vilhjalmur Stefansson, an explorer, sent expeditions to the island in 1921 and 1924 to claim it for Canada and dramatize the unreliability of the sector principle.[142] Canada asserted a claim to the island in 1922.[143] After the Soviet ship *Red October* removed Stefansson's party in 1924 and raised the Soviet flag, Canada disclaimed sovereignty. But as at 1928 the United States had not relinquished a claim of its own.[144]

According to the Soviet decree of 1926, all lands and islands already discovered or to be discovered in the future in the Arctic

135. p. 273.
136. p. 271.
137. L. Breitfuss, 'Territorial Division of the Arctic' (1929), 8 *Dalhousie Review*, 456 at 467.
138. A. van der Essen, 'Le problème politico-juridique de l' Antarctique' (1960), 20 *Annales de Droit et de Sciences Politiques*, 227 at 230.
139. Exchange of Notes between Canada and Norway respecting Sovereignty over the Otto Sverdrup Islands: (1930) Canadian Treaty Series No. 17.
140. M.M. Whiteman, *Digest of International Law*, Vol. 2 (1963), 1268.
141. T.A. Taracouzio, *Soviets in the Arctic* (1938), 69–70.
142. G.W. Smith in R. St.J. MacDonald (ed.), *The Arctic Frontier* (1966) 208.
143. W.H. McConnell, 'Canadian Sovereignty over the Arctic Archipelago', LL.M. thesis, University of Saskatchewan (1970) 54.
144. G.H. Hackworth, *Digest of International Law*, Vol. 1 (1940), 464–5. A recent State Department communication steered clear of an affirmation of US rights or recognition of Soviet sovereignty ((1978) 72 AJIL 894). This may be due more to concern at allegations of labour camps on the island rather than a desire to support a US claim.

Ocean between 32° 4' 35"E and 168° 49' 30"W were part of the Soviet Union.[145] Much was made of this act as a sector claim.[146] Some Soviet authors took the decree to cover part or all of the Arctic Ocean.[147] In retrospect the decree does not appear to bear that interpretation. Foreign sovereignty over islands in the area was permitted by the legislation if recognised by the Soviet Union. Soviet practice demonstrates an effective occupation adapted to the difficult conditions: meteorological observatories, scientific stations and prison camps. Despite recent Soviet textbook support, the official view refused endorsement of the sector principle.[148] The 12-mile territorial sea in the Arctic[149] is a practical confirmation of this approach. Sector lines are not State frontiers and the regime of the seas is not affected.[150] Refusal of transit to two United States icebreakers through the Vil'kitskii Straits in 1967 was based on the Soviet view that warships have no right of innocent passage.[151] Keeping the Northern Sea Route open with icebreakers and possessing a powerful navy, the Soviet Union has no need for a sector theory.

Canada is a puzzle. It was only in 1925 that official support for a sector appeared in a speech by the Minister of the Interior[152] prompted by plans for the US Navy expedition of MacMillan and Byrd.[153] In August 1925 Byrd was at Etah, Greenland. Bernier anchored his ship there and had an unrecorded conversation with Byrd. The US expedition then announced that it was to go to Baffin Island whose ownership was not disputed.[154] There have been a number of subsequent statements. Four recent Canadian Prime Ministers (St. Laurent, Diefenbaker, Pearson and Trudeau) have all given some degree of acceptance to the theory.[155] Since the agree-

---

145. Text in W. Lakhtine, 'Rights over the Arctic' (1930), 24 *AJIL*, 703 at 709.
146. 'Russia is the outstanding advocate of this system' (C.C. Hyde, 'Acquisition of Sovereignty over Polar Areas' (1934), 19 *Iowa LR*, 286 at 289).
147. Lakhtine, Korovin, Sigrist (T.A. Taracouzio, *Soviets in the Arctic* (1938) 348−9).
148. W.E. Butler, *Northeast Arctic Passage* (1978), 73.
149. W.E. Butler, *The Law of Soviet Territorial Waters* (1967), 111.
150. (1976−7) 48 *BYBIL*, 416.
151. D. Pharand, 'Soviet Union Warns United States Against Use of Northeast Passage' (1968), 62 *AJIL*, 927 at 933−4.
152. During the course of a debate on an amendment to the Northwest Territories Act to enable the Government to control scientists and explorers entering the Territories (15 and 16 Geo. V, Ch. 48).
153. J.-Y. Morin, 'Le progrès technique, la pollution et l'évolution récente du droit de la mer au Canada, particulièrement à l' égard de l'Arctique' (1970), 8 *CYBIL*, 158 at 235.
154. R.A.J. Phillips, *Canada's North* (1967), 107−8.
155. W.H. McConnell, 'Canadian Sovereignty over the Arctic Archipelago', LL.M.

ment with Norway on the Sverdrup Islands in 1930, there has been no real question of Canada's sovereignty over the islands of the Arctic Archipelago.[156] This resulted not from a reliance on the sector theory but from the exercise of government authority. In 1897 the first fishery patrol boat was sent to Baffin Island.[157] A particularly active role was played by the Royal Canadian Mounted Police, almost the least of whose duties were those generally associated with police work. They asserted sovereignty: 'At first their main concern was to carry the flag whether or not anyone was there to see it'.[158] In 1922 a new outpost of Canadian civilization at Craig Harbour on Ellesmere Island consisted of a police post, customs house and post office.[159]

In the same year Staff-Sergeant Joy, acting as policeman, coroner and magistrate, arrested three Eskimos accused of murdering a trader and carried out a preliminary enquiry. Most of the winter and spring were spent collecting the accused and witnesses who were scattered all over the northern part of Baffin Island.[160] A prime duty was occupation of the islands for the purpose of retaining sovereignty,[161] and police work in the Canadian Arctic was clearly designed to come within the effective occupation test. For these islands there was no need to invoke the sector theory. What has been at issue is whether Canada utilises the theory to claim offshore waters. The matter reached crisis proportions in 1970 when Canada asserted control over a 100-mile pollution zone under the Arctic Waters Pollution Prevention Act.[162] Official attitudes had never been clear, but they now became completely confused. Under pressure from parliamentarians to declare an outright sector claim, and attacked by the United States for denying the freedom of the high seas, the government took refuge in waffling.[163] It has been stated that the waters of

---

thesis, University of Saskatchewan (1970), 35.

156. As Canadian authorities generally agree. It is therefore puzzling to read in a number of modern Canadian studies discussion of the question of sovereignty over the islands themselves. Such Canadian perceptions of American intentions may arise from a more general concern for national identity (T.M. Tynan, 'Canadian-American relations in the Arctic' (1979), *The Review of Politics*, 402 at 426).

157. M. Zaslow, *The Opening of the Canadian North 1870–1914* (1971), 239.

158. R.A.J. Phillips, *Canada's North* (1967), 133.

159. J.D. Craig, *Canada's Arctic Islands* (1927), 10.

160. Later the practice developed of taking Eskimos accused of serious offences, and the witnesses, to distant courts (J. Sissons, *Judge of the Far North* (1968), 66, detailing Judge Sissons efforts to bring law courts to the Eskimo people).

161. RCMP, *Canadian Sovereignty in the Arctic* (n.d.).

162. See also Jurisdiction/*Crime*.

163. G.F. Graham, 'The Canadian Arctic Waters Pollution Prevention Act of 1970 and the Concept of Self-Protection', M.A. thesis, Carleton University (1974) 51.

the Archipelago are 'Canadian', but it is not clear which waters are referred to. Enactment of a 12-mile territorial sea and a 100-mile pollution zone suggest that seas are not claimed under the sector theory.

A Canadian case, *R* v. *Tootalik E4—321*,[164] supports a sector approach. On the basis of political statements and the exercise of responsibilities in the past by the RCMP, it was held that criminal jurisdiction existed over an offence committed on sea-ice at or near Pasley Bay, Boothia Peninsula. Taking into account the political quotations relied on by the court and reference to an offence the situs of which was sixty miles offshore the case is authority for a type of sector claim.[165] Subsequently the judge concerned took the judgment to include ice extending 'to the North Pole'.[166] But the case is only based upon two of the numerous (and conflicting) official views. Canadian practice does not support this interpretation and it has not been subsequently endorsed by the government.

There is no support for Arctic sectors in international litigation nor in the general practice of states. Only two nations can even arguably be identified with such claims, and in neither case is the argument persuasive. Canadian politicians have made statements of varying degrees of ambiguity favouring the principle, but no concrete action has been taken whether by legislation or by diplomatic notification.[167] The Soviet statute of 1926 could be construed as a sector, but state practice unequivocally contradicts such an interpretation.

Antarctic Sectors

Although designed for the Arctic, the principle has only been applied by claimants in the Antarctic.[168] Persuasive arguments may be put forward against the analogy. The circumstances are quite different, and there is only an outward resemblance between the two applications.[169] Arctic sectors are a prolongation of the mainland depending

164. (1969) 71 WWR, 435, reversed on other grounds (1970), 74 *WWR*, 740. See also Sovereignty/*Ice*.
165. F.M. Auburn, 'International Law-Sea-Ice-Jurisdiction' (1970), 48 *CBR*, 776 at 778.
166. W.G. Morrow, 'Law and the Thin Veneer of Civilization' (1971) 10, *Alberta LR*, 38.
167. 'The Government of Canada has never formally asserted sovereignty to Canadian Arctic waters under the sector principle' (L.S. Clark, Director, Legal Operations Division, Department of External Affairs, Canada in annex to letter dated 9 October 1979).
168. See map of Claims and Stations for Antarctic sector boundaries.
169. J.-F. da Costa, 'Le problème de la souveraineté sur les regions antarctiques', thesis, University of Paris (1948), 157.

upon national territory reaching the polar circle,[170] but in Antarctica this is not the case.[171] The principle cannot be fully implemented in Antarctica because the nearest land is far to the north.[172]

The analogy has substantial geographical flaws. Perhaps the most important of these is that the Arctic sector has natural baselines, whereas the Antarctic does not. If the polar circle were taken as the base for the Antarctic, there would be no sectors. At 50°S only Argentina and Chile could claim; at 40°S New Zealand and Australia could be added; at the Equator there would be a multitude of claimants.[173]

It is not surprising that the advancement of such a questionable theory led to dubious conclusions. Britain's Letters Patent of 1908 modified the Arctic concept to prevent considerable portions of Antarctica falling within the sphere of sovereignty of Argentina and Chile.[174] Base points were chosen arbitrarily.[175] Rather than leading to certainty application of sectors to the Antarctic invited additional claims.

Particularly difficult problems could arise in the South American sector. Theoretically claims could be advanced by Guatemala, Ecuador, Nicaragua, Costa Rica, Panama, Peru, Uruguay and Brazil.[176] Non-governmental references to possible claims by smaller countries such as Uruguay[177] may not pose a threat to the present equilibrium in Antarctica; but discussion of a suggested Brazilian claim to the area from 29° to 53°W between 1973 and 1975[178] was seen at the time as a serious issue.

---

170. C. Vallaux, 'Droits et prétentions politiques sur les régions polaires' (1932), 2 *Affaires Étrangères*, 14 at 23.
171. R.D. Hayton, 'The 'American' Antarctic' (1956), 50 *AJIL*, 583 at 603.
172. J. Daniel, 'Conflict of Sovereignties in the Antarctic' (1949), 3 *YBWA*, 241 at 259.
173. J.-F. da Costa, *Souveraineté sur l'Antarctique* (1958), 23.
174. Dominions Office (31 December 1931) in D.P. O'Connell and A. Riordan (eds.), *Opinions on Imperial Constitutional Law* (1971) 318.
175. H.J. Taubenfeld, 'A Treaty for Antarctica', 531 *International Conciliation* (Jan. 1961), 245 at 254.
176. J.B. Oerding, 'The Frozen Friction Point: a Geopolitical Analysis of Sovereignty in the Antarctic Peninsula', MA thesis, University of Florida (1977), 90. Because of the arbitrary nature of sector theory, one cannot give precise baselines for a putative division of this type. One theoretical approach suggests Brazil: 28°–49° 50'; Uruguay: 49° 50'–56° 40'; Argentina: 56° 40'–67°; Chile: 67°–81°; Peru: 81°–83°; Ecuador: 83°–90°. For an Argentinian interpretation of the unofficial Brazilian sector theory, see J.A. Fraga, *Introducción a la Geopolítica Antártica* (1979) 36.
177. L. Crawford, *Uruguay Atlanticense y los Derechos a la Antartida* (1974).
178. J.E. Greño Velasco 'La Adhesion de Brasil al Tratado Antartico' (1976), *Revista de Política Internacional*, 71 at 72–3.

For the Arctic there was some logic in drawing lines from mainland boundaries to the North Pole. Antarctic sectors do not have such a justification. Chile's claim is bounded by 90° longitude which is west of the island of Juan Fernandez but east of Rapa Nui (Easter Island).[179] Australia's Antarctic Territory extends far beyond the prolongation of the arguable limits of its metropolitan or island territories, as does the Ross Dependency. Only one explanation is possible for these and other divergences from the Arctic baseline idea. Antarctic sectors were planned with the purpose of including the more desirable continental areas available.[180] The baselines were then drawn to achieve this aim. Such inconsistency further undermines the geographical justification for Antarctic sectors.

Extension of the sector theory to Antarctica contradicts accepted means of acquisition of territory in international law. Apart from Argentina and Chile, Antarctic claims are based on discovery.[181] Yet sectors claimed include very substantial prior discoveries by nationals of other countries. An attempt to avoid the problem is found in the contention that the territory itself was discovered by one's own nationals but that some discoveries of particular parts of the principal groups of territory were made by others.[182] Such an argument may be acceptable for a small island but cannot apply to an area of continental proportions. Not only past but also future discoveries by other States are discounted.

Antarctic sectors violate the customary rule of establishing inchoate sovereignty over territory by right of discovery.[183] Contiguity and hinterland arguments, both rejected in international cases, reappear in the justification of claims. While these objections should be given weight, they are overshadowed by the vital flaw of sectors. Effective occupation is ignored.[184] Sectors are contrary to the general rule, and their purpose is to avoid it. However diluted effective occupation may have become, there is still a requirement of control of territory. This necessity is denied by sector claims.[185]

At the time when the sectors were proclaimed, there were no per-

179. F.M. Auburn, *The Ross Dependency* (1972), 27.
180. As in the case of Chile (E.W. Hunter Christie, *The Antarctic Problem* (1951), 277).
181. J.-F. da Costa, 'A teoria dos setores polares' (1951), 13–14 *Boletim da Sociedade Brasileira de Direito Internacional*, 87 at 109.
182. Application instituting Proceedings, *Antarctica Case* (*UK* v. *Argentina*) (1955), 12.
183. Secretary of the Navy (23 September 1929) in G.H. Hackworth, *Digest of International Law*, Vol. I (1940), 464.
184. S.C. Jain, 'Antarctica: Geopolitics and International Law' (1974), 17 *Indian Year Book of International Affairs*, 249 at 266.
185. C.C. Hyde, *International Law*, Vol. I (1947), 352.

manent stations on the continent itself. After bases had been established, it was argued that they constituted occupation of coastal strips, which were the foundations of the sectors.[186] However generously one concedes the ambit of control of coastal stations, it cannot be effective for hundreds of miles to east and west and as-far south as the Pole.

Special legal problems arise from attempts to define what a sector means in practice.[187] A popular view is that such a claim is 'shaped something like a triangle but with a conical base line with the apex of the triangle at the Pole'.[188] There is considerable support in official publications of claimant countries for the interpretation that lines drawn across the high seas are national boundaries. In 1913 the British government granted licences to Norwegian whaling firms to fish in waters of the Ross Sea outside the 3-mile limit which undoubtedly constituted high seas. The licences were transferred to New Zealand, which subsequently applied its own laws to the area.[189] This jurisdiction was criticised as a remarkable claim paralleled by that of the Stuart monarchs to dominion over the North Sea.[190] Although the regulations seemed to apply to all fishing in the Ross Sea, it was argued that official pronouncements confined application to territorial waters.[191] But the statements were made in 1930 after New Zealand had stopped enforcing its rules on whaling ships; previously New Zealand had licensed whaling on the high seas south of 60°S.[192] Similarly, Chile's claim relies on whaling licences.[193] Apart from various forms of state practice such as legislation, licences, official publication and stamps, there is considerable

---

186. C.H.M. Waldock, 'Disputed Sovereignty in the Falkland Islands Dependencies' (1948), 25 *BYBIL*, 311 at 340−1.
187. O. Svarlien, 'The Sector Principle in Law and Practice' (1960−1) 10 *Polar Record* 248.
188. *New Zealand's Gateway to the South, The Ross Dependency* (1962). Similarly the map in Central Office of Information (UK), *The Antarctic*, (1966), 16, shows the lines at 60°S as 'international boundaries'. Both maps appear in government publications.
189. (1926) *N.Z. Gazette*, 3139; (1929) *N.Z. Gazette*, 2747. The 1926 regulations were made because licensed whalers complained of unlicensed whaling beyond the three-mile limit (R.A. Swan, *Australia in the Antarctic* (1961), 196).
190. A.H. Charteris, 'Australasian Claims in Antarctica' (1929), 3(11) *Jo. Comp. Leg.*, 226 at 229.
191. I.L.M. Richardson, 'New Zealand's Claims in the Antarctic' (1957), *NZLJ*, 38 at 41.
192. 'Norwegian Sovereignty in the Antarctic' (1940), 34 *AJIL*, 83 at 85.
193. Mateo Martinić B., 'Interés, Preocupación y Presencia Antárcticos de Chile' in Francisco Orrego Vicuña and Augusto Salinas Araya (eds.), *El desarrollo de la Antártica* (1977), 43.

support by commentators for the interpretation that sector claims effectively cover the high seas.[194]

Claimants usually deny that there is any appropriation of the high seas. They are then faced with the task of explaining the legal significance of the lines drawn over the oceans, particularly those across the base of the 'pie-shaped' sector at 60°S. No such problem arose in the Arctic because the base there was the claimant-country's mainland territory. In Poirier's original scheme this was the essential justification of the theory. Even in the modified Antarctic format, the lines across the sea are intended to have some legal function.

It is generally argued that lines in water areas defined in treaties are not boundaries but a cartographic device to simplify description of the land areas involved. So the United States views the 1867 Alaska cession meridian as simply a line to the east of which all land or claim to land was ceded by Russia to the United States.[195] There is considerable force to the assertion that general international law attaches no significance to lines laid across the high seas and made to surround or bisect land arbitrarily.[196] But this does not help claimants. Sector lines must have some meaning in defining the extent of territory. A common justification is:

It is true that the sectors are expressed to begin north of the continent and that they even appear to include areas of the high seas. But the high seas are not in fact claimed and the projection of the sectors north of the continent only serves as a convenient means of bringing under a single geographical definition both the continental sector and individual islands to which *specific* titles are also professed.[197]

Here lies the dilemma. On the one hand, assertion of sovereignty over the high seas is denied; on the other, the lines must be invested with some meaning in law. Doubtless the geometrical form is convenient in making a claim, but that of itself does not give the lines legal standing. If it is argued that the geographical co-ordinates are 'merely a general description of where the named places lie',[198] the

194. For example, J.-F. da Costa, 'Le problème de souveraineté sur les regions antarctiques, thesis, University of Paris (1948), 160.
195. S.W. Boggs, 'Delimitation of Seaward Areas under National Jurisdiction' (1951), 45 *AJIL*, 240. The author, a Special Adviser on Geography to the State Department, had carried out the first comprehensive official US review of Antarctic policy in 1930 (B.M. Plott, 'The Development of United States Antarctic Policy', Ph.D. thesis, Fletcher School of Law and Diplomacy, Tufts (1969), 53).
196. R.D. Hayton, 'Chile, Argentina and Great Britain in the Antarctic' (1955–7), *Anuario Juridico Interamericano*, 119 at 124.
197. C.H.M. Waldock, 'Disputed Sovereignty in the Falkland Islands Dependencies' (1948), 25 *BYBIL*, 311 at 341.
198. United Kingdom Note to Argentina (17 December 1947) (1948), 5 *Polar Record*, 229 at 230.

validity of the land boundaries is also called into question. The ambivalent attitude of claimants to the legal status of sector lines over the high seas results from the illogical modification of a concept designed for a completely different geographical situation. A second defence is the argument that the lines are the most logical and equitable way of apportioning spheres of interest.[199] If the sector is not a means of acquiring sovereignty, it might then be invoked as a principle of delimitation.[200]

Sectors as a device for drawing boundaries are open to severe criticism. It is not equitable for claimants arbitrarily to define the limits to include the most desirable areas such as the Antarctic Peninsula. Nor is there much equity in the ultimate explanation for the principle: to claim lands not yet discovered. Antarctic practice has involved the assertion of rights over territory discovered by others,[201] reliance on discovery without any occupation whatsoever,[202] and the attempted discounting of what little effective occupation has actually taken place.[203]

Sectors are equally unsatisfactory in logic. Straight–line boundaries were drawn because the absentee boundary-makers[204] were ignorant of the geography of the area. Arbitrary claims to large areas meant that little of interest remained for future claimants.

Deficiencies of sector boundaries are best illustrated in the unclaimed 'American sector'. It is probable that claimants would welcome a United States proclamation over that area because it would add considerable weight to their own assertions.[205] This is the most inaccessible and least inviting area of the continent. Sector claims cover the Ross Sea region, which has been the focus of American activity since the expeditions of Admiral Byrd and the Antarctic Peninsula. There was no incentive for the United States to assert sovereignty over Marie Byrd Land alone without guaranteed access from the Ross Sea. From the east it would have been even more difficult. The sweeping and arbitrary nature of Antarctic sector boundaries is self-defeating.

Initially there was a strong relationship between the respective

199. Memorial of the Federal Republic of Germany, *North Sea Continental Shelf Cases*, Pleadings (1968), Vol. I., pp. 80–1.
200. R. Dollot, 'Le droit international des espaces polaires' (1949), 75(2) *Hague Recueil*, 114 at 170.
201. The Ross Dependency.
202. Definition of Australian Antarctic Territory in 1933 to exclude Adélie Land.
203. United Kingdom claim including Laurie Island which has been occupied by Argentina since 1904.
204. P.W. van der Veur, *Search for New Guinea's Boundaries* (1966), 125.
205. W. Sullivan, 'The International Geophysical Year' (1959), 521 *International Conciliation*, 324. See also National Interests/*The United States*.

attitude of some countries to territory in the two polar regions. United States policy-makers strongly opposed Antarctic sectors because of that nation's important interests in the Arctic.[206] Norway's Antarctic claim was confined to the coast to avoid prejudicing its Arctic position.[207] As sovereignty over Northern hemisphere polar land and islands has been essentially resolved, it is probable that such considerations will have little influence in the future.

The United Kingdom, New Zealand and Australia recognise each other's sectors which originated in a division of the continent for the British Empire. Proclamation of the Australian claim to exclude Adélie Land[208] indicated acceptance of the French sector, which was confirmed by the reciprocal grant of the free right of passage of French and British Commonwealth aircraft over each others' territory.[209]

Norway's specific rejection of sectors in the agreement with Canada relating to the Sverdrup Islands[210] culminated in the proclamation of an Antarctic claim over part of the mainland coast between the Falkland Islands Dependencies in the west and the Australian Antarctic Territory in the east 'with the land lying within this coast and the environing sea'.[211] Although there is reference to 'a wide tract of the mainland',[212] the southern boundary has not been defined. In 1929 Norway promised Great Britain not to raise claims to land brought under the dominion of the British Empire.[213]

It has been stressed that the region is not claimed as a sector like the British Dependencies.[214] Yet some commentators have regarded the Norwegian territory as a sector claim,[215] a view which has a measure of justification. Both the eastern and western limits are also the boundaries of other nations' sectors. In 1929 Norway officially

---

206. B.M. Plott, 'The Development of United States Antarctic Policy', Ph.D. thesis, Fletcher School of Law and Diplomacy (1969), 41.
207. J. Hanessian in T. Hatherton (ed.), *Antarctica* (1965), 21.
208. S.2, Australian Antarctic Territory Acceptance Act 1933.
209. Exchange of notes regarding Aerial Navigation in the Antarctic, 1938 UKTS No. 73.
210. '. . . [Norway] is anxious to emphasise that their recognisance of the sovereignty of His Britannic Majesty over these islands is in no way based on any sanction whatsoever of what is named 'the sector principle' (1930) Canadian Treaty Series No. 17.
211. 'Norwegian Sovereignty in the Antarctic' (1940), 34 *AJIL*, 83.
212. Ibid., at p. 85.
213. Ibid., at p. 84.
214. H. Bogen, 'Main Events in the History of Antarctic Exploration' (1957), *Norsk Hvalfangst Tidende*, 423.
215. C.H.M. Waldock, 'Disputed Sovereignty in the Falkland Islands Dependencies' (1948), 25 *BYBIL* 311; O. Svarlien, 'The Sector Principle in Law and Practice' (1960–1), 10 *Polar Record*, 248 at 252.

reserved its rights to the territory immediately circumjacent to the South Pole, of which Amundsen took possession in 1911 under the name of Haakon VII Plateau.[216]

Norway's interest in making the 1939 proclamation was to safeguard its whalers against the possibility of exclusion from the seas south of 60°S.[217] Having regard to previous Norwegian concern at the Ross Dependency whaling regulations, it may be argued that rejection of the sector principle related essentially to the Southern Ocean. If this interpretation is accepted, then Norway's claim may still extend to the South Pole.

Two further considerations must be taken into account. For some years Norway and the Soviet Union have been examining their boundary in the Barents Sea. On one configuration a sector division would substantially favour the Soviet Union; however there is no indication that the Soviet Union is using any arguments other than those based upon continental shelf delimitation rules.[218] In 1931 Norway claimed Peter I Island[219] in the 'American' sector. Even in theory this does not foreclose application of a sector on the continent.

The South American claimants advance a particular thesis to prefer their rights over those of the United Kingdom. Arctic sector theory is essentially based on proximity. One formula called for the attachment of sovereignty to littoral states according to a 'region of attraction'.[220] Support is thus provided for a variety of Antarctic arguments based on geographical continuity[221] and similarities of geological structure.[222] Those nations which are closest to Antarctica are best able to carry out economic exploitation and scientific work there.[223] On one Chilean view, proximity gives an incomplete root of title[224] which is perfected by legal and economic acts. Its justification is sought in a presumption that neighbouring States exercise sovereignty more frequently than other States, in national security, resource exploitation and the impossibility of other forms of delineation.[225] In proceedings between two parties advancing sector

216. G.H. Hackworth, *Digest of International Law* (1940), Vol. 1, pp. 453–4.
217. 'Norwegian Sovereignty in the Antarctic' (1940), 34 *AJIL*, 83 at 85.
218. J.C. Ausland, 'Spitsbergen: Who's in Control?' (Nov. 1978), *US Naval Institute Proceedings*, 63 at 65.
219. Naval War College (1948–9), 46 *International Law Documents* 239.
220. W. Lakhtine, 'Rights over the Arctic' (1930), 24 *AJIL*, 703 at 705.
221. G. Battaglini, *I Diritti degli Stati nelle Zone Polari* (1974), 78–80.
222. G. Kojanec, 'La situazione giuridica dell'Antartide' (1960), 15 *La Comunità Internazionale*, 21 at 26.
223. J.C. Puig, *La Antártida Argentina ante el Derècho* (1960), 50.
224. Apparently analogous to the role of discovery in effective occupation.
225. O. Pinochet de la Barra, *La Antártica Chilena* (1st. edn, 1948), 113.

claims the view that only neighbouring nations are entitled to make such assertions has some weight.[226]

United States denial of the validity of sectors must be linked to its general policy of non-recognition of Antarctic claims. Evidence that US rights could be converted into a sector exists. Admiral Dufek, when in command of the US Naval Support Force, Antarctica, recommended a sector claim to Marie Byrd Land and condominiums with Australia and New Zealand.[227] From 1946 onwards there had been considerable United States activity directed towards claims.[228] If a claim had been made, refusal by the United States to define a sector would have worked against it. Like much else in US Antarctic policy, this temporary expedient has hardened into general principle through inaction.[229] A policy change could well have brought an acceptance of sectors. Such a possibility explains the location of the South Pole station on the spot where the 'pie-shaped sectors claimed by other nations came together'.[230]

Claimants[231] support the sector theory. Although there are isolated statements from nationals of other countries to the effect that the theory is part of general international law,[232] the consensus of commentators from non-claimant states is firmly opposed to such acceptance, and correctly so. Sectors have no support from international tribunals. Effective occupation, and its constituent elements such as discovery, are contrary to the sector theory. Nor can it be advocated as a fair or effective method of drawing boundaries. It 'boils down to a somewhat elaborate way of asking for more'.[233] The sector theory is an Aunt Sally of international law, more of a political than a legal principle,[234] but even in politics it has significant drawbacks. A claimant is bound to the area defined, and concessions to new claimants would impugn the validity of the entire claim. Yet because of the defects of the principle it will be relied on in future. A sector is itself an admission of the failure to comply with the general standards of the law of nations.

226. D. Schenk, *Kontiguität als Erwerbstitel im Völkerrecht* (1978), 34.
227. Admiral Dufek to Dr R.V. Zander, Department of Defense (17 April 1957).
228. See, for instance, Acting Secretary of State to Secretary of Navy (14 December 1946) in M.M. Whiteman, *Digest of International Law*, Vol. 2 (1963), 1248.
229. See also National Interests/*the United States*.
230. H.M. Dater, 'Byrd Station; the first 2 years (1956–1958)' (1975), 10(3) *Antarctic Journal*, 96 at 108. The analogy comes from the resemblance to slices of a pie apparent in the map of Claims and Stations.
231. With the doubtful exception of Norway.
232. J.S. Reeves, 'Antarctic Sectors' (1939), 33 *AJIL*, 519 at 521.
233. Common Rejoinder of Denmark and the Netherlands, *North Sea Continental Shelf Cases*, Pleadings (1968), Vol. I, p. 472.
234. J.-F. da Costa, 'Le problème de la souveraineté sur les régions antarctiques', unpublished thesis, University of Paris (1948) 161.

Ice

Antarctica is unique as an ice-capped continent surrounded by an
ocean of ice. Ordinary rules for acquiring territory had to be adapted
to a new medium having many of the qualities of land. Explorers
remarked that once the floe froze around a ship, one lived to all
intents and purposes as if on land.[235] At least as far as travel is concerned, ice converts the sea to a terrestrial medium.[236] During the
Russo-Japanese War the Russians built a railroad over the ice of
Lake Baikal in winter,[237] and in April 1978 a Korean Airlines Boeing
707 carrying 106 passengers entered Soviet airspace by mistake and
landed on a frozen lake.[238] To suggest a legal regime for ice one must
examine its physical properties.

The Antarctic ice-sheet covers 11,500,000 sq. km. and has a mean
thickness of 2,000 metres. As there is virtually no rain in Antarctica,
the sheet is sustained by snow falls. The surface slopes down towards
the coast all over the continent and the ice flows everywhere towards
the sea.[239] On the coast there are ten large ice shelves forming part of
the ice-sheet and floating on the sea. The largest, the Ross Ice Shelf,
has an area of at least 325,000 sq. km. (though estimates vary
widely) is between 200 and 400 metres thick and projects approximately 30 metres above sea-level. Water depths under Antarctic ice
shelves reach 1,300 metres.[240]

Different parts of the ice move at various speeds. As a whole it
moves about 30 metres a year but the velocity of some glaciers has
been measured at several hundred metres a year. Most of the ice lost
from the sheet 'calves' (breaks off) the marginal shelves.[241] The
result is a vast volume of floating ice, including some very large
tabular bergs composed essentially of fresh water. One example,
Trolltunga, had an area of 4,650 sq. km. (nearly the size of
Delaware) and contained enough ice to supply nine times the total
yearly water requirements of the United States.[242] Even larger bergs,

235. R.N. Rudmose Brown, *The Voyage of the Scotia* (1906), 85.
236. W. Herbert, *A World of Men* (1968), 185.
237. T.W. Balch, 'The Arctic and Antarctic Regions and the Law of Nations' (1910),
     4 *AJIL*, 265 at 266.
238. 'Aboard Flight 902: "We Survived!" ', *Time* (8 May 1978).
239. G. de Q. Robin, *The Ice of the Antarctic* (Sept. 1962), 8.
240. T. Nagata, 'The Advancement of Scientific Research as the basis of Antarctic
     Development' in Francisco Orrego Vicuña and Augusto Salinas Araya (ed.), *El
     desarrollo de la Antártica* (1977), 87.
241. C. Embleton and C.A.M. King, *Glacial Geomorphology* (2nd edn, 1975),
     Vol. I, 51.
242. E. Paul McClain, 'Eleven Years Chronicle of one of the World's most gigantic
     Icebergs' (1978), 22(5) *Mariner's Weather Log*, 328 at 329.

of up to 34,000 sq. km.,[243] have been recorded.

A ring of pack-ice, several hundred miles wide in winter, surrounds the continent.[244] Most Antarctic sea-ice is very thin and lasts for one year only. It is the most variable large-scale feature on the surface of the earth.[245] Where coastal sea-water freezes, the resulting ice may be used in Antarctica for travel. But like the thin ice of the Arctic,[246] sea-ice is unpredictable and has to be treated with great care.[247]

Legal writers have not been able to reach any consensus on sovereignty over ice. Some of the difficulties are due to an attempt to impose general criteria applicable to other forms of territory. So it is argued that floating ice should be assimilated to open seas while more or less immovable formations should enjoy a legal status equivalent to polar territory.[248] But ice-shelves comply with both of the suggested tests.

Increased knowledge of the properties of various forms of ice and advances in technology must now be taken into account. Extensive scientific investigation of the Ross Ice Shelf only began during the International Geophysical Year, and the first photographs of the water underneath the thick ice-cover and 450 km. from open sea were taken in 1977[249] as part of a general scientific investigation of the Shelf.[250] Technical advances include the use of icebreakers to cut channels to coastal stations and enable supply ships to transit.[251] Arctic developments have shown the way. The ice-strengthened tanker *Manhattan* made the Northwest Passage in 1969.[252] Nuclear submarines have crossed the Arctic Basin under the ice and surfaced near the Pole.[253] Since 1937 scientists have worked on drifting ice stations.[254] Development of new techniques permits the occupation of some types of ice formation. International law should take note of

---

243. K.K. Markov, V.I. Bardin, V.L. Lebedev, A.I. Orlov and I.A. Suetova, *The Geography of Antarctica* (1970) 234.

244. 'Ring of Ice' (1973), 75 *Audubon*, 10 at 17.

245. National Academy of Sciences, *Antarctic Glaciology* (1974), 47.

246. R.K. Nelson, *Hunters of the Northern Ice* (1969), 13.

247. NZ Antarctic Research Programme, *Antarctic Field Manual* (1978), 12.

248. W. Lakhtine, 'Rights over the Arctic' (1930), 24 *AJIL*, 703 at 712.

249. J.W. Clough and B. Lyle Hansen, 'The Ross Ice Shelf Project' (1979), 203 *Science*, 433.

250. J.F. Splettstoesser, 'The Ross Ice Shelf Project' (1977), *Nebraska Blue Print*, 10.

251. US Naval Support Force, Antarctic, *Support for Science, Antarctica* (1968), 11–13.

252. B. Keating, 'North for Oil', *National Geographic* (March 1970), 374.

253. (1959), 9(61) *Polar Record*, 340.

254. Y. Tolstikov, 'Drifting over the Arctic' (1968), *Geographical Journal*, 1058.

such advances:[255] in particular, the possibility of beneficial use may enable ice to be subject to national appropriation.[256]

The ice-sheet overlying the continent itself does not present major legal difficulties. If the cap were removed, the land, which is depressed by the enormous weight of the ice, would rise (the process is known as isostatic rebound). A large proportion of Marie Byrd and Ellsworth Lands would be below sea-level. Part of the remainder would become islands, as would the Antarctic Peninsula.[257] Before the development of the ice-sheet, West Antarctica consisted of a series of islands and was separated from East Antarctica by the Shackleton Seaway.[258] As isostatic rebound is not likely to take place in the projected future of mankind, it lacks legal significance.[259] On such a long-term possibility we have to take Antarctica as it is.

Scientists have put forward the hypothesis that parts of the West Antarctic ice-sheet may be inherently unstable because they are grounded below sea-level and can respond drastically to moderate climatic warming.[260] Peripheral sections of the sheet could move rapidly.[261] On one view a greenhouse effect resulting from the exponential production of industrial carbon dioxide could trigger deglaciation within about fifty years.[262] While the resulting 5-metre rise in sea-level would have a drastic effect on populated coastal areas of other continents, the physical changes in Antarctica would not entail large-scale legal consequences.

Antarctic ice shelves raise peculiar issues.[263] Legal commentators emphasise that the shelves are firmly anchored to land and remarkably stable except for their margins. Permanent scientific stations have been established on them.[264] Shelf-ice has most of the physical

255. J. Machowski, *Sytuacja Antarktyki w Świetle Prava Miedzynarodowego* (1968), 143.
256. B.M. Carl, 'Claims to Sovereignty – Antarctica' (1955), 28 *Southern California Law Review*, 386 at 399.
257. J.F. Lovering and J.R.V. Prescott, *Last of Lands . . . Antarctica* (1979), 7.
258. W.J. Zinsmeister, 'Effect of formation of the west antarctic ice-sheet on shallow water marine faunas of Chile' (1978), 13(4) *Antarctic Journal*, 25.
259. J.P.A. Bernhardt, 'Sovereignty in Antarctica' (1975), 5 *California Western International Law Journal*, 297 at 307.
260. T. Hughes, 'Is the West Antarctic Ice-Sheet Disintegrating?' (1973), 78 *Journal of Geophysical Research*, 7884 at 7905.
261. I.M. Whillans, 'Radio-echo layers and the recent stability of the West Antarctic ice-sheet' (1976), 264 *Nature*, 153 at 155.
262. J.H. Mercer, 'West Antarctic ice-sheet and CO_2 greenhouse effect: a threat of disaster' (1978), 271 *Nature*, 321.
263. Arctic shelves are relatively minor coastal features which pose few problems (D. Pharand, *The Law of the Sea of the Arctic* (1973), 187).
264. J. Hanessian in T. Hatherton (ed.), *Antarctica* (1965), 8.

and utilitarian qualities of land and should be equated with it.[265] This argument is more attractive than the view that the same rule should apply to continental and shelf ice because there is no natural boundary between the two.[266] Such an approach is weakened by scientific investigation of the area beneath the ice which permits delineation of the boundaries of an ice-shelf.

It may be accepted that shelves have many of the physical properties of land. Whether they should be so viewed for legal purposes is a separate issue. Ice several hundred feet thick and having the area of a medium-sized country is not navigable by a ship[267] and cannot be regarded as high seas. But to infer that an ice-shelf must of necessity be equivalent to land would seem to go too far. The water area beneath a shelf may reach a substantial depth, is in some cases very extensive and is an inseparable physical constituent of the contiguous high seas.

A more acceptable conclusion is that such a shelf is neither land nor sea but rather a special form of territory *sui generis* and subject to physical appropriation.[268] Like the Rann of Kutch, a seasonally flooded marsh, the ice-shelf partakes of some of the characteristics of both land and sea, is a unique phenomenon, and should be so treated by the law.[269]

The special status of shelves relates directly to national claims in the form of sectors. It has already been pointed out that the high seas within the boundaries are said to be excluded, although state practice does not always coincide with public assertions. One form of claim refers to 'islands and territories'.[270] If 'territories' is taken in the usual connotation of land, such proclamations may be interpreted as excluding ice-shelves. This argument is particularly applicable to the Ross Dependency which covers the 'coasts of the Ross Sea, with the islands and territories adjacent thereto'.[271] If the Ross Ice Shelf were part of the Dependency, the test of adjacency would extend from the Barrier to the Pole, whereas the exclusion of the Shelf provides a much more acceptable interpretation.[272]

265. E.W. Cole, 'Claims of Sovereignty over the Antarctic', thesis, Judge Advocate General's School, US Army (1958), 37.
266. G. Smedal, *Acquisition of Sovereignty over Polar Areas* (1931), 30.
267. F.C. Alexander, 'A Recommended Approach to the Antarctic Resource Problem' (1978), 33 *University of Miami Law Review*, 371 at 385.
268. F.M. Auburn, *The Ross Dependency* (1972), 49.
269. A.L.W. Munkman, 'Adjudication and Adjustment – International Judicial Decision, and the Settlement of Territorial and Boundary Disputes' (1972–3), 46 *BYBIL*, 1 at 69.
270. e.g. S.2, Australian Antarctic Territory Acceptance Act 1933.
271. (1923) *NZ Gazette*, 2211.
272. F.M. Auburn, *The Ross Dependency* (1972), 53–4.

The seaward boundary of the ice-shelf is an unsolved problem. It is correct that legal principles governing the loss of land territory by processes such as avulsion do exist. But whether there is a similarity or possible analogy[273] may be questioned. One would be hard put to find a legal precedent for the regular loss of several thousand square kilometres of land territory.

It is argued that the repeated calving and advance of the shelf produce an overall structure with a relatively stable aspect.[274] Witnesses would not accept this view. On one occasion Admiral Byrd asked his meteorologist what he thought of the Barrier. Just as he did so, a quarter-of-a-mile of the cliff fell off with a sharp crack.[275] One reason for the absence of scientific investigation of calving is that the few glaciologists who have become involved in the process 'do not recommend close participation'.[276]

If the edge of a shelf is to be the baseline, a fixed boundary is desirable.[277] To avoid a constantly variable maritime frontier, the average seasonal maximum edge may be put forward as a possible baseline. This would imply the reduction of a State's area of sovereign rights (the term is used here to include land territory, internal waters, territorial sea and exclusive economic zone) in the case of a very large ice break-out. Most nations would not be prepared to accept such an eventuality.

The seaward margin of a shelf is unsuitable for establishing baselines. A normal baseline is the low-water mark along the coast.[278] Other methods of drawing baselines (straight baseline; archipelago principle) still depend on a coast, but an ice barrier is not a coast, nor does it have any feature similar to a low-water line. With the introduction of the exclusive economic zone, giving the coastal State resource jurisdiction up to 200 miles offshore, the relevance of establishing sea-boundaries has increased markedly. Traditional or proposed conventional rules do not provide for ice-formations, nor do they permit any useful analogy. As a tentative solution it is suggested that there could be a combination of two elements: first, the location of the ice edge, insofar as it is known, at a given date, and secondly, an allowance of an arbitrary figure, perhaps 50 miles, for

273. J.P.A. Bernhardt, 'Sovereignty in Antarctica' (1975), 5 *California Western International Law Journal*, 297 at 305.
274. W.H. McConnell, 'Canadian Sovereignty over the Arctic Archipelago', LL.M. thesis, University of Saskatchewan (1970), 64.
275. E.P. Hoyt, *The Last Explorer* (1968), 281.
276. W.F. Weeks and M. Mellor, *Some Elements of Iceberg Technology* (1978), 2.
277. J.F. Lovering and J.R.V. Prescott, *Last of Lands . . . Antarctica* (1979), 192.
278. Art 5. Informal Composite Negotiating Text, A/CONF. 62/WP 10/Rev. 2 (11 April 1980).

seaward extensions to deal with large losses within the previous ten years. The result would be a geographically fixed line which would prevail for the future regardless of the current location of the margin of the shelf.

Sea-ice attached to the land or shelf has been used for a number of purposes in the Arctic. For instance, Eskimos use a 35-mile-long ice bridge to cross Smith Sound between Danish Greenland and the Canadian Ellesmere Island.[279] The *Tootalik*[280] case has already been cited as an endorsement of a Canadian sector theory. Tootalik was accused of hunting a female polar bear with young contrary to the Game Ordinance 1960 (NWT). That ordinance applied within the Northwest Territories, defined as 'part of Canada north of the sixtieth parallel of north latitude'.[281] The incident took place in April 1969 on sea-ice more than 7 miles from the west coast of Pasley Bay, Boothia Peninsula,[282] and hence apparently regarded as outside the Canadian territorial sea.[283] Pasley Bay was frequently icebound even in summer.[284] As there was no discussion in *Tootalik* of the precise location of the offence, nor of baselines, internal waters or territorial waters, the assertion of jurisdiction and sovereignty must be taken as applicable to all fast sea-ice of a semi-permanent nature.[285]

It has already been pointed out, in discussing a Canadian sector, that the government statements cited in *Tootalik* cannot be relied on as representing the official position in 1969. In the absence of a claim by Canada to sea-ice beyond the territorial sea, patrols of the Royal Canadian Mounted Police relied on by the court could not be a display of sovereign rights.[286] Sea-ice over the high seas is part of the high seas.

A fortiori, such considerations are applicable to Antarctica which has thinner sea-ice and lacks a population of hunters like the Eskimos. One use may be noted. Outer Williams Field has two annual runways in McMurdo Sound between the Ross Shelf and Ross Island. It cannot be used after the annual ice breakup in early

---

279. W. Herbert, *Across the Top of the World* (1969), 76.
280. (1969) 71 WWR, 435, reversed on other grounds (1970), 74 WWR 740. See also *Sovereignty/Arctic Sectors*.
281. S.2(i) Northwest Territories Act 1952 (Can.).
282. W.H. McConnell, 'Canadian Sovereignty over the Arctic Archipelago', LL.M. thesis, University of Saskatchewan (1970), 88–9.
283. T.-P. Chen, 'International law – Arctic Sovereignty – Northwest Territories Act RSC 1906, c.62-R. v. Tootalik' (1970), 8 *Alberta Law Review*, 456 at 457.
284. (1969) 71 WWR 435 at 437.
285. F.M. Auburn 'International Law-Sea-Ice-Jurisdiction' (1970), 48 *CBR*, 776 at 778.
286. (1969) 71 WWR 435 at 439.

January.[287] On the previous argument this ice is not subject to sovereignty as such. Both runways, however, are situated on the minimal territorial sea appurtenant to Ross Island.[288]

After the tanker *Manhattan* transited the Northwest Passage in 1969 Canada, argued that it was idle to talk of the freedom of the high seas in an area large parts of which are covered by ice throughout the year. Local inhabitants travelling by dogsled and snowmobile use the frozen sea as an extension of the land.[289] But Canada has not asserted sovereignty on this basis. Difficulties of navigation in the pack-ice are more serious in the Arctic than in the Antarctic, and there does not appear to be any reason for accepting that pack-ice on the high seas can be subject to national appropriation.[290]

Polar Circumstances

Effective occupation requires less in the Antarctic than it does elsewhere because of the very small population, isolation and severe weather. How much less?

Occupation must correspond with local circumstances[291] and the nature of the territory.[292] Cases demand a manifestation of sovereignty 'normal for such a region'.[293] Some discontinuity is permissible. Sovereignty cannot be exercised at every moment on every point of a territory:[294] in a practically uninhabited area covered by dense tropical forests, acts of sovereignty need not be so open, public and frequent as in a densely-populated region rich in resources.[295] The *Eastern Greenland Case* stressed the inaccessible nature of the uncolonized parts of the island.[296] Antarctic claimants, stretching such dicta to their utmost extent, carried out formalistic

---

287. Bechtel Inc., *US Antarctic Research Program Scientific Support Study*, Vol. I (1972), 6.
288. Air New Zealand investigated tourism in 1969 but took no action due, *inter alia*, to lack of passenger terminal and accommodation facilities (Mr Gordon, *NZ Hansard* (17 June 1971) 978).
289. (1970) 9 ILM 611. See also Jurisdiction/*Crime*.
290. It may be noted that the Chilean Presidential Decree of 1940 covered pack-ice.
291. R. Dollot, 'Le droit international des espaces polaires' (1949), 75 *Hague Recueil*, 114 at 132.
292. J.L. Verner, 'Legal Claims to Newly Emerged Islands' (1978), 15 *San Diego Law Review*, 525 at 537.
293. *Island of Palmas Case* (1928) 2 UNRIAA, 829 at 856–7.
294. Ibid., at p. 840.
295. P.K. Menon, 'International Boundaries – a Case Study of the Guyana-Surinam Boundary' (1978), 27 *ICLQ*, 738 at 766.
296. 1933 PCIJ Ser. A/B No. 53; 22 at 50–1.

actions having a touch of comic opera;[297] there were coroners without inquests, justices of the peace without cases[298] and swastikas dropped from aeroplanes.

These excesses are properly criticised, but this does not necessarily mean that a relaxed legal standard for regions such as the Antarctic is itself invalid. The minimal control theory has been attacked as failing to specify what is required to establish title and encouraging sweeping claims.[299] It is suggested that some guidelines may be found, as can be shown by examining examples of issues peculiar to Antarctic claims.

Postage stamps have been regarded as one convenient way of expressing the animus or intent of the sovereign[300] or a form of symbolic administration.[301] Possibly acceptance of stamps showing claim boundaries is seen as a degree of recognition.[302] To issue them a country does not have to send an expedition to Antarctica or enforce its laws against recalcitrant foreign nationals. 'The philatelic effusion of a desolate region is due to various causes – frequently political, often financial sometimes philatelic, but rarely postal'.[303]

The earliest indication of the extent of Argentina's sector was contained in a note to the Universal Postal Union in 1927[304] and its precise delineation appeared on a stamp in 1946.[305] The United Kingdom, among others, has also issued stamps to support its claim[306] and they have been the subject of official protests; Argentina has regarded letters bearing these stamps as lacking postage.[307] Such trifling matters seem to assume importance in the absence of actual activity in Antarctica.[308]

National sensitivity to postal issues has not been frozen by the

297. E.K. Braybrooke, 'The Future of Antarctica' (1956), 10 *Landfall*, 330 at 331.
298. F.M. Auburn, *The Ross Dependency* (1972), 11.
299. E. Honnold, 'Thaw in International Law? Rights in Antarctica under the Law of Common Spaces' (1978), 87 *YLJ*, 804 at 821.
300. G. Battaglini, *La Condizione dell'Antartide nel Diritto Internazionale* (1971), 90.
301. J. Daniel, 'Conflict of Sovereignties in the Antarctic' (1949), 3 *YBWA*, 241 at 253.
302. H.J. Taubenfeld, 'A Treaty for Antarctica' (1961), 531 *International Conciliation*, 245 at 252.
303. R.W. Bagshawe and J. Goldup, 'The Postal History of the Antarctic, 1904–1949' (1951), 6 *Polar Record*, 45.
304. Naval War College (1948–9), 46 *International Law Documents* 218.
305. R.E. Wilson, 'National Interests and Claims in the Antarctic' (1964), 17(1) *Arctic*, 15 at 23.
306. Application instituting Proceedings, *Antarctica Case* (*UK* v. *Argentina*) (1955), 30.
307. M.M. Whiteman, *Digest of International Law*, Vol. 2 (1963) 1258–9 (see also Treaty/*Exchange of Information* on Rec. I-XII).
308. F.M. Auburn, *The Ross Dependency* (1972), 62.

Antarctic Treaty. At the Fifth Consultative Meeting in 1968 it was recommended that each country issue a commemorative stamp in 1971 for the tenth anniversary of the Treaty; the most prominent feature was to be the Antarctic Treaty emblem representing a map of Antarctica, and additional matter should be consonant with the provisions and spirit of the Treaty.[309] A newspaper editorialist observed that proof of title by printing stamps would be irrefutable if other claimants had not done the same,[310] but it is difficult to attribute much significance to the mere issuing of stamps depicting claims[311] other than to demonstrate an *animus occupandi*.

Intent is better demonstrated by other actions such as legislation, seen as one of the most obvious forms of exercise of sovereign power,[312] but the passing of laws does not suffice;[313] they must be enforced when the occasion arises.[314] Until a power is exercised, the statute can well be regarded as supporting a paper claim.[315] This may have been a reason contributing to the delay on the part of Australia and New Zealand in applying 200-mile fishery zones to their Antarctic territories. Claims are weakened by the lack of enforcement of laws relating to generally applicable topics such as entry permits, customs, health and aerial navigation.

Similar objections apply to the administration of claimed areas. A desert does not have to be governed like a great city, yet the minimum degree of control appropriate to polar areas is needed. For example, inquests on corpses are evidence of the exercise of jurisdiction,[316] and claimants – e.g. Australia and New Zealand – have made a practice of appointing coroners for Antarctic territories. New Zealand inquests on Antarctic fatalities have been carried out in New Zealand, as no doubt such proceedings would be inconvenient and expensive in Antarctica. But similar consideration did not impede the exercise of powers by the Canadian police in the Arctic. An Australian inquest has been scheduled at an Antarctic station.[317]

Emphasis is placed on cheap means of displaying administration which are not likely to require enforcement by law. Argentina points

309. Rec. V-I.
310. *New Zealand Herald* (4 January 1947).
311. As distinct from the use of stamps in Antarctica as evidence of annexation like flags (L.B. Quartermain, *New Zealand and the Antarctic* (1971), 13 and 19).
312. *Legal Status of Eastern Greenland* (1933), *PCIJ* Ser. A/B, No. 53, 22 at 48.
313. A.G. Roche, *The Minquiers and Ecrehos Case* (1959), 125.
314. I.L.M. Richardson, 'New Zealand's Claims in the Antarctic' (1957), *NZLJ*, 38 at 41.
315. L.F.E. Goldie, 'International Relations in Antarctica' (March 1958), *The Australian Quarterly*, 7 at 18.
316. *Minquiers and Ecrehos Case* (1955), *ICJ*, 47 at 65.
317. 'Polar storm victim dies', *West Australian* (8 August 1979).

to the existence of a postmaster at Laurie Island since 1904,[318] and New Zealand's Scott Base post office was set up for the same purpose.[319] Like stamps, post offices are easy to establish, and this is one of their main defects. Finn Ronne, leading a private US expedition in 1947–8 in the Antarctic Peninsula, used an abandoned American base at Stonington Island 200 yards from a British camp. British attempts discourage Ronne[320] only resulted in the State Department taking a leaf out of their book and appointing Ronne postmaster.[321] In an official protest at Byrd's reported establishment of a post office in the Ross Dependency in 1934, the British Ambassador in Washington had pointed out that such an act would infringe British sovereignty.[322] Apart from weakening New Zealand's claim,[323] the protest demonstrated the problems of administrative acts which were not intended to be backed up by practical action. Ineffective administration may serve a claimant worse than none at all.

Polar operations have undergone a revolution since the Second World War. Previously claimants could justify the absence of activity in Antarctica by the inhospitable nature of the region and the requirement that the exercise of sovereignty should be appropriate to the area concerned. During and since the IGY, a number of permanent stations have been established. Icebreakers and large cargo planes facilitate resupply, radio and satellites enable continuous communication through the southern winter. Stations are adequate if not comfortable. Introduction of additional facilities such as permanent runways[324] are often a question of cost rather than feasibility. Following the technological transition it is appropriate to demand a more normal standard of occupation.

The change is illustrated in the relaxation of the ban on women in Antarctica. In 1935 Karoline Mikkelsen became the first woman to set foot on the continent.[325] Twelve years later two women wintered over with the Ronne Expedition.[326] Subsequent requests met deter-

---

318. Primavera Acuña de Mones Ruiz, *Antártida Argentina, Isolas Océanicos, Mar Argentina* (1949), 44.
319. A.S. Helm and J.H. Miller, *Antarctica* (1964), 394.
320. Acting Secretary of State Acheson (27 December 1946) in M.M. Whiteman, *Digest of International Law*, Vol. 2 (1963), 1253–4. See also Treaty/*Origins*.
321. W. Sullivan, *Quest for a Continent* (1957) 271.
322. G.H. Hackworth, *Digest of International Law*, Vol. I (1940) 456.
323. By failing to take any action when the protest was not accepted (F.M. Auburn, *The Ross Dependency* (1972) 57–8).
324. US Naval Construction Battalion Reconnaissance Unit, *Applied Construction Feasibility Study, Marble Point, Antarctica* (1958).
325. H. Bogen, 'Main Events in the History of Antarctic Exploration' (1957) *Norsk Hvalfangst Tidende*, 365.
326. K.J. Bertrand, *American in Antarctica 1775–1948* (1971), 515.

mined resistance on the grounds of cost[327] or that facilities had been designed for 'male only' living.[328] In recent years official attitudes have undergone a complete revision, and substantial numbers of women take part in summer research programmes.[329] It has also become standard procedure to permit women to winter over at bases.[330] An explorer has written of women on the threshold who wait to colonise the continent.[331]

One may say that the presence of women of itself does not affect the acquisition of sovereignty because they are engaged in scientific research and logistic support as are men. This is not so. Relaxation of the effective occupation test is due to the special climatic and isolated nature of Antarctica. If technological change has overcome some of these handicaps, then the ordinary demands of international law should be reverted to insofar as possible. The introduction of women indicates a partial normalisation of living conditions.

Some degree of family life is now possible in Antarctica. It would be an indication of permanency in the fuller sense and would raise the general standard for sovereignty. In 1975 a plane landed at Spitsbergen carrying a group of Soviet women with double beds, accompanied by officials.[332] This was an unambiguous affirmation that the Soviet Union was there to stay. Some wives and children have lived in sub-Antarctic South Georgia,[333] and a French baby was born there in 1979.[334] So special significance attaches to the presence of Argentinian soldiers' wives and children from 1977 at Esperanza Base. The first child, Emilio Marcos Palma, was born to the wife of the base commander and baptised in January 1978.[335]

Colonization of Esperanza was intended to reinforce territorial claims. This purpose was underlined by a wedding which had to be carried out by an official commissioned by a government.[336] At least for some coastal areas, such as parts of the Antarctic Peninsula, it

327. J. Langone, *Life at the Bottom* (1977), 95.
328. Cf. Antarctic Division, Department of Scientific and Industrial Research, *Antarctic Operations Manual* (1975), 90.
329. 28 from the United States in 1978–1979 ('US Science Projects this Summer' (1978), 8(8) *Antarctic* 262).
330. 'Return of Sun to Ross Island' (1978), 8(7) *Antarctic*, 233 at 236.
331. W. Herbert, *A World of Men* (1968), 231.
332. J.C. Ausland, 'Spitsbergen: Who's in Control?' (Nov. 1978) *US Naval Institute Proceedings*, 62 at 68.
333. N. Brown, *Antarctic Housewife* (1971), 1–2.
334. 'Addition to French crew' (1979), 8(10) *Antarctic*, 362.
335. 'Antarctica's first baby warmly welcomed' (1978), 8(5) *Antarctic*, 169–70.
336. As was the case with the Canadian marriage on Fletcher's Ice Island in April 1973 when the RCMP Inspector concerned held an appointment as a Marriage Commissioner for the Northwest Territories (letter from Liaison Officer, RCMP (31 July 1973)).

would now appear that settlement by families may be possible. The fact that one claimant-State has undertaken such settlement raises the standard for effective occupation considerably.

A singular feature of polar claims is the assertion of sovereignty over vast areas in reliance upon small scientific stations most of which are situated on the coast. Sovereignty is the right to exercise functions to the exclusion of any other State.[337] A *jus excludendi alios* is particularly relevant in Antarctica. Between two parties, each of whom has a weak claim, it might possibly be arguable that one base suffices to support sovereignty if the area is uninhabited and there are no competing State acts.[338] On any general international law test this is not the case. Claimants tend to advance activity in one area of a sector as showing effective occupation hundreds or even 1,000 miles away[339] without any indication of the exclusion of non-recognising States.[340]

On the effective occupation test no current Antarctic claim can be fully justified. A major political defect of sectors is that there is no fall-back to a more acceptable position. Limited area claims, based on a moderate degree of activity, could well be upheld. Presuming for the moment that permanent stations on the continent comply with the sovereignty test, it may be conceded that they carry with them a reasonable adjacent zone.[341]

Commentators have failed to reach any degree of consensus on the ambit of putative limited area claims. One view supports a reasonable amount of hinterland which is easily controlled, such as a few hundred miles, but not any claims to the vast interior.[342] Control here presumably means that parties equipped for effective action can reach the area from manned bases. Another approach would restrict control to a small area,[343] emphasising that the actual domain around stations may extend no more than 200 metres.[344]

Clearly effective administration of an area 1,000 miles away cannot be supported.[345] It may be debated whether a search and rescue

337. *Island of Palmas Case* (1928) 2 UNRIAA 829 at 838.
338. D.J. Millard, 'Heard and MacDonald Islands Act 1953' (1955), 1 *Sydney Law Review*, 374 at 376.
339. E.W. Cole, 'Claims of Sovereignty over the Antarctic', thesis, Judge Advocate General's School, US Army (1958), 68 and 75.
340. R. Lagoni, 'Antarctica's Mineral Resources in International Law' (1979) 39(1) *Zeitschrift fur Ausländisches Öffentliches Recht und Völkerrecht*, 1 at 19.
341. 'Arctic and Antarctic Annexation' (1912), 37 *Law Magazine and Review*, 326 at 328.
342. J. Hanessian in T. Hatherton (ed.), *Antarctica* (1965), 10.
343. R.-J. Dupuy, 'Le statut de l'Antarctique' (1958) *AFDI*, 196 at 210.
344. R.E. Guyer, 'The Antarctic System' (1973), 139 *Hague Recueil*, 149 at 159.
345. I.M. Roggen, 'La position juridique des Belges en Antarctique' (1960), 11 *Aile et Roue*, 9 at 10.

capacity provides a form of control over an area of, say, 25,000 square miles. It is not available in winter, and even in summer is frequently interrupted by bad weather. Such an emergency procedure to save lives seriously disrupts regular activities if needed for any length of time. Rescue is a humanitarian operation and does not involve the enforcement or administration of laws. It is a traditional Antarctic principle that expeditions render all assistance feasible in an emergency.[346] If States wish to assert sovereignty over such large areas, they should be prepared to bear the cost. Inland bases such as Amundsen-Scott, Siple and Vostok are feasible. On the scale of other manifestations of international prestige, their expense is not high. Some particular limited areas may be claimed on an objective test. Argentina relies on an observatory maintained at Laurie Island since 1904.[347] Even this is not a clear case.[348] There is support for the United Kingdom's claim to individual territories within the sector,[349] but this would seem to be a relative title *vis-à-vis* other claimants. British interests are complicated by insistence on the critical dates of 1926 (South Orkneys) and 1937 (other Antarctic territory)[350] limiting reliance on permanent bases, all of which were established subsequently.

Can claims be made to the base areas? It may be contended that scientific activities cannot be a source of sovereignty.[351] Research has nothing in common with administration, and cannot contribute to claims.[352] The scientific character of activities does not necessarily deprive them of political effect. Mapping and exploring expeditions of this nature may be invoked.[353] Polar programmes are directly carried out, supported and funded by governments whose purpose is to preserve national interests.[354] Science may support claims albeit with a lesser degree of effectiveness than direct administrative or legal acts.

Antarctic stations may be occupied continuously, but their

346. Rec. X-8.
347. Carlos Aramayo Alzerreca, *Historia de la Antártida* (1949), 155.
348. The United Kingdom would cite negotiations between Britain and Argentina in 1912–14 for the British cession of the South Orkney Islands in return for a legation in Buenos Aires.
349. R.D. Hayton, 'The American Antarctic' (1956), 50 *AJIL* 582 at 610.
350. Application instituting Proceedings, *Antarctica Case (UK v. Argentina)* (1955), 32.
351. La Documentation Française, *L'Antarctide et les problèmes soulevés par son occupation* (24 March 1949), 5.
352. I. von Münch, 'Völkerrechtsfragen der Antarktis' (1958), 7 *Archiv des Völkerrechts*, 225 at 249.
353. *Legal Status of Eastern Greenland* 1933 PCIJ Ser. A/B No. 53 22 at 62–3.
354. F.M. Auburn, *The Ross Dependency* (1972), 5.

population is not fixed.[355] Settlements are scientific outposts with small, highly specialised, fluctuating populations.[356] There are no permanent residents. Do such bases constitute effective occupation?[357] There can be little doubt that guano collectors[358] and police forces suffice. A transient population could therefore comply with the requirements of international law. But the base itself must have some measure of permanent occupation. A substantial number of stations have been closed[359] or transferred to other States, particularly after the conclusion of IGY activities.[360] Once this has taken place, customary international law must regard the rights from the base as having ceased to accrue.

Manned polar stations are expensive. For this reason automated equipment has been utilized. Large nuclear-powered stations could collect data and transmit it by a real–time satellite link, replacing staff who would otherwise winter over.[361] A United States working group recommended a network of twelve unmanned geophysical observatories (UGOs). A complete UGO, including power supply and fuel for one year, could be carried in a C-130 plane. Although one may question the cost-saving to be achieved in practice, the advantages of flexibility and speed are of considerable interest to scientists.[362]

Automatic stations would save manpower at bases. If this led to temporary vacation of a base, it would reduce support for territorial claims.[363] This view has particular force for a country putting forward a large claim and only having stations on the coast. Having regard to the very limited forms of national activity exercised in the Antarctic, closure of any permanent base could weaken sovereignty. An unmanned observatory does have some legal significance although it is less than that of even a small conventional station. Close analogies may be found in sea-beacons and buoys.[364] The

355. S.O. Butler, 'Owning Antarctica' (1977), 31 *Journal of International Affairs*, 35 at 36.
356. E. Honnold, 'Thaw in International Law? Rights in Antarctica under the Law of Common Spaces' (1978), 87 *YLJ*, 804 at 820.
357. D.L. Soden, *A Political and Legal Analysis 'The Antarctic Treaty'*, Institute for Marine and Coastal Studies, University of Southern California (1978), 27.
358. *Whiton* v. *Albany City Insurance Co.*, 109 Mass., 24 at 27 (1871).
359. G. Battaglini, *I Diritti degli Stati nelle Zone Polari* (1974), 78.
360. For example the United States handed over Ellsworth (to Argentina) and Wilkes (to Australia) in 1959 (F.M. Auburn, *The Ross Dependency* (1972), 42).
361. 'Will nuclear giant replace Antarctic men?' (1970), 5(10) *Antarctic*, 434.
362. National Academy of Sciences, *Upper-Atmosphere Physics Research in the Antarctic* (1974), 22–3 and 29.
363. Report of the Advisory Committee on Antarctic Programs (Australia), Vol. II *Automatic Stations: Past Experience and Future Applications* (1974).
364. *Minquiers and Ecrehos Case* (1953) ICJ 47 at 69.

weight to be attached to an unmanned observatory would depend upon the magnitude and expense of the undertaking.[365]

If one assumes that a title is valid for the area immediately around permanent bases, the perimeter controlled could expand with the exercise of administrative jurisdiction. Despite Antarctica's continental proportions, the number of points in it that are suitable for stations is quite small. This is due to the persistence of pack-ice blocking vessel access to certain coastal areas (notably Marie Byrd Land) even in summer. Only a small proportion of the coast of the continent is ice-free and relatively easy to approach by ship.

So Deception Island, in the South Shetland Islands, which has an almost completely landlocked harbour in a volcanic crater, has been utilised since 1820.[366] It was a focus for sealers in the nineteenth century and for pelagic whaling in the early twentieth century. The island was the centre of British activity, involving the presence of a resident magistrate, in the polar summer between 1910 and 1930[367] and is vital to the United Kingdom's claim to the Antarctic Peninsula.[368] Establishment of an Argentine base on the island and its formal destruction by Britain in 1953 contributed substantially to the tension in the area and the filing of the *Antarctica Cases* with the International Court of Justice. Three nations maintained bases[369] within 5 km. of each other. In February 1969 the British and Chilean bases were destroyed by a volcanic eruption and the Argentine station was evacuated.[370] One could not attribute control beyond the base area where three stations were in such close proximity. The neighbouring bases were apparently intended to cancel each other out by denying an element of sovereignty, the ability to exclude other States.[371]

In 1820 Edward Bransfield took formal possession of King George Island, also in the South Shetland group, for Britain.[372] The first Soviet base in the South American sector, Bellingshausen, was established on Fildes Peninsula in February 1968. Chile quickly set

365. *Grisbadarna Case* (1910) 4 AJIL 226 at 234.
366. K.J. Bertrand, *Americans in Antarctica 1775–1948* (1971), 124–5.
367. Application instituting Proceedings, *Antarctica Case* (*UK* v. *Argentina*) (1955), 19.
368. C.H.M. Waldock, 'Disputed Sovereignty in the Falkland Islands Dependencies' (1948), 25 *BYBIL*, 311 at 330.
369. Decepción (Argentina), Presidente Pedro Aguirre Cerda (Chile) Deception Island (United Kingdom).
370. 'Deception Island Eruption' (1969), 4(3) *Antarctic Journal*, 87.
371. J. Kish, *The Law of International Spaces* (1973), 52.
372. Application instituting Proceedings, *Antarctica Case* (*UK* v. *Argentina*) (1955), 11.

up Presidente Frei Station next to the Russians.[373] Eleven years later Poland built Arctowski Base on the same island. Perhaps the most interesting example is that of Ross Island, site of New Zealand's Scott Base and the US McMurdo complex.[374]

373. Discussed under Environment/*Specially Protected Areas.*
374. See National Interests/*the United States.*

3

NATIONAL INTERESTS

The South American Sector

The South American sector presents the most complicated political issues of Antarctic sovereignty, a wide range of legal arguments and the most extensive literature, mostly in Spanish. Britain's views are formally documented in its case presented to the International Court of Justice in 1955. Beginning with the annexation of South Georgia by Cook in 1775, British sailors and naval officers carried out acts of formal possession on a number of islands. Such acts purported to extend to undefined contiguous lands,[1] although the islands themselves were located in the northern reaches of the Antarctic Peninsula and the sub-Antarctic.

Letters Patent of 1908[2] and 1917[3] were put forward as boundary delimitations for the Falkland Islands Dependencies.[4] For periods between 1909 to 1930 magistrates resided at South Georgia and Deception Island. Reliance is also placed upon whaling licences and legislation applicable to the area. Permanent scientific bases date from 1944.[5]

Argentina's occupation of the observatory at Laurie Island in 1904 was not followed by any further settlement, although there were early negotiations with Chile, discussions with the United Kingdom, and formal protests.[6] An expedition by the vessel *Primero de Mayo* in 1942 set up plaques on islands off the northern Antarctic Peninsula proclaiming the boundaries of the Argentine territory as 25° and 68° 34′W, south of 60°S.[7] Since 1947 stations have been established.

1. Application instituting Proceedings, *Antarctica Case* (*UK* v. *Argentina*) (1955), 12.
2. (1912) 101 BFSP 76.
3. (1921) 111 BFSP 16.
4. Including the South Sandwich Islands, South Georgia and Shag Rocks north of 60°S. In 1962 these islands were declared to be the Falkland Islands Dependencies and the sector south of 60°S was denominated the British Antarctic Territory.
5. Application instituting Proceedings, *Antarctica Case* (*UK* v. *Argentina*) (1955), 16–29.
6. Letter to the Director of the Universal Postal Union (14 September 1927) (1948–9) 46 US Naval War College, International Law Documents 218.
7. Argentina did not publish a decree defining the claim (R.D. Hayton, 'The American Antarctic' (1956), 50 *AJIL*, 583 at 589). From 1947, 74°W was adopted as the western boundary.

Like Argentina's, Chile's claim is based on an imperfect title inherited from Spain.[8] Whaling and fishing concessions were granted between 1902 and 1914.[9] A Presidential Decree in 1940 gave the limits as 53°W and 90°W without a northern boundary.[10] The first permanent station, Soberania, was set up on Greenwich Island, in the South Shetland group, in 1947 as a manifestation of effective occupation under the decree of 1940.[11]

Apart from the general issues of Antarctic law previously reviewed, the South American sector claimants invoke doctrines particularly applicable to that area. Argentina and Chile trace their rights to the Bull Inter Caetera of Pope Alexander VI of 1493 demarcating the sphere of influence between Portugal and Spain, and the Treaty of Tordesillas of 1494 between the two countries which moved the boundary 270 leagues further west. Opponents regard the Bull as a hopeless root of title today, and to have been difficult to uphold even in the fifteenth century.[12] Another view argues that the Bull represented the ruling law of Europe at the time, a similar grant having been given to Henry II over Ireland.[13] Properly read, the Bull applies only to lands and islands discovered or to be discovered by one of the two countries.[14] 'At the time, the legal validity of these letters patent, as we may well designate them, seems to have been unquestioned'.[15]

It is not argued that the Bull and Treaty of Tordesillas are part of modern international law. Chile[16] and Argentina contend that they inherited the rights of Spain on attaining independence. Central and South American countries support the *uti possidetis juris* by which each adheres to the former Spanish Provincial boundaries. Thus at a time when vast areas of the subcontinent were unexplored, no territory remained without a sovereign. The doctrine was specifically intended to forestall attempted occupation by European powers.[17]

---

8. O. Pinochet de la Barra, *La Antártica Chilena* (4th edn, 1976), 136.
9. Mateo Martinić B., 'Interés, Preocupación y Presencia Antárticos de Chile' in Francisco Orrego Vicuña and Augusto Salinas Araya (eds.), *El desarollo de la Antártica* (1977), 38 at 42–7.
10. (1948–9) 46 US Naval War College, International Law Documents, 224.
11. Oscar Vila Labra, *Chilenos en la Antártica* (1947), 189–90.
12. Having been disregarded by Catholic powers (France and England) at the time (C.H.M. Waldock, 'Disputed Sovereignty in the Falkland Islands Dependencies' (1948), 25 *BYBIL*, 311 at 321).
13. H. Harisse, *The Diplomatic History of America* (1897), 40.
14. Ibid., at p. 74.
15. J. Goebel, *The Struggle for the Falkland Islands* (1927), 50.
16. O. Pinochet de la Barra, *La Antártica Chilena* (4th edn, 1976), 158.
17. J.B. Scott, 'The Swiss Decision in the Boundary Dispute between Columbia and Venezuela' (1922), 16 *AJIL*, 428 at 429.

All land in Spanish America, however remote or inhospitable, is deemed to have been part of one of the former administrative divisions of colonial rule.[18]

Uti possidetis has been vigorously attacked[19] and even categorised as an 'exotic argument'.[20] But the concept has general support in Latin American practice and arbitration as an intra-American international law rule.[21] Difficulties within the region arise not from any questioning of the validity of *uti possidetis* but from the lack of trustworthy information during colonial times with respect to much subsequently disputed territory and the absence of any semblance of administrative authority in such areas.[22] Boundaries on paper often differed materially from those of actual occupation.[23]

Uti possidetis is particularly helpful to the South American Antarctic claims. If it is a rule of international law, then the South American sector was not *res nullius* at the time when Britain's various acts of sovereignty were carried out. Britain would argue, first, that a regional custom is subordinate to general international law. It is therefore not opposable against third parties[24] and for this reason was rejected in the *Clipperton Island Case*.[25] *Uti possidetis* can only apply to territory over which Spain had title in 1810, and there is little evidence of a Spanish claim to any part of Antarctica.[26] It may be concluded that *uti possidetis* is a valid rule of intra-American customary international law, although its extension to the Antarctic is objectively dubious – but no more questionable, it might be argued, than the sector principle which it resembles in a number of ways.

The United Kingdom places considerable reliance on the argument that activities after 1925 for the South Orkney Islands and 1937 for the other Antarctic areas should be disregarded. Once sovereignty to territory has been established, actions subsequent to the

---

18. *Beagle Channel Arbitration* (1978) 17 ILM 632 at 645.
19. E. Honnold, 'Thaw in International Law? Rights in Antarctica under the Law of Common Space' (1978), 87 *YLJ*, 804 at 814.
20. S.O. Butler, 'Owning Antarctica' (1977), 31 *Journal of International Affairs*, 35 at 42.
21. Judge Gros in *Beagle Channel Arbitration* (1978) 17 ILM 632 at 675. The concept of regional custom peculiar to Latin American States has been accepted in principle. (*Asylum Case* (1950) ICJ 266 at 276) and expounded in detail by Judge Alvarez (dissenting opinion, *Asylum Case* at pp. 293–4).
22. *Honduras Boundaries Arbitration* (1933) 2 UNRIAA 1308 at 1325.
23. G. Ireland, *Boundaries, Possessions and Conflicts in South America* (1971), 329.
24. G. Cohen Jonathan, 'Les Îles Falkland (Malouines)' (1972), 18 *AFDI*, 235 at 239.
25. (1932) 2 UNRIAA 1105 at 1109, where Mexico's claim as successor to Spain was presumably based on the doctrine.
26. cf. J.C. Puig, *La Antártida Argentina ante el Derecho* (1960), 115–21.

critical date should be disregarded to prevent window – dressing.[27] The doctrine has much support in cases.[28] One may agree that the concept is useful where, as in *Palmas* and *Eastern Greenland*, the critical date is obvious. Difficulties arise, however, when various dates are possible. Then, it is contended, one must take the date of crystallization of the dispute as the time at which means of settlement were proposed.[29] On the latter approach the United Kingdom's filing of the *Antarctica Cases* may be seen as an attempt to stop the clock running in the face of the expanding network of Chilean and Argentinian bases.

In such complicated cases selection of a critical date virtually determines the issue.[30] Even decisions utilizing the concept have relied on subsequent events, for example to cast light on the immediately preceding period[31] or because special circumstances, such as the gradual development of activity over centuries, have continued without interruption after the critical date.[32] Territorial rivals find difficulty in resisting the temptation to rely both on the critical date and later events. One may conclude that judicial adoption of this test will not preclude admission of subsequent facts in special circumstances.

In many cases even a sovereign is not certain precisely when title to territory accrued.[33] Various dates may be relevant but none decisive. In such instances the critical date is of little value.[34] It should be seen as a technique of analysis but not as a rule of law.[35]

Directly contrasting with the argument for a precise point in time at which title accrues is the concept of a slow evolutionary process of establishment of sovereignty[36] by historical consolidation.[37] Since

27. For example: *Island of Palmas Case* (1928) 2 UNRIAA 829 at 839, 845 and 864; *Legal Status of Eastern Greenland* (1933) PCIJ Ser. A/B No. 53 22 at 45 and 64.
28. L.F.E. Goldie, 'The Critical Date' (1963), 12 *ICLQ*, 1251 at 1266.
29. G.G. Fitzmaurice, 'The Law and Procedure of the International Court of Justice 1951–1954' (1955–6), 32 *BYBIL* 20 at 24–5 and 29. Fitzmaurice's article discusses the critical date in great detail and has direct relevance to his contemporaneous application of it in the *Antarctica Cases* (Application instituting Proceedings, *Antarctica Case* (*UK* v. *Argentina*) (1955) 100). It may be noted that Fitzmaurice's invocation of the critical date for Antarctica precludes any consideration of subsequent facts.
30. T. Cheng, 'The Sino-Japanese Dispute over the Senkaku Islands and the Law of Territorial Acquisition' (1971), 14 *Virginia Journal of International Law*, 221 at 229.
31. *Island of Palmas Case* (1928) 2 UNRIAA 829 at 866.
32. *Minquiers and Ecrehos Case* (1953), *ICJ*, 47 at 59–60.
33. *A.G. for British Honduras* v. *Bristowe* (1880), 6 App. Cas., 143 at 148.
34. *Argentine-Chile Frontier Arbitration* (1966) 38 ILR 10 at 80.
35. R.Y. Jennings, *The Acquisition of Territory in International Law* (1963), 34.
36. Judge Levi Carneiro in *Minquiers and Ecrehos Case* (1953), ICJ, 47 at 104.
37. *Anglo-Norwegian Fisheries Case* (1951), ICJ, 116 at 138.

the *Anglo-Norwegian Fisheries Case*, commentators have paid considerable attention to this view.[38]

Consolidation emphasises the element of prolonged establishment of rights prominent in offshore jurisdiction cases[39] requiring validation by historic processes.[40] Numerous examples may be advanced of illegal acts giving rise to lawful situations.[41] Although the doctrine is extensively relied on by Antarctic claimants,[42] its defects are patent. Suggesting that none of the particular rules of international law suffices, consolidation does not provide a substitute. There is no indication of the content of the doctrine to guide judicial tribunals in resolving territorial disputes.[43] Consolidation does not have a firm basis in the cases and should not be relied on as an additional root of title to territory.

Any consideration of the South American sector must take account of the long-standing dispute between Argentina and the United Kingdom over the Falkland (Malvinas) Islands situated 400 miles east of Argentina. Their area is about that of Northern Ireland, and, as the Argentinians recognise,[44] the population of 1,800 is strongly pro-British. Exports consist almost entirely of wool.[45] It is a bleak treeless little world where a howling gale blows one day out of every six.[46]

According to the Argentinian view, Article 8 of the Treaty of Utrecht guaranteed Spanish possessions in the Americas against further British action. In 1770 Spain compelled British settlers on the Falkland Islands to leave. The crisis was resolved in 1771 by a secret agreement by Britain to abandon the islands.[47] This was carried out in 1774 but a plaque was left purporting to preserve British rights. If Britain's occupation had been illegal *ab initio*, the plaque could have no effect; in any case, a mere notice of this nature could not constitute effective occupation. Louis Vernet, appointed Governor by

38. e.g. D.H.N. Johnson, 'Consolidation as a Root of Title in International Law' (1955), *CLJ*, 215.
39. *US* v. *Alaska* 422 US 184 at 190 (1975).
40. cf. D.P. O'Connell, 'Bays, Historic Waters and the Implications of *A. Raptis & Son* v. *South Australia*' (1978), 52 *ALJ*, 64 at 67.
41. J. Crawford, 'The Criteria for Statehood in International Law' (1976–7), 48 *BYBIL*, 93 at 171 and 174.
42. See F.M. Auburn, *The Ross Dependency*, (1972) 22–3.
43. Ibid., at p. 22.
44. Jose Manuel Moneta, *Nos Devolvéran las Malvinas*? (1972), 32.
45. Central Office of Information, 'The Falklands Islands and Dependencies' (September 1968).
46. O.J. Pettingill, 'People and Penguins of the Faraway Falklands' (1956), 91(3) *National Geographic Magazine*, 387.
47. J. Goebel, *The Struggle for the Falkland Islands* (1927), 286.

the Buenos Aires government, established a settlement at Port Soledad in 1826. He seized American ships for sealing without a licence, which led to reprisals by the United States. Finally in 1833 the British warship *Clio* expelled the Argentinian garrison. Since then Argentina has protested against the occupation on numerous occasions.[48]

From the time of Lord Palmerston such remonstrances have fallen on deaf ears. Argentinian public interest in the issue has always been significant. In demonstrations of support an Argentinian pilot landed at Port Stanley in 1964 with a national flag,[49] and in 1966 a group calling itself 'Condor' hijacked an Argentinian Airlines plane carrying Admiral Jose Maria Guzman, Governor of Tierra del Fuego, Antarctica and the South Atlantic Islands, and forced it to land at Port Stanley.[50]

Argentinian official pressure in the United Nations led to a General Assembly Resolution[51] inviting the two nations to enter into negotiations for a pacific solution of the dispute in accordance with the principles of self-determination embodied in Res. 1514/XV of 1960.[52] Argentina emphasised that ninety-four countries voted for the 1965 resolution, fourteen abstained and none voted against it.[53] Prolonged discussions have continued since then. At first the islanders were convinced that Argentina would prevail,[54] and this tendency appeared to have been borne out by an agreement in 1971 enabling them to travel to Argentina and providing for a regular shipping and air service to that country.[55] An airfield was built by Argentina at Stanley in 1972. Integration seemed to be only a matter of time.[56] Then further agreements in 1974 facilitated trade and allowed the Argentine state petroleum company to supply petrol to the Falklands.

As long as the dispute related only to a group of distant islands with a small population and little economic attraction, a gradual

48. J. Pedrero, 'América, las Malvinas y el Derecho Internacional' (1954), 270 *Argentina Austral*, 2 at 5.
49. Jose Manuel Moneta, *Nos Devolverán las Malvinas*? (1970), 53.
50. Juan Carlos Moneta, *La Recuperación de las Malvinas* (1973), 280.
51. Res. 2065/XX of 1965.
52. Argentina argues that regard must be had to the 'interests' but not the 'wishes' of the Falkland Islanders because it was deprived of the islands by an illegitimate act of force. Therefore the governing principle is that of territorial integrity under paragraph 6 of Res. 1514 (UN Doc. A.AC. 109/520 (7 May 1976)).
53. Ezequiel Federico Pereyra, *Las Islas Malvinas* (1968), 36.
54. R. Gott, 'Imperial Sunset over the Falklands', *Guardian Weekly* (5 December 1968).
55. UN Doc. A/8368 (27 August 1971).
56. G. Cohen Jonathan, 'Les Îles Falkland (Malouines)' (1972), 18 *AFDI*, 235 at 262.

settlement appeared feasible, but by 1974 considerable interest had developed in the hydrocarbon reserves of the continental shelf. Numerous licence requests had been made. Jurisdiction over off-shore resources served as a catalyst for escalation of the dispute.[57] Professor Donald Griffiths of Birmingham University prepared a report on possible oil deposits off the islands for the British government. There were rumours of an important oilfield between the islands and Argentina. In December 1974 the Falkland Islands Legislative Council urged that licences be issued.[58] Argentina protested to the Committee of Twenty-four, stating that the Griffiths Report concerned possible petroleum deposits on the Argentine continental shelf near the Malvinas and that no foreign country had the right to explore for or extract hydrocarbons in the area.[59]

Not surprisingly, Argentina considered the British assessment of offshore oil potential to be an indication of an intention to retain sovereignty. Despite the expression of Argentinian concern, in October 1975 the British government commissioned Lord Shackleton to carry out the Falkland Islands Economic Survey.[60] Argentina then withdrew its Ambassador from London.

One would have thought that Argentina's opposition to Falkland continental shelf research had been made abundantly clear in March 1975, and it is in this light that subsequent events must be viewed. On 4 February 1976 the British research vessel *Shackleton* operated for the National Environment Research Council, carried out geo-physical research 80 miles south of the Falklands.[61] An Argentinian warship *Almirante Storni* ordered the British vessel to heave to and steam to Ushuaia. Ignoring the order, the *Shackleton*, which was carrying explosives, went to Port Stanley followed by the *Almirante Storni*.[62]

With considerable justification Argentina regarded government-sponsored research on the disputed continental shelf as a provocation, analogous to, if not as severe as, the Turkish seismic research in the Aegean.[63] While the *Shackleton*'s mission was presumably not so

57. R.L. Fahrney, 'Status of an Island's Continental Shelf Jurisdiction: A Case Study of the Falkland Islands' (1979), 10(4) *Journal of Maritime Law and Commerce*, 539.
58. UN Doc. A/10023/Add. 8 (Part III) (31 October 1975).
59. UN Doc. A/AC. 109/482 (28 March 1975).
60. Economist Intelligence Unit, *Economic Survey of the Falkland Islands* (1976).
61. 'The Shackleton incident could profit international law' (1976), 259 *Nature*, 435.
62. The *Almirante Storni*, carrying guns, torpedoes and depth charges and with a maximum speed three times that of its quarry, could easily have stopped the *Shackleton* ('British ship fired on by Argentine warship', *The Times*, (5 February 1976)).
63. *Aegean Sea Continental Shelf Case* (1978) ICJ 3 at 10.

intended, its timing was inept. Argentina argued that the situation was made more serious because of its previously stated attitude to offshore research. The *Shackleton*'s action in ignoring Argentine instructions, although carrying explosives, was 'reckless and provocative' and clearly indicated an intention to conceal its activities.[64]

Disputed sovereignty in the Falklands is directly related to Antarctica. Argentina regards the islands as situated on its continuous continental shelf[65] which by parity of reasoning extends to South Georgia, the South Sandwich and South Orkney groups. Argentina puts forward a legal argument that these islands are a geological continuation of the Andes reappearing as the Antartandes.[66] In geopolitical terms the Southern Atlantic and Antarctic are seen as a single region. Within a year of the Antarctic Treaty coming into force, the United Kingdom detached the area south of 60°S from the Falkland Islands Dependencies to form the British Antarctic Territory,[67] insulating its Antarctic claim from the effect of any future settlement with Argentina in the Falklands. In practice a transfer of sovereignty over the islands would tend to weaken Britain's position in South Georgia leading to a ripple effect. Much of the United Kingdom's case for the Antarctic depends on administrative acts carried out in the Falklands.

A further piece for the South American jigsaw puzzle of law and politics is the Argentine/Chile doctrine of an 'American Antarctic'. Despite their overlapping claims, the two countries have repeatedly put forward a united front against Britain. Politically, the 'American Antarctic' has the attraction of involving the United States whose rejection of outside interference in Latin America dates back to the Monroe Doctrine.

Chile and Argentina carried on inconclusive Antarctic delimitation discussions as early as 1906.[68] Major impetus for an American Antarctic came from President Roosevelt. In 1939 the United States decided to set up bases to further its claims, but at the same time the State Department was most concerned not to antagonise the Latin American nations. In an initiative which appears to have been the personal decision of Roosevelt, Argentina and Chile were informed that the United States' activities in the South American sector would be carried out on behalf of all the other American Republics. If the sector proved valuable, its sovereignty could be managed by an inter-American Republic governing body. In May 1940 Secretary of State

64. Argentine letter dated 23 February 1976 (UN Doc. A/31/55 (24 February 1976)).
65. F.A. Milia and others, *La Atlantártida* (1978), 248.
66. J.A. Fraga, *Introducción a la Geopolítica Antártica* (1978), 25.
67. British Antarctic Territory Order-in-Council 1962, No. 400.
68. J.C. Puig, *La Antártida Argentina ante el Derecho* (1960), 177.

Cordell Hull spoke of the imperative need for the American Republics to have a clearer title than non-American countries in the sector on defence considerations.[69]

After the Chilean claim of November 1940, representatives of Argentina and Chile agreed that a South American Antarctic existed and only their two countries had exclusive rights of sovereignty over it.[70] A communiqué in 1947 in a similar vein led to the Donoso-La Rosa declaration of 1948. Each country recognised the other's indisputable rights of sovereignty. Common accord was to govern action for the juridical protection and defence of rights. Demarcation of boundaries in the Antarctic was to be negotiated.[71] An indication of the strength of the joint front is the Act of Puerto Montt of February 1978 (at the height of the Beagle Channel confrontation) by which the Presidents of both countries reaffirmed their defence of legal rights in Antarctica.

Roosevelt's initiative, with its apparent disregard for relations with the United Kingdom, was a mistake. Its full effect became clear on the signature of the Inter-American Treaty of Reciprocal Assistance (Rio Treaty)[72] in 1947. Parties agreed that an armed attack by any State against an American State should be considered an attack against all American States.[73] Article IV defined the region covered by the Treaty as extending to the South Pole. South of South America the boundaries were 90°W and 24°W[74] Aggression included violation of the integrity of territory by means other than an armed attack.[75] Argentina and Chile made declarations reserving their rights over, *inter alia*, their Antarctic territories. A corresponding United States declaration recorded its position that the Treaty had no effect upon the sovereignty or international status of the territories in the region. On signing the Antarctic Treaty Chile, Argentina and the United States declared that it did not affect their obligations under the Rio Treaty.[76]

The Rio Treaty was a considerable achievement for Argentina and Chile. President Videla of Argentina made it clear that it covered the Antarctic, and that Britain's conduct constituted aggression against

69. R.D. Hayton, 'Polar Problems and International Law' (1958), 52 *AJIL*, 746 at 756.
70. R.E. Wilson, 'National Interests and Claims in the Antarctic' (1964), 17 *Arctic*, 15 at 22.
71. (1948–9) 46 US Naval War College, *International Law Documents*, 226–7.
72. 21 UNTS 78.
73. Art. III (1).
74. The western boundary of Chile's claim is 90°W and the eastern limit of Argentina's Antarctic Territory is 25°W (see Map).
75. Art. VI.
76. Department of State, *Conference on Antarctica* (1960), 68–9.

all the Americas within the meaning of the Treaty.[77] Clearly the South American countries had laid the basis for an American Antarctic doctrine involving the United States. As a source of title, the Rio Treaty must be ignored;[78] the agreement was a collective security treaty.[79] However, it applied to the Antarctic in terms intended to allow Argentina or Chile to invoke it against Britain. At least, the Treaty prevented the United States from supporting Britain in any confrontation with the South American countries.[80]

The claims of Argentina and Chile overlap. Furthermore the region claimed by both is the most desirable part of the sector. Yet each country supports the indisputable rights of the other. As the United Kingdom has emphasised, both claims could not be valid even if either were.[81] Had this been solely an Antarctic boundary problem, the demarcation contemplated in 1948 by the Donoso-La Rosa Declaration might have been achieved. However, both countries regard Antarctica as a continuation of their South American territory; for instance President Pinochet, visiting the Antarctic in January 1977, declared that his country's Antarctic territory was merely an extension of Chile proper. Prolonged and severe dispute over the southernmost portion of this boundary, in the Beagle Channel, directly affects any possible Antarctic delimitation.

In 1881 the countries signed a Boundary Treaty. Article III provided that:

In Tierra del Fuego a line shall be drawn, which starting from the point called Cape Espiritu Santo, in parallel 52° 40′, shall be prolonged to the south along the meridian 68° 34′ west of Greenwich until it touches Beagle Channel. Tierra del Fuego, divided in this manner, shall be Chilean on the western side and Argentine on the eastern. As for the islands, to the Argentine Republic shall belong Staten Island, the small islands next to it, and the other islands there may be on the Atlantic to the east of Tierra del Fuego and of the eastern coast of Patagonia; and to Chile shall belong all the islands to the south of Beagle Channel up to Cape Horn, and those there may be to the west of Tierra del Fuego.

Under a compromis of 1971 the British Sovereign was requested to act as arbitrator regarding the sovereignty of Picton, Nueva, Lennox and adjacent islands and islets in the Channel. An appointed Court of Arbitration found for Chile. Argentina's case was based on

77. E.W. Hunter Christie, *The Antarctic Problem* (1951), 284.
78. I. von Münch, 'Völkerrechtsfragen der Antarktis' (1958), 7 *Archiv des Völkerrechts*, 225 at 240.
79. J.C. Puig, *La Antártida Argentina ante el Derecho* (1960), 226.
80. See also the Stonington Island episode (Treaty/*Origins*).
81. Application instituting Proceedings, *Antarctica Case* (*UK* v. *Argentina*) (1955), 35.

the view that the words 'to the east' cannot be read literally but must mean 'on the eastern side of the archipelago'. Argentina contended that it was to have any islands on the Atlantic side.[82] The validity of Argentina's views depended on the 'Atlantic' principle[83] according to which Chile's territory was limited to the Pacific Ocean and Argentina's to the Atlantic. The Court specifically rejected the Argentinian arguments in this regard.[84] Argentina declared the award a nullity in January 1978 on the grounds (*inter alia*) that the Court erred in rejecting the Atlantic principle.[85] Troops were massed on both sides of the border, blackout exercises were carried out in Buenos Aires, and units of the Argentinian Navy went on manoeuvres in the South Atlantic in November. Possible armed conflict was avoided only when both parties agreed to the Pope's mediation.[86]

Both Argentinian and Chilean commentators regard any Antarctic delimitation as linked with the Beagle Channel boundary.[87] Introduction of 200-mile Exclusive Economic Zones, development of krill trawling[88] and potential offshore oil resources are all politically volatile issues. Argentina sees Chile as aspiring to extend the Pacific Ocean to South Georgia and the South Sandwich, South Orkney and South Shetland Islands,[89] and to utilise the demarcation to expand Antarctic territory at Argentina's expense.[90] As Argentina is well aware, Chile places emphasis on a handwritten note of Bernardo O'Higgins dated 1831 which was found in the British Foreign Office in 1918. According to this note, Chile has the key to the Atlantic extending to the South Pole and the Pacific,[91] raising the prospect of a bioceanic projection of Chile.[92]

82. *Beagle Channel Arbitration* (1978) 17 ILM 632 at 658.
83. Ibid., at p. 662.
84. Ibid.
85. (1978) 17 ILM 738 at 748. Although Argentina relied on a variety of arguments its political concern centred on this issue (D.M. Himmelreich, 'The Beagle Channel Affair' (1979), 12 *Vanderbilt Journal of Transnational Law*, 971 at 986 and 997).
86. (1979) 18 *ILM* 1. An interim settlement in 1979 involved Chilean acceptance of the oceanic principle.
87. J.-F. da Costa, 'A Teoria dos Setores Polares' (1951), 13 & 14 *Boletim da Sociedade Brasileira de Direito Internacional*, 87 at 107.
88. V. Palermo, 'Una Argentina bicontinental y biocéanica' (1978), 82 *Discusión*, 50 at 56.
89. R.F. Huáscar, 'Un análisis a fondo de la cuestión de límites con Chile en la zona austral', *Clarin* (21 August 1977).
90. A.L. Aufranc, 'Antecedentes históricos y estado actual-del litigio con Chile', *La Nacion* (24 December 1978).
91. O. Pinochet de le Barra, *La Antártica Chilena* (4th edn, 1976), 77.
92. At best O'Higgins' note can have little legal effect, but its political significance for Argentina is considerable.

So far the South American sector has been seen as involving the three claimants. Direct interest of the superpowers in Antarctica will be discussed separately. Here one must add Brazil. South American concepts of Antarctic issues are based upon large-scale geopolitical considerations. Expression of interest in the continent by a major rival such as Brazil is seen as a serious political issue.

In 1958 Brazil reserved its rights to formulate a claim and refused to recognise existing claims.[93] Considerable support was voiced for such action. The theory of '*defrontaçao*', an adaptation of the sector,[94] would extend land boundaries in the area of the South American Antarctic corresponding to the Security Zone of the Rio Treaty. On one interpretation this would give Argentina most of the Antarctic Peninsula, leaving Brazil with a much less attractive sector in the Weddell Sea.[95] Another proposal would have extended from 28°W to 53°W.[96]

Given the rivalry between Argentina and Brazil there was cause enough for concern, exacerbated by Brazil's demonstration of an actual interest in Antarctic affairs. In 1972 a group of private citizens established the Brazilian Institute of Antarctic Studies (IBEA).[97] It was reported that an engineering club from that country was planning a thirty-man expedition to the Antarctic Peninsula.[98] In response to the Brazilian plans,[99] President Lastiri and the entire Argentinian Cabinet flew to Marambio Base, which was proclaimed the temporary capital of Argentina as an affirmation of sovereignty.[100] Chile insisted on its sovereignty,[101] and Uruguayans complained of a violation of rights over their sector.[102]

93. J.E. Greño Velasco, 'La Adhesion de Brasil al Tratado Antártico' (1976), *Revista de Politica Internacional*, 71 at 81.
94. R. Platzöder, *Politische Konzeptionen zur Neuordnung des Meeresvölkerrechts* (1976), 161.
95. J.A. Fraga, *Introducción a la Geopolítica Antártica* (1978) 36. (28°W to 49 50′W, allowing for an Uruguayan sector).
96. Enrique Gajardo Villarroel, 'Brasil y la Antártida Sudamericana', *El Mercurio* (1 March 1973).
97. J.A. Wiltgen, 'Instituto Brasileño de Estudios Antárticos: Objetivos y Politicas' in Francisco Orrego Vicuña and Augusto Salinas Araya (eds.), *El desarrollo de la Antártica* (1977), 324.
98. 'Brazil may send expedition' (1973), 6(12), *Antarctic* 436.
99. 'Argentina en la Antártida', *El Mercurio* (10 August 1973).
100. 'Base Marambio: Capital Accidental de la República' (1974), *Antártida*, 19 at 23 (see also Treaty/*Claims* and Treaty/*Third Parties*).
101. J.N. Goodsell, 'South American Nations again take Interest in Antarctica's Future', *Otago Daily Times* (2 November 1973).
102. There has not been any official claim by that country nor (despite recent press discussion) by Peru. Uruguay acceded to the Antarctic Treaty in 1980 ((1980) 19 ILM 547).

In explanation of its accession to the Antarctic Treaty in 1975, it was stated that, having the largest South Atlantic coastline, Brazil had direct and substantial interests in Antarctica[103] and had responsibilities for the area's security under the Rio Treaty. This rationale is uncomfortably similar, from the Argentinian viewpoint, to the *defrontaçao* argument. Argentina took a serious view of Brazil's Antarctic plans before Brazil adhered to the Treaty.[104] Any future Antarctic crisis in the South American sector may now implicate Brazil.

Examining the comparative stance of the claimants, the disadvantaged position of the United Kingdom is apparent. Its Antarctic Territory was claimed in 1908 at a time when British naval power and the concomitant resolve to use it if necessary were at their height. The voyage of the Argentinian ship *Primero de Mayo* in 1942 and the subsequent establishment of rival stations in the Antarctic Peninsula area directly challenged the United Kingdom's claim. Thirty years ago British commentators pointed out that every year in which the Argentine and Chilean bases were maintained saw a progressive weakening of the British position.[105] Since then there has been a considerable acceleration in the process. An influential former British diplomat suggested in 1977 that the United Kingdom should look upon itself as a non-claimant 'in all but name' for resources.[106]

Chile and Argentina see Antarctica as a major issue close to home. This is not the case for the United Kingdom. It is difficult to envisage Britain resorting to military means to defend its claim, but Argentina and Chile could well do so if they thought it necessary. Chile's effort is enterprising, audacious and sustained. Every opportunity is taken to reiterate its claim.[107] But it is overshadowed by Argentina which has a population of 26,000,000 (as against 11,000,000 for Chile) and larger military forces.

Argentina is the key to the South American sector. It has the resources and the power, and the determination to use them if needed. In the 1977 Antarctic winter season Argentina had seven stations open (more than any other country), while the United Kingdom

103. J.E. Greño Velasco, 'La Adhesion de Brasil al Tratado Antártico' (1976), *Revista de Politica Internacional* 71 at 72.
104. B.N. Rodriguez, 'Soberania Argentina en la Antártida' in F.A. Milia and others, *La Atlantártida* (1978), 195.
105. E.W. Hunter Christie, *The Antarctic Problem* (1951) 290.
106. B. Roberts, 'International Co-operation for Antarctic Development: the Test for the Antarctic Treaty' (1978), 19(119) *Polar Record*, 107 at 112.
107. See, for example, Statement by Ambassador Zegers, Opening Session, Ninth Antarctic Treaty Consultative Meeting (1977) and cf. the apparently politically-motivated Chilean campaign for Marine SPA and SSSI designations (Treaty/*Area*).

had four and Chile three.[108] Chile's bases are concentrated on a relatively small area of the Antarctic Peninsula north of 63°S. Argentina and the United Kingdom have winter stations in this area and also much further south, at 68°S and on the coast of the Weddell Sea, but since 1965 United Kingdom personnel wintering over have declined from approximately 100[109] to fifty-five, while Chile has fifty and Argentina 154.[110] In 1978 Argentina took delivery of the *Almirante Irizar*, a very costly icebreaker with a crew of 133 and capacity for 100 passengers.[111] Argentina has reached agreement with New Zealand for the operation of a regular polar air service between Buenos Aires and Christchurch by Aerolineas Argentinas.[112]

Mention has already been made of the presence of wives, the birth of a baby and the celebration of a wedding at Esperanza Base.[113] Eight families with a total of twelve children were provided with a school run by the colony's priest. Described by the Argentinian press as a new era in Argentinian sovereignty, the venture underlined determination to take all possible measures to assert its claim. Behind these actions was a view of the Antarctic as having geopolitical and strategic relevance on a global scale,[114] a type of manifest destiny[115] and a value as a cultural and educational project related to a mystic harmony between man and nature[116] with a feeling for tradition. Argentinians are also concerned at the long-range issues of policy[117] in marked contrast with the *ad hoc* decision-making of some other Antarctic nations.

The United States

United States policy presents a number of problems. Why did the nation having the most extensive record of Antarctic activities not make a claim? What are the objectives of the United States in

108. (1979) 63 *SCAR Bulletin*, 106.
109. Earthscan Press Briefing Document No. 5 (1977), 15.
110. National Science Foundation. *US Antarctic Program Draft Environmental Impact Statement* (1979) 2–11 (taken from Antarctic Treaty Exchange of Information Reports for 1977–8).
111. ' "Almirante Irizar" – most powerful icebreaker in the South' (1979), *Shipbuilding and Marine Engineering International*, 194.
112. 'Argentine proposals for polar air route' (1979), 8(10) *Antarctic*, 367.
113. Sovereignty/*Polar Circumstances*.
114. J.E. Fraga, *Introducción a la Geopolitica Antártica* (1978), 54–7.
115. V. Palermo, 'Espacio Continental y Espacio Antártico' (1978), 21 *Revista Escuela de Defensa Nacional*, 81 at 90.
116. V. Palermo, 'El Espacio Antártico en la formacion de la Conciencia geopolitica Argentina', MS (1979).
117. C.J. Moneta, 'Antártida Argentina: Los problemas de 1975–1990' (1975), 1 *Estrategia* 5.

Antarctica? Is there a grand design to obtain access to all the continent's resources?

American involvement dates back to a sealing venture in South Georgia in 1790.[118] Subsequently sealers worked extensively in the Antarctic Peninsula, including Captain Palmer of the *Hero* whose voyage in 1820–1 gave rise to claims of first discovery of the continent and a heated debate on priority.[119] In 1840 Wilkes' United States Exploring Expedition, financed by Congress, surveyed the coast of part of what is now the Australian Antarctic Territory in poorly-equipped sailing ships, but did not land. Although Wilkes' expedition was a government venture, its aims were scientific and no claims were made.

There is a gap of nearly ninety years until the next significant American activity, Admiral Byrd's private expeditions. The first, between 1928 and 1930, established a base at Little America on the Ross Ice Shelf and carried out scientific work in the Queen Maud Mountains and flights to the South Pole and Marie Byrd Land. A geological expedition claimed part of the area east of 150°W (the eastern boundary of the Ross Dependency). From 1933 to 1935 the Admiral's second private expedition worked in the same area expanding activities in Edward VII Land and Marie Byrd Land.

Lincoln Ellsworth flew across the continent from Dundee Island in the Antarctic Peninsula to Little America in 1935, claiming the land between 80°W and 120°W for the United States as James W. Ellsworth Land.[120] A further flight 240 miles inland in 1939 brought a claim to the area south of 70°S. in the Australian Antarctic Territory, covering 150 miles south, east and west of 79°E, which was the line of flight.[121] Although Ellsworth's flights were private, his 1939 claim had the covert support of the Department of State.[122]

The first official United States expedition to the continent itself, led by Byrd from 1939–41, was intended to support claims. West Base at Little America was used for work in King Edward and Marie Byrd Lands, and East Base on Stonington Island served to explore the south-east and south-west coasts of the Antarctic Peninsula. Claims sheets were deposited at various points in rock cairns marked by a United States flag.

Operation Highjump, a navy training exercise in 1946–7, was the

118. K.J. Bertrand, *Americans in Antarctica 1775–1948* (1971), 25.
119. J.F. Lovering and J.R.V. Prescott, *Last of Lands . . . Antarctica* (1979), 115–16.
120. K.J. Bertrand, *Americans in Antarctica 1775–1948* (1971), 365.
121. L. Ellsworth, 'My Four Antarctic Expeditions' (1939), 76(1) *National Geographic*, 129 at 137.
122. M.M. Whiteman, *Digest of International Law*, Vol. 2 (1963), 1245.

largest Antarctic expedition and involved thirteen ships including icebreakers and an aircraft-carrier, numerous land vehicles, 4,700 men and eleven reporters. Aerial photography was carried out on a vast scale around much of the coast from Alexander Island through Marie Byrd Land and the Ross Dependency to the Australian Antarctic Territory. In this expedition and Operation Windmill in 1947, claims papers were again deposited and dropped from aircraft.

For the International Geophysical Year seven bases were established: 1) Amundsen-Scott at the South Pole, which had the political purpose of establishing a toe-hold in each sector; 2) McMurdo on Ross Island, the US logistics centre and the staging post for supplies to inland stations; 3) Little America V at Kainan Bay on the Ross Ice Shelf, closed in 1959 at the end of the IGY; 4) Hallett at Cape Adare in the Ross Dependency, jointly operated with New Zealand – finally ceased operations in 1973; 5) Wilkes in the Australian Antarctic Territory, established with minimum facilities in the approximate projected longitude of the planned Soviet inland base of Vostok to counter any Soviet claim, and handed over to Australia at the end of the IGY[123] (this transfer effectively marked the withdrawal of US permanent bases from East Antarctica[124] and is remarkable because all six Russian IGY bases were in that portion of the continent); 6) Ellsworth on the Filchner Ice Shelf in the Weddell Sea, planned so as effectively to strengthen US rights in the area,[125] and handed over to Argentina in 1959; and 7) Byrd, situated centrally in Marie Byrd Land at 80°S and 120°W, and closed in 1967. In 1969 Siple (now at 79° 55′S and 83° 55′W) was established as a summer station, turned into a winter base in 1973 and rebuilt with supplies from McMurdo, 2250 km. away, in 1979.[126] In 1966–7 the United States constructed the small Palmer Base at Anvers Island, marking its determination to maintain operations on the Antarctic Peninsula, the main site for rival bases. With a budget of $55,000,000 in 1980,[127] the United States has one of the two largest Antarctic programs.[128]

123. Wilkes was manned until 1969 when operations were moved to a new Australian station, Casey, 2 km. away (E. Chipman, *Australians in the Frozen South* (1978), 21).
124. Plateau Station, in the interior of the Norwegian claim (79° 15′S., 40° 30′E), was occupied from 1965–9 (National Science Foundation, *US Antarctic Program Draft Environmental Impact Statement* (1979), D-3).
125. Secretary of Defense (Special Operations) to Secretary of the Navy (14 March 1955).
126. 'Airlift to new station in West Antarctica' (1979), 8(9) *Antarctic*, 312.
127. *Congressional Quarterly* (12 May 1979), 902.
128. Precise comparisons with the Soviet Union are difficult because of the problems of costing (e.g. the US budget does not include all research expenses), and the difference in logistics (the United States relies extensively on air supply to McMurdo: the Soviet Union sends materials and men by sea) and research (the

If actions such as the transfer of Wilkes and Ellsworth Stations in 1959 suggest some confusion, one can only conclude that this is a reflection of the meanderings of policy. Attempts to formulate US thoughts date from the opinion of Secretary of State Hughes expressed in 1924 that 'the discovery of lands unknown to civilization, even when coupled with a formal taking of possession, does not support a valid claim of sovereignty unless the discovery is followed by an actual settlement of the discovered country'.[129] In the same letter Hughes pointed out that the Antarctic Peninsula claimed by the United Kingdom had no permanent population, although whalers anchored there in summer.[130] With considerable justification it has been argued that Hughes' opinion did not constitute a policy but rather a belief in the inability of other nations to fulfil what the State Department took to be the contemporary international law criteria.[131] The Hughes doctrine unsettled all claims[132] without giving the United States any benefit. Furthermore it later worked against American interests by requiring a higher standard than that adopted by the actual claimants.

After 1924 came *Palmas*, *Clipperton* and *Eastern Greenland*. It is curious that at least the *Eastern Greenland Case* did not change the State Department's attitude.[133] A departmental study in 1939 concluded that the Hughes view gave insufficient consideration to climatic conditions and over – emphasised the degree of occupation required. But the expedition sent in that year was still planned to set up two permanent stations.[134]

In essence the State Department was unable to make up its mind either then or later. One sign of this confusion was the direction to make claims but keep them secret.[135] Instructions were given to deposit claims in cairns and drop them from aircraft[136] with little conception of the legal effect of such acts. Ellsworth's claim to the American Highlands, based on overflight, was expressly stated to

United States has a large summer programme: the Soviet Union operates all the year round at a more even level).

129. Letter to A.W. Prescott in G.H. Hackworth, *Digest of International Law*, Vol. I (1940), 399.
130. Ibid., at p. 453.
131. B.M. Plott, The Development of United States Antarctic Policy, Ph.D. thesis, Fletcher School of Law and Diplomacy (1969), 24.
132. C.H. Grattan, *The Southwest Pacific since 1900* (1963), 613.
133. J. Hanessian in T. Hatherton (ed.), *Antarctica* (1965), 41.
134. B.M. Plott, 'The Development of United States Antarctic Policy', Ph.D. thesis, Fletcher School of Law and Diplomacy (1969), 76 and 77.
135. Ellsworth (1938); US Antarctic Expedition (1939); Operation Highjump (1946).
136. M.M. Whiteman, *Digest of International Law*, Vol. 2 (1963), 1249 for Operation Highjump.

operate 'so far as this act allows',[137] an expression taken at the suggestion of the State Department from an aerial claim by Wilkins in 1929 on behalf of Britain,[138] even though Britain's views on title to *res nullius* were contrary to those of the United States. One puzzled American polar veteran was unable to find anyone who could interpret just what the words meant.[139]

From 1938 until 1957 there was ample evidence of US intentions to make claims, but none was advanced. America continues to refuse recognition of any other country's sovereignty over any portion of Antarctica and to reserve its own 'basic historic rights'.[140] This official view emerged by default. There is little justification in denying claims to any portion of the continent and at the same time asserting undefined US rights. Whatever may be the merits of American historic rights, it must be conceded that other countries have interests of equivalent validity in certain parts of the continent. The United States has been the most vigorous opponent of claims by other countries. Even US officials have had difficulty in interpreting the nation's policy on claims. Admiral Abbott stated: 'We don't own the continent. Nobody does'.[141] A similar view is that Antarctica is not amenable to claims,[142] which can hardly be reconciled with the continued existence of US rights.

How can there be a claim which has never been asserted?[143] Here lies the central weakness of the American approach. There has been no ratification of claims such as that of Byrd, and it is therefore difficult to argue for an inchoate title.[144] No clear official indication has been given as to the areas which would be claimed. There has been no intent to occupy on behalf of the United States.[145] If a claim were to be made, surely the United States would have to adopt all the relevant activities of its nationals. It cannot have its cake and eat it. So, for instance, Byrd's apparent recognition of the Ross Dependency

137. L. Ellsworth, 'My Four Antarctic Expeditions' (1939), 76(1) *National Geographic*, 129 at 137.
138. M.M. Whiteman, *Digest of International Law*, Vol. 2 (1963), 1246.
139. L.M. Gould, *The Polar Regions in their relation to Human Affairs* (1958), 17.
140. Department of State in 'US Antarctic Policy', Hearing, Subcommittee on Oceans and International Environment, Committee on Foreign Relations, Senate 94th Cong., 1st Sess. (1975), 18.
141. D. Ballantyne, 'When Hardy Souls go South' *Auckland Star* (18 Dec. 1967).
142. Advanced as one possibility in B.H. Oxman, 'The Antarctic Regime: An Introduction' (1978), 33 *University of Miami Law Review*, 285 at 290.
143. Sen. Hickenlooper in 'The Antarctic Treaty' Hearings, Committee on Foreign Relations, Senate, 86th Cong., 2nd Sess. (1960) 31.
144. S.C. Jain, 'Antarctica: Geopolitics and International Law' (1974), 17 *Indian Yearbook of International Affairs*, 249 at 262.
145. J.P.A. Bernhardt, 'Sovereignty in Antarctica' (1975), 5 *California Western International Law Journal*, 297 at 325.

66   *Antarctic Law and Politics*

claim could well bind the United States if his activities were to be relied upon generally.[146]

A peculiarity of American activity in the Antarctic has been the practice of dropping claims papers from aircraft and depositing them in cairns without making them public. The procedure of aerial claims was taken up in earnest by US pilots. Papers were scattered over the continent like confetti with scant regard for prior discovery exploration or claims. By direction of the President of the United States, Lieutenant J.H. Roscoe claimed 'Ross Island and the areas about McMurdo Sound' on 29 January 1948, declaring that he had surveyed and investigated the territory.[147] On 13 January 1956 Lieut.-Col. H.R. Kolp intimated that he had explored and investigated from McMurdo Sound to the South Pole and claimed 'this territory'.[148] Next day R.C. Spann claimed '90° 00'S lat. and 200 miles either side of course to Weddell Sea' on the same basis. Even under the relaxed tests advanced by Antarctic claimants, this type of activity is hard to justify. Much of the area claimed by such US papers had previously been discovered, explored and investigated by others, for example McMurdo Sound and the South Pole. If the United States were to rely on claims by overflight, it would have to concede equally extravagant pretensions by other nations. There is certainly little trace of the Hughes doctrine in such assertions. The juridical value of these secret acts is most doubtful. Neither the State Department nor the men filling in the forms[149] appeared to have had any intelligible plan.

This incoherence, due to the failure to focus interest on particular areas, has been a persistent feature of US policy. It has already been pointed out that the area discovered by Wilkes has not been the site of a permanent American station since 1959. In 1954 the National Security Council thought the time might have come to announce a claim in the Antarctic Peninsula area to protect potential claims against those of 'more active' countries.[150] Presumably, as in 1939,

146. F.M. Auburn, *The Ross Dependency* (1972), 58.
147. 'Discovery' was crossed out and 'surveyed' inserted. For the printed form used in Highjump and Windmill see M.M. Whiteman, *Digest of International Law*, Vol. 2 (1963), 1249. Subsequently different formulas were employed.
148. The exploration and investigation were presumably carried out during the flight time from McMurdo to the Pole. There is no indication of the boundaries of the area claimed.
149. Significant variations are apparent in the definition of the area claimed. Some forms refer to a geographical feature and the surrounding area others to coordinates, or a line of flight.
150. Statement of Policy by the National Security Council on Antarctica (16 July 1954).

fear of the expected bitter reaction of Chile and Argentina prevented such an assertion.

Marie Byrd and Ellsworth Lands, the 'United States sector',[151] have been previously examined as examples of the deficiencies of sector boundaries. Part of the area east of 150°W was claimed in 1929 by Gould's party in Byrd's expedition.[152] Chile explicitly recognised the United States' right to claim west of 90°W in 1940,[153] and other claimants have given America tacit priority in the area.[154] But the reason why it has not been claimed by other States is the same reason which prevented US action: it is the least accessible and valuable of the sectors. Were America to claim the area it would constitute renunciation of other rights.[155]

That sector is, from the US point of view, inseparable from the Ross Dependency. Since 1929 the Ross Sea has been the area of greatest interest to the United States. McMurdo, by far the largest American base and logistics centre with a summer population of up to 1,000,[156] is situated on Ross Island, and both the South Pole and Siple Stations are supplied from there. Apart from the Antarctic Peninsula, McMurdo Sound is the most useful part of the continent: its advantages include ice-free sites, reliable sea access, relative proximity to the South Pole and the 'United States sector' and (today) the best harbour facilities for Ross Sea oil and gas exploration. Scientific interest centres on the nearby Ice Shelf and Dry Valleys. New Zealand's activities, essentially conducted from Scott Base, are on a much smaller scale than those of the United States.

The relationship between the two countries' Antarctic programmes is close. By a Memorandum of Understanding signed in 1958, New Zealand agreed to provide facilities in New Zealand itself in connection with US operations in Antarctica. Operational headquarters (in Christchurch), transit of personnel, ships and aircraft, and a military radio station were permitted. It will be noted that there was no mention of New Zealand permission for US operations in the Ross Dependency. US logistic support was to be given for New Zealand operations in Antarctica.[157] This agreement, which expired

151. *Martin* v. *Commissioner of Internal Revenue* (1969), 63 *AJIL*, 141 at 142.
152. K.J. Bertrand, *Americans in Antarctica 1775–1948* (1971), 310.
153. Note to Japan in (1948–9), 46 US Naval War College, *International Law Documents*, 225.
154. H.J. Taubenfeld, 'A Treaty for Antarctica' (1961), 531 *International Conciliation*, 245 at 249.
155. R.E. Wilson, 'National Interests and Claims in the Antarctic' (1964), 17(1) *Arctic*, 15 at 17.
156. National Science Foundation, *US Antarctic Program Draft Environmental Impact Statement* (1979), 1–17.
157. (1958) NZTS No. 2.

on 31 December 1959, was renewed indefinitely in 1960, and further provision was made for prior notification of operations planned for each season.[158]

The treaties represent a formalisation of prior practice.[159] Mutual assistance extends well beyond the bare agreement.[160] New Zealand field activities are largely dependent on US air support. Search and rescue facilities in the Ross Dependency are provided by the Americans who maintain aircraft landing facilities on a sea-ice runway and snow skiways at Williams Field. New Zealand would have great difficulty operating Scott Base if McMurdo were closed.[161] An accident to a US Hercules plane in 1975 forced the cancellation of one-third of New Zealand's 1975–6 research programme.[162] Benefits to New Zealand include US expenditure of $2,000,000 each year on purchases in New Zealand,[163] which makes a significant contribution to overseas currency reserves. Advantages to the United States are the politically dependable facilities in New Zealand (and their denial to the Soviet Union), assistance with cargo-handling in Christchurch and at Williams Field, [164] and the transport of cargo and passengers by Royal New Zealand Air Force planes to the Antarctic.

Cooperation between the two countries frequently involves both the United States and New Zealand in far-reaching international programmes such as RISP and DVDP. Until its closure in 1973, Hallett Station in Northern Victoria Land was jointly operated by the US and New Zealand. This is a unique example involving a claimant and a nation specifically disputing the claim.[165] Ross Island in McMurdo Sound has the United States McMurdo facility and New Zealand's Scott Base only a couple of miles apart. Even in winter New Zealanders can travel on foot or by vehicle to McMurdo which has amenities such as a dentist and a store.[166] The Scott Base site was selected by Hillary in 1957 when accessibility was the over-

158. (1961) NZTS No. 3.
159. An agreement between Dufek, Fuchs and Hillary (*NZ External Affairs Review* (August 1955)).
160. A. Hayter, *The Year of the Quiet Sun* (1968), 22.
161. M.M. Prebble, 'New Zealand's Antarctic Field Programme 1957–1965', MA thesis, Victoria University (1965), 84.
162. 'NZ programme cut about one-third' (1975), 7(8) *Antarctic* 232.
163. 'US Support Force reduces spending in New Zealand' (1973), 6(10) *Antarctic* 351.
164. *Report of Operation Deep Freeze* (1976), IV-4.
165. Correspondence between British Ambassador in Washington and Secretary of State in 1934 (G.H. Hackworth, *Digest of International Law*, Vol. I (1940), 456–7.)
166. L.B. Quartermain, *South from New Zealand* (1964), 51.

riding consideration. A channel had been carved by the US ice – breaker *Glacier* towards the US station. Scott Base is not a desirable focus for scientific research, as seismic observations are limited by hills to the north and west, and areas of interest to geologists are some 200 miles away.[167] The site was chosen because of the necessarily interwoven nature of New Zealand and American activities.[168]

McMurdo is self-contained in winter and has the equipment of a small industrial town[169] with its own hospital, fire station, library, post office, gymnasium, theatre, clubs and dial-telephone system.[170] Fifty personnel are assigned to Public Works in the summer.[171] As the two stations are on a peninsula, the expanding McMurdo with its extending fuel and power lines, roads and lighting could have swamped Scott and rendered the scientific recording for which it was designed almost useless.[172]

Informal discussions in 1965 between the United States National Science Foundation (NSF) and the New Zealand Department of Scientific and Industrial Research (DSIR) led to the drawing up of a map of the Peninsula setting aside science reserves, logistic work areas, central station complexes, historic sites and future logistics and science areas.[173] In 1967 the McMurdo Land Management and Conservation Board, consisting of representatives of the DSIR, NSF and the US Navy, was formed.[174]

The Board's responsibilities were defined in 1975 as including the monitoring of: the protection and preservation of buildings and objects of historic interest in the McMurdo area; the protection and preservation of special science benchmarks at McMurdo Station; station support activities to insure non-interference with scientific projects; efforts to reduce or eliminate environmental pollution in the McMurdo area; and conservation of Antarctic fauna and flora. The Board is intended to be supervisory and advisory, a responsive means for producing rapid and responsible resolution of problems. 'In most cases it is expected that conflicting land usage problems will

167. Conversation between Secretary, New Zealand Embassy, Washington and Dr. J.E. Mooney (21 May 1957).
168. A.S. Helm and J.H. Miller, *Antarctica* (1964), 151.
169. G.F. Stuart and M.J. Sites, 'A radio noise survey of the McMurdo Area' (1973), 8(1) *Antarctic Journal* 1.
170. W.J. Cromie, 'The Navy's Stake in Antarctica' (Oct. 1968) *US Naval Institute Proceedings*, 36 at 42.
171. *Report of Operation Deep Freeze* (1976), V-12.
172. A. Hayter, *The Year of the Quiet Sun* (1968), 124.
173. Area Development Plan, Hut Point Peninsula (July 1965).
174. R.B. Thomson, 'United States and New Zealand Cooperation in Environmental Protection' (1971), 6(3) *Antarctic Journal*, 59.

be resolved by the mutual agreement of cognizant Board Members'.[175]

In practice the Board exercises effective authority over the area around the two bases. So relocation of the McMurdo Amateur Radio Facility in 1973 required its consent, and the designation of the Cape Royds penguin rookery as a Site of Special Scientific Interest was approved by the Board in 1975. Although primarily concerned with matters such as rubbish disposal, roads, power lines and historic huts on Ross Island, the Board has discussed issues related to Marble Point,[176] the Dry Valleys and Hallett Station.[177]

At the Board's recommendation a two-man party was set up to study the considerable contamination of Hut Point Peninsula by radio noise, earth currents, light, haze and vibrations. The investigation recommended establishment of a quiet experimental station and administrative procedures to permit effective control over both scientific and support activities.[178] Unless strict control of all equipment and experiments at Scott and McMurdo was initiated, noise levels might increase to the point where it became impracticable to carry out sensitive experiments anywhere around the Hut Point Peninsula.[179]

At the Seventh Consultative Meeting in 1975, an electromagnetically quiet area was designated as a Site of Special Scientific Interest for this purpose at Arrival Heights, Hut Point Peninsula.[180] Only personnel with prior permission will be permitted within the site.[181] For these two stations, situated on a peninsula, an area of control has been jointly demarcated. Although the Board's activities are directed primarily at McMurdo Station and the surrounding area,[182] it is difficult to avoid an inference of joint administration at least for this part of the Ross Dependency.

New Zealand has always been a lukewarm claimant. Initiative for

175. Commander, Naval Support Force, Antarctica, Instruction 11010.2A (22 December 1975).
176. Minutes of McMurdo Land Management and Conservation Board Meeting (8 February 1979).
177. R.B. Thomson, 'United States and New Zealand Cooperation in Environmental Protection' (1971), 6(3) *Antarctic Journal*, 59.
178. M.J. Sites and G.F. Stuart, *An Electromagnetic Interference Survey of the Hut Point Peninsula and Adjacent Regions* (1971), 80.
179. G.F. Stuart and M.J. Sites, 'A radio noise survey of the McMurdo Area' (1973), 8(1) *Antarctic Journal*, 1 at 4.
180. Rec. VIII-4.
181. Antarctic Division, DSIR, *Antarctic Operations Manual 1975* (1975), 97.
182. Minutes of McMurdo Land Management and Conservation Board Meeting (21 January 1976). Another instance is the US/New Zealand agreement in 1963 on limiting access to the Cape Royds penguin rookery (see discussion of Jurisdiction/*Treaty Regime*).

its claim came not from New Zealand but from the United Kingdom:[183] an Order-in-Council of 1923[184] placed the Ross Dependency under the administration of the New Zealand Governor-General, but did not make it part of New Zealand. Apparent absence of any subsequent transfer of sovereignty from the United Kingdom to New Zealand is a legal embarrassment[185] and an indication of the government's lack of interest in the Dependency:

If, in 1923, we acquired an empire in Antarctica, we scarcely proved to be born imperialists. We appointed Administrators to the Ross Dependency but they never set foot in the territory. . . . Our chief administrative acts were attempts to regulate whaling. But as we had no gunboats in the Dependency to enforce our edicts, they appear to have been for the most part disregarded.[186]

New Zealand government departments often view the Dependency as not being part of New Zealand.[187] It is the sole claimant which has publicly stated its desire to relinquish sovereignty in favour of an international regime.[188]

Sir Douglas Mawson suggested that the United States should have claimed the Pacific sector, and there would have been no difficulty with New Zealand in extending it to the Ross Ice Shelf with territorial adjustments elsewhere.[189] Admiral Dufek, Commander of the US Naval Support Force during the IGY, considered that a tacit condominium had existed in the area for many years.[190] It has been suggested that such a condominium could be reconciled with the Antarctic Treaty.[191]

To understand why this was not done one must examine the various attempts within the US government to define a claims policy. Byrd's expedition of 1939 was directed to take the coast between 72°W and 148°W as its principal objective. Secondary interests were the west coast of the Weddell Sea and the area between the Sentinel Range and Horlick Mountains in the interior of the US sector.[192] But US action was not intended in any way to prejudice the rights or

183. C. Beeby, *The Antarctic Treaty* (1972), 5.
184. (1923) *NZ Gazette*, 2211.
185. F.M. Auburn, *The Ross Dependency* (1972), 66.
186. J.H. Weir, Counsellor to the New Zealand Embassy in Washington, 'New Zealand in the Antarctic' (1964), 5(8) Bulletin of the US Antarctic Projects Officer, 6 at 7.
187. For example, see F.M. Auburn, *The Ross Dependency* (1972), 62–3.
188. 'The Antarctic Treaty' (1972), 22(6), *NZ Foreign Affairs Review*, 19 at 25.
189. L.M. Gould, *The Polar Regions in their relation to Human Affairs* (1958), 32.
190. Letter to Dr. R.V. Zander, Office of the Secretary of Defense (17 April 1957).
191. F.M. Auburn, 'A Sometime World of Men: Legal Rights in the Ross Dependency' (1971), 65 *AJIL* 578 at 581–2.
192. K.J. Bertrand, *Americans in Antarctica 1775–1948* (1971), 472.

interests of any American Republic in the Antarctic.[193] It was not clear how this compromise was to be achieved, particularly since the Chilean and Argentinian boundaries were only delineated subsequently.

In 1947 and 1948 the United States discussed with the claimants the concept of a trusteeship or a multiple condominium. One State Department draft contemplated a claim over 35°W to 135°W between 68°S and 81°S, 135°W, − 140°E except the area around the Pole claimed by Amundsen in 1911 and 140°E to 18°E, north of approximately 75°S. At least part of the draft claim was apparently intended to cover the areas explored or mapped only by US expeditions. So vast a claim, to most of the coast of the continent, apart from the northern Antarctic Peninsula and part of Queen Maud and Coats Lands, would have been difficult to justify on any criteria of discovery, exploration or state activity. It would certainly have been unacceptable to those countries to whom a condominium was being proposed. Luckily for the State Department, its initiative failed for other reasons.

More careful thought was then given to US interests. Detailed records of American Antarctic expeditions were compiled.[194] In July 1954 the National Security Council considered that the United States was not at that time in a position to make a wise choice of areas to include the localities best suited to its possible needs. To protect potential claims, an announcement should be made 'as soon as possible'. US rights should be publicly asserted in the Antarctic Peninsula and islands south at least to 82°S and west to include Little America, Byrd's former base on the Ross Ice Shelf. Selection of the specific area should be governed by compactness and should include significant areas where US rights could be at risk in the near future (presumably in the north Antarctic Peninsula); where US rights were obviously superior or uncontested (apparently intended to cover Marie Byrd Land); where potential US requirements had been identified; and where early nineteenth-century Russian and subsequent Soviet interests made a Soviet claim most probable.[195]

Particular interest attaches to a map of Antarctic Exploration and Claims apparently relied on by opponents to ratification of the Antarctic Treaty, who argued that the United States had solid claims

193. M.M. Whiteman, *Digest of International Law*, Vol. 2 (1963), 1247.
194. These may be the 'other Antarctic projects;' mentioned in K.J. Bertrand, *Americans in Antarctica 1775–1948* (1971), XIV, and may also be connected with the Advisory Committee on Antarctic Names of the US Board on Geographic Names, whose research was linked with sovereignty issues. See also P. Siple, *90° South* (1959), 88.
195. National Security Council, Statement of Policy (16 July 1954).

to most of the continent.[196] This map was drawn by Raymond Butler, a cartographer working in the US Antarctic Projects Office, in 1956.[197] It was based on earlier maps drawn by Butler showing national exploration in Antarctica from 1772 to 1956.[198] The 1959 version of the map used three colours: grey for 'areas seen only by US explorers', pink for 'areas seen by US explorers and by explorers of other countries', and yellow for 'areas seen by other explorers but not seen by US explorers'. Most of the continent was coloured grey, representing to a large degree US overflight. Much of the Antarctic Peninsula, Victoria Land and the coast of the Australian and French claims were pink, as was Amundsen's route to the Pole. The map, having regard to its origin, appears to represent US official thinking.[199] If so, a good proportion of US rights would have been based on overflight, a conclusion which supports the previous interpretation of the claims papers dropped in secret.

Another version of this map was prepared for Admiral Dufek, the US Antarctic Projects Officer, in 1957. On it 90°W to 20°W was labelled 'Sector 1', the Norwegian Claim, 'Sector 2' and so on to the unclaimed 'Sector 7'.[200] Dufek's proposal was for a US – New Zealand condominium over Sectors 7 and 6 (the Ross Dependency), if New Zealand agreed. Should Australia also consent, there was to be a triple condominium including the Australian Antarctic Territory. The eastern boundary should extend as far to 74°W as bargaining would permit. Should Australia disagree, the United States should offer recognition of the Australian claim in return for inclusion of the smaller Australian sector in the US – New Zealand condominium.[201] Subsequent inter-agency discussion considered that negotiations could be taken up in phases beginning with Australia and New Zealand,[202] leading eventually to a multiple

196. Senator Engle, Congressional Record (8 August 1960) 15981.
197. Letter from Center for Polar and Scientific Archives, General Service Administration (26 June 1979).
198. Butler's map in Hayton records details up to 1 February 1956, although the book was published in 1959. The 1959 version is stated to be one of a series.
199. Confirmation may be found in references to the same colours, legend and proportion on a map of Antarctic exploration and claims (Senator Gruening in 'The Antarctic Treaty' Hearings, Committee on Foreign Relations, Senate, 86th Cong., 2nd Sess. (1960) 15).
    The map was attached to the report of the US Antarctic Projects Officer for 1956 (ibid. at p. 82 per Elizabeth A. Kendall).
200. Other variations from the map in Hayton were the lesser extent of areas seen only by US explorers and the division of those areas into two categories, one for areas seen from land or sea or ice, the other for areas seen from the air.
201. Letter to Dr. R.V. Zander, Office of the Secretary of Defense (17 April 1957).
202. H.M. Dater, Staff Historian, US Antarctic Program, Memorandum of OCB Antarctic Working Group Meeting of 9 July 1957 (11 July 1957).

condominium. Having regard to the failure of a similar attempt in 1948, it is not surprising that nothing came of this proposal.

It has been argued that an American claim was never a realistic solution.[203] In 1960 the Senate Committee on Foreign Relations considered that the only feasible claim was to the unattractive American sector. Broader demands would result in conflict with friendly countries. Exercise of the option over the unclaimed sector would require recognition of other claims, jeopardize free access, and possibly stimulate further claims by others including the Soviet Union.[204] On this issue the Committee endorsed the position of the State Department[205] advanced to obtain ratification of the Antarctic Treaty. Had it been accepted that a United States claim was still feasible, there would have been a most persuasive cause to deny ratification. At the same time the Department argued that Article IV did not 'relinquish in one iota any claim or basis of claim of the United States of America. It is so stated categorically'.[206] Such an assurance was needed to answer criticisms that the Treaty surrendered American interests. But if the United States could not make a claim to the areas of interest in 1960, it must have been apparent that the same situation would prevail in 1991. The two basic elements in the State Department's argument were incompatible.

Previous analysis suggests that the State Department's contention that a viable claim was impractical in 1960 was wrong. New Zealand was prepared totally to relinquish its sovereignty, and in return for US recognition it is probable that Australia would have been prepared to make concessions. Between 80°W and 90°W there is only the Chilean claim. From 74°W to 80°W the British and Chilean claims overlap. There were prospects for moving the United States sector boundary to at least 80°W in return for US recognition. Therefore a claim from 142°E to 80°W, including a partial condominium with New Zealand over the Ross Dependency, was within the bounds of possibility. The United States would then have obtained most of the area discovered by Byrd, together with the desirable Ross Sea sector. The reason for not making a claim before 1959 was not the political difficulty but rather the inability of the United States to formulate a claims policy.

What then are the 'rights' reserved by the United States? It has been pointed out that they rest on shaky foundations, especially in

203. B.M. Plott, 'The Development of United States Antarctic Policy', Ph.D. thesis, Fletcher School of Law and Diplomacy (1969), 275.
204. *Congressional Record* (8 August 1960), 15981.
205. 'The Antarctic Treaty' Hearings, Committee on Foreign Relations, Senate, 86th Cong., 2nd Sess. (1960), 40.
206. Ibid., at 39.

light of the Hughes Doctrine. One government paper examined the issue in detail:

14. A US claim could take one of several forms. Delineation of a US claim to full sovereignty, even if we could identify our major interests at this time, might prove to be an abortive effort because of the lack of internationally agreed rules for acquiring sovereignty in the Antarctic. It would also be a sharp break with our past policy of refusing to recognize claims to sovereignty when not accompanied by occupation. More important, the principles underlying any selection of the precise areas of superior US 'rights' would be applied elsewhere as a yardstick of comparison by other powers, possibly to our disadvantage. Inferior US 'rights' outside the area of a 'sovereignty' claim would be impaired, at least by implication, even though they might eventually acquire significance as the result of further US activities, or through default by other powers.

15. A more desirable step might be to claim 'all US rights' without imputing relative value to them, either separately or in the aggregate. We would not assert that our 'rights' necessarily add up to sovereignty now, nor would we deny that possibility. The difficulty with such a claim would be to explain accurately just what it would mean, between full sovereignty at one extreme and mere reservation of rights at the other. The general outline of this kind of claim on the part of the US would have to include practically all coastal areas and islands of Antarctica within an area larger than the US. A third possibility would be an initial claim to 'all US rights' within a defined area, while reserving them everywhere else in the Antarctic. Because it would avoid certain of the difficulties outlined above, this is the preferred course.[207]

The State Department policy on sovereignty was to have no meaningful policy.[208] It is not surprising that there has been difficulty in defining US 'rights', because the government itself did not, and still does not, know what they are. Its safeguarding of rights which are largely devoid of international legal validity is an empty reservation.[209] Asked what the US would do if other States asserted claims more actively, the Legal Adviser to the National Science Foundation said in 1977 that the 'United States would probably attempt to protect its interests in some other way'.[210]

So far we have seen that the United States was unable to make up its mind on the issue of sovereignty. But this indecision also extends to other policy issues. Commentators have made reference to American strategy.[211] One may say that Argentina has an Antarctic

207. National Security Council, Statement of Policy (16 July 1954).
208. Congressman Pillion in 'The Antarctic Treaty' Hearings, Committee on Foreign Relations, Senate 86th Cong., 2nd Sess. (1960), 25.
209. J.P.A. Bernhardt 'Sovereignty in Antarctica' (1975), 5 *California Western International Law Journal*, 297 at 326.
210. E. Honnold, 'Thaw in International Law? Rights in Antarctica under the Law of Common Spaces' (1978), 87 *YLJ*, 804 at 814.
211. G. Skagestad, 'Small States in International Politics – a Polar-Political

strategy, but this can hardly be said of the US. Public statements of policy purport to reiterate an unchanging approach. Yet an analysis of various formulations shows wide differences. In 1965 Harlan Cleveland, then Assistant Secretary of State for International Organization Affairs, enunciated policy as follows:

1. The United States supports the principles of the Antarctic Treaty, and will do what is necessary to insure that Antarctica is used for peaceful purposes only.
2. We foster international cooperation among the nations active in Antarctica, seeking further areas for agreement whereever that is possible.
3. We continue to attach major importance to programs of scientific research for which Antarctica affords unique conditions.
4. We pursue vigorously our efforts to explore and chart the south polar region.
5. We shall not overlook the possibility that Antarctica may, at some indiscernible time, disclose resources which the world needs.
6. As part of the attempt to master Antarctica's difficult environment, we give special attention to the technicality of transport and other logistics.
7. In all our activities, we make special efforts to preserve Antarctic animal and plant life.[212]

Five years later President Nixon noted objectives as:

To maintain the Antarctic Treaty and ensure that this continent will continue to be used only for peaceful purposes and shall not become an area or object of international discord.
To foster cooperative scientific research for the solution of worldwide and regional problems, including environmental monitoring and prediction and assessment of resources.
To protect the Antarctic environment and develop appropriate measures to ensure the equitable and wise use of living and non-living resources.[213]

In 1975 Dixy Lee Ray, Assistant Secretary of State and Chairman of the Antarctic Policy Group, told a Senate sub-committee that:

Throughout the history of our involvement in Antarctica, the US policy has consistently held that:
Antarctica shall be used for peaceful purposes only and shall not constitute a source of international discord;
US rights and interests must be protected;
Freedom of exploration and scientific research should be guaranteed;

Perspective' in F. Sollie (ed.), *New Territories in International Politics* (1974), 136.

212. 'Antarctic Report 1965' Hearings, Subcommittee on Territorial and Insular Affairs, Committee on Interior and Insular Affairs, H. Rep. 89th Cong., 1st Sess. (1965), 30.
213. Office of the White House Press Secretary (13 October 1970) in 'US Antarctic Policy' Hearing, Subcommittee on Oceans and International Environment, Committee on Foreign Relations, Senate, 94th Cong., 1st Sess. (1975), 30.

Activities in Antarctica should be guided by established, non-preferential rules;
Orderly administration of the area should be established;
Free access to develop natural resources; and establish uniform and nonpreferential rules applicable to all countries and nations for any possible development of resources in the future.[214]

Even when one takes into account that the 1975 statement related to resource exploration, the differences between the views of 1965, 1970 and 1975 were substantial and apparently passed unnoticed by the US government. 'Plant and animal life' was to be protected in 1965; in 1970 this became 'the Antarctic environment', and by 1975 any such clause had been omitted. Only the 1975 formulation mentioned US rights and then in an ambiguous manner, in relation to undefined 'interests'. Guarantees for freedom of exploration first appeared in the 1975 formula but that formula no longer specified maintenance of the Antarctic Treaty as an objective. Perhaps the most striking aspect of the testimony of Dixy Lee Ray was the affirmation that the stated objectives had been consistently held throughout the history of US involvement in Antarctica.

One cause of American policy thus seeming to have no memory is frequent personnel changes in the State Department. Another is the fragmentation of effort. The Navy does not have a military mission in Antarctica and has been compelled, unwillingly, to provide logistic support.[215] The Natural Science Foundation is concerned with research, but has no major role to play in resource exploration. In recent years interest has also been expressed by the National Oceanic and Atmospheric Administration of the Department of Commerce and by the Department of Energy. Until 1977 there was no continuing oversight of Antarctic policy.[216] Since that date much work has been done, but there has been a strong tendency to react to the initiatives of government departments rather than to take an overall view. For several years legislation to establish an Antarctic Commission to coordinate US efforts was proposed.[217] It foundered, in part, due to the opposition of agencies then engaged in Antarctic

---

214. Ibid., at p. 5.
215. Navy personnel also fear that a long tour of duty in Antarctica will affect their chances of promotion (Mr Harkin in 'US Antarctic Program', Hearings, Subcommittee on Science, Research and Technology, Committee on Science and Technology, H. Rep. 96th Cong., 1st Sess. (1979) 61).
216. F.M. Auburn, 'United States Antarctic Policy' (1978), 12(1) *Marine Technology Society Journal*, 31 at 36.
217. Richard E. Byrd Antarctic Commission Act in 'Antarctica Legislation – 1961' Hearings, Subcommittee on Territorial and Insular Affairs, Committee on Interior and Insular Affairs, H. Rep. 87th Cong., 1st Sess. (1962), 1–6.

work. An independent body of this nature is needed to ensure that the United States adopts and carries out a coherent Antarctic policy.

The Soviet Union

For a complete contrast one may turn from American policy to that of the Soviet Union. Between 1819 and 1821 Bellingshausen and Lazarev in the ships *Vostok* and *Mirnyy* discovered islands of the South Sandwich Group, Peter I Island[218] and Alexander Island, and explored the South Shetlands. It is contended that the continent was sighted in the course of these voyages. Since 1949 there has been considerable controversy over this issue. In the Soviet view, Bellingshausen discovered the continent,[219] but other commentators have held that no claim of such a discovery was made by the expedition because of insufficient evidence.[220] This historical dispute, complicated by modern finding of additional facts, is not merely academic. Priority is important to the Soviet Union because rights are said to accrue from it.[221]

No Russian or Soviet ship visited the Antarctic for the next 125 years.[222] Apart from a protest note to Norway in 1939, the next Soviet activity in the Antarctic was that of the *Slava* whaling fleet in 1946. In reaction to the discussion initiated by the United States, a memorandum was sent to that power and six claimants (excluding Chile) in 1950, according to which the services of Bellingshausen and Lazarev were no less important than those of later explorers on the continent itself. An Antarctic regime should not be settled without the participation of the Soviet Union. Any separate solution of state ownership would be unlawful.[223]

The Soviet Union has considerable concern with Antarctica. Whaling is a dying industry but it pioneered experimental krill trawling in 1961.[224] It is a leader in all aspects of research, technology and marketing relating to that crustacean. Soviet sources have frequently emphasised Antarctic minerals.[225] More recently it has been

218. In the high seas of the 'American' sector, Norway claimed the island in 1931 (1948–9)46 US Naval War College, *International Law Documents* 239).

219. E.M. Suzymov, *A Life Given to the Antarctic* (1968), 3.

220. T. Armstrong, 'Bellingshausen and the Discovery of Antarctica' (1971), 15(99) *Polar Record*, 887 at 888.

221 B.V. Kostritsin cited in W.W. Kulski, 'Soviet Comments on International Law' (1951), 45 *AJIL*, 762 at 767.

222. E. Pruck, 'Die Sowjets in der Antarktis' (1958), 8 *Osteuropa*, 658.

223. (1956) 50 *AJIL* 624–5.

224. G.O. Eddie, *The Harvesting of Krill* (1977), 5.

225. S.B. Slevich, *The Antarctic Must Become an Area of Peace* (1960, translated

made clear that the economic interests of the Soviet Union in the Antarctic in the immediate future include fishing, krill, seals and minerals. Particular stress has been placed on offshore oil and gas, but even metals have not been ignored.[226] Druzhnaya Base, on the Weddell Sea, was occupied in 1975 with an official announcement of the non – ferrous mineral prospects and potential oil and gas reserves of the area.[227] Pronouncements on minerals and other resources are official, frequent and optimistic, in marked contrast to the caution shown by US experts.

The Soviet Union has unparalleled experience in polar technology. Its Arctic regions have a population of millions, a number of cities with a population of more than 100,000,[228] agriculture, timber and mineral production.[229] Siberia has extremely large oil and gas reserves. Development of the Northern Sea Route has entailed the regular passage of large vessels from June to January, aided by ice-breakers.[231] Year-round shipping will be accomplished in the near future. The Soviet nuclear icebreaker *Artika* became the first surface vessel to reach the North Pole in 1977. Transit of the Northeast Passage by a cargo ship assisted by the icebreaker *Sibir* was effected in May 1979 at a time of maximum ice thickness.[232]

For an indication of Soviet intentions one may examine the location of bases. Beginning with Mirny (1956), several stations were occupied during the IGY in the larger Australian sector, including one (Vostok) in the interior. Novolazarevskaya, on the centre of the coast claimed by Norway, was established in February 1961. Molodezhnaya (January 1963)[233] followed in the Australian Antarctic Territory approximately 40 miles from the boundary with the Norwegian claim, a short distance by Antarctic standards.

Bellingshausen, set up on the now rather crowded King George Island in the South Shetland group in 1968, was the first Soviet base in East Antarctica, adding to the already large number of stations in

1967), 4; M.G. Ravich quoted in N. Potter, *Natural Resource Potentials of the Antarctic* (1969), 16–17.

226. S.B. Slevich, *Basic Problems of Antarctic Exploitation* (1973, translated 1974), 8 and 17.

227. 'Filchner ice shelf stations major project this summer' (1975), 7(7) *Antarctic*, 211.

228. Including Murmansk (374,000) and Arkhangelsk (391,000).

229. R.A.J. Phillips, *Canada's North* (1967), 289.

230. T. Armstrong, G. Rogers and G. Rowley, *The Circumpolar North* (1978), 46.

231. W.E. Butler, *Northeast Arctic Passage* (1978), 60–1.

232. G.R. Harrison, 'Exploratory Drilling: The Polar Challenge' Tenth World Petroleum Congress, Bucharest (1979).

233. G. Vane, 'Soviet Antarctic Research, 1972–1973' (1973), 8(6) *Antarctic Journal*, 325 at 328.

the north Antarctic Peninsula. Its hasty establishment[234] followed the building of the US Palmer Station in 1966−7 on another island in the Peninsula.

Molodezhnaya has been remarked upon for its placement near the boundary of two claims. In January 1970 Leningradskaya was built in the smaller Australian Antarctic sector, again about 40 miles from a boundary, that of the Ross Dependency. It is the only base in this portion of the Australian claim, apart from the US station at the South Pole. Despite the provisions of the Treaty and recommendations for notice of activities, the establishment of the base was accompanied by reticence.[235]

Soviet positioning of stations assumed a clear pattern with the announcement in 1972 of a projected base at Cape Burks, Hobbs Coast, Marie Byrd Land, to be named Russkaya[236] and to be used all the year round. This station was occupied for two weeks in 1973 but attempts to establish it on a permanent footing were not pursued at the time,[237] presumably due to severe ice conditions. The station was re-established in 1980,[238] and one can hardly envision a clearer challenge to American interests than an all-year base on the coast of the 'United States' sector. Russkaya is situated in Cordell Hull Bay, so named by Byrd in 1940. Hobbs Coast had previously been an area of US activity,[239] and this was followed up with a detailed geological survey in 1977−8.[240] It is intended that Russkaya will be a permanent winter station.[241] The only current American winter base in the sector, Siple, is much further east near the foot of the Antarctic Peninsula. Russkaya has additional significance. Taken with Leningradskaya, the Soviet Union will have two stations in the vicinity of the Ross Sea, which is the most promising sector for oil and gas exploration.[242]

Druzhnaya was built in 1975 on the Filchner Ice Shelf in the Weddell Sea near the substantial all-year Argentinian base General Belgrano and the site of the former US and Argentinian Ellsworth Base. Its purpose was to prospect for minerals over a five-year

234. See Environment/Specially Protected Areas.
235. F.M. Auburn, 'The Case of the Leningradskaya Nunatak' (1970), 5(8) *Recent Law*, 251 at 254.
236. 'New Soviet Station on Icebound Hobbs Coast' (1972), 6(7) *Antarctic*, 238.
237. 'Russkaya station not yet manned' (1976), 7(10) *Antarctic*, 327.
238. 'Russkaya established by cargo ship Gizhiga' (1980), 9(3) *Antarctic*, 95.
239. US Antarctic Service Expedition 1939−1941, Field Operations Map in K.J. Bertrand, *Americans in Antarctica 1775−1948* (1971), 425.
240. F.A. Wade, 'Geological Survey of Ruppert-Hobbs Coasts sector, Marie Byrd Land' (1978), 13(4) *Antarctic Journal*, 4.
241. 'Possible change in plan for Russkaya' (1979), 8(11) *Antarctic*, 395.
242. See Oil and Gas/*Location*.

period.[243] Although originally set up as a temporary and seasonal station, Druzhanaya is of considerable significance. It has been the largest base devoted solely to summer research. US geologists discovered and explored the Dufek Intrusion in the Pensacola Mountains, some 500 miles south of Druzhnaya, considered to be of 'possibly great economic potential',[244] an opinion which Soviet sources have also expressed.[245] Study of the Dufek Intrusion has been a particular task of geologists at Druzhnaya.[246] The Soviet Union began construction of a new winter station, Druzhnaya II, on the Ronne Ice Shelf near the base of the Antarctic Peninsula in 1980.[247] West Germany's new base will be situated near Berkner Island[248] in reasonable proximity to the Druzhnaya site. Apart from their importance for mineral exploration, Druzhnaya and the other bases in the area are of political concern. The concentration of stations in the Southern Weddell Sea is the most dense in Antarctica after the Antarctic Peninsula. As with the Peninsula, one must infer that the explanation is political rather than scientific.

Soviet establishment of bases since 1956 demonstrated an initial concern with the Australian claim but has now progressively expanded to cover all sectors. The thrust is apparent but not the aim. Early discussion of the interests of the Soviet Union emphasised the demand to participate in any agreement on the basis of historic rights.[249] Attempts to delineate a possible claim could only be guesses. One list included fourteen islands in the South Shetlands and proximate areas.[250] It was pointed out that Queen Mary Land in the Australian Antarctic Territory had been renamed Pravda Coast, and future territorial claims on a grand scale could not be excluded.[251] But doctrine could not support an inchoate title in 1819–21 with a gap between discovery and occupation of at least 125 years until the earliest arguable taking of possession through the

243. 'Filchner ice shelf station major project this season' (1975), 7(7) *Antarctic*, 211. In 1980 the summer station was extended and improved.
244. N.A. Wright and P.L. Williams, *Mineral Resources of Antarctica* (1974) 17 (see Oil and Gas/*Minerals*).
245. S.B. Slevich, *Basic Problems of Antarctic Exploitation* (1973, translated 1974), 17.
246. '265 men wintering at six permanent stations' (1978), 8(6) *Antarctic*, 189.
247. 'Soviet plans for another winter station' (1980), 9(2) *Antarctic*, 56.
248. 'West German design for first base' (1979), 8(10) *Antarctic*, 350.
249. P.A. Toma, 'Soviet Attitude toward the Acquisition of Territorial Sovereignty in the Antarctic' (1956), 50 *AJIL*, 611 at 612.
250. S. Wolk, 'The Basis of Soviet Claims in the Antarctic' (1958), 5 *Bulletin of the Institute for the Study of the USSR*, 43 at 46.
251. V.N. Petrov, 'Soviet Participation in .the International Geophysical Year' (1957), 4 *Bulletin of the Institute for the Study of the USSR*, 3 at 8.

activity of the *Slava* fleet in 1946.[252]

Unlike the United States, there had been no unofficial Soviet claims nor any unambiguous official statement of the particular parts of the continent which might be the object of future claims. US commentators were therefore of the view that Soviet interests took the form of a demand for participation in decision-making in the region rather than a specific territorial claim.[253] This interpretation has been adopted by the Central Intelligence Agency.[254] It is further supported by the argument that the two superpowers hold similar positions and act in a like manner.[255]

For the United States government this 'stake not claim' interpretation is tempting. If the Soviet Union wishes only to assert a right to participate in decision-making for the Antarctic generally, then the scale and location of its research and logistics are of only secondary importance. Once bases and programmes are established and are to be maintained, Soviet aims have been accomplished.

In 1958 the Soviet Union stated that it reserved all rights based on discoveries and explorations of Russian navigators and scientists, including the right to present corresponding territorial claims.[256] One would have thought that this position, reiterated at the Washington Conference in 1959,[257] gave a clear indication of the Soviet Union's intentions. At that time Soviet stations were confined to the Australian Antarctic Territory. From the number of bases, their geographic spread and the scale of activities, the Soviet Union had already achieved enough for a stake in Antarctic affairs, and the subsequent steady expansion of activity and strategic positioning of stations can no longer be ascribed to a desire for a generalised participation in decision-making. Soviet programmes since 1961 appear to be aimed at coverage of the entire continent and at expanding the feasibility of territorial claims should the need arise.

There are nations–for example, South Africa and Japan–which have a stake in the continent but not a claim, and for lack of decisive action the United States appears to be drifting into an analogous position. For example, at the conclusion of the IGY it decided to reduce costs: Ellsworth Station was handed over to Argentina and Wilkes to Australia, both friendly nations. A year later United States officials considered that it was to America's national benefit that the

---

252. I. von Münch, 'Völkerrechtsfragen der Antarktis' (1958), 7 *Archiv des Völkerrechts*, 225 at 246.

253. J. Hanessian in T. Hatherton (ed.), *Antarctica* (1965), 30.

254. Central Intelligence Agency, *Polar Regions Atlas* (1979), 43.

255. R.E. Guyer, 'The Antarctic System' (1973), 139 *Hague Recueil*, 149 at 161.

256. M.M. Whiteman, *Digest of International Law*, Vol. 2 (1963), 1254–5.

257. Mr. Kuznetsov in Department of State, *Conference on Antarctica* (1960), 23.

Belgian station be maintained without assistance from the nearby Soviet expedition. In both instances friendly nations were seen as surrogates for the United States. But the activities of the three countries concerned, especially the two claimants, could not support American territorial rights. Quite the contrary.

By contrast, the Soviet Union transferred the Oazis Station on the coast of the Australian Antarctic Territory between Mirny (Soviet Union) and Wilkes (United States) to Poland in January 1959.[258] If the base now becomes permanent, the territorial position of the Soviet Union, with its main base (Mirny) and an inland station (Vostok) in the sector, will be unimpaired. Sixteen years later Poland set up the permanent Arctowski Station on King George Island, a few miles from Bellingshausen which is the only Soviet base in the Antarctic Peninsula. The Soviet Union clearly does not regard allies as surrogates for its Antarctic interests. Not only has it continuously extended its sphere of interest, but it has also directly challenged the United States by establishing a base in the 'United States' sector and working on the Dufek Massif.

Since 1959 the Soviet Union has advanced and the United States has retreated. The case of Alaska provides a useful contrast. There the US government was criticised for purchasing a vast area from Russia because it had no apparent value. The gold rush and Prudhoe Bay oil proved otherwise. Failure to take timely action in Antarctica may well have cost America a claim to a substantial part of the continent.

---

258. J. Machowski, *Sytuacja Antarktyki w Świetle Prawa Miedzynarodowego* (1968), 34, The station was not subsequently manned by Poland and was closed. Since 1978 Poland has re-occupied the site as a summer base (Dobrowolski).

4
TREATY

Origins

The Antarctic Treaty is unique in international affairs. The continent is dedicated to peaceful purposes. Freedom of scientific investigation is guaranteed. Claims are frozen for the duration of the agreement. Nuclear explosions and waste disposal are forbidden. All areas covered by the Treaty, including stations, are open to aerial and ground inspection. The original parties' representatives meet at two yearly intervals to recommend policy measures. Although open to review in 1991 the regime will, in the absence of amendments, continue after that date.

Development of the Antarctic Treaty may be traced from 1939. President Roosevelt's initiative had the unintended effect of provoking the Chilean claim in 1940. Argentina's *Primero de Mayo* expedition in 1942 led to the British Operation Tabarin establishing permanent bases. Chile and Argentina (which has had a post at Laurie Island since 1904) followed suit in 1947. January 1948 saw Argentinian navy ships in the Antarctic and Britain sent the cruiser *Nigeria*.

This particular aspect of the issue was dealt with by an agreement between the three countries not to send warships south of 60°S, apart from routine movements.[1] Regarded at the time as a 'mere expedient',[2] the agreement was renewed annually. It may be seen as an antecedent to both the non-militarisation provision in the Treaty[3] and the interim nature of the Treaty settlement. Subsequent disputes, including incidents at Hope Bay in 1952 and Deception Island in 1953, showed that the potential for conflict was still present in the Antarctic Peninsula.

By the end of 1947 the United States was faced with the problem of a confrontation between the United Kingdom and two major South American countries. It has already been shown how Argentina and Chile used the Rio Treaty of 1947 in an attempt to involve the United States in their dispute with Britain.

But this was not the end of American worries. There was also a

1. M.M. Whiteman, *Digest of International Law*, Vol. 2 (1963), 1238.
2. C.H.M. Waldock, 'Disputed Sovereignty in the Falkland Islands Dependencies' (1948), 25 *BYBIL*, 311.
3. G. Fahl, *Internationales Recht der Rüstungbeschränkungen* (1975), 6.

potential conflict between Britain and the United States, exemplified by the Stonington Island incident. Byrd's East Base on that island had been hurriedly evacuated in March 1941, leaving behind equipment and supplies. In February 1946 Britain, resolved to expand its activities, set up a base on the site, tidying up East Base in the process. In the same year Finn Ronne's private US expedition made plans to utilize East Base. When the State Department enquired of the British government as to the condition of its property, the British replied that there was insufficient space for two full-sized expeditions, not enough seals for dog-food,[4] and that East Base was in poor repair.

Ronne took the British note as an attempt to discourage him from re-occupying East Base. When the expedition arrived, there was tension due to his belief that the British had caused damage, and because of the political problems of United States occupation of a base in British territory.[5] Ronne has been appointed as a postmaster to demonstrate US administration.[6] Later, as a result of friendly relations with the British leader, agreement was reached on a joint sledging expedition.[7] The agreement, which was preserved by Ronne, was an interesting document. It provided for the British to name geographical features along the Weddell Coast from Darlington Island to Mount Tricorn and the Americans to name features further south.[8] As with the previously discussed example of US rights carrying corresponding duties,[9] the Ronne agreement would have a bearing on any US rights arising from his expedition.

Necessity compelled a US initiative. This came in 1948 in the form of alternative proposals for a United Nations trusteeship or a multiple condominium of the claimants and the United States. Both drafts were of a very sketchy nature. Once agreement was reached, so the British Ambassador was informed in June 1948, the United States would make its own claim. The trusteeship concept under Chapter XII of the United Nations Charter was primarily intended to advance the interests of the inhabitants of a territory,[10] but

---

4. M.M. Whiteman, *Digest of International Law*, Vol. 2 (1963) 1253–4. See also Sovereignty/*Polar Circumstances*.
5. J.H. Lipps, 'The United States "East Base" Antarctic Peninsula' (1976), 11(4) *Antarctic Journal*, 211 at 217.
6. W. Sullivan, *Quest for a Continent* (1957), 271
7. Ronne quoted in J.H. Lipps, 'East Base, Stonington Island, Antarctic Peninsula' (1978), 13(4) *Antarctic Journal* 231 at 232.
8. 'Agreement for British-American Weddell Coast Party': K.J. Bertrand, *Americans in Antarctica 1775–1948* (1971), 529.
9. Byrd's admission of the validity of New Zealand's claim (see National Interests/*The United States*).
10. Art. 76(*b*), UN Charter.

Antarctica did not comply with this requirement. Although the American proposals had special appeal to Britain, whose situation in the Antarctic Peninsula was steadily deteriorating,[11] the very word condominium brought shivers to the Foreign Office.[12] But the major drawback of the American proposals was that none of the claimants knew what areas would be claimed by the United States. Nor did the State Department. Britain and New Zealand, having no real choice, supported the initiative, but it was opposed by the other claimants. After the Soviet Note of June 1950 and the outbreak of the Korean War, negotiations ceased.

But like its predecessor of 1939 this United States move had unforeseen results. As part of its international solution the State Department had proposed the promotion of scientific investigation and research in the area,[13] and this was ultimately incorporated into the Treaty. Chile's response to the American proposals was put forward in July 1948 by Professor Escudero in the form of a *modus vivendi* providing for scientific research and exchange of information. No new bases, expeditions or activities south of 60°S would prejudice rights of sovereignty. The arrangement would last for five years, and six months before its expiry consultations for an Antarctic Conference would begin.[14] The Chilean reply contained most of the basic principles of the future Treaty. Apparently the State Department added the concept of a consultative committee with one member for each country.[15]

If the theoretical framework of the Antarctic Treaty is to be found in the Escudero proposals, the practical aspect comes from the International Geophysical Year's. Scientific research had already been suggested in 1948 as the major activity in the Antarctic. At the instigation of the State Department the National Academy of Sciences prepared a report in 1949 outlining a programme on a continental scale.[16] It was therefore no accident that the proposal of a number of geophysicists for a polar year was advanced in 1950. Berkner, an American, and Chapman, an Englishman, presented the idea to the Mixed Commission on the Ionosphere, which com-

11. B.M. Plott, 'The Development of United States Antarctic Policy', Ph. D. thesis, Fletcher School of Law and Diplomacy (1969), 134.
12. Presumably due to the intractable problems detailed in D.P. O'Connell, 'The Condominium of the New Hebrides' (1968–9), 43 *BYBIL*, 71.
13. Department of State Press Release (28 August 1948).
14. Enrique Gajardo Villarroel, 'Apuntes para un libro sobre la Historia Diplomática del Tratado Antártico y de la participación chilena en su elaboración' (1977), 10 *Revista de difusión INACH* 40 at 46–7.
15. J. Hanessian, 'The Antarctic Treaty 1959' (1960), 9 *ICLQ*, 436 at 445.
16. Ibid., at p. 438.

mended it to the International Council of Scientific Unions (ICSU). The latter established a Special Committee for the IGY, the Comité Spécial de l'Année Géophysique Internationale (CSAGI). The IGY was to run for eighteen months from 1 July 1957 to 31 December 1958 to coincide with an expected peak of sunspot activity and several eclipses.[17]

The IGY became a programme of global cooperation directed at world- or area-wide synoptic measurements.[18] It covered geophysics, meteorology, geomagnetism, aurora and air glow, ionosphere, cosmic rays, longitudes and latitudes, glaciology and climatology, oceanography, rockets and satellites, seismology and gravimetry,[19] and nuclear radiation. Emphasis was placed on intensive observation of the sun with increased observations on regular world days.[20] At its second full meeting in Rome in 1954, CSAGI formulated principles for the IGY. Programmes were to be selected with a view to solving specific planetary problems of the earth. Antarctic research was a major objective:

B. Problems requiring special attention during the IGY should be selected according to the following criteria:
(*a*) Problems requiring concurrent synoptic observations at many points involving co-operative observations by many nations.
(*b*) Problems of branches of geophysical sciences whose solutions will be aided by the availability of synoptic or other concentrated work during the IGY in other geophysical sciences.
(*c*) Observations of all major geophysical phenomena in relatively inaccessible regions of the Earth that can be occupied during the IGY because of the extraordinary effort during that interval, in order to augment our basic knowledge of the earth and of the solar and other influences acting upon it.
(*d*) Epochal observations of slowly varying terrestrial phenomena, to establish basic information for subsequent comparison at later epochs.

Priority was to be accorded to item B(*a*).[21]

The official programme of the IGY did not cover a number of activities carried out in Antarctica at that time such as biology and geology.[22] Icebreaker exploration and aerial photography of the

17. W. Sullivan, *Assault on the Unknown* (1961), 27.
18. T.O. Jones, 'Developing the US Antarctic Research Programme' (1970), 26(10) *Science and Public Affairs*, 81.
19. W. Buedeler, *The International Geophysical Year* (1957), 25.
20. S. Chapman, *IGY: Year of Discovery* (1959), 102–3.
21. H.S. Jones, 'The Inception and Development of the International Geophysical Year' (1959), 1 *Annals of the IGY*, 393.
22. T. Nagata, 'The Advancement of Scientific Research as the Basis of Antarctic Development' in Francisco Orrego Vicuña and Augusto Salinas Araya (eds.), *El desarollo de la Antártica* (1977), 74.

Amundsen and Bellingshausen Sea areas was proposed by the US Navy in 1956 to 'enhance the US claims position in relation to other countries engaged in scientific and exploratory efforts during the International Geophysical Year'.[23] Cartography had been specifically rejected as an IGY discipline[24] because of its connection with politics, and US funding was refused because it was outside the IGY's programme.[25] However the Soviet Union went ahead with an extensive photography surveying and mapping programme covering half the continent.[26] Like some other parts of the Soviet Antarctic programme, this was outside the IGY assignment.[27]

The most publicised extra – IGY activity was the Commonwealth Trans-Antarctic Expedition (TAE) of Fuchs and Hillary. This project had clearly recognised political implications.[28] Although TAE was structured as a private limited liability company, it received substantial donations from the United Kingdom and New Zealand governments. Members of the New Zealand TAE committee included representatives of the Treasury, Department of External Affairs, Navy and Air Force.[29] Buildings for Scott Base and the use of the vessel *Endeavour* and aircraft[30] were provided to TAE by the New Zealand government.

ICSU and CSAGI were private scientific organizations. The international budget was little more than $250,000 out of a total expenditure of approximately $2,000 million for the IGY. The United States outlay alone was $500 million.[31] In essence IGY consisted of national scientific programmes and this was the reason for its generous funding. The international coordination provided by CSAGI was a minor element in the overall effort.

Scientists had presented IGY to their governments as a 'one-shot affair' and for this reason were reluctant to ask for more assistance when it ended.[32] Bases, such as those of New Zealand[33] and the

23. Chief of Naval Operations to Commander-in-Chief, US Atlantic Fleet (19 September 1956).
24. W. Sullivan, *Assault on the Unknown* (1961), 295.
25. B.M. Plott, 'The Development of United States Antarctic Policy', Ph. D. thesis, Fletcher School of Law and Diplomacy (1969), 170.
26. W. Sullivan, "The International Geophysical Year' (1959) 521 International Conciliation 322.
27. J.D. Roscoe, US Antarctic Programs, to OCB Antarctic Working Group (7 June 1956).
28. A.S. Helm and J.H. Miller, *Antarctica* (1964), 330.
29. L.B. Quartermain, *New Zealand and the Antarctic* (1971), 83.
30. L.B. Quartermain, *South from New Zealand* (1964), 49.
31. H. Bullis, *The Political Legacy of the International Geophysical Year* (1973), 13–16.
32. P. Briggs, *Laboratory at the Bottom of the World* (1970), 16.
33. 'Antarctic Anniversaries' (1977), 8(1) *Antarctic* 9.

United States,[34] had been built as temporary structures to be closed at the end of 1958. The initial US appropriation had been obtained with the assurance that no more would be required and that IGY funds would not be spent beyond the fiscal year 1960.[35]

It was the Soviet decision to maintain its stations after the end of the IGY which forced the United States and other nations to remain[36] and was the catalyst for the negotiation of the Treaty. The Soviet Union's entry into Antarctic politics and the consolidation of its presence on the continent[37] were the most significant effects of the IGY.[38]

Article IV of the Treaty was preceded by a gentlemen's agreement during the IGY. At the plenary session of the 1955 IGY Conference in Paris, it was accepted that the Conference had 'exclusively scientific' overall aims and a technical character. Financial and political questions were not its concern:

The Argentine and Chilean delegations give their accord to the recommendations for the co-ordination of existing and new bases, with the proviso that, agreeing to the goal and spirit of the resolution taken at the first plenary meeting of the Conference, these are temporary measures calculated to achieve the best results of the IGY and adopted in the interests of scientific development, and that these resolutions do not modify the existing status in the Antarctic regarding the relations of the participating countries.[39]

Acceptance by the Conference of this declaration has been taken as constituting the gentlemen's agreement,[40] but such an undertaking would have been rather limited. The Conference itself was taken as being purely scientific, but there was no indication that the same held for IGY activities. Even if the Argentinian and Chilean declaration is taken as having general application to all participants, it only specifically applies to bases and not to activities. In terms it only covers the effect of the recommendations of IGY Conferences. *Prima facie*, non-IGY activities were not covered. If the gentlemen's agreement is to be taken from the Paris Conference, its ineffectiveness is apparent. As the Conference declared its own exclusively

34. US Naval Support Force, Antarctica, *Introduction to Antarctica* (1967) 33.
35. G.B. Baldwin, 'The Dependence of Science on Law and Government – The International Geophysical Year – A Case Study' (1964), *Wisconsin Law Review*, 78 at 109.
36. R.D. Hayton, 'The Antarctic Settlement of 1959' (1960), 54 *AJIL*, 349 at 353.
37. R.-J. Dupuy, 'Le Statut de l'Antarctique' (1958), *Annuaire Française de Droit International,* 196 at 197.
38. D.L. Soden, *A Political and Legal Analysis 'The Antarctic Treaty'*, Institute for Marine and Coastal Studies, University of Southern California (1978), 16.
39. M.M. Whiteman, *Digest of International Law*, Vol. 2 (1963), 1242–3.
40. B.M. Plott, 'The Development of United States Antarctic Policy', Ph.D. thesis, Fletcher School of Law and Diplomacy (1969), 164.

scientific aims and character, any political statements at the Conference were outside its ambit.

There are clear indications that the terms of the gentlemen's agreement are wider than those of the Paris Conference. Diplomats who took part in the drafting of the Antarctic Treaty had a much more expansive view of its terms. Ambassador Paul Daniels of the United States contended that 'the various governments concerned had reached a sort of gentleman's agreement not to engage in legal or political argumentation during that period, in order that the scientific program might proceed without impediment.'[41] Professor van der Essen, Director of the Belgian Ministry of Foreign Affairs, held that the scientific agreement that activities did not affect sovereignty was totally respected by governments.[42] Commentators state that the understanding was between governments and was not written.

The legal effect of the gentlemen's agreement is important. It could be argued that tacit adoption of the Argentinian and Chilean declaration by governments gave rise to interdependent attitudes in a manner analogous to the Ihlen Declaration.[43] This approach would be supported by the acceptance in the *Nuclear Test Cases* of France's declaration that it would cease atmospheric testing. The Court held that declarations given publicly by way of unilateral acts could create obligations if there was an intention to be bound.[44] This could be taken as a form of estoppel.[45] Form is not decisive but the intention must be clear.[46] So far the doctrine has only applied to statements.[47] In the case of the Argentinian and Chilean declaration, it is not the wording itself which is invoked but its tacit acceptance by governments of other countries. The IGY saw the establishment of permanent stations by the United States and the Soviet Union among others, and a vast expansion of research and logistic support. In the absence of contrary agreement, such activities would clearly have supported claims. Two-and-a-half years after the end of the IGY Article IV of the Antarctic Treaty came into force. From June 1961 such activities no longer counted, at least in legal theory. Reliance on IGY activities would therefore be of considerable relevance in any ultimate resolution of claims.

41. P.C. Daniels, 'The Antarctic Treaty' (1970), 26(10) *Science and Public Affairs*, 11 at 12.
42. A. van der Essen, 'Le problème politico-juridique de l'Antarctique et le Traité de Washington' (1960), 20(3) *Annales de Droit et de Sciences Politiques*, 227 at 236.
43. *Legal Status of Eastern Greenland* (1933) PCIJ Ser. A/B No. 53, 22 at 70–1.
44. *Nuclear Tests Case (Australia* v. *France)* (1974) ICJ 253 at 267.
45. S. Fur, 'Les Affaires des Essais Nucléaires' (1975), 79 *RGDIP*, 972 at 999.
46. *Temple of Preah Vihear Case (Preliminary Objections)* (1961), *ICJ*, 17 at 32.
47. T.M. Franck, 'Word Made Law: the Decision of the ICJ in the Nuclear Test Cases' (1975), 69 *AJIL*, 612 at 617.

Scientists at the 1955 IGY Conference represented private organizations. Their statements did not bind governments. Even if the declaration could be held to bind governments as a unilateral act or by estoppel, it has previously been argued that the terms of the understanding were too narrow to encompass all IGY activities. If a wider, unwritten standstill agreement is invoked, one faces serious difficulties. What were its terms? When did it start and finish? Did it apply to all activities during the IGY[48] or only to those carried out within the IGY programme?[49] There does not appear to be a satisfactory answer to any of these questions. It is suggested that the tacit agreement is too vague to have legal effect. Nor was it intended to have such effect if it was a gentlemen's agreement.[50]

Despite numerous protestations to the contrary, claims staking continued. The official map of US discovery previously discussed depicted discoveries up to 1 February 1956. US claims papers were being deposited as late as December 1956. In July 1957 the Antarctic Working Group of the US Operations Coordination Board discussed various claims possibilities. It has already been pointed out that Wilkes Station was established to forestall the Soviet Union.

Nor was the United States the only nation to utilize the IGY for political objectives. Bases of the Soviet Union and all claimants may be taken as wolves in the sheeps' clothing of scientific research.[51] The scientific aims of the IGY required stations along the three meridional pole-to-pole lines, adequate coverage of the continent and representative coverage of the interior.[52] This demanded careful consideration of the geographical distribution of observing stations to detect gaps and recommending combination or elimination where unnecessary duplication might occur.[53] It will be recalled that Argentina and Chile made a declaration regarding IGY base coordination in 1955. The statement related to a Conference resolution in the following terms:

2. The Antarctic Conference RECOGNIZES that in consideration of the IGY programme, it is of importance that the stations be established in such a way that they are adequately distributed all over the Antarctic, but CONSIDERING

48. J. Hanessian, 'The Antarctic Treaty 1959' (1960), 9 *ICLQ*, 436 at 449.
49. J.-F. da Costa, 'Antártida: O Problema Político' (1961), 4(15) *Revista Brasileira de Política Internacional*, 85 at 87.
50. E. Lauterpacht, 'Gentleman's Agreements' in W. Flume, H.J. Hahn, G. Kegel and K.R. Simmonds (eds.), *International Law and Economic Order* (1977), 381 at 396.
51. L.F.E. Goldie, 'International Relations in Antarctica' (1958), 30 *Australian Quarterly*, 7 at 23.
52. M. Nicolet, 'The IGY Meetings' (1958), 2A *Annals of the IGY*, 176–7.
53. H.S. Jones, 'The Inception and Development of the International Geophysical Year' (1959), 1 *Annals of the IGY*, 393.

that certain primary requirements may well necessitate certain stations being established close to each other, RECOMMENDS that, in such exceptional cases, the stations should be located, as far as feasible, in such manner that their respective situations will permit, in the best possible way, the study of the geophysical phenomena which are the object of the IGY.[54]

'Certain primary requirements' could not be of a scientific nature. It may be inferred that they were political. So Ellsworth (United States) and General Belgrano (Argentina) Stations were established next to each other on the Weddell Sea. Scott (New Zealand) was sited on Ross Island because of its proximity to McMurdo (USA). The north Antarctic Peninsula and neighbouring islands had as many stations as all of the rest of the continent, including three on the small but strategic Deception Island. All claimants' bases were within the area claimed. CSAGI could only accept whatever nations wished to do about the gaps (Princess Astrid Coast, Knox Coast and Vahsel Bay),[55] having neither the funds nor the political influence to do otherwise.

The IGY ended on 31 December 1958, and it is therefore presumed that the effect of the gentlemen's agreement expired with it.[56] However, the State Department considered that it had been extended for a year.[57] In August 1958 CSAGI agreed to a further geophysical year to be known as International Geophysical Cooperation – 1959 (IGC). United States scientists had obtained government funding on the basis that the IGY was a specific time-limited undertaking, and therefore could not agree to an extension of the IGY.[58] IGC was organised by a new committee and the extent of participation was up to each member. This was a compromise between Soviet desires for a prolongation of the IGY and American concern at additional unforeseen expenditure.[59] If IGC was not an extension of the IGY, then the 1955 Conference resolution did not continue in effect during 1959. On the 'tacit consent of governments' interpretation of the gentlemen's agreement, it would be doubtful whether the understanding remained in force because it was implied for the IGY only. The Argentinian and Chilean declarations, which referred to temporary measures, appeared inapplicable to IGC the purpose of which was to establish activities on a permanent basis.

Application of the gentlemen's agreement during IGC is of some

54. M.M. Whiteman, *Digest of International Law*, Vol. 2 (1963), 1242.
55. M. Nicolet, 'The IGY Meetings' (1958), 2A *Annals of the IGY*, 178–81.
56. R.D. Hayton, 'The Antarctic Settlement of 1959' (1960), 54 *AJIL*, 349 at 359.
57. J. Hanessian, 'The Antarctic Treaty 1959' (1960), 9 *ICLQ*, 436 at 455.
58. H. Bullis, *The Political Legacy of the International Geophysical Year* (1973), 33–4.
59. W. Sullivan, *Assault on Antarctica* (1961), 409.

relevance to claims. It has been argued previously that the agreement was without legal effect. If the contrary view were to prevail, 1959 assumes a special place in territorial arguments because a number of stations of strategic significance were closed or transferred in that year. Assuming a wide interpretation of the gentlemen's agreement, no activities between July 1955 (the date of the Paris Conference) and 31 December 1959 would count. Therefore IGY stations transferred during IGC, such as Ellsworth and Wilkes, would not assist a possible sovereignty claim by the transferor.

The IGY can be seen as a practical exercise largely codified by the Treaty. It established scientific research as the currency of Antarctic politics, and large-scale national funding initiated for this purpose was maintained. Permanent bases, previously confined to the northern Antarctic Peninsula, were now established around the continent and inland. Emphasis on national activities and international cooperation continued. Numerous specific features of the Treaty framework made their appearance. Examples are the exchange of scientists, freedom of movement and exchange of information.

But the IGY was only planned as a temporary programme. Frozen into the Antarctic Treaty, the defects of the IGY as a permanent fixture became apparent. CSAGI was perhaps effective in coordinating a national effort at minimal cost, but its successor, SCAR, was inherently unsuited to the wider problems raised by a continuing research effort. Sovereignty issues could be avoided for a short period, but became inevitable in the long term. The basic defects of the Antarctic Treaty can to a large degree be traced to the IGY.

Negotiation

Two factors dictated the necessity for some form of agreed regime for Antarctica. First, the IGY had been planned as a coordinated effort over a limited and short period of time, and secondly, the Soviet Union made it clear in that its own activities would continue after the end of IGY. A secret British initiative for an international consortium, including the Soviet Union, was made public and rejected by Chile and Argentina in February 1958.[60] US negotiations then led to secret preparatory meetings between June 1958 and October 1959.[61]

There was considerable support for internationalization of the continent, New Zealand was the prime advocate, and the United

---

60. J. Hanessian, 'The Antarctic Treaty 1959' (1960), 9 *ICLQ*, 436 at 454.
61. Ibid., at p. 461.

Kingdom, the United States and the Soviet Union also favoured this solution.[62] But Argentina and Chile were absolutely opposed to any derogation from their sovereignty.[63] France and Australia would not accept an international regime.[64] New Zealand, a reluctant claimant, had publicly advocated a UN trusteeship in 1956. Previous review of Argentinian and Chilean interests has shown that their claims were not, and are not, subject to waiver. This policy has not been pursued merely for internal political purposes, as is evident in the routine functioning of the Treaty regime.

Invitations to the negotiations preceeding the Conference were issued by the United States to each country having 'a direct interest in Antarctica',[65] interpreted as meaning every nation active on the continent during the IGY. This was the easy solution, and it had far-reaching implications. An international regime was in effect ruled out before the negotiations began because four of the twelve participants would not accept it. In basing invitations on IGY activity, the possibility that some nations would subsequently cease their Antarctic programmes was not taken into account. Inclusion of twelve States with conflicting interests led to a lowest common denominator of agreement − preservation of the *status quo*.[66]

Peaceful Purposes

Exclusive dedication of Antarctica for peaceful purposes[67] is a remarkable innovation, for Antarctic research has military applications. During the Second World War Byrd's men constituted the only major US reservoir of knowledge of Arctic problems.[68] Operation Highjump, a US expedition in 1946, had as one of its objectives the training of Navy personnel and testing of equipment under Antarctic conditions.[69] After the Treaty had come into force, Admiral Tyree agreed that any country operating in Antarctica obtained military knowledge by observing the impact of extreme weather on men and machinery, particularly aircraft.[70]

62. A. Scilingo, *El Tratado Antártico* (1963) 49.
63. D.L. Soden, *A Political and Legal Analysis 'The Antarctic Treaty'*, Institute for Marine and Coastal Studies, University of Southern California (1978), 21.
64. C. Beeby, *The Antarctic Treaty* (1972), 8.
65. Identical notes dated 3 May 1958 from the United States to each of the governments (Department of State, *Conference on Antarctica* (1960), 3).
66. Mr. Casey (Australia) in Department of State, *Conference on Antarctica* (1960), 26.
67. Art. I(1), Antarctic Treaty.
68. E.P. Hoyt, *The Last Explorer* (1968), 357.
69. K.J. Bertrand, *Americans in Antarctica 1775−1948* (1971), 484.
70. 'Antarctica Report 1965' Hearings, Subcommittee on Territorial and Insular

Clearly Antarctica had no role to play in super-power conflict in 1959. But Article I is a renunciation of the exercise of military purposes, which constitute an important aspect of national sovereignty. Before the Treaty there had been naval patrols and even minor clashes in the South American sector. For the South American countries the Article represented a major concession.

The larger powers automatically reap military advantages. Much has been learned about the special problems of practising medicine in cold weather and about psychological screening of men for difficult duty in isolated conditions, such as aboard nuclear submarines.[71] Experience in ice-breaking and building runways on sea-ice can be applied to Arctic operations.[72]

Article I(2) specifically permits the use of military personnel or equipment for scientific research or any other peaceful purpose. This proviso was primarily inserted to enable continuation of US logistic support by the Navy,[73] but it also enures to the benefit of countries such as Argentina whose programme is directed by naval officers and whose bases belong to branches of the military. New Zealand and other countries at the 1959 Conference were unhappy with this provision, a derogation from the principle of non-militarisation, but accepted it because the scientific expeditions of most Antarctic nations (including New Zealand) could not be mounted without military and naval support.[74] On publicly known facts, present logistic support appears to comply with the requirement of peaceful purpose in Article I(2). Polar training is not the primary interest in Antarctic work by the military forces of various nations.[75]

There has been Soviet comment on the high ratio of enlisted men and officers to each US scientist.[76] In 1968–9 the American winter programme comprised 213 military personnel, as against thirty scientists.[77] By 1975–6 the proportion of civilians had been sub-

Affairs, Committee on Interior and Insular Affairs, H. Rep., 89th Cong., 1st Sess. (1965), 147.

71. Commander R. Spaulding, Staff Psychiatrist, Bethesda Naval Hospital, quoted in (1963), 5(4) *Bulletin of the US Antarctic Projects Officer*, 4.

72. W.J. Cromie, 'The Navy's Stake in Antarctica' (October 1968), *US Naval Institute Proceedings*, 37 at 44.

73. J. Hanessian, 'The Antarctic Treaty 1959' (1960), 9 *ICLQ*, 432 at 468.

74. C. Beeby, *The Antarctic Treaty* (1972), 13.

75. Y.K. Fedorov, 'Antarctica: Experimental Proving Ground for Peaceful Coexistence and International Collaboration' (1970), 26(10) *Science and Public Affairs*, 22 at 24.

76. Ibid.

77. US Navy Task Force 43, *Report of Operation Deep Freeze 69* (1969), 45.

stantially increased[78] due to the National Science Foundation
operating some support services through a contractor.[79] On a formal
level, the actual funding of operations had been vested in the
National Science Foundation in 1970.[80] Although a number of
factors (lack of Navy interest in the absence of military objectives
and a political desire to reduce government involvement and to
increase the participation of private enterprise) contributed to the
reduction of the Navy's role, concern at outside criticism based on
the Treaty was no doubt relevant. Other nations made extensive use
of military personnel and continue to do so.

More difficulty is posed by research projects with military implications. Antarctic upper atmosphere physics studies may be useful
for defence communications systems.[81] Antarctic research on
multiplication of very low frequency (VLF) radio emissions has been
examined by the US Department of Defense.[82] Noise transmission
under sea-ice could be of relevance to naval communications. However even if research is funded by a branch of the military,[83] this in
itself does not imply a breach of Article I. There can only be a contra-
vention if the purpose is not peaceful as might be indicated, *inter alia*
by the results not being published openly. Deletions from the
Congressional testimony on appropriations for the former nuclear
reactor at McMurdo[84] in the 1968 financial year raise questions
under Article I. A more serious issue arises from extensive censoring
of a 1975 Senate subcommittee hearing 'in the interests of natural
security'.[85] Scrutiny of the context of the deletions suggests that the
reason given for excision is incorrect. It seems likely that the relevant
passages concerned the development of US policy on politically
sensitive issues[86] of a non-military nature.

On the general meaning of Article I there is considerable room for

78. Sixty Naval personnel and twenty-nine civilians (US Navy Task Force 199,
    Report of Operation Deep Freeze 76 (1976), IX-8).
79. 'Contractor gains expanded role' (1974), 9(1) *Antarctic Journal*, 31.
80. 'US Antarctic Policy' Hearing. Subcommittee on Oceans and International Envi-
    ronment, Committee on Foreign Relations, Senate, 94th Cong., 1st Sess. (1975),
    30.
81. 'Antarctica Legislation – 1961' Hearings, Subcommittee on Territorial and
    Insular Affairs, Committee on Interior and Insular Affairs, H. Rep. 87th Cong.,
    1st Sess. (1962), 20.
82. L. Ponte, *The Cooling* (1976), 169.
83. O. Wilkes, *Protest* (1973), 43.
84. O. Wilkes and R. Mann, 'The story of Nukey Poo' (Oct. 1978), *Science and
    Public Affairs*, 32 and 34.
85. US Antarctic Policy' Hearing, Subcommittee on Oceans and International Envi-
    ronment, Committee on Foreign Relations, Senate, 94th Cong., 1st Sess. (1975),
    II.
86. E.g. page 16 (Antarctic resources as the common heritage of mankind).

differences of opinion. Almost every technological device is capable of being put to some military use,[87] and it is not generally possible to draw a sharp line between warlike and peaceful.[88] When asked whether Soviet Antarctic activities represented any military use, Admiral Tyree said he did not know of any but 'it is awfully hard . . . to say what . . . potentially can be used for military purposes.'[89]

Although 'peaceful purposes' is vague, it specifically excludes the establishment of military bases and fortifications, the carrying out of military manoeuvres and the testing of any type of weapons.[90] So military rockets could be used to carry out scientific research but not to test weapons systems. The measures specified in Article I convey an objective test. Military fortifications cannot be for peaceful purposes.

'Peaceful purposes' should be naturally construed. To argue that it should include all activity not clearly identified as military[91] has little justification in the Treaty text and goes against the linking of peaceful purposes and the prevention of international discord.[92] A US naval officer has contended that the only defence experiments forbidden by the Treaty are those related to weapons.[93] But other types of defence research could be 'of a military nature' contrary to Article I. Narrow interpretations of 'peaceful purposes', especially from well-informed commentators, are a cause for concern.

Several bases were set up, and are maintained by various branches of the armed forces of the countries concerned. Article I specifically prohibits the establishment of military bases. It is suggested that the stations are not contrary to the provisions of the Treaty. Article I preserves the continent for peaceful purposes. The test is the purpose for which the base was founded; furthermore, the ban on military bases is cited by the Treaty as an example of measures of a military nature. The stations mentioned are bases of the military, but for peaceful purposes. This consideration is necessary because Article I(2) permits the use of military personnel and equipment for peaceful purposes but does not mention bases.

'Peaceful purposes' relates to Antarctica as defined by Article VI.

---

87. J.E.S. Fawcett, *International Law and the Uses of Outer Space* (1968), 30.
88. D.G. Brennan in L.P. Bloomfield (ed.), *Outer Space* (1968), 174.
89. 'Antarctica Legislation – 1961' Hearings, Subcommittee on Territorial and Insular Affairs, Committee on Interior and Insular Affairs, H. Rep. 87th Cong., 1st Sess. (1962), 65.
90. Art. I(1).
91. J. Hanessian, 'The Antarctic Treaty 1959' (1960), 9 *ICLQ*, 436 at 468. Mr Hanessian participated in US planning for the IGY.
92. Preamble.
93. B.M. Plott, 'The Development of United States Antarctic Policy, Ph.D. thesis, Fletcher School of Law and Diplomacy (1969) 245.

Although the Treaty applies to the area south of 60°S, high seas freedoms are preserved; Article VI specifies that 'nothing in the present Treaty shall prejudice' these freedoms; therefore the dedication to peaceful purposes in Article I is subordinate to Article VI.[94] Article I does not apply north of 60°S. So, even if the allegation that Operation Deepfreeze at Christchurch Airport is a general purpose military exercise[95] were upheld, there would be no violation of the Treaty because that activity is outside the Treaty area.

It is common to refer to the Treaty as demilitarising the continent. Antarctica has not been militarised and the Treaty ensures that this situation will continue. There are wide differences of opinion on the political significance of Article I. On one view the Cold War has been kept out of Antarctica when it was a potentially explosive area of the world.[96] Another approach is that the continent is of 'most minimal strategic significance'.[97] The real test would only come in an international crisis or if war broke out.[98] To date there has been no support for warlike uses of the continent.

Discussion of the American Antarctic has raised the relevance of the Rio Treaty. On signing the Antarctic Treaty the United States, Argentina and Chile made a declaration, which is in law a reservation,[99] that it did not affect their obligations under the Rio Treaty.[100] A further Chilean declaration in relation to Article I interpreted that Article as not derogating from its legitimate right of collective and individual self-defence under the United Nations Charter.[101] On the views previously advanced, 'any measures of a military nature' are prohibited. The declarations would rewrite Article I to say that measures of a military nature in individual or collective self-defence are 'peaceful purposes'. Taking into account the expansive nature of the various modern doctrines of self-defence, little would be left of Article I in a crisis involving Argentina or Chile. It has already been pointed out that the two countries were close to war in 1978 over the Beagle Channel boundary. That issue is directly connected with their rival claims in the Antarctic Peninsula.[102]

94. See further discussion under Treaty/*Area*.
95. O. Wilkes, *Protest* (1973), 50.
96. B. Roberts, 'International Co-operation for Antarctic Development: the Test for the Antarctic Treaty' (1978), 19(119) *Polar Record*, 107 at 108.
97. W.T. Burke, 'Law and the New Technologies' in L.M. Alexander (ed.), *The Law of the Sea* (1967), 224.
98. M.W. Mouton, 'The International Regime of the Polar Regions' (1962), 107 *Hague Recueil*, 175 at 236.
99. See Treaty/*Reservations*.
100. Department of State, *Conference on Antarctica* (1960), 68–9.
101. A. Scilingo, *El Tratado Antártico* (1963), 89.
102. See National Interests/*South America*.

Scientific Investigation

Establishment of a foundation for the continuation and development of cooperation on the basis of freedom of scientific investigation[103] is a major purpose of the Treaty. Scientific activities are relatively non-controversial[104] and were demonstrated during the IGY to defuse sovereignty issues. The reason that Antarctica is uniquely dedicated to science does not therefore arise from its particular suitability for research but rather from political necessity. Scientific activity is fundamental to maintaining the IGY framework. The Treaty was not designed to deal with mining, commerce or industry, nor is it suitable for adaptation to these purposes.

Article II deals with scientific 'investigation'. Elsewhere scientific 'research' is used.[105] From the context the two terms may be taken to have the same meaning.[106] Scientific investigation is not defined. It may be assumed that research such as the taking of cores in the vicinity of the Ross Sea continental shelf to provide data relating to ice conditions, the influence of tectonic elements on terrigenous sedimentation and 'the hydrocarbon potential of the continental margin'[107] is within Article II because of the remoteness of the connection between the research and any eventual recovery of minerals. For several years basic US earth science research in Antarctica has been justified as necessary to provide the geological background data to assess potential resources.[108] Scientific exploration for economically exploitable resources is arguably not excluded because the Treaty does not warrant the drawing of a line between pure and applied science.[109] So long as the investigation is scientific, it is within the ambit of Article II.

The Soviet Union had proposed an unqualified freedom of investigation throughout Antarctica.[110] Such a wide formula was

103. Preamble.
104. G. Skagestad, 'The Frozen Frontier: Models for International Co-operation' (1975), 10 *Co-operation and Conflict*, 167 at 169.
105. Art. IX (1)(*b*).
106. Scientific research facilitation (Art. IX(1)(*b*)) can only refer to the activities protected by Art. II. This view is supported by the ordering of Art. IX(1), which follows that of the substantive treaty provisions: peaceful purposes (Art. I); scientific research (Art. II); international scientific cooperation (Art. III); inspection (Art. VII).
107. 'US Antarctic Research Program 1978–1979' (1978), 13(3) *Antarctic Journal*, 1 at 8–9.
108. National Research Council, *Antarctic Geology and Solid-Earth Geophysics* (1974), 1.
109. E. Hambro 'Some Notes on the Future' of the Antarctic Treaty Collaboration' (1974), 63 *AJIL*, 217 at 222–3.
110. Enrique Gajardo Villarroel, 'Apuntes para un libro sobre la Historia

unacceptable, and the Treaty restrictions are intentional and significant.[111] A literal interpretation of 'continue' would require that the same arrangements prevail. But the IGY was a temporary and limited non-governmental venture in scientific cooperation. The Antarctic Treaty has a life of at least thirty years and is an arrangement between governments. Article II does not continue the gentlemen's agreement, because that topic is dealt with by Article IV. One could posit that those scientific activities carried out during the IGY are protected by Article II, but this interpretation would not cover non-IGY activities, such as biology, adopted by SCAR after the IGY and seems unlikely. Perhaps the better view is that scientific research will be continued in the manner in which it has previously been carried out.

Article II is subject to 'the provisions of the present Treaty'. Any limitations must be found in the Treaty text. At the 1977 Consultative Meeting, governments were recommended to endeavour to ensure that no activity should be conducted to explore Antarctic mineral resources pending the timely adoption of an agreed regime.[112] This part of the purported moratorium could not apply to exploration for minerals as part of a scientific investigation conforming with the Treaty. A recommendation under Article IX cannot amend the Treaty. So a by-product of the 1978–9 US investigation of the Dufek Massif was an appraisal of its mineral resource potential,[113] and this research was not subject to the 1977 moratorium.

Freedom of scientific investigation is also subject to the freezing provisions of Article IV. It has been argued that the United States' true motivation in initiating the Treaty was to gain access to the whole continent.[114] An official view is that 'as things stand, we are at liberty to investigate anywhere, build anywhere, fly anywhere, traverse anywhere in this vast and still mysterious southland.'[115] US freedom of movement throughout Antarctica does not arise from Article II or IV but from its own policy of non – recognition of

Diplomática del Tratado Antártico y la participación chilena un su elaboración' (1977), 10 *Revista de Difusión INACH*, 40 at 64.
111. A. Scilingo, *El Tratado Antártico* (1963), 51.
112. Rec. IX-I examined in Oil and Gas/*Moratorium*.
113. 'US Antarctic Research Program 1978–1979' (1978), 13(3) *Antarctic Journal*, 1 at 5.
114. O. Wilkes, 'Antarctica: The New Frontier' (1974), 20 *Canta*.
115. H. Cleveland, Assistant Secretary of State for International Organization Affairs in 'Antarctica Report – 1965', Hearings, Subcommittee on Territorial and Insular Affairs, Committee on Interior and Insular Affairs. H. Rep., 89th Cong., 1st Sess. (1965), 29.

claims. Access under Article II is not available for non-scientific purposes such as purely commercial resource exploitation.

Exchange of Information

Two categories of international information exchange appear in the Treaty. In order to promote international cooperation, scientific observations and results shall be exchanged and made freely available.[116] For the same purpose, and to permit maximum economy and efficiency of operations, plans for scientific programs shall be exchanged.[117] Advance notice of expeditions, stations, military personnel and equipment[118] is provided for in the Article dealing with inspection. At the First Consultative Meeting a single recommendation,[119] purportedly framed under Article VII(5), expanded on the requirements of both Articles. By 1975 there were numerous recommendations on the topic, partly consolidated[120] in a Standard Format for Annual Exchanges of Information.[121]

There is a significant difference between the two categories of information. Article III is concerned with science. Plans, observations and results are to be made available 'to the greatest extent feasible and practicable'.[122] Absence of an absolute obligation follows from the intent to promote international cooperation in scientific investigation. In contrast, Article VII(5) clearly requires that each Contracting Party 'shall give . . . notice in advance'. This is related to the inspection provisions in the same Article whose purpose is to 'ensure the observance . . . of the Treaty'.[123]

Telecommunications (apart from military equipment), a basic element of Antarctic cooperation, does not fall within either the scientific or the diplomatic exchange provisions. For a number of years there was no exchange on the topic,[124] which is now governed by Recommendation X-3 of 1979. Failure to comply with this measure, in relation to non-military facilities, would not be a breach of the information exchange requirements of the Treaty.

116. Art. III(1)(*c*).
117. Art. III(1)(*a*).
118. Art. VII.(5).
119. Rec. I-VI.
120. For an example of a recommendation not covered, see Rec. I-XIII (nuclear equipment and techniques).
121. Rec. VIII-6.
122. Art. III(1).
123. Art. VII(1).
124. H.M. Dater 'The Antarctic Treaty in Action 1961–1971' (1971), 6(3) *Antarctic Journal*, 67 at 70.

Diplomatic information shall be given 'in advance'.[125] In 1961 this was taken to mean as early in each year as possible and in any case before the end of November.[126] Despite the absence of the 'in advance' requirement from Article III, the 1961 measure also applied to scientific information.[127] A United States declaration in 1959 interpreted this provision as not forbidding alterations to items notified under Article VII(5).[128] Modifications of previously reported activities are to be notified as soon as possible and not later than 30 June.[129] The Recommendation refers to subsequent notice of changes and is contrary to Article VII(5). Instead of the mandatory prior notification required by the Treaty, a delay of at least ten months is permitted, from the first flight to the continent at the end of August until 30 June the following year. The Standard Format for the Annual Exchanges confirms the confusion between Articles III and VII(5). By demanding advance notice of such a lengthy list of items, the Consultative Parties have in effect encouraged non-observance of prior reporting under Article VII(5) on the excuse that modifications need only be reported by 30 June.

The Standard Format was intended to reduce overlapping and lack of coordination between the recommendations which had been adopted piecemeal.[130] But it became essentially a consolidation rather than a revision. The expansion of reporting was emphasised by the adoption at the same Consultative Meeting of yet another category.[131] There have been repeated problems of reports being too late, evidenced by complaints which have continued from 1961 to the present.[132] In 1962 the adoption of Recommendation II – VI on modifications was intended to resolve the issue. Yet the 1966 Consultative Meeting again recommended timely compliance.[133] According to an official source, only the United States, Argentina and Japan complied with the 30 November deadline for the 1974–5 Antarctic season. South Africa and France reported in December 1974; New Zealand, Norway and the Soviet Union in March 1975; Australia and the United Kingdom in April. Most, if not all, of the Consultative Parties were in breach of Article VII(5) of the Treaty and the

125. Art. VII(5).
126. Rec. I-VI.
127. Rec. I-VI, items (6) and (7).
128. A. Scilingo, *El Tratado Antártico* (1963), 94.
129. Rec. II-VI, codified in Rec. VIII-6. (Roman numerals were used for the first three Meetings and Arabic ones thereafter).
130. R.E. Guyer, 'The Antarctic System' (1973), 139 *Hague Recueil* 149 at 202.
131. Reports by Tour Organisers (Rec. VIII-9).
132. B. Roberts, 'International Co-operation for Antarctic Development: The Test for the Antarctic Treaty' (1978), 19(119) *Polar Record*, 107 at 109.
133. Rec. IV-23.

time-limit set by Recommendation I-IV. Late reporting is not merely a technical defect. It prevents monitoring of Treaty observance and may limit scientific and logistic cooperation.

Considerable evidence also exists of failure to report. Australia complained in 1962 that it had little information on the Soviet Molodezhnaya station, and initial data on Leningradskaya was defective. Article XII of the Agreed Measures for the Conservation of Antarctic Fauna and Flora of 1964 provide for discussion of exchange of statistics on native birds and mammals killed and captured. In 1966 Interim Guide Lines laid down particular reporting requirements for seals.[134] Returns were furnished on seals and birds apparently under both provisions. Between 1964 and 1969 a maximum of only six out of ten expected returns were made each year. Some countries provided no information. Quite large numbers of seals were taken but not reported.[135] At the Tokyo Meeting in 1970 exchange of information was extended to ships carrying out substantial oceanographical research programmes,[136] but there have been omissions of such data. Marine biology concerned with krill and fish resources is generally not dealt with. It does not therefore appear likely that the information exchange provisions of the treaty can be confidently applied to valuable resources.[137]

Not only is there considerable evidence of failure to carry out reporting requirements, but there is little desire to ensure compliance. Recommendation VIII-6, which contains the Standard Format, is essentially similar to a US proposal. But paragraph 6 of the American draft was omitted. It suggested that 'they request that the host government for the forthcoming Consultative Meeting assume the responsibility to monitor the completeness and timeliness on the reports exchanged and to notify reporting governments in case of failure to provide complete or timely information.'[138] Why,

134. Rec. IV-21.
135. R.M. Laws, 'Seals and Birds Killed, and Captured in the Antarctic Treaty Area, 1964–1969', (1972), 41 *SCAR Bulletin*, 847 at 848. In 1974–5 only seven out of ten expected returns had been made (R.M. Laws and E.C. Christie, 'Seals and Birds Killed or Captured in the Antarctic Treaty Area' (1980), 65 *SCAR Bulletin*, 21).
136. Rec. VI-13.
137. In April 1979 the Director of the Division of Polar Programs, National Science Foundation, stated that the most recent work done by the Soviet Union at the Dufek Massif had been carried out two years before. It apparently had not yet been published but the Director assumed it would be published eventually ('US Activities in Antarctica' Hearing, Committee on Energy and Natural Resources, Senate, 96th Cong. 1st Sess. (1979), 40). On the significance of the Dufek Massif see Oil and Gas/*Minerals*.
138. US Position Paper for Eighth Consultative Meeting on Agenda Item 5, Exchanges of Information.

then, are there such a number of recommendations dealing with the exchange of information? One observer regarded such decisions as expedients to escape from the real issues.[139] A Treaty precedent is the provision for discussion of jurisdiction,[140] inserted because the United Kingdom's substantive proposals on this topic were not accepted.[141] One example of such a recommendation covers advice of opportunities for forwarding mail.[142] Another is the provision of information on experiments involving radio – isotopes[143] which arose from an attempt to deal with conflicting individual uses.

Claims

Article IV is the cornerstone of the Treaty. Its origin has been traced to the Escudero proposal of 1948 and the IGY gentlemen's agreement. Although Article IV is taken to be a continuation of the IGY agreement, the Treaty provision differs from its predecessor. The Article is detailed, inter-governmental and long-term. But it still bears the hallmark of the IGY understanding as an agreement to disagree. Article IV was deliberately drafted to enable States with conflicting interests to adopt differing views as to its meaning.

Advocating ratification, a State Department representative contended that objections to the Treaty were based on a failure to comprehend its provisions.[144] At the same hearings Senator Gruening stressed the negative aspects of Article IV: it stated what it did not mean, and did not state what it did mean. Such vague language left considerable doubts as to interpretation.[145] The Senator's objections are justified. Treaty negotiators desired to 'simply photograph' the current gentlemen's situation,[146] and an analogy is commonly made with freezing. The metaphors are taken from physical processes fixing a picture or a substance in a particular state. But Article IV was intended to preserve interests of at least three differing types: those of claimants, potential claimants and non-claimants. If a physical comparison has to be made, then there would be three

---

139. B. Roberts, 'International Co-operation for Antarctic Development: the Test for the Antarctic Treaty' (1978), 19(119) *Polar Record*, 107 at 109.
140. Art. IX(1)(e).
141. A. Scilingo, *El Tratado Antártico* (1963), 96.
142. Rec. I-XII, for the British proposal, strongly opposed by Argentina, see the United Kingdom Delegation's Statement at that Consultative Meeting.
143. Rec. VI-6.
144. 'The Antarctic Treaty' Hearings, Committee on Foreign Relations, Senate, 86th Cong., 2nd Sess. (1960), 39.
145. Ibid., at p. 13.
146. Prof. A. Gros, Antarctic Conference (29 October 1959).

different photographs or frozen objects. It may be doubted whether such simple analogies are useful in relation to a complex legal conflict.

Article IV(1) stipulates that nothing in the Treaty shall 'be interpreted as' affecting rights and claims. It is not clear why this phrase was inserted. Immunity from jurisdiction of observers and exchange scientists is the Treaty provision most likely to be affected, but Art. VIII(1) has its own separate safeguard.[147] As it is, the phrase suggests the possibility of an unambiguous treaty provision affecting claims not requiring interpretation and therefore falling outside the ambit of Article IV(1). There is no such clause.

Yet subheads (*a*), (*b*) and (*c*) bear the mark of lengthy debate. Without access to the Conference proceedings one may tentatively suggest that the discussions on this issue served a political purpose. Governments could feel that national interests had been vigorously defended. Although Article IV(1) does not actually affect Treaty interpretation, some interesting questions arise from the complicated wording of subheads (*b*) and (*c*). Reference to 'any basis of claim'[148] is intended to cover matters which are not 'previously asserted rights'.[149] Therefore subhead (*b*) is intended to protect prior activities which could be used to make a future claim, such as those which the United States would rely on. This basis of claim may be found in a Contracting Party's actions 'or those of its nationals', a reference to claims made before 1961 but not ratified by the State concerned.

The basis of claim may arise from the activities of the State, its nationals 'or otherwise'. It may be argued that this refers to the sector theory.[150] In relation to passage of time, the State Department expressed the view that as long as a possible claimant having a basis for a claim continues to assert that it is not surrendering the basis, international law recognises that it exists and is not lost.[151] This construction is contrary to accepted views of discovery and inchoate title. Can one then infer that Article IV(1) protects all US rights? The answer is that one cannot. Claims such as those based on Wilkes' voyage, which were extremely doubtful before the Treaty, remain so. References to dubious arguments founded on the Article only

---

147. 'Without prejudice to the respective positions of the Contracting Parties relating to jurisdiction over all other persons in Antarctica'.
148. Art. IV(1)(*b*).
149. Art. IV(1)(*a*).
150. G. Kojanec, 'La situazione giuridica dell' Antartide' (1960), 15 *La Comunita Internazionale*, 21 at 45.
151. 'The Antarctic Treaty' Hearings, Committee on Foreign Relations, Senate, 86th Cong., 2nd Sess. (1960), 58.

preserve a State's right to make such points but not to have them accepted.

Subsection (2) is the vital part of Article IV. 'Acts or activities' carried out while the Treaty is in force are not to have any effect. *Prima facie* omissions are not covered. So it could be contended that the failure of a State to ratify its nationals' claims since 1961 would constitute a basis for denying its title. On the other hand, ratification would be an 'act' and therefore of no effect. One solution would be to regard the ratification requirement as a relevant rule of inter-national law applicable in the relations between the parties to the Treaty[152] and construe acts as including omissions. Such an inter-pretation might be supported by the reference to 'its nationals' in Article IV(1)(*b*).

Article IV(1) deals with interpretation of the Treaty. It must there-fore yield to the clear meaning of the text. One view of Article IV(1)(*b*) is that the word 'may' could be construed to signify a possibility or likelihood in the future.[153] This construction is difficult to accept because subhead (*a*) refers to 'previously asserted rights' and there is no other indication in Article IV(1) of covering future actions. If 'may' refers to the future, then it does not refer to the past; so any pre-existing basis of claim would not be protected, a result which seems contrary to the intention of Article IV(1) to pre-serve the *status quo* for claims (subhead (*a*)), potential claims (subhead (*b*)) and recognition (subhead (*c*)). The reference in Article IV(1)(*b*) is to any basis of claim which a Contracting Party may have (on its own view of international law) or may not have (on a contrary view).

If, despite the above argument, it were accepted that Article IV(1)(*b*) referred to the future, then nothing in the Treaty shall be interpreted as a renunciation or diminution of any basis of claim to territorial sovereignty which any Contracting Party may have in the future. The future, for the purposes of Article IV, is the time when the Treaty is in force. Such an interpretation would reduce the ambit of Article IV(2) and give a special status to 'any basis of claim' or, in other words, US and Soviet interests.

Article IV(2) requires some form of action by a State. A new claim, or an enlargement of an existing claim, shall not be 'asserted'. Therefore an expansion of territorial rights which does not involve an assertion may be permissible. It is on this footing, *inter alia*, that

---

152. Art. 31(3)(*c*), Vienna Convention on the Law of Treaties.
153. J.P.A. Bernhardt, 'Sovereignty in Antarctica' (1975), 5 *California Western International Law Journal*, 297 at 313.

claimants would support the declaration of 200 mile offshore zones since 1961.[154]

Claimants' positions are sometimes taken to be the same for the duration of the Treaty, regardless of the activities of others.[155] On the termination of the Treaty the legal situation would return to the *status quo ante*.[156] This view has been officially advanced by Chile[157] and appears to have gained wide credibility as a justification for ratification. But the political realism of an attempt to fix a current situation is questionable.[158] Is it credible that there will be a freezing of sovereignty and that one will be able to revive the situation in its entirety after a lapse of thirty years?

Activities wholly carried out within the Treaty period, such as the maintenance of the strategic US Plateau station from 1965 to 1969, may not present any difficulty. They would not count. But actions before the Treaty came into force or after termination would not be frozen. Serious problems arise from continuing activities. On one view the existence of bases could not be ignored because it would be irrational to presume that the 'investment' of Treaty years would be surrendered on termination.[159] Coming from a State Department official, with the usual statement that the views expressed are not necessarily those of the US Government, this approach requires careful scrutiny. One cannot accept a legal argument that activities carried out while the Treaty is in force are relevant to claims, because this would contradict Article IV(2). But that provision is specifically related to the currency of the Treaty. An expedition sent to Antarctica after termination of the Treaty would assist a claim, even if it were a continuation of similar activities within the Treaty period. Similar reasoning applies to the continued occupation of bases.

Such an interpretation clearly erodes the effect of Article IV(2). To regard continuing activities as constituting a basis for claims is not far removed from saying that the same programmes carried out while the Treaty was in force may be relied upon. This is most apparent in the instance of large stations such as McMurdo which have taken years to build and equip. Withdrawal of a party to the Treaty,

154. See also Treaty/*Area*.
155. Mr Osborne, House of Representatives Debates (Australia) (28 September 1960) 1435.
156. US Note to Chile (24 March 1958) in Enrique Gajardo Villarroel, 'Apuntes para un libro sobre la Historia Diplomática del Tratado Antártico y la participación chilena en su elaboración' (1977), 10 *Revista de Difusión INACH*, 41 at 54.
157. A. Scilingo, *El Tratado Antártico* (1963), 98.
158. H.J. Taubenfeld, 'A Treaty for Antarctica' (1961), 531 *International Conciliation*, 245 at 284.
159. J.P.A. Bernhardt, 'Sovereignty in Antarctica' (1975), 5 *California Western International Law Journal*, 297 at 315.

apart from Article XII, could occur at any time in reliance upon a number of international law doctrines. To provide for such a possibility, parties could well prefer to maintain a sustained level of activity.

Although the *status quo ante* approach may have been used to persuade governments to ratify the Treaty, it is submitted that the continuing activities interpretation is preferable. In case of need it would no doubt be advocated by those countries which would benefit from it, especially the Soviet Union. Article IV(2) is an exercise in unreality. Taking into account continuing programmes goes part of the way towards mitigating this political criticism. What effect has Article IV(2) had during the time the Treaty has been in force? Examination of bases during the IGY has shown that their location was due to political rather than scientific motives. The same trend has been evident since 1961 as shown, for example, by the spread of Soviet stations.

Behind closed doors, the sovereignty issue has been repeatedly raised at Consultative and related meetings. The first discussion of historic sites[160] led to Argentinian fears of preservation of large sections of the Antarctic Peninsula by the United Kingdom to limit Argentinian activities. Under the Agreed Measures for the Conservation of Antarctic Fauna and Flora, permits are issued to carry out research, and this was one of a number of matters relating to sovereignty which gave rise to controversy between the parties both before and after 1964.[161] Discussion of the Marine Living Resources regime entailed endless arguments over sovereignty.[162] From these known examples one may safely conclude that publication of the proceedings of Preparatory and Consultative Meetings would reveal a number of additional instances in which sovereignty issues played a major role.

Political assumptions directly contradict the view that once the Treaty was ratified a nation could retreat from Antarctica without losing any rights.[163] Parties consider that maintenance of activities is necessary while the Treaty is in force. In 1978 an Australian Commonwealth Parliamentary Committee stated: 'To give the claim for sovereignty over the area of the Antarctic Territory greater international validity, Australia must obviously demonstrate a

---

160. Rec. I-IX. It is presumably for this reason that a subsequent recommendation was headed 'historic monuments' (Rec. VII-9).
161. For the Chilean attempt to delete 'appropriate authority' in 1966, see Environment/*Agreed Measures*.
162. 'Control of Marine Resources' (1978), 8(7) *Antarctic*, 237.
163. R. Lewis, 'Antarctic Dilemma' (February 1963), *Bulletin of the Atomic Scientists*, 37.

greater interest in the Territory.'[164] Unequivocal evidence of acts and activities taking place while the Treaty is in force and intended to support territorial sovereignty is freely available in the recent history of the South American sector.

From the previous examination of sovereignty in that area two illustrations may be selected: first, the visit of the President and Cabinet of Argentina to Marambio Base in August 1973 to proclaim the station the temporary capital of the Republic and issue an Act of Affirmation of Sovereignty in the Argentinian Antarctic;[165] and secondly, the presence of wives and children at Esparanza Station, the birth of a child, a wedding and other manifestations of regular settlement to reinforce territorial claims.[166] Chile and Argentina have stated that they intend to continue to strengthen their claims to sovereignty. It has been contended that activities such as those at Marambio and Esperanza appear to be technical violations of Article IV, at least in intent.[167] This argument may be put very simply; namely that the first sentence of Article IV(2) is negated by such actions. Argentina has publicly affirmed at the highest level of government that specific acts and activities carried out while the Treaty is in force support its claim to sovereignty. This is a breach of a vital Treaty provision.

Argentina and Chile declare their purpose openly. Other nations take a similar position without publicity. Despite the apparent protection of Article IV(2), claimants and potential claimants have maintained their Antarctic programmes. Only one such State, Norway, ceased its activities after IGY, but it has now resumed research. In assessing Article IV one must take into account that most of the sovereignty issues arising under the Treaty have been of a relatively minor nature. With the exception of krill, no substantial economic resources have yet been discovered within the Treaty area. Yet rights have been insisted upon with vigour even on quite insignificant matters such as permits under the Agreed Measures.

Article IV is essentially an agreement to disagree. Claims were swept under a convenient rug.[168] Adoption of the 'homely principle of not crossing a river until one comes to it'[169] may provide the easiest

164. Joint Committee on Foreign Affairs, Interim Report, *Australia, Antarctica and the Law of the Sea* (1978), 74.
165. 'Base Marambio: Capital Accidental de la Republica' (1974), *Antartida*, 19 at 23.
166. 'Antarctica's first baby warmly welcomed' (1978), 8(5) *Antarctic*, 169 at 170.
167. J.B. Oerding, 'The Frozen Friction Point: A Geopolitical Analysis of Sovereignty in the Antarctic Peninsula', MA thesis, University of Florida (1977), 74.
168. C.H. Grattan, *The Southwest Pacific since 1900* (1963), 662.
169. Lord McNair, Debates, House of Lords (18 February 1960) 182.

way out at the time. But it leaves the basic question unresolved. Sovereignty disputes become much more difficult to deal with when resources are at stake. A hope that claims would eventually disappear[170] has not eventuated. Article IV is an illusory safeguard. Territorial sovereignty serves the purpose of allocating exclusive jurisdiction among States. In the absence of an indigenous population and valuable resources, there has been no urgent need for a resolution of the claims issue. Once economic issues arise the temporary *status quo* becomes vulnerable.

Inspection

Treaty rights of inspection and observation are far-reaching.[171] Observers designated by Consultative Parties have complete freedom of access at all times[172] to all areas of Antarctica[173] including stations, installations and equipment. Consultative Parties have an unlimited right of aerial inspection.[174] Inspection may be exercised even if no measures for facilitation have been agreed upon.[175] Great significance was attached to the inspection provisions by the State Department. Refusal by the Soviet Union to accept effective inspection had been a principle stumbling — block in disarmament negotiations. The Antarctic Treaty was seen as a valuable source of practical experience. Hesitation by the United States in ratifying the first international agreement affording an unlimited right of inspection would, the Department urged, have been unfortunate.[176] This was the first time that the Soviet Union had accepted free aerial inspection by treaty[177] and a weighty argument for ratification.

When inspections were carried out, they were not based on any anticipation of treaty violations.[178] None has apparently been undertaken by the Soviet Union.[179] Reports have consistently concluded that there was no evidence to indicate any breach of the

170. H.J. Taubenfeld, 'A Treaty for Antarctica' (1961), 531 *International Conciliation*, 245 at 300.
171. D.W. Wainhouse, *International Peace Observation* (1966), 528.
172. Art. VII(3).
173. Art. VII(2).
174. Art. VII(4).
175. Art. IX(5).
176. 'The Antarctic Treaty' Hearings, Committee on Foreign Relations, Senate, 86th Cong., 2nd Sess. (1960), 38.
177. C.P. Economides, 'Le Statut International de l'Antarctique résultant du Traité du 1 Décembre 1959' (1962), 15 *Revue Hellénique de Droit International*, 76 at 82.
178. Department of State Press Release (1964), 58 *AJIL*, 166.
179. F.V. Rigler, 'Navy's continuing commitment in Antarctica' (June 1975) US Naval Institute Proceedings 101 at 105.

Treaty.[180] Despite official advocacy of the provisions as a precedent, the United States did not carry out inspections in the first two Antarctic summers after the Treaty came into force.[181] It was not until November 1963 that New Zealand undertook what was reported to be the first inspection.[182]

Initial lack of interest may well be explained by the stress placed on Article VII as a precedent. Governments had no real fear of violation of the Treaty by secret means. Once the Treaty came into force there was no incentive to carry out inspections. In September 1963 the United States announced its intention to inspect, at least in part to reassure the Senate which was considering the Partial Test Ban treaty.[183] The right was exercised in order to prevent it from falling into desuetude.[184]

Continuing apathy towards inspection may also be due to restricted economic capability.[185] Each trip requires transport, and logistic and material support; 'one can't just hop a cab or fly from one base to another.'[186] Only fairly powerful States have the resources to carry out more than purely nominal or sporadic inspections.[187] One means of dealing with this limitation is for the inspected State to provide transport, as the United States did when New Zealand, Australia and the United Kingdom examined South Pole and Byrd in 1963. But one can hardly regard this type of visit as an effective inspection. Had the United States violated the Treaty there would have been adequate warning to permit concealment.

Precisely what can be inspected? Although the terms of the Treaty are very wide, they are not unlimited. Inspection is permitted in relation to stations, installations and equipment in all areas of Antarctica. People and dogs cannot be searched. Ships may be inspected at points of discharging or embarking cargoes or personnel

180. For example, US Arms Control and Disarmament Agency, *Report of the 1975 United States Antarctic Inspection* (1975), 4.
181. 1961–2 and 1962–3.
182. Historical Studies Division, Department of State, *United States Antarctic Policy and International Cooperation in Antarctica* (1964), 19.
183. H.J. Taubenfeld, 'The Antarctic Treaty of 1959' (1964), 2(2) *Disarmament and Arms Control*, 136 at 140.
184. H.M. Dater, 'The Antarctic Treaty in Action 1961–1971' (1971), 7(3) *Antarctic Journal*, 67 at 72.
185. R.N. Bing, 'The Role of the Developed States in the Formulation of International Controls for Unoccupied Regions, Outer Space, the Ocean Floor and Antarctica', Ph.D. thesis, Tufts University (1972), 74.
186. Mr Pillion, 'The Antarctic Treaty' Hearings, Committee on Foreign Relations, Senate, 86th Cong., 2nd Sess. (1960), 28.
187. E. Hambro, 'Some Notes on the Future of the Antarctic Treaty Collaboration' (1974), 68 *AJIL*, 217 at 220.

in Antarctica,[188] but floating or submerged equipment not coming within the definition of a 'ship' could not be examined; this may exclude oil rigs, which cannot be independently navigated.[189] Ships at sea within the Antarctic Treaty area would not appear to be covered by Article VII(3), a view reinforced by the reservation of the high seas rights of States in that area.[190]

The purposes of inspection are not clearly defined. Ensuring observance of Treaty provisions prevents little conceptual difficulty. But inspections are also intended 'to promote the objectives' of the Treaty.[191] On a wide interpretation,[192] objectives which are mentioned in Article IX(1) are measures recommended at Consultative Meetings which have come into force. However, inspections have examined compliance with the Agreed Measures before they came into effect.[193] This is difficult to reconcile with Article IX. The assumption that a recommendation is automatically a ground for inspection[194] is not necessarily justified. It is quite conceivable that a recommendation could be contrary to the objectives of the Treaty.

The right of inspection has not been widely used. Only the United States has included a large number of stations over a substantial area.[195] Whether the inspections carried out so far have been effective is moot; it has already been suggested that an inspection utilising the transport of the inspected State is hardly likely to discover violations. From the text of Article VII(1) it may be inferred that the required communication of observers' names to all Consultative Parties connotes prior notice. This has been the practice. Where, as with the United States, a separate agency carries out inspections, observers must be transported to the Antarctic for that specific purpose. In addition, US standard routine has been to notify stations to be inspected in advance by radio.[196] In 1971 the American inspection, utilising a ship, visited Dumont d'Urville on February 18, Casey on 21 February, Mirny on 24 February and Mawson on 28

188. Art. VII(3).
189. F.M. Auburn, 'Offshore Oil and Gas in Antarctica' (1977), 20 *German Yearbook of International Law*, 139 at 171.
190. Art. VI.
191. Art. VII(1).
192. Discussed below (Treaty/*Third Parties*).
193. US Arms Control and Disarmament Agency, *Report of the 1975 United States Antarctic Inspection* (1975), 3.
194. M. Voelckel in G. Fischer and D. Vignes, *L'Inspection Internationale* (1976), 233.
195. F. Sollie, 'The Political Experiment in Antarctica' (1970), 26(10) *Science and Public Affairs*, 16 at 18.
196. Arms Control and Disarmament Agency and Department of State, *Report of the 1971 Antarctic Inspection* (1971), 2.

February.[197] News of the inspections could be routinely transmitted by radio between the bases. In any case, Antarctic conditions require advance notice of any such visit unless the inspection is from a neighbouring station.

It is still surprising that no violations of the Treaty or recommendations have been reported. The 1971 US inspection compared activities with those reported under Article VII(3). Reference has already been made to State Department complaints four years later that only five States had reported on their 1974–5 expeditions by March 1975.[198] In February 1971 the United States inspected stations belonging to France, Australia and the Soviet Union. France was the only one of these countries that had reported before the same month in 1975. Insofar as inspections examine the advance reports due under Article VII(5), one must ask whether the observers had reports from the inspected country for the current season when they made their inspection. In at least one case they did not. Argentina, Chile, the Soviet Union and the United Kingdom were inspected by the United States in January 1975.[199] Of the four nations only Argentina had submitted its advance report by that time. Furthermore, the inspection report is dated 1 April 1975. The United Kingdom only submitted its information at an unspecified date in April, and Chile did not do so until later. In the two latter cases compliance with Article VII(5) could not have been monitored. This instance suggests that a detailed correlation of the dates of receipt of reports under that Article with the dates of inspections and inspection reports is needed in order to ascertain the extent to which inspections have been unable to monitor information supplied under Article VII(5).

There are other indications of defects in inspection procedures. The 1971 US Report concluded that all observed activities complied with the letter and the spirit of the Treaty and its associated regulatory regime.[200] At Casey two dogs were seen apparently wandering about the station at will. One was observed feeding on a freshly killed penguin.[201] Three dogs at Mirny were not restrained.[202] Allowing dogs to run free is harmful interference which must be minimised.[203] A *prima facie* violation of the Agreed Measures

197. Ibid., at p. 1.
198. Treaty/*Information Exchange*.
199. US Arms Control and Disarmament Agency, *Report of the 1975 United States Antarctic Inspection* (1975), 1.
200. Arms Control and Disarmament Agency and Department of State, *Report of the 1971 Antarctic Inspection* (1971), 3.
201. Ibid., at p. 36.
202. Ibid., at p. 61.
203. Art. VII, Agreed Measures which were the object of US inspection.

requires at least some comment.

Reviewing the US inspection of 1975, a State Department official concluded that the location of stations visited did not appear to have an adverse effect on the environment.[204] Two of the bases were Bellingshausen (the Soviet Union) and Frei (Chile) in what had been the Fildes Peninsula Specially Protected Area.[205] There is considerable evidence[206] that the establishment of the bases completely changed this area of outstanding scientific interest.

One means of testing the effectiveness of the procedures would be to carry out the same type of inspection on one's own bases as is performed in relation to those of other States, and compare the findings with those of a full-scale and detailed examination based on a comprehensive review of departmental files. On the basis of the relatively scanty information at present available, it is suggested that more cases of non-compliance would be discovered.[207]

Assessment of inspection practice is of general interest for disarmament negotiations. It was suggested that the Soviet Union might be hard pressed to reject military inspection in the Arctic if the Antarctic were similarly treated by the same international agency.[208] Even with a national inspection system, the same contention could have been put forward. It is correct that on-site and aerial observation have not set precedents because Antarctica is unpopulated and remote from the vital interests of the major powers, and sovereignty is contested.[209] But such inspection remains of wider use, notwithstanding the special status of Antarctica,[210] because of the lack of precedents. If comprehensive provisions are not effective in Antarctic practice, then they are not likely to function in areas of high political concern.

Even on the basis of the available official reports, it cannot be said that the Antarctic inspection experience has been an unqualified success. It has been doubted whether the conclusions regarding compliance with the Agreed Measures can be supported. The practice of providing advance warning of inspection, while frequently justified

204. R.D. Yoder, 'United States inspects four Peninsula stations' (1975), 10(3) *Antarctic Journal*, 92 at 93.

205. Rec. IV-12.

206. Discussed later (Environment/*Specially Protected Areas*).

207. It may be surmised that some observers have already inspected their own stations.

208. R.D. Hayton, 'Polar Problems and International Law' (1958) 52 AJIL, 746 at 765.

209. J. Goldblatt, 'The Arms-Control Experiment in the Antarctic' (1973), *SIPRI Yearbook*, 477 at 481.

210. J. Simsarian, 'Inspection Experience under the Antarctic Treaty and the International Atomic Energy Agency' (1966), 60 *AJIL*, 502 at 510.

by polar logistics, permits concealment of possible violations. Independent inspection of distant stations by smaller nations is not feasible. Few States share the US interest in periodic inspections.[211] Formality and impracticality are sometimes evident. In 1963 New Zealand inspected McMurdo, and in 1964 the United States examined Scott Base. Personnel from the two stations, which are only two miles apart, regularly exchange visits; so McMurdo staff would be well aware of activities at Scott (and vice versa), and better qualified to report than government officials specially flown in from the United States.

The air of unreality is compounded by the exchange of scientists. Of special interest is the US-Soviet agreement for the annual exchange of a scientist wintering over.[212] Such experience[213] is a much surer indication of compliance than a one- or two-day visit by an official contingent of observers.

Third Parties

Consultative Parties claim exclusive competence over Antarctic affairs. This monopoly is manifested in the refusal to cooperate with international agencies whose intentions are seen as politically motivated, a fear of activities by States which are not parties to the Treaty, and concern regarding private expeditions and tourism. It might have been thought that the regular functioning of cooperation since 1961 would have consolidated the Treaty system. The first decade from 1961–71 passed without a major political crisis. Yet since 1972, when the possibility of territorial claims by non-parties was raised,[214] there have been repeated official and unofficial statements and activities related to outside States, international organisations and individuals.

If one turns to the plans and actions of outsiders, at first sight the apprehensions of the Consultative Parties appear somewhat out of place. There has been no third party territorial claim or substantial independent expedition. Italian[215] and Spanish tourist ships in the Antarctic Peninsula may raise problems when large numbers of people visit stations,[216] but pose no special threat to the regime itself.

211. Central Intelligence Agency, *Polar Regions Atlas* (1979), 44.
212. Historical Studies Division, Department of State, *United States Policy and International Cooperation in Antarctica* (1964) 8.
213. G. Vane, 'Soviet Antarctic Research, 1972–1973' (1973), 8(6) *Antarctic Journal*, 325.
214. Final Report of the Seventh Antarctic Treaty Consultative Meeting (1972), 5.
215. 'More "Day Trips" to Antarctic' (1978), 8(8) *Antarctic*, 292.
216. Rec. VIII-9 (see Environment/*Tourism*).

In January–February 1976 a privately-sponsored Italian expedition to the Antarctic Peninsula set up a base in Admiralty Bay, King George Island, and carried out scientific research and mountain climbing.[217] As one purpose of the venture was to persuade the Italian government of the need for accession,[218] it was intended to promote the Treaty.

Two developments did involve political repercussions. The plan for a Brazilian private expedition in 1972 and subsequent reactions have been examined previously.[219] A proposal for a European Antarctic Expedition was put forward by a Polar Research Working Party of the Committee on Science and Technology of the Council of Europe. Baron de Gerlache de Gomery of Belgium was Chairman of the Working Party and the research would have been carried out in the Norwegian sector.[220] It is only recently that Norway has resumed operation of Antarctic stations in summer. Belgium and Norway are the only Consultative Parties which do not currently have winter stations open. The proposal would have provided a partial solution to this problem by sharing the five-year cost of $17,000,000 between ten States: Austria, Belgium, France, Holland, Italy, Norway, West Germany, United Kingdom, Sweden and Switzerland.

Five of the countries were not parties to the Treaty at the time. The Executive Committee of the Scientific Committee on Antarctic Research (SCAR) recommended that such States should regard themselves as signatories for the duration of the expedition.[222] Had the project gone ahead, the political implications would have been widespread. It is possible that East Germany's accession in 1974 was partly prompted by the European plan. Even if the SCAR solution were adopted there would have been a substantial presence of officially-supported non-Treaty nationals on an independent expedition. Projects sponsored by the Committee on Science and Technology are intended to have political value by various criteria including strengthening European scientific and technological potential.[223]

---

217. Mountaineering in the Antarctic, Appendix to the Report of the First Italian Expedition to Antarctica 1976.
218. Press Office of the Expedition, First Italian Expedition to Antarctica (n.d.)2.
219. See National Interests/*South America*.
220. G. de Gerlache de Gomery, 'A proposed European Antarctic Expedition' (1973), 8(1) *Antarctic Journal*, 15.
221. 'Belgium associated with European research plan' (1974), 7(3) *Antarctic*, 89.
222. J. Capelle, Explanatory Memorandum, Consultative Assembly, Council of Europe, Doc. 3257 (29 January 1973), 5 at 18.
223. Parliamentary Assembly, Council of Europe, 'Report on the Exercise in Scientific Cooperation: Situation and Prospects' Doc. 3840 (15 September 1976), 10.

Brazil acceded to the Treaty, and the European programme was not carried out. Absence of an actual threat is underlined by the frequent presence of scientists from non-Treaty nations carrying out research in cooperation with Consultative Parties. They have come from East and West Germany (before accession), India, Austria and Canada.

A fundamental cause of the Consultative Parties' feeling of insecurity relates to the question of the general acceptance of the Treaty regime. Each Contracting Party undertakes to exert appropriate efforts consistent with the United Nations Charter to the end that no one engages in any activity in Antarctica contrary to the principles or purposes of the Treaty.[224] As a general rule, treaties do not bind third States without their consent,[225] and it would therefore appear that any steps taken to ensure compliance by third parties can not have a legal basis.

But it has been argued that the Treaty can be enforced against third parties.[226] It has been seen as a regional arrangement established under Chapter VIII of the UN Charter.[227] However, the Charter authorises such agreements without making them binding on non-parties. There is no evidence of derogation from the primary rule that only parties are bound by treaties.[228]

An argument that has found some favour is that the Treaty affects the territorial status of Antarctica, creating an objective regime opposable against all States.[229] It is presumably on this basis that two diplomats involved with the drafting of the Treaty suggest that the Treaty powers have generated a certain legislative right in reference to the region.[230] A similar view is that a mandate and authority to promulgate international legislation for the Antarctic arises from Article IX.[231] The short answer is that the concept of an objective regime is not supported by international law.[232] If such a doctrine does exist, the Antarctic Treaty is not an example. Article IV was

224. Art. X.
225. Art. 34, Convention on the Law of Treaties.
226. Mr Phleger, Department of State, 'The Antarctic Treaty'. Hearings, Committee on Foreign Relations, Senate, 86th Cong., 2nd Sess. (1960), 42–3.
227. R.D. Hayton, 'The Antarctic Settlement of 1959' (1960), 54 *AJIL*, 349 at 366.
228. M.W. Mouton, 'The International Regime of the Polar Regions' (1962), 107 *Hague Recueil*, 175 at 258–9.
229. R.-J. Dupuy, 'Le Traité sur l'Antarctique' (1960), *AFDI*, 111 at 122.
230. R.E. Guyer, 'The Antarctic System' (1973), 139 *Hague Recueil*, 149 at 224–5; A. van der Essen, 'L'Antarctique et le Droit de la Mer' (1975–6), 5–6 *Iranian Review of International Affairs*, 89 at 96.
231. Ambassador Hambro, Prepared Remarks, Nansen Conference on Minerals in Antarctica (1973), A8 at A16.
232. P. Cahier, 'Le Problème des Effets des Traités a l'égard des États Tiers' (1974), 143 *Hague Recueil*, 589 at 677.

intended to ensure that there would be no objective regime. It was not an agreement on territorial status but rather a decision not to press claims. Because sovereignty over the continent is disputed between the parties to the Treaty, it can hardly be argued that there is a regime binding others.

Current international law does not support the turning of the Antarctic system into a legally recognised regime. This does not mean that an international form of government is undesirable. There is much to be said for a generally accepted framework, whether in the form of a type of condominium of the Consultative Parties or in an expanded form with internationalised status.[233] One cannot rule out the future evolution of international law in this direction, but the current political situation suggests that such a development would be opposed by the Consultative Parties.

Because Article X does not bind third parties, what does it mean? If it only affects parties, the provision would be superfluous. One interpretation is that the Contracting Parties would have to consider jointly what action they would take in self-defence consistent with the UN Charter.[234] Self-defence is hard to justify in the Antarctic context. There is no present fear of armed attack. Could the United States come to the aid of a claimant defending territorial sovereignty which it, the United States, did not recognise?

Article X refers to 'each' of the Contracting Parties. This emphasis on individual action may be contrasted with the Consultative Meetings under Article IX. Joint action by Contracting Parties would be a precedent for breaking the monopoly of decision-making of the Consultative Parties. It may also be argued that Article IX provides an exclusive method of policy formulation under the Treaty.

Article X refers to any activity contrary to the 'principles or purposes' of the Treaty. Clearly this covers peaceful purposes.[235] But the ambit of the principles and purposes is held to be far wider than the strict obligations of the Treaty text. A similar phrase, 'principles and objectives of the Treaty', defines the subject-matter of recommendations of Consultative Meetings.[236] Inspection is intended to promote the 'objectives' of the Treaty and ensure the observance of its provisions.[237] These vague words are of considerable importance,

233. J. Tinker, 'Antarctica: towards a new internationalism', *New Scientist* (13 September 1979), 799 at 801.
234. R.E. Guyer, 'The Antarctic System' (1973), 139 *Hague Recueil*, 149 at 224.
235. Art. I.
236. Art. IX(1).
237. Art. VII(1). The dichotomy between direct obligations arising from the Treaty and 'objectives' may be noted.

since Article X is seen in some quarters as a source of quasi-legislative competence. Article IX defines the scope of recommendations. Much use is made of the words 'principles', 'purposes' and 'objectives' at Consultative Meetings,[238] and to begin the search for a definition, one may review the list of examples in Article IX(1). The first four items are within the terms of the Treaty itself. Article IX(1)(e), questions relating to the exercise of jurisdiction, was inserted because a proposal to deal with the matter in the Treaty had met strong opposition. Preservation and conservation of living resources[239] does not relate to any other provision of the Treaty.

It might be argued that jurisdiction and living resources can only be dealt with at Consultative Meetings in furtherance of specific principles and objectives of the Treaty. But the wording of Article IX(1) appears to define the two topics as measures in furtherance of the Treaty. Practice of the Consultative Parties supports the construction that 'principles and objectives' are not words of limitation. Many recommendations have no foundation in any Treaty obligation.[240] The Consultative Parties seem to consider that any effective recommendation is automatically in furtherance of the principles and objectives of the Treaty.[241] On this approach the only real limitation may be that recommendations cannot be contrary to the Treaty itself.

There does not seem to be any logical difference between the 'principles and objectives' of Article IX and the 'principles or purposes' of Article X. Article IX(1)(a) specifically includes 'peaceful purposes', so that it may be inferred that 'purposes' are equivalent to 'objectives'. This is the interpretation of the Consultative Parties illustrated in part of the preamble of a recent recommendation:

Aware of the responsibilities of the Consultative Parties to ensure that any activities in Antarctica, including mineral exploration and exploitation, should they occur, should be consistent with all the principles and purposes of the Antarctic Treaty system, including its objectives that activities in Antarctica should not become the cause of international discord, endanger the unique Antarctic environment, or disrupt scientific investigation.[242]

'Principles and purposes'[243] include 'objectives'.[244] It may be

238. See also Rec. V-1 and X-9 (stamps commemorating the Tenth and Twentieth Anniversaries of the entry into force of the Treaty should be consonant with its provisions and 'spirit').
239. Art. IX(1)(f).
240. For example, Rec. X-7 (Oil Contamination of the Antarctic Marine Environment).
241. Final Report of the Special Antarctic Treaty Consultative Meeting (July 1977).
242. Rec. X-1.
243. Taken from Art. X.
244. From Art. IX.

assumed that 'principles' has the same meaning in both Articles. Laudable though it may be, the preservation of the Antarctic environment – as distinct from conservation of living resources[245] – is not mentioned in the Treaty.

Attempts to persuade third parties to observe recommendations in reliance on Article X would have a very weak basis both in general international law and on Treaty practice. It is the view of the Consultative Parties that effective recommendations do not bind existing and new Contracting Parties and new Consultative Parties without their specific acceptance.[246] Once it is admitted that such parties to the Treaty are not bound by measures which are in force, it is difficult to assert that third parties should be under any greater obligation.

Principles, purposes and objectives appear repeatedly in recent recommendations, and multiple references occur in the recommendations on mineral exploitation.[247] Other examples are to be found with regard to activities of States that are not Consultative Parties.[248] A common thread is the lack of clear authority in the Treaty text. Invocation of these terms suggests that the Consultative Parties themselves are unsure of the legal basis of their actions.

International organisations have made a number of attempts to carry out activities related to Antarctica. So far undesired incursions have been successfully resisted. Pre-treaty proposals for United Nations or international trusteeship or administration, although rejected, still have outside support.[249] In the light of these proposals it is significant that the Treaty does not allot a direct function to the United Nations in Antarctic affairs. There can be no doubt that this was a deliberate omission. A provision giving jurisdiction to the International Court of Justice[250] is subject to the consent of all parties to the dispute. Article III enables cooperation with Specialised Agencies of the UN, but even here there are a number of limitations.

The primary reach of that Article is an agreement by Contracting Parties to promote international cooperation in scientific investigation by the exchange of information, scientific programmes,

---

245. Art. IX(1)(*f*).
246. Rec. III-VII. Nor does the text of Article X show an intention to bind third parties (on both, see Antarctic System/*Recommendations*).
247. Rec. VIII-14, IX-1, X-1.
248. Rec. VIII-8.
249. E. Honnold, 'Draft Provisions of a new International Convention on Antarctica' (1977), 4 *Yale Studies in World Public Order*, 123.
250. Art. XI(2).

scientific personnel, observations and results.[251] Cooperation with Specialised Agencies and other international organisations is only for the purpose of implementing Article III. Such bodies are most restricted by the terms of the Treaty. Exchange of plans, personnel and results is essentially a matter for States carrying out Antarctic research. The Treaty confines promotion of international scientific cooperation to that applied during the IGY.[252]

Agencies cannot function on their own; their participation is dependent upon encouragement and the establishment of working relations.[253] The interest of the organisation in Antarctica must be scientific or technical.[254] So the Universal Postal Union could be categorised as a technical agency, but if it were to lay down rules for Antarctica, the Consultative Parties would presumably take that interest to be political.[255] Practice indicates that 'scientific or technical' means whatever is desired by the Treaty powers.

There is a contradiction between the purpose of the Treaty — to establish a firm foundation for international scientific cooperation[256] — and the attitude of the Contracting Parties. If such cooperation is so important, it would seem that international organisations are vital. This objection has been met by the establishment of a specific scientific organisation parallel to the Antarctic Treaty in the form of SCAR, which is the scientific advisor of the Treaty Nations. Resort to SCAR permits the Consultative Parties to avoid relevant international organisations if desired. SCAR is the primary vehicle for exchange of scientific plans[257] and information.[258] Consultative Parties regard the Committee as responsible for development of the scientific aspects of the Antarctic Treaty system.[259] SCAR is an unusual scientific body. Although it is a committee of ICSU, the latter organisation does not control its plans. On the other hand SCAR is to a large degree dependent on the Consultative Parties to the Treaty.

Despite the substantial extent of Antarctic scientific research, cooperation with international organisations other than SCAR has been the exception rather than the rule; when relations do exist, they are usually carried out with SCAR as an intermediary. The most

251. Art. III(1).
252. Art. II.
253. Art. III(2).
254. Ibid.
255. Compare Rec.I-XII and statement of United Kingdom Delegation at that Meeting.
256. Preamble.
257. Rec.I-I.
258. Rec. I-IV.
259. Rec. X-9 (the relationship is analysed under Antarctic System/*SCAR*).

extensive and continuous effort at cooperation has been with the World Meteorological Organization (WMO), and from the First Consultative Meeting,[260] the need for rapid and effective transmission of weather information has been stressed. As weather information constitutes a large percentage of Antarctic messages, much of the discussion at the three Treaty Meetings on Telecommunications has been devoted to meteorology. Requirements for raw and processed meteorological data in terms of the number of receptions per day were prescribed in 1970. In complete contrast with their attitude to other international agencies, the Consultative Parties invited the WMO to review these needs from time to time.[261] Even in this case, the initiative remains with the Treaty system. This exceptional instance of cooperation arises from the technical necessity for maintaining compatible and effective transmission of information essential to Antarctic operations with minimal delay.[262]

Apart from the WMO, there have been arrangements with other international organisations, but only on a modest scale. An example is the Co-ordinating Group for the Southern Ocean set up by the Intergovernmental Oceanographic Commission (IOC). The Group's proposed gradual development of a comprehensive study, with the participation of SCAR, was welcomed.[263] Much more emphasis was placed by the Consultative Parties on the role of SCAR than on that of the IOC.

In general the Parties have either omitted to cooperate with a relevant international organisation or they have taken active steps to frustrate outside plans. Several instances of omission may be cited from recommendations. Exchange of information on the application of nuclear equipment and techniques[264] was not specified to include the International Atomic Energy Agency. Discussion of a proposed cooperative air transport system[265] made no mention of the International Civil Aviation Organization. Initial examination of marine living resources[266] did not refer to the Food and Agriculture Organization. Oil pollution from ships was covered with reference to international agreements[267] but not to the Intergovernmental Maritime Consultative Organization which drafted the treaties.

With increasing interest in Antarctica over the last ten years, there

260. Rec. I-V.
261. Rec. VI-3 and X-3.
262. Rec. VI-I.
263. Rec. V-3.
264. Rec. I-XIII.
265. Rec. VII-8 and VIII-7.
266. Rec. VIII-10.
267. Rec. X-7.

have been a number of proposals for action by various UN Agencies. So far all suggestions emanating from sources outside the Antarctic Treaty system have been defeated, usually by the Treaty powers. In 1971 the Committee on Natural Resources of the Economic and Social Council (ECOSOC) was asked whether it would consider development of a systematic approach to the exchange and dissemination of experience and information on the development, utilisation and conservation of natural resources. One cited example of an area about which insufficient information was available was the natural resources of Antarctica.[268] In a brief annex to the submission[269] it was pointed out that any worldwide assessment of resources would be incomplete without Antarctic data. The Committee on Natural Resources might request such information from member-States actively pursuing studies on the region, from SCAR and from all other States that had conducted analyses and experiments on the basis of Antarctic data and specimens. The Committee could rely on 'the spirit and practice of international cooperation exemplified in the Antarctic Treaty'.[270]

One would have thought such a proposal should be acceptable. It was carefully related to the sensitivities of the Consultative Parties. Primary sources of information would be States 'actively pursuing studies in the region' (essentially confined to the Consultative Parties) and SCAR; ECOSOC would only have collected data, and would not have carried out any activity on the continent. Yet even this minor proposal to insert an item on the agenda of a committee of a UN body was rejected because SCAR was said to be dealing with the matter.[271]

Another approach was much bolder. In 1964 the Consultative Parties stated that they considered the Treaty Area to be a Special Conservation Area.[272] For the past decade they have stressed the need to strengthen the protection of the Antarctic environment,[273] which was viewed as a responsibility assumed by them.[274] It was not surprising that the Second World Conference on National Parks, meeting in the United States in September 1972, saw Antarctica as a special opportunity for implementation of the world park concept.

268. Note by the Secretary-General, 'Natural Resources Information and Documentation: General Issues', UN Doc. E/C.7/5 (25 January 1971), 4.
269. Ibid, 'Information on Natural Resources in Antarctica'.
270. Ibid.
271. Mr Bunge (Argentina) in Summary Records of the Committee on Natural Resources (UN Doc. E/C.7/SR. 12–29 (2 March 1971), 50).
272. Preamble, Agreed Measures for the Conservation of Antarctic Fauna and Flora.
273. Rec. VII-1.
274. Rec. X-9.

Antarctic Treaty nations were urged to establish the continent and the surrounding seas as the first world park under the auspices of the United Nations. Although this initiative was supported by the International Union for Conservation of Nature and Natural Resources (IUCN),[275] which drew it to the attention of the Consultative Parties,[276] they did not act upon it. Three years later the South Pacific Conference on National Parks and Reserves, sponsored by the New Zealand government, South Pacific Commission and IUCN, cited the 1972 Recommendation and proposed a world park in the region to protect significant marine ecosystems, to be put to the UN Conference on the Law of the Sea.

The two themes of natural resources and protection of the environment were brought together in a proposal to the United Nations Environment Program (UNEP) in February 1975 to extend the Antarctic Treaty to ensure full protection of the environment particularly in relation to possible resource exploitation. Consideration of the matter was blocked by quiet diplomacy by the Consultative Parties which were members of the UNEP Governing Council.[277] The Executive Director of UNEP, Maurice Strong, suggested a moratorium on exploitation.[278] It must be emphasised that the UNEP proposal to expend $100,000 per year for three years was intended to be carried out in cooperation with the Treaty powers.

Strong was not discouraged by the Governing Council's action. He sent a telegram to the Chairman of the Eighth Consultative Meeting, Ambassador Hambro. Despite exclusion of the Antarctic proposal for the coming year, Strong stated that informal discussions with Treaty countries indicated general acceptance of UNEP interest and willingness to have it participate in scientific and technical activities. Advice as to the means by which UNEP might most usefully cooperate with 'your committee' (i.e. the Consultative Parties) was requested.[279]

At the Consultative Meeting a recommendation entitled 'The Antarctic Environment' was adopted as a response.[280] This item was not on the agenda for the Meeting. However another item, 'Man's

275. See also Antarctic System/*Secrecy* on the exclusion of the Union from substantive participation in the 1980 Living Resources Conference.
276. Earthscan, 'The Future of Antarctica' (1977), 31.
277. Argentina, Australia, Chile, France, Japan, the UK, the USA and the Soviet Union (G.P. Wilson, 'Antarctica, the Southern Ocean and the Law of the Sea' (1978), 30 *JAG Journal*, 47 at 61).
278. S.O. Butler, 'Owning Antarctica' (1977), 31 *Journal of International Affairs*, 35 at 49.
279. ANT/INF/4 (10 June 1975).
280. Rec. VIII-13.

impact on the Antarctic Environment', gave rise to Recommendation VIII-11. In commenting on the latter item, the State Department supported a suggestion of SCAR. If opposition developed it should be pointed out that positive and meaningful steps were needed 'if the Antarctic is to be kept outside the ambit of direct UNEP control'. Attention should also be drawn to the 1972 Recommendation of the World Conference on National Parks.

Recommendation VIII-13 had all the hallmarks of an improvised response to UNEP. There was no obvious need for two discussions of the same topic. The agenda item had adopted, with changes, the SCAR Code of Conduct for Antarctic Expeditions and Station Activities. Recommendation VIII-13 was essentially a defence of the Antarctic Treaty system against outsiders. The preamble recognised the prime responsibility of the Consultative Parties for Antarctic matters, including environmental protection. Their good works in drafting the Agreed Measures, Sealing Convention and Code of Conduct were recalled, and Article III(2) and Strong's cable were noted. The actual content of the recommendation was vague: measures to protect the Antarctic environment must be consistent with the interests of all mankind, and no activity with an inherent tendency to modify the environment over wide areas within the Antarctic Treaty area should be undertaken unless steps were taken to exercise appropriate controls.

The only mention of UNEP in the substantive portion of the recommendation was to welcome the offer of cooperation and invite SCAR to continue work with the Scientific Committee on Problems of the Environment (SCOPE). SCOPE is affiliated to ICSU, and SCAR had already been asked to cooperate with SCOPE in Recommendation VIII-11. This recommendation was part of a continuing series, VIII-13 had no predecessor and no successor. It was not intended to deal with actual problems of the environment, but to ward off an attempt by UNEP to intrude into Antarctic affairs.

A much broader threat to the Antarctic Treaty arrangements had been expected from the developing countries. The New International Economic Order (NIEO) was declared by the UN General Assembly in 1974, and the seabed beyond national jurisdiction has been accepted as the common heritage of all mankind with particular consideration for the interests of the developing countries.[281] Elaboration of the common heritage idea since 1970 raised the spectre of an international body capable and willing to administer part of the area south of 60°S. United States government depart-

281. Art. 140, Informal Composite Negotiating Text, UN Doc. A/Conf. 62/WP.10/Rev. 2 (11 April 1980).

ments regarded the suggestion that Antarctic resources be the common heritage of all mankind, or even that the issue be raised at the Law of the Sea Conference, as very sensitive − as is evidenced by deletions in testimony before a Senate Subcommittee in 1975.[282]

In 1976 a board meeting of the non-aligned nations in Algiers discussed the matter, but reached no conclusion. Several Arab countries considered the inclusion of the Antarctic within the jurisdiction of the proposed International Seabed Authority.[283] Antarctica was not discussed at the Law of the Sea Conference,[284] apparently due to efforts behind the scenes by Treaty nation diplomats to head off attempts to introduce the issue formally.[285]

This is not necessarily the end of the matter. Representatives of developing countries have expressed forceful views on the need for international control. Ambassador Pinto of Sri Lanka stated that living and non-living resources of the area should be made subject to a management regime to secure optimum benefits for mankind as a whole and, in particular, the developing countries in accordance with appropriate global arrangements and within the framework of the New International Economic Order.[286] Failure of the Conference to consider Antarctica will not preclude an International Seabed Authority from asserting jurisdiction over seas south of 60°S.[287] There is no need for a specific mandate in the final text of the Law of the Sea Convention. Seabed beyond national jurisdiction will automatically come within the scope of the proposed Authority.

Furthermore, the Authority could well argue that its control extends to the coast of the Antarctic continent. On the US view, there is no recognised sovereign for the 'land' area, and therefore no continental shelf inheres in any State.[288] Nor can there be a territorial sea. This argument leads to the logical inference that the seas around Antarctica are high seas and all the bed of the sea is beyond national jurisdiction. Should substantial oil fields be discovered in the area,

282. 'US Antarctic Policy', Hearing, Subcommittee on Oceans and International Environment, Committee on Foreign Relations, Senate, 94th Cong., 1st Sess. (1975), 16 and 22 (see also Treaty/*Area*).
283. B. Mitchell, 'Antarctica: a special case?', *New Scientist* (13 January 1977), 64 at 65−6.
284. G.P. Wilson, 'Antarctica, The Southern Ocean and the Law of the Sea' (1978), 30 *JAG Journal*, 47 at 51.
285. D. Shapley, 'Antarctic Problems: Tiny Krill to Usher in New Resource Era' (1977), 196 *Science*, 503 at 504.
286. Earthscan Press Briefing Seminar (1977).
287. E. Honnold, 'Thaw in International Law? Rights in Antarctica under the Law of Common Spaces' (1978), 87 *YLJ*, 804 at 854.
288. Department of State, 'Legal Status of Areas South of 60°S latitude' in 'US Antarctic Policy', Hearing, Subcommittee on Oceans and International Environment, Committee on Foreign Relations, Senate, 94th Cong., 1st Sess. (1975), 18 at 19.

the International Seabed Authority would have a claim to resources which could sustain it until manganese nodules[289] in the North Pacific yielded revenue. Control of Antarctic oil could also assist producers to maintain high prices.

The Food and Agriculture Organization (FAO) was responsible for the most ambitious proposal by an outside body. In 1974 fisheries experts from Australia, Denmark, West Germany, Japan, Norway, Spain, Britain, the United States and the Soviet Union were invited by the FAO Department of Fisheries to an informal consultation in Rome. FAO was endorsed as an information centre on krill research. The Organization was to assume responsibility for sounding out international agencies for funding if needed to advance international coordination in research.[290] For the next two years the FAO carried out the Southern Ocean Fisheries Survey Programme[291] funded by the UN Development Programme at a cost of $200,000.

On the basis of this research the FAO proposed a ten year Antarctic marine living resources programme for the area south of 45°S to cost $45,000,000. At this stage the Treaty nations took action to stop the plan. Reasons given included disturbance to the Antarctic Treaty system, failure to take into account political realities, special problems of jurisdiction and rejection by countries with the technological capacity to fish of possible control of the project by developing countries.[292] It is significant that some delegations (presumably those of developing nations) at the FAO Committee on Fisheries session in 1977 viewed the project as a great contribution to the NIEO.

Why did SOFSP get as far as it did? The initial FAO meeting consisted of fisheries specialists, not diplomats, and six of the Consultative Parties were represented. SCAR has always had difficulties raising funds for special projects and the FAO was prepared to seek finance itself. There was little likelihood of the Consultative Parties providing money for a large-scale fully international project on krill. Support for BIOMASS, a comprehensive marine living resources investigation designed by SCAR,[293] was lukewarm as is evidenced by the phrasing of the relevant recommendation at the 1977 Consul-

---

289. Manganese nodules are potato-sized lumps of minerals (including manganese, nickel, copper and cobalt) found in vast quantities on the deep seabed. Under the Draft UN Convention on the Law of the Sea, their extraction would be licensed by the Authority, which would use the revenue for international purposes.

290. 'Informal Consultation on Antarctic Krill' (1975), 153 *FAO Fisheries Reports*, 3.

291. SOFSP.

292. B. Roberts, 'International Co-operation for Antarctic Development: the Test for the Antarctic Treaty' (1978), 19(119) *Polar Record*, 107 at 114.

293. Discussed under Krill/*Conservation Principles*.

tative Meeting.[294] However, the FAO initiative may well have had an effect in contributing to the decision to draft a definitive living resources regime as a matter of urgency.

Experience has shown that the Treaty nations have been capable of resisting the intrusions of unwanted international organisations. Non-signatory States would present a more formidable problem. The issue arose at the 1972 Consultative Meeting, apparently due to Brazilian plans for a private expedition.[295] It has already been pointed out that Argentina took a serious view of the matter. Discussion by an Argentinian diplomat in 1973 of a hypothetical new participant, without prior activities, making new territorial claims not based upon discovery[296] may be taken to refer to Brazil.

Possible substantial or continuing activities or territorial claims by non-signatories would make it advisable for governments to consult together as provided for by the Treaty and to be ready to urge or invite the State or States concerned to accede to the Treaty. The principles and purposes of the Treaty were recalled, in particular that the area should continue to be a zone of peace and scientific cooperation and not become the scene or object of international discord. Attention was drawn to Article IV.[297] As the representatives were concerned with the possibility of non-cooperating third party expeditions,[298] it was far from clear what, if anything, the Consultative Parties considered could be done to stop such a State.

In 1972 this matter came under the heading of 'Activities of Countries not Contracting Parties'. Three weeks before the following meeting, Brazil acceded to the Treaty. Under the rubric 'Activities of States that are not Consultative Parties', the principles set forth at the previous meeting were affirmed.[299] The Preamble and Article X of the Treaty were invoked, but there was no indication of what action might be taken. At the Ninth Meeting in 1977, the question of 'Activities in the Antarctic of other States' was widely discussed. The statement made in 1972 was repeated.[300]

Although there seems to have been lengthy discussion of third party State expeditions no practical means for coping with them has yet emerged. Accession to the Treaty was advocated in 1972 and was the eventual means of dealing with the Brazil issue. But there is no

294. Rec. IX-2.
295. See National Interests/*South America*.
296. R.E. Guyer, 'The Antarctic System' (1973), 139 *Hague Recueil*, 149 at 225.
297. Final Report of the Seventh Antarctic Treaty Consultative Meeting (1972), 5.
298. Closing Address by F.H. Corner (New Zealand).
299. Rec. VIII-8, discussed in detail in relation to Contracting Parties (Antarctic System/*Recommendations*).
300. Final Report of the Ninth Antarctic Treaty Consultative Meeting (1977), 6.

legal method by which a non-cooperating third party can be compelled to sign the Treaty. Appropriate efforts[301] could involve the refusal of logistic support and assistance.[302] However, even relatively small expeditions, such as that of the Italians in 1976, have been able to operate independently.

The Treaty nations have not taken steps to regulate the entry of non-governmental groups and tourists; measures taken relate only to visits to stations.[303] In the past there has been neither general agreement nor a will to prevent third parties sending expeditions. Any concerted attempt by the Consultative Parties to lay down rules would directly raise the issue of sovereignty.

It has been suggested that resort could be had to the United Nations.[304] This would be a departure from the recent stubborn resistance of the Treaty nations to UN interest even on quite minor matters. There would have to be a strong case to invoke the powers of, say, the Security Council. Assuming that the third party intended to exploit offshore resources, the legal argument for violation of the Treaty would not be strong.[305] Action taken by the Security Council would probably not be for the enforcement of the Treaty but rather for international security generally. Nations such as the United States would be hard put to argue that oil exploitation in an area not claimed by it was a threat to peace. Even if a Security Council resolution were obtained, there would be a serious likelihood of disobedience by the third party concerned.

Area

The zone of application of the Treaty is specifically defined.[306] It has been the practice of the Consultative Parties to use the term 'Antarctic Treaty Area'.[307] Particular importance must be attached to Article VI. On the face of it, this provision purports to lay down territorial limits applicable to all other Articles. Like Article IV, the Antarctic Treaty Area is hard to understand, and the explanation in both cases is an underlying disagreement between the signatories. Having regard to the controversy at the time of drafting over the breadth of the territorial sea, the question of what were the high seas

301. Art. X.
302. C. Beeby, *The Antarctic Treaty* (1972), 17.
303. Rec. X-8.
304. J. Hanessian, 'The Antarctic Treaty 1959' (1960), 9 *ICLQ*, 436 at 473.
305. See discussion of Treaty/*Area*.
306. Art. VI.
307. For example; Rec. III-1; VI-12; X-8. 'Treaty Area' is also referred to with the same meaning (Rec. III-II; VI-12; X-8).

was left indefinite.[308] Choice of the 60°S boundary was not dictated by geographical or scientific considerations but rather by the northern limits of claims.[309]

The peculiar wording of the high seas exception to Article VI has given Consultative Parties continual problems. Its full implications have still not been finally determined.[310] One argument holds that the waters south of 60°S are excluded from the Treaty.[311] In support it may be pointed out that the definition of 'area' as including ice shelves suggests that such formations would not otherwise be covered by the term 'area'. Land and its equivalent was included, and the specific reference to ice shelves clarifies the moot point of their status for Treaty purposes.

Yet there would be no need to reserve high seas freedoms if the Treaty did not apply to offshore waters. Inspection of ships[312] is intended to take place in the Antarctic equivalent of internal waters or the territorial sea. Provision for measures regarding the preservation and conservation of living resources[313] is another indication of an intention to cover water areas. However, practical considerations militate against the argument. If the Treaty Area were confined to land and ice shelves there would be no agreed regime for the immediately adjacent sea, and disputed sovereignty claims and assertions would continue in relation to offshore areas. At the other end of the spectrum is the interpretation that the Antarctic continent has jurisdiction over marine areas exercised by Consultative Meetings.[314] This is a variant of the objective regime construction discussed and rejected previously.[315] A further difficulty is that such a jurisdiction would not be vested in an internationally recognised entity.

Treaty practice regarding offshore areas has undergone considerable change. Examining Article VI, it would seem that the Treaty does apply to all the waters south of 60°S, but cannot affect high seas freedoms. There is however no such prejudice when the Consultative Parties freely agree with each other[316] to limit the exercise of their rights. If this were not so, it is difficult to understand how any parties

---

308. Mr Phleger, State Department, 'The Antarctic Treaty' Hearings, Committee on Foreign Relations, Senate, 86th Cong., 2nd Sess. (1960), 66.
309. G. Fahl, *Internationales Recht der Rüstungsbeschränkungen* (1975) 10.
310. F. Sollie, 'The Legal Status of the Antarctic', MS (1976), 12.
311. R.E. Guyer, 'The Antarctic System' (1973), 139 *Hague Recueil*, 149 at 163.
312. Art. VII(3).
313. Art. IX(1)(f).
314. A. van der Essen, 'L'Antarctique et le Droit de la Mer' (1975–6), 5–6 *Iranian Review of International Relations*, 89 at 96.
315. See Treaty/*Third Parties*.
316. Under Art. IX(1).

to the High Seas Convention could also participate in fisheries treaties limiting gear, effort or catch. Yet there is evidence of such a view in the early practice of Consultative Meetings.

The Agreed Measures for the Conservation of Antarctic Fauna and Flora were embodied in a recommendation.[317] Article I of these Measures provides for the same area of application as the Treaty itself.[318] However, diplomats and scientists connected with the Treaty system took the view that the Agreed Measures apply to terrestrial and ice shelf areas only.[319] Seals are covered by the Agreed Measures;[320] therefore, separate concurrent discussion of pelagic sealing[321] suggested a similar restriction of the Measures. Yet there are good grounds for contending that the Agreed Measures do apply to offshore waters. First, one may invoke the previous arguments based on Article VI of the Treaty which are equally relevant to the Agreed Measures. Definition of 'native mammals' to exclude whales[322] strongly suggests that the Measures are not confined to land. Lesser indications are the extreme emergency exception for the safety of ships,[323] the taking of steps to alleviate pollution of waters adjacent to the coast,[324] and arrangements for observation of the Measures by ships' crews.[325]

Recommendations made pursuant to the Agreed Measures have applied to marine areas. Ross seals, whose habitat is sea – ice, were declared a Specially Protected Species under Annex A of the Measures.[326] Definition of the Cape Crozier Specially Protected Area covered land on the coast of Ross Island. The area 'is also deemed to include the locality occupied at any time by the rookery of Emperor Penguins'.[327] This curious description of floating sea – ice .was apparently adopted in an attempt to avoid legal difficulties about applying the Agreed Measures to coastal waters. Diplomats may have been satisfied with this device, but lawyers could hardly regard it as appropriate. If the Measures did not apply to offshore waters,

317. Rec. III-VIII.
318. This is redundant because a recommendation is made under the Treaty and therefore subject to Article VI. The explanation is to be found in the original proposal which took the form of a separate convention.
319. SCAR Working Group on Biology, Report of Thirteenth Meeting of SCAR (1975), 49 *SCAR Bulletin*, 69 at 74.
320. Art. II(*a*), Art. VII(2)(*c*) and (*d*), Agreed Measures.
321. Rec. III-XI.
322. Art. II(*a*), Agreed Measures.
323. Art. V, Agreed Measures.
324. Art. VII(3), Agreed Measures.
325. Art. XI, Agreed Measures.
326. Rec. IV-17.
327. Rec. IV-6.

they were equally inapplicable to floating penguin rookeries.

From 1970 onwards Chile put forward repeated proposals for Specially Protected Areas (SPAs) and Sites of Special Scientific Interest covering land and adjacent marine areas. Coppermine Peninsula, Robert Island,[328] became a SPA, but the offshore waters were deleted. At the same Consultative Meeting Chile also proposed that Deception Island, 'including its neighbouring sea', become a SPA.[329] As has been previously pointed out[330] this small island had long been a focus of sovereignty disputes. At the time of the 1969 volcanic eruption, stations of Chile, Argentina and the United Kingdom were sited in close proximity. This Chilean suggestion was based on the need to prevent contamination and enable scientific observation of the re-establishment of life after the eruption. To avoid the sovereignty and offshore issues, a recommendation was passed that new islands formed by geological processes (a new islet had been created in Telefon Bay, Deception Island, by an eruption in December 1967) should be the subject of immediate consultation. The governments should use their best endeavours to avoid contamination by human interference.[331]

Following a review by SCAR of Specially Protected Areas the 1972 Consultative Meeting laid down guidelines requiring representative samples of major land and 'freshwater' ecological systems[332] excluding sea areas by implication. Agenda items on 'Specially Protected Marine Areas' and 'Marine Sites of Special Scientific Interest' were deleted at the 1975 Meeting.[333] There was considerable support for these items, and opposition from the United States was significantly not based on Article VI of the Treaty. At the next Meeting Chile proposed Bahia South, Doumer Island, as a Marine SSSI covering a bay, and the entire Foster Bay, Deception Island, as a SSSI for similar reasons to those advanced in 1970.[334] Chile also submitted and withdrew a draft recommendation inviting SCAR to propose Marine SSSIs.[335] In the Final Report the opinion was expressed that SCAR should be invited to examine the matter and Representatives noted Chile's intention to propose two Marine SSSIs to SCAR 'following agreed procedures'.

328. Rec. VI-10.
329. ANT/4 (19 October 1970).
330. See Sovereignty/*Polar Circumstances*.
331. Rec. VI-II.
332. Rec. VII-2. At this Meeting Chile expressed regret that seal conservation had been dealt with by a separate Conference.
333. Final Report of the Eighth Antarctic Treaty Consultative Meeting (1975), 2.
334. ANT/IX/75 (29 September 1977).
335. ANT/IX/84 (7 October 1977).

At the 1975 Meeting an informal working group of legal experts, instructed by the Chairman, met the President of SCAR to advise him with respect to legal matters arising from SCAR's concern with the need to reserve certain marine areas for scientific purposes. This working group considered a statement by SCAR that 'a number of SCAR National Committees have expressed interest in the possibility of designating inshore marine areas either as Specially Protected Areas or as Sites of Special Scientific Interest. However, at present this is not possible under the Agreed Measures for the Preservation of Flora and Fauna as they apply to terrestrial and ice shelf areas only.' The group agreed that the interpretation of Article VI of the Treaty and Article I of the Agreed Measures by SCAR was 'too restrictive'; a marine area could be a SPA or a SSSI[336] No reasons were given. In form this was a reversal of a SCAR interpretation. In fact it related to the Consultative Parties. At its 1978 Meeting SCAR adopted Chile's proposal for a Marine SSSI at Chile Bay, Greenwich Island. Port Foster, Deception Island, was referred back to Chile for revision because it included a natural anchoring ground.[337] It may be noted that the SCAR statement referred to 'inshore marine areas', and that Chile's proposals related to bays. But there is no apparent reason for differentiating between such areas and other offshore waters.

The extent of the departure from previous interpretations may be measured by the negotiation of the Antarctic Sealing Convention of 1972.[338] For a number of years the Consultative Parties discussed pelagic sealing,[339] and interim voluntary guidelines were adopted in 1966.[340] It was recognised that a binding international agreement might be required in the future.[341] At the 1968 Consultative Meeting a detailed draft was recommended to governments for consideration at the next Meeting,[342] and its examination was listed on the agenda for the 1970 Meeting. It was then decided to consider the matter outside the Treaty framework because the conservation of seals did not fall within its scope and was of interest to third parties.[343]

336. ANT 41 (10 June 1975).
337. Rec. XV-BIOL 9 (397 *SCAR Circular* (3 July 1978)). The 1979 Consultative Meeting had insufficient time to fully consider concerns relating to the designation of Marine SSSI areas and therefore did not recommend their immediate adoption. This covered both Chile Bay and the marine portion of the Admiralty Bay proposal (the land area became SSSI No. 8 under Rec. X-5).
338. Substantive provisions are examined below (Krill/*Sealing Convention*).
339. The first recommendation was Rec. III-XI.
340. Rec. IV-21.
341. Ibid.
342. Rec. V-8.
343. Final Report of the Sixth Antarctic Treaty Consultative Meeting (1970), 3.

The legal difficulties apparently dominated the entire 1966 session.[344] One approach was that Article VI limited the competence of Consultative Meetings[345] because the hunting of seals is a freedom of the high seas. The United States view was that Consultative Meetings were not appropriate fora for concluding an agreement derogating from such a right, but Meetings could prepare a draft. Both interpretations are suspect. If Article VI did apply to the conclusion of a treaty, it must also have applied to discussion and drafting. Decisions of a Consultative Meeting are recommendations which require the further assent of all Consultative Parties. There does not seem to be any obvious justification for differentiating between the drafting of a treaty by a Meeting and its acceptance by a Meeting in the form of a recommendation; neither binds governments. One may conclude that the prolonged discussion of pelagic sealing at Consultative Meetings was due to differing interpretations of Article VI.

The absence of a clear dividing line between drafting and decision-making has become evident in negotiations on minerals and marine living resources. In 1977 four principles on minerals were endorsed.[346] Similarly elements of a living resources regime were enunciated.[347] From the viewpoint of legal competence under the Treaty, these recommendations on essential constituents of resource regimes would bind Consultative Parties after unanimous assent of governments in the same manner as formal treaties. Therefore the requirement for a separate convention must be ascribed to a need to permit accession of non-Antarctic Treaty signatories, or other reasons such as territorial ambit north of 60°S.

Interpretation of Article VI by the Consultative Parties has undergone major revision. Originally a narrow construction was adopted, as reflected in the opinion that the Agreed Measures did not extend to pelagic seals. It appears that this somewhat constrictive approach was not held by all the Consultative Parties. From the history of the negotiation of the Sealing Convention, one may infer that a wider approach was gaining support but could not finally prevail. The advice given to SCAR in 1975 on Marine SPAs was a major change of interpretation by the Consultative Parties. For the United States and other nations not recognising claims, one is hard put to find a logical distinction between offshore zones, because no territorial, sea or other form of jurisdiction is accepted. Given the desire of the Consultative Parties to monopolise Antarctic decision-making, they had little choice but to assert competence offshore. It was no longer

344. R.E. Guyer, 'The Antarctic System' (1973), 139 *Hague Recueil*, 149 at 197–8.
345. Ibid., at p. 197.
346. Rec. IX-I. The main concern is with offshore hydrocarbons.
347. Rec. IX-2.

possible to resort to such semantic devices as that shown in the discussion of the Cape Crozier SPA. Otherwise krill and hydrocarbons might be regulated by international organisations with no stake in the Treaty regime.

Similar reasoning may compel the Consultative Parties to cover areas north of 60°S. For the purpose of SCAR the Antarctic is bounded by the Antarctic Convergence. SCAR may also include sub-Antarctic islands outside the Convergence such as Amsterdam, Crozet and Macquarie.[348] With the advent of 200 mile fishery zones and interest in oil and gas exploration,[349] areas north of 60°S have assumed substantial political importance. Although SCAR covered at least the islands, the Antarctic Treaty regime did not. Again the Treaty powers feared a vacuum.

The method adopted to deal with the issue was interesting. Reference has already been made to the instance of the Cape Crozier SPA, defined as the site of a penguin rookery to avoid mention of its offshore location.[350] In laying down principles for a living resources treaty, the 1977 Consultative Meeting specified that it should extend north of 60°S where that was necessary for the effective conservation of the species of the Antarctic ecosystem without prejudice to coastal state jurisdiction.[351] The magnitude of the reversal of opinion may be measured by contrast with the four-nation statement in 1970 (by Argentina, Australia, Belgium and the United Kingdom) that references to areas outside the Treaty Area in annual exchanges of information do not affect rights or claims to such areas.[352]

In this case there is a double limitation confining consideration to the area south of 60°S. First, there is Article IV, and secondly, discussion of the preservation and conservation of living resources is in terms limited to 'Antarctica',[353] which is the Treaty Area. In refashioning the Treaty on an *ad hoc* basis, the Consultative Parties have not taken full account of the reason for the 60°S boundary. Based on claims, it was intended to apply to the disputed territory of the Antarctic continent and associated islands. Application north of the boundary can only be viewed as a dangerous precedent raising additional problems for resource regimes.

Article VI specifically mentions ice shelves. Does this alter their

348. *SCAR Manual* (2nd. edn), (1972), 13 (discussed under Antarctic System/*SCAR*).
349. For example the ERAP (France) application for a prospecting licence over the Gaussberg-Kerguelen Plateau (5416 *Journal Officiel*, 28 May 1972).
350. Rec. IV-6.
351. Rec. IX-2.
352. Final Report of the Sixth Antarctic Treaty Consultative Meeting (1970), 4.
353. Art. IX(1)(*f*).

status? Surely not. Article VI does not define the legal position of territory, but deals with the area to which the Treaty applies. To make ice shelves subject to the Treaty regime does not convert them into land or sea; if anything the provision emphasises the distinctive nature of such formations. Nor does Article VI decide whether the waters below shelves are high seas. The continental shelf south of 60°S is part of the Treaty Area, and claimants will regard the shelf as the natural prolongation of their Antarctic land territory. Article IV(2) will not operate to prevent the declaration of such rights,[354] since the coastal state's rights are inherent and do not require any special legal acts to be performed.[355] The fact that the Continental Shelf Convention has not been ratified by certain parties to the Antarctic Treaty does not affect the rule which has its source in customary international law.

The logical implication of the non-claimants' position would leave the Antarctic continental shelf open to the jurisdiction of the International Seabed Authority.[356] The State Department has affirmed that the status of the shelf is 'unclear'.[357] Not so. If the United States does not recognise a sovereign on land, the same applies to rights over the shelf. Invocation of the Treaty is beside the point because the Treaty does not affect the territorial status of the area. An International Seabed Authority may well inform nations such as the United States that there will be no intrusion on sovereignty, but claims must be made if they are to be respected. This approach applies with greater force to those parts of the seabed south of 60°S beyond the continental shelf as defined by a Law of the Sea Convention.

Emergence of the Exclusive Economic Zone (EEZ) raises serious problems. Krill and other resources are concentrated within 200 miles of the continent.[358] Is such a proclamation by a party to the Antarctic Treaty a breach of Article IV(2)? *Prima facie* it constitutes the enlargement of an existing claim to territorial sovereignty, the assertion of which is forbidden by that Article. But a number of Treaty parties invoke an EEZ.[359]

---

354. cf. J.M. Marcoux, 'Natural Resource Jurisdiction on the Antarctic Continental Margin' (1971), *Virginia Journal of International Law*, 374 at 398.
355. *North Sea Continental Shelf Cases* (1969) *ICJ*, 3 at 22.
356. See the previous discussion under Treaty/*Third Parties*.
357. 'Legal Status of the Area South of 60° South Latitude' in 'US Antarctic Policy', Hearing, Subcommittee on Oceans and International Environment, Committee on Foreign Relations, Senate, 94th Cong., 1st Sess. (1975), 18 at 19.
358. F. Pallone, 'Resource Exploitation: The Threat to the Legal Regime of Antarctica' (1978), 8 *Manitoba Law Journal*, 597 at 603.
359. F. Zegers, 'El Sistema Antártico y la Utilización de los Recursos' (1978), 33 *University of Miami Law Rev.*, 426 at 461.

Enlargement of claims does not conflict with Article IV(2) if it is not 'asserted'.[360] Whether the EEZ is inherent or requires proclamation has not yet been clarified by State practice.[361] It will be argued that sovereignty over land automatically carries title to adjacent sea areas as an overriding general principle.[362] Extending the arguments used for reservations, one can contend that the ambit of territorial status expressed in a treaty expands with the development of international law.[363]

Widespread endorsement of a Law of the Sea Convention would provide a strong argument that the EEZ inheres in the coastal State. The Revised Informal Composite Negotiating Text reiterated that continental shelf rights do not require express proclamation.[364] There is no such provision for the EEZ.[365] But the same applies for the territorial sea[366] which is undoubtedly part of customary international law. Having regard to the overlap between the continental shelf concept and the EEZ, both of which are essentially offshore resource zones appurtenant to a State, it will be strongly argued that the EEZ is also inherent in coastal sovereignty.

Once the EEZ becomes part of general international law in this way, less comprehensive forms of 200 mile resource jurisdiction, such as fishing zones, will cease to constitute a breach of Article IV(2) of the Antarctic Treaty. This would still leave the possibility of the 200 mile territorial sea contravening the Treaty. Future examination of this issue will require detailed analysis of each case to conclude whether a particular instance, especially the older claims ante-dating the Third Law of the Sea Conference, will be classified as a territorial sea or an EEZ. Pre-1961 200 mile zones, such as that of Chile, are not affected by Article IV(2).

Claimants contend that Article IV(2) is limited to claims to territorial sovereignty, and this term does not apply to offshore jurisdiction.[367] However, the Article also prohibits utilisation of acts as a basis to support a claim or to create any rights of sovereignty. It is a common misconception that the Treaty does not apply to high sea areas.[368] But the text only protects high seas rights under inter-

360. See Treaty/*Claims*.
361. S.J. Burton, 'Legal/Political Aspects of Antarctic Iceberg Utilization' in A.A. Husseiny (ed.), *Iceberg Utilization* (1978), 604 at 606.
362. *Beagle Channel Arbitration* (1978), 17 *ILM*, 632 at 672–3.
363. *Aegean Sea Continental Shelf Case* (1978), *ICJ*, 3 at 32.
364. Art. 77, UN Doc. A/CONF. 62/WP.10 Rev. 2 (11 April 1980).
365. Ibid., Part V.
366. Ibid., Part II.
367. 'Antarctica: A Continent of Harmony?' (1980), 51(2) *Australian Foreign Affairs Record*, 4 at 10.
368. Department of State, *Draft Environmental Impact Statement for a Possible*

national law from being affected by 'the present Treaty'.[369] It has already been pointed out that the exception cannot prevent a voluntary agreement between parties to the Antarctic Treaty which limits a freedom of the high seas.

Article VI must be superimposed upon each obligation of the Treaty. For this reason naval manoeuvres on the high seas south of 60°S would not contravene Article I[370] even if they were declared not to be for peaceful purposes. If nuclear testing does indeed constitute a high seas freedom, States which are not signatories to the Partial Nuclear Test Ban Treaty could carry out such tests in the offshore waters of the Antarctic Treaty area. It has been suggested that a nuclear test took place near Prince Edward Island, South Africa or Antarctica in September 1979, but the nature of the occurrence recorded by an American Vela satellite is in dispute, as is its location.[371]

Radioactive wastes from the former nuclear reactor at McMurdo Sound were shipped back to the United States to comply with the Treaty.[372] In theory they could have been dumped at sea, despite Article V(1). Rumours of the presence of a Soviet submarine in the Antarctic Ocean in 1971 led to a statement by the New Zealand Prime Minister that no imputation could be made against the Soviet Union.[373] At best this was an ambiguous stand. Even a submarine firing nuclear warheads would not contravene the Antarctic Treaty. For the foreseeable future the main focus of Antarctic activities will be offshore and on the coast. Article VI is a serious limitation on the apparently wide provisions of the Treaty, and in particular on Article I.

Dispute Settlement

Dispute settlement under the Treaty is dependent on the consent of all parties.[374] A majority at the 1959 Conference, including the United States, supported the compulsory jurisdiction of the International Court of Justice.[375] The Soviet Union, Argentina, Chile and

---

Regime for Conservation of Antarctic Living Marine Resources (February 1978), 10, corrected in the *Final Statement* (June 1978) 16; M. Booker, *Last Quarter* (1978), 119.

369. Art. VI.
370. 'The Antarctic Treaty' (1972), 22(6) *NZ Foreign Affairs Review*, 19 at 23.
371. 'Navy Lab Concludes the Vela Saw a Bomb' (1980), 209 *Science*, 996.
372. F.M. Auburn, *The Ross Dependency* (1972), 40.
373. (1971), 21(11) *NZ Foreign Affairs Review*, 70.
374. Art. XI.
375. Report of the Committee on Foreign Relations on the Antarctic Treaty, *Congressional Record — Senate* (8 August 1960), 15980.

one other nation (not named) objected.[376] But Article XI is not merely an ineffective means of dealing with possible disagreements; it turns back the clock.

One can well argue that the Article removes the effect of general agreements between signatories to submit disputes to the International Court.[377] France and the United Kingdom did not accept this approach.[378] Consent to refer to the Court is required 'in each case', and there is mention of 'failure to reach agreement on reference'. Both phrases support the view that special agreement of all parties is required in each instance. Article XI also can be read as constituting an agreement to a method of peaceful settlement within the meaning of the declarations of those Consultative Parties which have submitted to the general jurisdiction of the Court.

Under Article XI(2), disputes may only be referred to the Court with the consent 'of all parties to the dispute'. Because the controversy must concern the interpretation or application of the Treaty and is not limited to two parties,[379] there would be cause for any Consultative Party to intervene in an existing disagreement. To take a hypothetical example, assume that the United States complains that a French Antarctic 200 mile zone contravenes Article IV(2) of the Treaty. Both countries agree to submit the case to the Court under Article XI(2). Argentina protests that it is a party to the dispute because it claims a 200 mile zone in the Antarctic, and it will not submit to the Court. The Argentinian contention that it is directly affected by the dispute between the two other countries is strong. This would be the case for the vast majority of problems to which Article XI could apply. The dispute settlement procedure has been aptly termed the worst solution imaginable.[380]

Is the Treaty little more than a gentlemen's agreement?[381] At best the sanctions are psychological in the form of pressure from the possible adverse opinion of other States.[382] But it is questionable whether the Consultative Parties would risk controversy by attempting to put pressure on a violator.[383] An additional deterrent would

376. Mr Phleger, 'The Antarctic Treaty', Hearings, Committee on Foreign Relations, Senate, 86th Cong., 2nd Sess. (1960), 63.
377. R.D. Hayton, 'The Antarctic Settlement of 1959' (1960), 54 *AJIL*, 349 at 364.
378. A. Scilingo, *El Tratado Antártico* (1963), 97.
379. 'Two or more' (Art. XI(1)).
380. R.-J. Dupuy, 'Le Traité sur l'Antarctique' (1960), *AFDI*, 111 at 126.
381. J.B. Oerding, 'The Frozen Friction Point: a Geopolitical Analysis of Sovereignty in the Antarctic Peninsula', M.A. thesis, University of Florida (1977), 73.
382. G. Battaglini, *I Diritti degli Stati nelle Zone Polari* (1974), 144.
383. T. Hanevold, 'Inspections in Antarctica' (1971), 6 *Cooperation and Conflict*, 103 at 112.

occur in the situation where the breach was attributed to a Consultative Party. This is the most likely case, because the Contracting Parties carry out very little research, and because, when they do so, it is usually as part of an expedition sent by a Consultative Party. There would be no practical possibility of sanction within the framework of the Treaty. Recommendations under Article IX are the only method of formal action available to the Consultative Parties. Opposition to such a proposal would come from the offending State. Under the unanimity principle, this would suffice to prevent adoption of a recommendation.

Have there been violations of the Treaty or recommendations made under it? The Treaty itself provides the means of verification of observance in the form of exchange of scientific[384] and diplomatic information[385] and inspection.[386] Salient conclusions may be selected from the examination of practice. There have been complaints of incomplete and delayed information. A proposal to monitor and report on such failures was rejected at the 1975 Consultative Meeting.[387] With the exception of the United States, the Consultative Parties have shown little interest in carrying out inspections. It may be doubted whether, in their present form, inspections can be guaranteed to reveal violations, because advance notice is usually given. A prerequisite of inspection is the timely provision of information, but there is evidence that this has not always been available. Several cases have been cited in which apparent violations were not commented upon by observers. Experience to date suggests that inspection is not a sufficient guarantee of compliance.

Discovery of any breach would not be easy. Scientific research and logistic support are generally the function of governments, and to a large degree access to the continent is a monopoly of the Consultative Parties. Journalists are usually invited by governments. Much of the information on Antarctica flows directly from public affairs officers and other officials.

The previous analysis of information exchange has shown that Article VII(5) has been repeatedly contravened. It is difficult to argue that the exchange of scientific information has been carried out to 'the greatest extent feasible and practicable'.[388] More particularly, a detailed review of the annual exchanges of information under the numerous recommendations codified in the Standard

384. Art. III.
385. Art. VII(5).
386. Art. VII.
387. See discussion of Rec. VIII-6 under Treaty/*Information Exchange*.
388. Art. III(1).

Format[389] would reveal repeated failures in compliance. Later discussion in relation to the Environment will suggest that observation of the Agreed Measures has not always been satisfactory, even in the form of interim guidelines to be carried out 'as far as feasible'.[390] Some countries have incorporated the Measures into municipal law, and enforced their provisions by demanding permits for the import of Antarctic fauna. As far as can be deduced from the open literature, there has been no formal notification of non-compliance.

Probably the clearest case for Treaty violation arises in relation to the first sentence of Article IV(2) examined previously. One may take as clear examples two Consultative Parties, Chile and Argentina, which have repeatedly stated that acts since 1961 have been carried out to support their claims. But it has also been argued previously that other claimants, the United States and the Soviet Union, effectively operate under the same assumption.

The Treaty requires that every encouragement shall be given to the establishment of cooperative working relations with Specialised Agencies and other international organisations having a scientific or technical interest in Antarctica.[391] Yet SCAR has been used as the scientific arm of the Treaty system. Contrary to the terms of the Treaty, the Consultative Parties have made vigorous and successful efforts to deter UNEP and FAO from proposals for cooperation. Acquisition of Consultative status under Article IX(2) has been made solely dependent upon the establishment of a winter station, despite the clear words of the Treaty.[392] The Consultative Parties, apart from the United States, have not evaluated the environmental effect of their planned major operations.[393] There is evidence that the interim moratorium on mineral exploration under Recommendation IX-1 has not been observed.[394]

From the open record, compliance of the Consultative Parties with the Treaty and recommendations leaves much to be desired. One may infer that further violations will emerge if the full proceedings of Consultative Meetings and national documentation are published, but even on the available information the record of the Consultative Parties is not good. The Treaty contains few clear obligations; some are merely agreements to refrain from actions which were not seriously contemplated in any case. Recommendations

---

389. Rec. VIII-6 (for details and the argument that Rec. II-VI is contrary to the Treaty, see Treaty/*Information Exchange*).
390. Rec. III-IX.
391. Art. III(2).
392. See Antarctic System/*Consultative Status*.
393. Under Rec. VIII-11 (Environment/*Impact Assessment*).
394. Examined in Oil and Gas/*Moratorium*.

require unanimous approval of the Consultative Parties, and do not impose very burdensome requirements.

Interpretation

Treaty interpretation raises some fundamental issues. US critics argued that the Soviet Union would use semantics that serve its purposes even when American understanding of the words might be completely contrary.[395] Although the text is brief, a lengthy list of varying constructions has emerged. Perhaps the best example is the vexed question of the extent to which the Treaty applies offshore. It has been contended that Article I permits all activities not clearly identified as military.[396] A vital difference of opinion arises from the view that the *status quo ante* applies on effluxion of the Treaty.[397] Is accession to Consultative status automatic? To what extent do recommendations already in force bind such a new entrant?[398] Are Contracting Parties bound by recommendations? Does Article IX permit discussion of any topic not contrary to the Treaty, or must it be limited to subjects such as scientific research specifically covered in the text?[399] Does the Treaty prevent commercial mining?[400] It must be stressed that all the issues of construction mentioned have either arisen in Treaty practice, or have been put forward by commentators involved in drafting the Treaty or in advising governments and thus having an inside knowledge of national policy and the Antarctic system. Whether such an approach can be supported by the Treaty text or not, it could well represent the attitude of one or more of the Consultative Parties. Indeed one interpretation[401] has wide support, even though it is contrary to the words of the Treaty.

Divergent constructions may go even further. It has been argued that the Treaty can be interpreted in all significant respects in two plausible ways – one consistent with the claimant view and the other one with the non-claimant view.[402] This stance is difficult to

---

395. Senator Lausche in 'The Antarctic Treaty' Hearings, Committee on Foreign Relations, Senate, 86th Cong., 2nd Sess. (1960), 35–6.
396. See previous discussion of Treaty/*Peaceful Purposes*.
397. Examined under Treaty/*Claims*.
398. Both points are dealt with later under the Antarctic System.
399. For previous discussion, see Treaty/*Third Parties*.
400. The opposing views were stated at the 1973 Nansen Conference on Antarctic Resources discussed under Oil and Gas.
401. That Art. IX(2) requires new Consultative Parties to establish a winter station (see Antarctic System/*Consultative Status*).
402. S.J. Burton, 'New Stresses on the Antarctic Treaty' (1979), 65 *Virginia Law Review*, 421 at 467 and 478. Mr Burton worked for the State Department and was on the US delegation to the 1975 Consultative Meeting.

accept. For instance, Article IV(2) should be construed in the same manner by all parties. But the fact that such a striking interpretation is advanced by a lawyer with inside knowledge of the Antarctic regime suggests that it might represent the position of at least one Consultative Party.

The Treaty draftsmen foresaw that there would be disputes on interpretation,[403] but failed to provide any workable means of resolution. Amendment requires Consultative Party unanimity.[404] Where opposing views are insisted upon, one can foresee an unsatisfactory outcome. An example is the Meeting at which Poland's Consultative status was accepted.[405]

Termination

Proposals for the duration of the Treaty ranged from ten years to an indefinite period.[406] Although the result was a compromise, critics held that it was for all practical purposes perpetual.[407] At the 1959 Conference, Chile, supported by Argentina and France, argued against all other participants who desired an indefinite time-span. Had the majority view prevailed, the protection of claims afforded by Article IV would have been illusory. Failing to achieve a fixed period, the minority took Article XII as going some way towards meeting the objections raised.[408]

The sole method of termination in the Treaty is linked with the amendment procedure. Modification at any time is permitted with the unanimous consent of the Consultative Parties.[409] A Contracting Party which has not ratified the amendment within two years of its coming into force is deemed to have withdrawn from the Treaty.[410] After the expiration of thirty years from the date of entry into force of the Treaty,[411] any Consultative Party can require the calling of a review conference of all Contracting Parties.[412] Amendments must

403. Art. XI(1).
404. Art. XII(2)(*b*).
405. Final Report of the Special Antarctic Treaty Consultative Meeting (July 1977). (See Antarctic System/*Consultative Status*).
406. F. Sollie, 'The Political Experiment in Antarctica' (1970), 26(10) *Science and Public Affairs*, 16 at 21.
407. Mr Pillion, 'The Antarctic Treaty' Hearings, Committee on Foreign Relations, Senate, 86th Cong., 2nd Sess. (1960), 28.
408. A. Scilingo, *El Tratado Antártico* (1963), 67–8.
409. Art. XII(1)(*a*) The particular provision for nuclear explosions and waste disposal (Art V(2)) also depends on unanimity.
410. Art. XII(1)(*b*), which constitutes a significant deterrent to amendment (see Oil and Gas/*Treaty*).
411. 23 June 1961.
412. Art. XII(2)(*a*).

be approved by a majority of all parties present, including a majority of Consultative Parties at the conference. Entry into force requires the unanimous consent of all Consultative Parties.[413] If the modification has not become effective in this manner, then any Contracting Party may, within two years of all parties receiving notice of it, give notice of withdrawal, which takes effect two years after receipt by the depositary government.[414] It is unlikely that the minority at the 1959 Conference were satisfied with a termination provision dependent upon a majority vote in another thirty years.

On the other hand the Treaty only deals with termination arising from amendment. There is no exclusion of the otherwise applicable rules of customary international law. So duress and fraud could invalidate a State's consent to be bound by the Treaty. Two doctrines are of particular relevance. There is little doubt that there have been changes in Antarctic politics since 1959 and those to be expected in the future will be substantial. Will they provide a basis for invocation of *rebus sic stantibus*? The relevant circumstances must have existed at the time of conclusion of a treaty, and have been an essential basis of the consent of the parties to be bound.[415] The Antarctic Conference did not have a mission to change or alter anything,[416] hence the Treaty was deliberately intended to maintain the *status quo*.[417] Because the continuation of these circumstances was a major purpose of the agreement, a fundamental change in the situation could provide a ground for termination or withdrawal.[418] An example of such a change could be the development of equipment for exploiting offshore oil in Antarctica. This rule has special relevance to the Antarctic Treaty and was recently mentioned in relation to resources by the State Department's Officer in Charge of Marine Resources and Polar Affairs.[419]

At the time of United States ratification of the Treaty, relations with the Soviet Union were at a low level. There was widespread mistrust, and the violation of agreements was feared. To counter this apprehension, the State Department affirmed that a Soviet breach

413. Art. XII(2)(*b*).
414. Art. XII(2)(*c*).
415. Art. 62(1)(*a*), Convention on the Law of Treaties, which may be taken to represent custom on this point.
416. Mr Scilingo in Department of State, *Conference on Antarctica* (1960), 31.
417. See the previous discussion of Treaty/*Negotiation*.
418. G. Battaglini, *I Diritti degli Stati nelle Zone Polari* (1974), 123.
419. 'If a State chose, it could argue at any time that circumstances had so changed since the treaty had been negotiated that it had the right under general international law to withdraw' ('US Antarctic Program', Hearings, Subcommittee on Science, Research and Technology, Committee on Science and Technology, H. Rep., 96th Cong. 1st Sess. (1979), 39).

would release the United States from its obligations.[420] The Report of the Senate Committee on Foreign Affairs even inferred that any breach would suffice.[421] Actual instances of violations have been cited previously. Should a party wish to opt out of the Treaty this argument will presumably also be available in the future.

Actual withdrawal would have drastic consequences and could well lead to a breakdown of the entire regime. An intermediate possibility is that the threat of such action might be used. For example, assume that a Consultative Party were to grant its national oil company an exploration licence in the Amundsen Sea off Marie Byrd Land. One course open to the United States would be to view the permit as a breach of Article IV(2), regarding such an assumption of jurisdiction as supporting a claim; the State concerned would then be informed that unless the licence was cancelled, the United States would withdraw from the Treaty and immediately claim the sector and its continental shelf. Should a serious dispute arise, the Treaty would not afford any mechanism for its resolution. Termination, or the threat of it, could well be the only available sanction.

Reservations

There is no express provision on reservations in the Treaty. *Prima facie*, it may therefore be assumed that they are permissible.[422] Exclusion of reservations by reference to the intent of the parties[423] has not been supported by arguments based on inference from the text or the 1959 Conference. None of the substantial number of declarations made have been categorised as reservations by the States concerned. Of itself this is not conclusive. A reservation may be made 'however phrased or named'.[424] For present purposes, the test is whether the statement excludes or modifies the actual terms or the legal effect of any provision of the Treaty in its application to the State making the declaration.[425] So the Belgian view that none of the declarations on Article IV modified its dispositions on the rights of parties[426] means that the statements were not

---

420. Mr Phleger, 'The Antarctic Treaty' Hearings, Committee on Foreign Relations, Senate, 86th Cong. 2nd Sess. (1960), 42.
421. Congressional Record-Senate (8 August 1960), 15981. Contrast the much more acceptable view of Senator Fulbright ('violation in any substantial manner', ibid., at p. 16113).
422. *Reservations to the Genocide Convention Case* (1951) ICJ 15 at 22.
423. J. Hanessian, 'The Antarctic Treaty' (1960), 9 *ICLQ*, 436 at 474.
424. Art. 2(1)(*d*). Convention on the Law of Treaties incorporating customary international law.
425. *Anglo-French Continental Shelf Arbitration* (1979) 19 ILM 397 at 418.
426. A. Scilingo, *El Tratado Antártico* (1963), 90.

regarded by that country as reservations.

Most of the declarations may be taken as having no legal effect. So the views of France and others that Article VII did not affect their general support for international methods of disarmament control[427] were purely political. Australia's declaration on Article IV was a paraphrase of the Article[428] and therefore not a reservation. The United States declaration interpreting Article V as permitting the peaceful use of nuclear materials (in reactors)[429] is clearly consonant with the terms of the Article.

A few of the declarations would appear to be reservations. The statement made for United States, Argentina and Chile — the only declaration in the official public Conference report — has been previously discussed.[430] Its purported subordination of the Antarctic Treaty to the Rio Treaty has been severely criticised as a form of wishful thinking having no legal effect. It was argued that such a statement could not dissolve real contractual incompatibilities between the two treaties.[431] The Rio Treaty made provision for joint defence against armed attack, but such measures would have to be of a military nature and therefore contrary to the express terms of the Antarctic Treaty.[432] This was a reservation, and the specific Chilean declaration on Article I, invoking the right of individual and collective self-defence,[433] has the same status.

In relation to Article VIII, France specified that it did not renounce any of the privileges of sovereignty over Adélie Land, particularly in regard to its general power of jurisdiction.[434] It is difficult to see how this declaration can be reconciled with Article IX(1)(f), empowering Consultative Meetings to recommend measures regarding questions relating to the exercise of jurisdiction. If France retained all jurisdictional rights, apart from the special case of Article VIII, the exercise of these rights in Adélie Land could not be discussed under Article IX.

427. Ibid., at p. 93.
428. Ibid., at p. 90.
429. Ibid., at p. 92.
430. See National Interests/*South America* and Treaty/*Peaceful Purposes*.
431. R.D. Hayton, 'The Antarctic Settlement of 1959' (1960), 54 *AJIL*, 349 at 366.
432. Art. I(1).
433. A. Scilingo, *El Tratado Antártico* (1963), 89.
434. Ibid., at p. 95.

5

THE ANTARCTIC SYSTEM

Consultative Status

The Treaty was a compromise between opposing views. Some claimants were adamantly opposed to any form of internationalisation, and even the unanimous decision of the representatives of the Consultative Parties has only the form of a recommendation requiring approval of all governments to become effective.[1] There is no governing body only the clumsily named Antarctic Treaty Consultative Meeting. On the international level these Meetings, together with the operations of SCAR, carry out the functions of the Treaty. Consultative Parties use the not entirely apt term 'Antarctic Treaty system'[2] or 'Antarctic system'.[3] Inevitably the form and functions of this system have evolved and changed during the twenty years that the Treaty has been in force. Originally devised as a framework for cooperation in scientific research, the system has increasingly been required to deal with the much more difficult issues raised by other activities, particularly resource exploration.

Consultative status is the key to the functioning of the Antarctic system. Much of the recent criticism of the Treaty has centred on the heavy burden demanded of new entrants to the decision-making group. Although a number of States have acceded, the granting of Consultative rights has been most restricted, lending support to remarks that an exclusive club has been created.[4] It was only after sixteen years that the first new Consultative Party, Poland, was admitted.[5]

That decision raised basic issues on the meaning of Article IX(2), which provides that each Contracting Party by accession[6] (thus excluding the original twelve signatories, who do not have to fulfil any test) 'shall be entitled' to Consultative status during such time as it demonstrates its interest in Antarctica by conducting substantial scientific research there, such as the establishment of a scientific

---

1. Art. IX(4). The discussion under this head is based upon F.M. Auburn, 'Consultative Status under the Antarctic Treaty' (1979), 28 *ICLQ*, 514.
2. Rec. X-1.
3. R.E. Guyer, 'The Antarctic System' (1973), 139 *Hague Recueil*, 149.
4. G. Skagestad, 'The Frozen Frontier: Models for International Cooperation' (1975), 10 *Cooperation and Conflict*, 168 at 179.
5. Final Report of the Special Antarctic Treaty Consultative Meeting (July 1977).
6. Art. IX(1).

station or the despatch of a scientific expedition. It also required the laying down of requirements and procedures for acquisition of the status.

Circumstances leading to the July 1977 Meeting did not encourage the development of clear criteria for admission. Poland had established an all-year base in February 1977. Discussion of a marine living resources regime was scheduled for September that year, and Poland's participation was essential since that country was a leader in krill research. Failure to agree on Poland's request at a Preparatory Meeting in March left little time to carry out international negotiations on major issues of principle.

Article IX(2) indicates that there is an entitlement to Consultative status if the criteria are met. Does this mean that, once the test has been passed, participation is automatic? Or must there also be a recommendation with the possibility of a veto by any one of the existing Consultative Parties? Argentina, for instance, pressed for the latter solution, because it was concerned at the possibility of a Brazilian application. Resort to the Treaty text lends considerable support to the automatic interpretation: so, if a scientific station has been established, Consultative status arises as a matter of entitlement. One participant in the Washington Conference of 1959 relied upon the Treaty discussions (which were secret)[7] as evidence that Article IX(2) is mandatory.[8] In nominating an observer – a prerogative of Consultative Parties – [9] in 1975–6,[10] Poland had originally adopted the same argument. Yet the application of the unanimity rule has been required by another commentator who took part in the drafting of the Treaty.[11]

The July 1977 Meeting reported on the general principles and on the particular case of Poland. The outcome was intentionally obscure. A Contracting Party considering itself entitled to the status shall provide information for evaluation by the Consultative Parties, who may conduct appropriate enquiries including inspection. Within twelve months of communication of the information to the Consultative Parties, a Special Consultative Meeting shall be convened to determine whether to 'acknowledge' that the require-

---

7. See previous analysis of Treaty/*Negotiation*.
8. B. Roberts, 'International Co-operation for Antarctic Development: the Test for the Antarctic Treaty' (1978), 19(119) *Polar Record*, 107 at 117.
9. Art. VII(1).
10. S. Rakusa-Suszczewski, 'Preliminary Report from the first Polish Marine Research Antarctic Expedition on the RV *Professor Siedlecki* and the MS *Tazar*', International Conference on Living Resources of the Southern Ocean, Woods Hole (August 1976).
11. A. Scilingo, *El Tratado Antártico* (1963), 63.

ments of Article IX(2) have been met. Such acknowledgement must be unanimous. With regard to Poland, the establishment of a permanent scientific station, approval of all recommendations and compliance with Article X was noted and it was acknowledged that Poland had fulfilled the requirements of Article IX(2) and therefore had the right to Consultative status.[12]

The Meeting did not decide whether to adopt the automatic interpretation or not. On the one hand, the use of 'entitled' and 'acknowledgement' suggest that the role of the Consultative Parties is confined to ascertaining whether the scientific activities objectively conform with Article IX(2). On the other hand, the convening of a Special Consultative Meeting and the requirement of unanimity at such a Meeting indicate that political considerations can be taken into account. Although the outcome was ambiguous in theory, in practice a veto could be cast on such a wide variety of grounds – e.g. non-compliance with the principles and purposes of the Treaty; refusal to adopt recommendations; the use of an ostensibly scientific station for commercial exploration – that a decision could be subjective.

On the general issues, the operative words used were 'unanimously decide', and for the particular case of Poland they were 'record their acknowledgement'. Recommendations have otherwise used the term 'recommend', because Consultative Meetings only have powers to make recommendations to governments.[13] This is apparent evidence of the automatic interpretation. Another possibility is that the governments departed from precedent by empowering their representatives to make recommendations and also to approve them on the spot. Less persuasively, the general decision may be taken as a matter of procedure rather than substance. Against the automatic view, it will be pointed out that there was no doubt that a Consultative Meeting had been convened. Such a Meeting only has the power to make recommendations. So basic an issue can hardly be dealt with as a mere question of procedure. The redundant requirement of unanimity of the representatives at future Special Meetings is evidence of the unresolved conflict over the meaning of Article IX(2). Absence of any specific requirement of approval by all the governments is noteworthy. Yet the Special Meeting is still governed by Article IX(4), and therefore such approval is needed. But there is nothing to prevent immediate effectiveness if all the representatives have been duly empowered by their governments.

The July 1977 decision has been interpreted as favouring a discre-

---

12. Final Report of the Special Antarctic Treaty Consultative Meeting (July 1977).
13. Art. IX(1).

tionary admission test, but substantial weight should be given to the textual grounds for the automatic construction. Introduction of subjective or political elements can only lend support to outside criticism of the Consultative Parties' monopoly.

If admission to Consultative status is not automatic, a further rewriting of Article IX(2) is involved. New Consultative Parties only have that status during such time as they conduct substantial scientific research activity in Antarctica. On the automatic admission construction, the right would arise immediately the test had been complied with. Under the discretionary approach adopted in July 1977 admission depends upon unanimous agreement at a Special Consultative Meeting. Twelve months may pass between the date of communication of the requisite information to all the Consultative Parties and the convening of the Meeting,[14] during which period the applicant is not entitled to participate in Consultative Meetings, despite having satisfied the requirements of Article IX(2). This is difficult to reconcile with the clear words of the Treaty, which gives the entitlement 'during such time' as substantial scientific research activity is conducted.

There is no mention in the decision of July 1977 of the mechanism for depriving the new entrant of status, but it would seem logical to infer that a similar procedure would be required. This follows from the rejection of the automatic test. It would also be contended that because the admission requires a recommendation, its reversal must be carried out in the same manner. Again the discretionary test contradicts the text of the Treaty. Entitlement would continue for a period in which research is no longer being carried out.

Since both lines of argument require unanimity, it would be impossible to deprive the new entrant of Consultative status without the consent of the country itself. If a recommendation is needed, political reasons alone would suffice to justify non-approval because there are no conditions limiting the exercise of the discretion of governments. Refusal might also be supported by a range of arguments: suspension of research might be of a temporary nature due to financial stringency; or the new entrant could reject the other Consultative Parties's interpretation of substantial research and hold that its continued activity in the form of participation in the expeditions of another country sufficed; despatch of a fishery research vessel could also be relied upon. There would probably be no need for the nation concerned to take such an approach alone,

14. Final Report of the Special Antarctic Treaty Consultative Meeting (July 1977). As time begins to run from the date of communication by the depositary government to the other Consultative Parties, the time lapse between the date of satisfying the test of Art. IX(2) and the Special Meeting could exceed twelve months.

because new entrants can expect assistance from political allies in the form of disagreement with the draft recommendation or non-approval of the measure. Even the standard delay of two years in obtaining unanimous consent to recommendations would enable the inactive country to cause serious problems at the intervening Consultative Meeting.

If these logical inferences from the outcome of the July 1977 Meeting are adopted by the Consultative Parties, as would seem likely, the effect would be to substitute 'after' for 'during such time as' in Article IX(2). There is much to be said for such a partial amelioration of the position of new entrants in relation to that of the original signatories.

Although the 1959 Conference had not been able to agree on an exhaustive definition of 'substantial scientific research',[15] the effective practice has been to require the establishment of an all-year station.[16] This view may be traced to a request by Poland in April 1959 to take part in the Treaty preparatory meetings on the basis of its use of the Russian Oazis Station. However, Poland did not occupy the base permanently, and presumably its application was rejected for this reason.[17] Poland seems to have acted on this view: although it initially relied upon the 1975–6 marine expedition,[18] the formal diplomatic communication stated that Article IX(2) was complied with on 26 February 1977, the date of permanent establishment of its Arctowski Station.[19] West Germany acceded to the Treaty in February 1979 with the intention of becoming a Consultative Party,[20] but only planned to acquire the status after establishment of a station on the Filchner Ice Shelf.

The requirement of a winter station may be seen as the lowest common denominator in the absence of unanimity. There can be no argument that this is the sole test. Article IX(2) does not demand that the research be carried out on an independent expedition. Before the Fourth Consultative Meeting a test of one-third participation was

---

15. B. Roberts, 'International Co-operation for Antarctic Development: the Test for the Antarctic Treaty' (1978), 19(119) *Polar Record*, 107 at 116.

16. Foreshadowed in J. Hanessian, 'Der Antarktis-Vertrag vom Dezember 1959' (1960), 12 *Europa-Archiv*, 371 at 381, presumably as a result of the Polish application in 1959.

17. Poland had been advised that it could adhere to SCAR from the date of disembarking a wintering party ((1959) 3 *SCAR Bulletin*, 591). At this time SCAR criteria were similar to what became Treaty practice (see also Antarctic System/*SCAR*).

18. Discussed previously in this section.

19. Note of Polish Ministry of Foreign Affairs to States Parties to the Antarctic Treaty (2 March 1977).

20. (1979) 1 *BMFT Newsletter*, 6.

suggested, to cover an inquiry regarding the Netherlands, but was not taken up. Had the Council of Europe project gone ahead, it is suggested that the Netherlands could have demanded Consultative status provided its own contribution was 'substantial'. Reliance on another country for logistic and other support is not a legal disqualification. Politically it could only be regarded as a further and unjustifiable attempt to exclude eligible nations. From 1964 to 1967 Belgium and the Netherlands conducted joint expeditions. Belgium was a Consultative Party, yet the Netherlands would not have been given the status had it applied. In 1975 East Germany had eleven scientists taking part in the Soviet programme.[21] At the same time Norway had no independent scientific expedition.[22] Substantial scientific research with the logistic support of another country would enable less affluent countries to become Consultative Parties and take the sting out of a major criticism of the Antarctic system.

It is not clear precisely how 'substantial' the research must be. Presumably the wintering-over criterion is based on the words 'during such time' in Article IX(2), but most research is carried out in summer. Taking the test to be the actual activity of the Consultative Parties in the IGY, essential reliance on summer research would seem justified.

Status can only be acquired if the research is scientific. Previous discussion[23] has underlined the difficulty of distinguishing between scientific research and resource exploration. Shortly before the July 1977 Meeting, the State Department made internal inquiries as to whether Arctowski Station was a science activity. Although both the Polish and West German work covers scientific investigation, the main interest of the two countries is in living resources. Poland's claim to status in 1976 was actually based on a krill expedition, but a request relying only on commercial exploration, and so categorised, would presumably be rejected. It has been contended that Article IX allows discussion on any topic and therefore provides the framework for drafting a resource regime. But the effective discouragement of participation by countries concerned solely with resources, while original signatories with no capacity or interest in the field have Consultative status, is a major hindrance in dealing with such matters under the Treaty. Not only is the high entry fee of 'substantial scientific research' a hindrance to seeking status, but it is also a disincentive to any such nation even acceding to the Treaty when it can have no say in decision-making.

21. 'Major traverse to Dome C and Dumont d'Urville' (1976), 7(10) *Antarctic*, 326 at 327.
22. 'Second Norwegian expedition' (1978), 8(5) *Antarctic* 170.
23. See Treaty/*Scientific Investigation*.

The ambiguities of the attitude of the Consultative Parties to new entrants were reinforced when West Germany became a Consultative Party in March 1981. That country had to invest DM260,000,000,[24] much of it for purposes remote from its main interest in krill. It was accepted on the basis of its having approved all effective Recommendations. As its station was established on 24 February, and Consultative status was granted a week later, there was presumably no real opportunity to inspect the base; but in spite of this, it was concluded that West Germany's activities complied with the principles and purposes of the Treaty. It would appear that the Consultative Parties acted essentially on the basis of information supplied by the applicant State. It is not suggested that West Germany did not comply with the test, but rather that the Consultative Parties will take the word of the country in question. As with Poland, the Consultative Meeting recorded its 'acknowledgement' that West Germany had fulfilled the requirements of Article IX(4).[25]

It has been argued that Poland and West Germany are primarily interested in krill exploitation. To gain Consultative status they have taken it upon themselves to set up winter stations presumably because they were prepared to comply with the lowest common denominator of interpretation. The only practical site for such bases was near the major krill concentrations in the South American sector. Closure of a new entrant's single station would put its Consultative rights in question. The net result was that those Parties whose main interest is in resources were under a strong inducement to establish permanent bases in the sector most sensitive to sovereignty disputes. Once established it will be difficult to close such a station. There were two winter stations on King George Island[26] when Poland's Arctowski Base was opened in 1977. Even though Poland and West Germany are not claimants, the policy of the original signatories has forced them to establish stakes which will further complicate any future possibility of a settlement in that sector.

Meetings

The formal framework of Treaty cooperation is provided by the meetings held under Article IX known as the Antarctic Treaty ˙Consultative Meetings.[27] Held at intervals of approximately two

24. 'Bonn joins select band of Antarctic powers', *Der Tagesspiegel* (7 March 1981).
25. Final Report, Third Special Antarctic Treaty Consultative Meeting (1981).
26. Bellingshausen (Soviet Union) and Presidente Frei (Chile) discussed later under Environment/*Specially Protected Areas*.
27. Rule 1, Rules of Procedure.

years and lacking the formal power to make decisions, the Consultative Meetings are inadequate to deal with numerous issues and detailed drafting. In practice most negotiations are carried on at preparatory meetings which cannot make recommendations. Even the early Consultative Meetings sometimes required very lengthy preliminary discussions,[28] and this has placed a heavy burden on the smaller countries, which have to make available diplomats and scientists with knowledge of the issues. A recurring problem has been the absence of a mission at the capital city concerned.[29] With the advent of resource regime negotiations, these procedural defects in a system requiring unanimous decision can only make agreement more difficult.

Various devices have been adopted to overcome this basic deficiency which is due to the lack of a secretariat and a single meeting-place. In 1973 the Nansen Foundation in Norway held an informal meeting of experts on Antarctic minerals. Although it was stated that participants were invited in their individual capacities, this was in effect a preparatory meeting.[30] Meetings on single topics, such as the 1976 Special Preparatory Meeting on minerals, the July 1977 Special Consultative Meeting on Poland and the two Special Consultative Meetings on living resources in 1978, have become frequent. But merely to increase the number of sessions only compounds the representational problems of the smaller States.

Meetings of experts are convened from time to time to discuss practical problems relating to Antarctic activities, and unless otherwise agreed, the reports of these conferences are submitted to the subsequent Consultative Meeting for consideration.[31] Such meetings have been held on logistics[32] and telecommunications, but although there have been three meetings on the latter topic, the essential result seems to be that defects and delays in the transmission of data and lack of uniformity still persist.[33] For the Consultative Parties to convene specialists on non-political topics also raises questions as to the role of SCAR.[34]

28. e.g. for the drafting of the Agreed Measures for the Conservation of Antarctic Fauna and Flora, 1964.
29. An example is New Zealand (Second Consultative Meeting at Buenos Aires).
30. F.M. Auburn, 'Offshore Oil and Gas in Antarctica' (1977), 20 *German Yearbook of International Law*, 139 at 144–5.
31. Rec. IV-24.
32. Rec. IV-25.
33. Rec. X-3.
34. See below (Treaty System/*SCAR*).

Secretariat

The Treaty did not set up even the most minimal form of international organisation. Consultative Meetings are rotated between capital cities. Originally, the only material that had to be forwarded from one host government to the next was a certified copy of the final report with all documents agreed and adopted by the Consultative Meeting,[35] but it was resolved in 1972 that a complete set of all documents circulated should also be sent.[36] There is still no common archive,[37] nor do any formal means exist of monitoring the completeness and timeliness of reports made under the Treaty.[38] Between sessions there is no official spokesman for the Consultative Parties.

This major deficiency in the Treaty system was deliberate-Argentina, Australia and Chile were opposed to any form of international administration – and fear of a super-government has not lessened over the years. Repeated attempts have been made to raise the issue at Consultative Meetings, but without success. The existing framework is rudimentary but any change is regarded as extremely controversial.[39] Proposals for a secretariat at early Consultative Meetings were rejected, their opponents including Argentina, Belgium, Chile, France, America and the Soviet Union. Lengthy and stubborn debates underlined the impossibility of achieving consensus. Even very modest later proposals, such as that of the United States in 1975 for an archivist and for the next host to be spokesman, have not been welcome.

Consultative Parties cannot have their cake and eat it. If they claim exclusive responsibility for Antarctic decision-making, then they must carry out their assumed duties with at least some semblance of order. To regulate completely all matters dealing with a whole continent, even one as uninhabited and inclement as Antarctica, there must be an organisation and a continuous exercise of responsibility. Failing this, they are quite correctly open to outside criticism.

---

35. Rec. I-XIV.
36. The Final Report of the Seventh Antarctic Treaty Consultative Meeting (November 1972), 8.
37. E. Hambro, 'Some Notes on the Future of the Antarctic Treaty Collaboration' (1974), 68 *AJIL*, 217 at 224.
38. See previous analysis of Rec. VIII-6 (Treaty/*Information Exchange*).
39. B. Roberts, 'International Co-operation for Antarctic Development: the Test for the Antarctic Treaty' (1978), 19(119) *Polar Record*, 107 at 118.

Secrecy

The Washington Conference of 1959 was conducted behind closed doors,[40] and its proceedings have not been published. This has been carried over to the Consultative Meetings. The opening plenary session is held in public, but other sessions are held in private unless the Meeting determines otherwise.[41] The plenary session is devoted to speeches of a general nature. Recommendations are published in the final report, which should also contain a brief account of the proceedings of the Meeting.[42]

Inevitably some details of the Washington Conference became public. State Department testimony before a Senate Committee revealed the conflicting positions on compulsory jurisdiction of the International Court of Justice and inspection.[43] The head of the Argentinian delegation described the opposing views on the duration of the agreement.[44] It is not surprising that commentators were able to discuss the position of countries on particular issues.[45]

Publication of information is to a large degree a function of the general significance attached to the discussions, and perhaps because there was no such wider concern with the mundane functioning of the system for the first fifteen years, little is available. But since 1975 there has been a considerable amount of detail from the deliberations of the Consultative Parties. An informal New Zealand working paper submitted to the Paris Preparatory Meeting in 1976 has been cited.[46] But the main focus of interest has been living resources, and on this issue there has been more information than any other to date, with even the full text of the draft Convention reached the public.[47] Ongoing and outstanding issues have been the subject of commentary,[48] but the availability of information did not indicate any change in attitude by the Consultative Parties. When an article referred to reservations of Chile and France on the living resources issue at the 1977 Consultative Meeting,[49] those countries

40. J. Hanessian, 'The Antarctic Treaty' (1960), 9 *ICLQ*, 436 at 461.
41. Rule 7, Rules of Procedure.
42. Rule 24, Rules of Procedure.
43. 'The Antarctic Treaty', Hearings, Committee on Foreign Relations, Senate, 86th Cong., 2nd Sess. (1960), 63 and 67.
44. A. Scilingo, *El Tratado Antártico* (1963), 67.
45. e.g. J.-F. da Costa, 'Antártida: O Problema Político' (1961), 15 *Revista Brasileira de Política Internacional*, 85 at 95 on Art. V.
46. B. Mitchell, 'Resources in Antarctica' (April 1977), *Marine Policy*, 91 at 101.
47. (1979) 5 Environmental Policy and Law, 58.
48. J.N. Barnes in 'Antarctic Living Marine Resources Negotiations', Hearing, National Ocean Policy Study of Committee on Commerce, Science and Transportation, Senate, 95th Cong., 2nd Sess. (1978), 30.
49. 'Voluntary restraints planned for Antarctic krill catch' *Financial Times* (29

protested at the revelation. As long as the policy of secrecy exists, publication of details given by sympathetic delegations or as part of national reports to legislators cannot provide an adequate substitute for full and regular divulgence.

The general veil of secrecy gives additional interest to the writings of diplomats, civil servants and scientists who have attended Consultative Meetings or taken part in the formulation of national policy, and similarly those of authors permitted to use restricted materials. Diplomats with personal experience of the Antarctic system include A. van der Essen, Guyer, Hambro, Gajardo, Roberts and Scilingo; all of them took part in the Washington Conference. Particular significance may be attached to the discussion by insiders of apparently theoretical problems because of the possibility that they refer to actual instances[50] or represent official thought on an important topic.[51]

Another aspect of secrecy in Antarctic affairs is the large measure of control over information exercised by governments. It has previously been suggested that this contributes to the difficulty of discovering any breach of the Treaty.[52] Some journalists invited to Antarctica consider that they are being asked to write an account of the positive aspect of research programmes.[53] Reporters and scientists frequently present uncritical accounts. There is much discussion of why Antarctic science is valuable in principle, but little of whether it is valuable in fact. Modern Antarctica is represented as a challenging environment, but little is said of the miscalculations, errors and waste of money inevitable in government enterprises of this size. The few critical descriptions of Antarctic life and research, such as that of Finne Ronne,[54] are in contrast with most contemporaneous works.[55]

The original procedural rule applied to 'sessions' of the Consultative Meeting, and this has been interpreted to cover the official documents of the Meeting.[56] According to the State Department,

---

September 1977).

50. R.E. Guyer, 'The Antarctic System' (1973), 139 *Hague Recueil*, 149 at 225 giving the hypothetical example of a new participant making claims immediately before adhering to the Treaty. This could well refer to Brazil (see National Interests/*South America*).

51. J.P.A. Bernhardt, 'Sovereignty in Antarctica' (1975), 5 *California Western International Law Journal*, 297 at 312–3 (see Treaty/*Claims*).

52. See Treaty/*Dispute Settlement*.

53. J. Langone, *Life at the Bottom* (1977), 6.

54. *Antarctic Command* (1961).

55. e.g. G.J. Dufek, *Operation Deepfreeze* (1957).

56. The Final Report of the Seventh Antarctic Treaty Consultative Meeting (November 1972), 8.

this 'agreed practice' cannot be altered by US dissent alone; confidential treatment must be given to all documents submitted by other governments expecting secrecy.[57] However, the United States has been prepared to release some of its own working papers.

The legal basis for the secrecy of documents of Consultative Meetings is not clear. At the 1975 Consultative Meeting it was declared that all the conference documents of that Meeting were confidential. However, fifteen documents required for further discussion with SCAR and other non-governmental organisations should not be so regarded. They included the SCAR response to Recommendation VII-3 and extracts from the *SCAR Manual*:[58] both documents had previously been seen by persons not attending the Consultative Meeting, as had a cable from the Executive Director of UNEP.[59] It is illogical to declare material confidential when it must, of necessity, either originate from or be sent to another body and is freely available in that form. From the declaration of secrecy in 1975 one may infer that all documents are covered, and provided that the United States regards itself as bound by this interpretation, it would seem that even its own working papers could not be made public. An American paper in 1977, proposing a new rule of procedure by which documents should be available unless made confidential by the submitting government or a consensus,[60] was not accepted,[61] but was itself published by the US government.[62] The United States and other countries proposed open negotiation and publication of texts of the marine living resources negotiations, but there was no consensus for the view.[63] Although the IUCN and other international organisations were invited to the 1980 Conference, they were excluded from the substantive debate.[64]

The usual justification for secrecy is that acceptable compromises can be thus reached uninhibited by political considerations;[65] some

57. 'Exploration of Antarctic Resources', Hearing, Subcommittee on Arms Control, Oceans and International Environment, Committee on Foreign Relations, Senate, 95th Cong., 2nd Sess. (1978), 28–9.
58. ANT/INF/22 (19 June 1975).
59. ANT/INF/4 (10 June 1975).
60. ANT/IX/42 (26 September 1977).
61. Final Report of the Ninth Antarctic Treaty Consultative Meeting (October 1977), 6.
62. 'Exploration of Antarctic Resources', Hearing, Subcommittee on Arms Control, Oceans and International Environment, Committee on Foreign Relations, Senate, 95th Cong., 2nd Sess. (1978), 29.
63. J.N. Barnes, 'The Emerging Antarctic Living Resources Convention' (1979), *ASIL Proc.*, 272 at 274.
64. R.A. Boote, Vice-President, IUCN, Observations in Final Plenary Session, Conference on the Conservation of Antarctic Marine Living Resources (1980).
65. R.E. Guyer, 'The Antarctic System' (1973), 139 *Hague Recueil*, 149 at 189.

delegations are able to submit working papers which they could not discuss in their own countries or even with certain officials in their foreign ministries.[66] However, these arguments, put forward by senior diplomats, are surprising, because from what is known of the proceedings of Consultative Meetings, it appears that politics play a very large role. Examples are the negotiations on the Agreed Measures and marine living resources. Rather than acting independently, representatives have been closely restricted by their instructions.

Diplomatic secrecy is hard to reconcile with the freedom of scientific investigation and promotion of international cooperation to that end[67] required by the Treaty. The status of SCAR as a non-governmental international organisation dedicated to science means that its operations are public: SCAR reports may be classified at Consultative Meetings, but can still be published in the *SCAR Bulletin*.[68] Exchange of scientific information between parties is seen as a means of reducing suspicion. In the absence of any detail on the proceedings of Consultative Meetings, the claim that they are acting in the interests of all mankind[69] will be viewed with suspicion.[70]

Unanimity

Recommendations only become effective after approval by all Consultative Parties.[71] Although the representatives could be empowered by their governments to take this step at the Meetings, there appears to be only one instance in which this may have been done.[72] From the legal viewpoint the provision ensures that no Consultative Party will be bound by a recommendation without its consent, and that a single nation can prevent such a measure coming into force. It is noteworthy that, despite a very complete protection of minority interests, recommendations must be approved by all representatives present.[73] This is the only Rule of Procedure which requires the consent of all representatives present for amendment.[74]

There are hints that the veto may also apply to acceptance of the

66. R.C. Brewster in Transcript of Public Meeting on Antarctic Living Resources (20 December 1977) in Department of State, *Final Environmental Impact Statement for a Possible Regime for Conservation of Antarctic Living Marine Resources* (1978), B21.
67. Art. II and III.
68. R.E. Guyer, 'The Antarctic System' (1973), 139 *Hague Recueil*, 149 at 189.
69. Rec. X-9.
70. B. Mitchell, 'Attention on Antarctica', *New Scientist* (22 September 1977), 714.
71. Art. IX(4).
72. At the Special Consultative Meeting in July 1977.
73. Rule 23, Rules of Procedure.
74. Rule 25, Rules of Procedure.

agenda. The host-country for the next Meeting is required to consult with the other participants in regard to the provisional agenda.[75] Adoption of the agenda is a matter taken up by the Meeting itself, but generally this is a formality,[76] because any controversial issues will have been disposed of at the preparatory meetings. Although there is no indication of the procedure of these sessions, the final decision on inclusion will turn on the Consultative Meeting Rules. Votes on matters of procedure are taken by a majority of representatives present,[77] but separate Rules govern the number of votes required for approval of recommendations, the final report and amendment of the Rules.[78] It may be inferred that there are matters of substance other than those specifically covered by Rules 23–25, such issues not being provided for by any Rule. At the Second Consultative Meeting, the United Kingdom withdrew a proposed agenda item on jurisdiction, protesting that it had been the subject of a veto by one nation, Argentina. Taken with the usual practice of adoption of the entire agenda, the incident suggests that unanimity is also applied at this stage.

Article IX(4) may be seen as the major safeguard of the claimants. The additional requirement introduced by the Rules of Procedure gives a second veto, and agenda approval may be a third. This legally redundant protection serves the purpose of giving further political bargaining counters, but the flexibility provided by an ordinary or even a two-thirds majority is not available.

The veto makes the outlook for rapid agreement on any controversial issue appear rather bleak.[79] It took more than eight years to negotiate the minor resource regime on pelagic seals. Very intensive discussions led to the Agreed Measures, the lax standards of which were approved by the United States after fifteen years. Only the fear of outsiders prompted urgent action on marine living resources. Inability to resolve differences has sometimes resulted in evasion by recommending the exchange of information.[80]

A sufficiently determined State could utilise Article IX(4) to bring the Treaty system to a halt. To take a hypothetical instance, if very large oil reserves were discovered before a minerals regime had been concluded, OPEC could view their exploitation as a threat to the

75. Rec. I-XIV.
76. An exception was the deletion of Items 9 and 10 (Marine Areas) at the Eighth Meeting (discussed previously in relation to Treaty/*Area*).
77. Rule 20, Rules of Procedure.
78. Rules 23–25.
79. R.D. Hayton, 'The Antarctic Settlement of 1959' (1960), 54 *AJIL*, 349 at 364.
80. See Treaty/*Information Exchange*.

maintenance of high prices. A member-State of that organisation, such as Saudi Arabia, could establish a winter station and scientific programme – in support of iceberg exploitation research, for example – to gain Consultative status and then veto an effective regime. Another and cheaper alternative would be the coercion of an existing Consultative Party with the threat of an oil embargo.

Procedure

The sketchy nature of the Antarctic Treaty system is particularly evident in its procedure. Delay is inherent in any negotiating process where the results have subsequently to be endorsed by governments, but one can understand the use of such a process for the drafting of a treaty. However, this has been carried to extremes for Antarctica in its application to each and every administrative decision, however minor. Two procedural causes of delay are the inability of representatives to take binding decisions and the necessity for subsequent and unanimous government approval.

Repeated procrastination on controversial issues suggests that the Treaty system is often incapable of prompt and adequate action. Reference has already been made to the lengthy delays preceding conclusion of the Sealing Convention. The mineral resource issue was first put forward in 1970 by New Zealand, but in spite of its importance, it was not mentioned in the Final Report of that Consultative Meeting. The 1972 recommendation[81] merely put the matter on the next agenda. Three years later SCAR was invited to assess the environmental impact of possible mineral exploration and exploitation.[82] The first serious and formal discussion of a mineral regime appears to have taken place at the unsuccessful Paris Special Preparatory Meeting in July 1976. Finally, in October 1977, the initial concepts emerged.[83] Thus only after seven years had the Consultative Parties begun to discuss the real issues. The rest of the world will not wait while the Treaty governments drag their feet.[84]

The lapse of time in endorsement of recommendations is even more difficult to excuse. Approval well before the following Meeting used to be the general rule, but the final national consent to the November 1968 recommendations was given on 14 October 1970, five days before the opening of the next Meeting. Since then delays have increased.[85] While numerous excuses may be advanced, parti-

81. Rec. VII-6.
82. Rec. VIII-14.
83. Rec. IX-1.
84. B. Roberts, 'International Co-operation for Antarctic Development: the Test for the Antarctic Treaty' (1978), 19(119) *Polar Record*, 107 at 112.
85. ANT/IX/INF 13 (28 September 1977).

cularly the well-worn argument of satisfying constitutional processes, the obvious explanation is that such delays in acceptance of measures which have been agreed upon by national representatives indicate that Antarctic affairs occupy a low priority in the national policy of States.

One result of the above has been that recommendations are acted upon before they have become effective. For instance, the June 1975 Consultative Meeting recommended that a special preparatory meeting on minerals be held in 1976, and that SCAR be asked to assess the environmental impact.[86] Both actions were necessary well before the following Consultative Meeting, and were taken even though the recommendations had not become effective as at September 1977.

As long as the Consultative Meetings dealt with non-controversial or low level political issues, procedural points of this nature were not important. However, a Consultative Party would be fully within its rights in asserting that no action could be taken on a recommendation until it had become effective. The present practice is contrary to the Treaty.[87] Provided that there is continued and total acceptance of the procedure, its invalidity will raise few difficulties, but once a protest is made, States will be forced to take a stand on principle. Claimants, particularly those for whom sovereignty is a vital issue, cannot publicly renounce the unanimity safeguard in the Treaty without damaging their position. The additional protection provided by the Rules of Procedure is secondary to the Treaty provision. There can be no doubt that the current practice is sensible and indeed the only means of carrying on business efficiently. But it was not the intention of the draftsmen of the Treaty, and is one of the vulnerable links in the weak chain of Antarctic administration.

Apart from recommendations, the major source of official information on Consultative Meetings is the Final Report, which has assumed increasing interest since 1970.[88] Secrecy has its drawbacks, and from the initial Meeting it was realised that something more than the recommendation had to be released. Representatives unwilling to take the extreme step of imposing a veto still needed the opportunity of publishing their differing views. For instance, Argentina stated in the Final Report of the 1968 Meeting that its approval of the measures concerning pelagic sealing was not a precedent affecting the application of Article VI of the Treaty.

Recommendations are formal and inflexible, and require unanimous approval. Because, in the absence of an executive, the

86. Rec. VIII-14.
87. Art. IX(4).
88. R.E. Guyer, 'The Antarctic System' (1973), 139 *Hague Recueil*, 149 at 189.

Antarctic system has had to develop other modes of resolution of internal disputes, there has emerged the agreed statement embodied in the Final Report but not elevated to the status of a recommendation. There are various categories of this statement. A particularly interesting one, which gives the outsider some insight into the internal workings of the system, may be called the failed recommendation. At the 1966 Meeting, agreement was reached on considerations pertinent to applying Recommendation III-VII, dealing with the fundamental issue of which States are bound by effective recommendations. Detailed analysis[89] indicates that the recommendation was regarded by the United States as an unsatisfactory result. An initiative for review did not gain approval, and the result was a compromise of dubious juridical standing.

Recent developments have emphasised another type of agreement which may be called a prototype recommendation. When the statement also refers to principles of interpretation, the question of the legal status of the agreement becomes relevant. For example, the Final Report of the 1977 Meeting included a Working Group understanding[90] that a particular meaning should be attached to the word 'conservation' in the draft of Recommendation IX-2 on marine living resources. This was a major concession to the krill-fishing nations, and must be taken as a consensus on the construction of the recommendation. Had the interpretation been inserted in the body of the recommendation, environmental organisations would presumably have made strong efforts to block approval. The interim mineral exploration moratorium of 1977[91] was taken from a statement at the previous Meeting, which noted that all governments there represented urged such action.[92]

Inevitably there has been pressure to utilise the Final Report to circumvent the clumsy recommendation procedure. Instances of purported amendment may be cited. At the First Consultative Meeting, interim provisions were made for transmission of documents from one Meeting to the next,[93] and in the absence of any subsequent measure on the topic, this original recommendation was taken to remain in force.[94] However, in 1972 it was agreed that the host would send a complete set of all circulated documents to the next host-country.[95] Errors in a Specially Protected Area and Site of

89. See Antarctic System/*Recommendations*.
90. For the substantive discussion see Krill/*Conservation Principles*.
91. Rec. IX-1.
92. Final Report of the Eighth Antarctic Treaty Consultative Meeting (June 1975), 5.
93. Rec. I-XIV.
94. Presumably by interpreting 'present meeting' as 'current meeting'.
95. The Final Report of the Seventh Antarctic Treaty Consultative Meeting (November 1972), 8.

Special Scientific Interest[96] were corrected in the next Final Report.[97] One can understand why the representatives would not wish to have to obtain government approval for such insignificant but embarrassing mistakes, but it is difficult to accept that any legal effect can be given to these amendments.

The Treaty was concluded in English, French, Russian and Spanish, each version being equally authentic.[98] These are also the official languages of the Consultative Meetings.[99] It may be inferred that the Treaty provision has thus been extended to the text of recommendations, and this view is supported by State practice. Again the formal approach used in treaties is applied to routine administrative matters. In theory each recommendation should be approved by the representatives present in all the four languages, and can only become effective after each government has agreed in the same manner.

Belgium approved Recommendation IV-27 in the English language text but could not accept part of the French version. With regard to Recommendation IV-21, the whole French text was specifically rejected,[100] whereupon the State Department compared the three other language texts with the English version,[101] and twenty-four discrepancies were found, some of them significant. For example, the English text of Recommendation IV-18 read 'to cooperate as far as practicable in limiting the issuance [of permits] . . .' whereas the French was translated as 'to coordinate, to the extent possible [*sic*], the issuance . . .'.[102] The State Department's solution was to exclude the French-language version when notifying other nations of approval of the recommendations, and to bring the differences to the attention of France with the hope that an agreed text could be developed.[103] The United Kingdom approved the recommendations of the Fourth Meeting 'as set out in English in the Final Report'. There have been other cases of differences between texts. For instance, Chile contended that the Spanish version of the Rules of Procedures contained errors.[104]

The United States, as depositary government, prepares a chart for

96. Rec. VIII-1 and VIII-4.
97. Final Report of the Ninth Antarctic Treaty Consultative Meeting (October 1977), 6–7.
98. Art. XIV.
99. Rule 21, Rules of Procedure.
100. Note of Belgium to the United States (5 December 1967).
101. Memorandum of B.P. Manfull, State Department (23 April 1968).
102. Memorandum of M.F. Woerheide, State Department (11 April 1968).
103. Memorandum of B.P. Manfull, State Department (23 April 1968).
104. Point 5 of the Agenda, 'Approval of the Regulations' presented by the Chilean Delegation, P. 1 (17 July 1962).

each Consultative Meeting showing the approval of the recommendations of all Meetings for each country. No indication has been given of the language limitations for the Fourth Consultative Meeting,[105] and it may well be that detailed comparison of the four versions of the recommendations of other Meetings would also reveal discrepancies. While the attitude of the State Department in seeking to settle textual differences with France was sensible, it is difficult to justify legally. The recommendations to be approved by governments are the measures agreed by the representatives at the Consultative Meetings, each language version being equally authentic. Amendments to recommendations are a matter for Consultative Meetings, not for bilateral negotiations between governments.

If only one language version has the unanimous approval required by Article IX(4), then the others do not comply with the Article and cannot be effective. But as all four texts of a measure have equal validity, it may well be that none of the recommendations of the Fourth Meeting has become effective under Article IX(4).

The status report on approval of recommendations is not conclusive. Whether or not a particular measure is effective must depend on an objective analysis of the facts of each case, and this will require a textual comparison of the recommendation in its four versions as drafted by the representatives and a further check on the wording as approved by the governments, in case there have been any intervening alterations. Finally, all the diplomatic notes conveying approval will need scrutiny. However, although the last step is necessary, it may well prove unrewarding. Examination of the twelve notifications of acceptance relating to the Sixth Meeting shows that all refer simply to approval of the recommendations without any distinction as to language versions. Should textual divergences be discovered, governments would have to be asked which language or languages each country adopted.

Due to the secrecy of the Consultative Meetings, discussion of procedure can only deal with a small proportion of the topics. Three have been selected: delay, the final report and official languages. A common thread is the very limited nature of administrative procedures set up under the Treaty, both in theory and in practice.

Recommendations

Which States are bound by recommendations in force? The Treaty

---

105. ANT/IX/INF 13 (28 September 1977).

provides that the measures 'shall become effective',[106] but does not specify against whom. Clearly all Consultative Parties which have actually approved recommendations are bound by their agreement. How far, if at all, any further effect is obtained may be seen as one of the fundamental legal issues of the Antarctic system. The Treaty was a minimal consensus, and deficient in many respects; there exists only one practical means of supplementing its provisions, short of amendment, and that is in the outcome of the Consultative Meetings.

On the widest view, it has been argued that the Treaty may bind even States which are not parties. The various forms of this approach have been examined and rejected.[107] Reliance has been placed on Article X to contend that all Contracting Parties must carry out effective recommendations. It has previously been accepted[108] that 'principles or purposes' in that Article are equivalent to 'principles and objectives' in Article IX. However, Article X does not purport to make the principles and purposes binding. It merely requires Contracting Parties to 'exert appropriate efforts' consistent with the UN Charter to the end that no one shall contravene the principles and purposes. Had there been an intention to make recommendations binding on all Consultative Parties, surely Article X would have specifically mentioned measures under the previous Article.

The adoption of a recommendation does not constitute an authoritative decision that it is in fact a measure in furtherance of the principles and objectives of the Treaty. An example has previously been cited of a recommendation contrary to the express terms of the Treaty.[109] On these general grounds one may conclude that the Treaty provides no indication of an intention to have Contracting Parties affected by recommendations.

At the Third Consultative Meeting it was recommended that any new Consultative Parties should be 'urged to accept' effective recommendations as part of the overall structure of cooperation established by the Treaty; existing and new Contracting Parties were to be 'invited to consider' such acceptance.[110] Together with the Consultative Parties' construction of Article VI, this recommendation must rank as a major step in Treaty interpretation. The result is quite clear: namely that only existing Consultative Parties are bound by effective recommendations, and that no State is under

106. Art. IX(4).
107. See Treaty/*Third Parties*.
108. Ibid.
109. Rec. II-VI codified in Rec. VIII-6 (see Treaty/*Information Exchange*).
110. Rec. III-VII.

a duty to carry out a recommendation unless it has undertaken to do so. At the same Meeting the point was emphasised in the Agreed Measures which, when approved by all Consultative Parties, 'shall become effective for those Governments'.[111]

United States approval of Recommendation III-VII and its entry into force were only forthcoming in 1979.[112] Presumably, the American representative had consented to the recommendation at the Meeting due to one US view that only Consultative Parties are bound by approved recommendations. A Belgian proposal to amend the Treaty to make acceptance mandatory on other parties met general opposition, including that of the United States, because of the inherent difficulties of amendment.[113]

US refusal to approve arose from a division on policy within the government. One opinion held that acceding States are bound by approved recommendations, while the second US approach, which was also the interpretation of the other Consultative Parties, was embodied in Recommendation III-VII. To accomodate both positions, the United States proposed at the Fourth Meeting to revise the Recommendation. The outcome was an Explanatory Statement incorporating part of the US proposal.[114] However, the alterations were of major significance: instead of taking the form of a recommendation, the statement was presented as agreed considerations pertinent to the application of Recommendation III-VII – in other words, a non-binding interpretation. The US draft's operative portion would have urged acceding parties active in Antarctica formally to notify the depositary of their acceptance of those approved recommendations which prescribe practices to be followed under the Treaty and of their intention to apply and be bound by the specific provisions of the accepted recommendations. Non-active acceding parties would have been invited to take similar action. Apparently it was believed that there would be more support if emphasis were placed on recommendations laying down general rules of conduct. This position had the merit of not insisting on acceptance of the large number of recommendations of a trivial or essentially non-binding nature. But the absence of any list of the measures seen to be within the intention of the draft would have led to lengthy arguments.

The US proposal, which was in the form of a proposed recommendation, referred to acceding parties active in Antarctica, or, in other words, candidates for Consultative status. Had the draft been

111. Art. XIII, Agreed Measures which also refers to Rec. III-VII in relation to the accession of Contracting Parties.
112. (1979) 18 ILM, 1414.
113. Such as the need for domestic legislation.
114. Items 1–4, Explanatory Statement concerning Recommendation III-VII.

adopted, it would have been taken as an amendment of Recommendation III-VII, and would have opened the way for a requirement that new Consultative Parties accept such recommendations as a condition of attaining status. In place of the operative portion of the American proposal, the Explanatory Statement read: 'Approved Recommendations are to be viewed in the light of the obligation assumed by Contracting Parties under the Treaty and in particular Article X'.[115]

Instead of a potentially binding recommendation altering the effect of Recommendation III-VII, there emerged what was essentially an interpretation devoid of legal effect. Reference to Article X has little meaning in this context, because it is clear from the Recommendation that there is no duty on any State to obey an approved recommendation unless that State has specifically agreed to do so either as an existing Consultative Party or otherwise. In one respect the Statement suggests an even weaker approach than the Recommendation. In the US draft there was a differentiation between potential Consultative Parties and inactive Parties similar to that made in Recommendation III-VII; but the Statement appears to apply to all Contracting Parties, a tendency particularly evident in Item 5 which speaks of Contracting Parties' obligations under Article X in relation to approved recommendations. If there is a case for imposing such measures on any category of States, the most obvious instance is that of new Consultative Parties. Such a condition would have been possible under Recommendation III-VII and the US draft, both of which distinguished between the two types of parties. The Explanatory Statement supports the interpretation that whatever duty is imposed by approved recommendations (the nature of the duties was not made clear) applies to all Contracting Parties. There is no means of forcing Contracting Parties to accept any obligation under a recommendation, but potential Consultative Parties could have been put under such a compulsion as a condition of acquiring status.

In 1972 the question of possible activities of non-Contracting States was considered,[116] and the principles enunciated then became part of a recommendation in 1975.[117] The recommendation was not, however, confined to third parties, although this seems to have been the original intention of the agenda item.[118] There are two portions

115. Ibid., Item 5.
116. The Final Report of the Seventh Antarctic Treaty Consultative Meeting (November 1972) 5. Presumably this was due to fears of a Brazilian expedition (see previous discussion under Treaty/*Third Parties*).
117. Rec. VIII-8.
118. Agenda Item 15, 'Activities of countries not parties to the Treaty'.

of the Recommendation dealing with the position of Contracting Parties. It was considered desirable for acceding States to approve existing and future recommendations which form an integral part of the Treaty regime.[119] In the operative portion of the Recommendation, States that 'have or will become Parties' were urged to approve effective recommendations. The text supports the argument that only third parties were originally intended to be covered, and those portions dealing with Contracting Parties seem to have been tacked on at the Meeting, perhaps in some haste. It is unusual for a recommendation on a particular topic not to cite previous pertinent recommendations in the Preamble, yet Recommendation III-VII was not mentioned. The definition of approved recommendations in the operative portion is clumsy and that in the Preamble is ambiguous.[120] The text refers to all parties to the Treaty, and they are urged to approve effective recommendations. Recommendation III-VII urged new Consultative Parties and invited Contracting Parties: there is no apparent difference in the legal effects of the two recommendations, but the later one is more emphatic in its request to Contracting Parties. Perhaps it is for this reason that the United States has approved Recommendation VIII-8.

One possible explanation for the sudden introduction of Contracting States at the 1975 Meeting may have been the knowledge that Poland intended to despatch an expedition in December 1975 and claim Consultative status. In declaring its entitlement, Poland stated that it had accepted all recommendations of the first eight Meetings.[121] This approval was recalled at the July 1977 Meeting,[122] which also laid down the procedure for acquisition of status. The Preamble reiterated that effective recommendations are in terms of Article IX(1) measures in furtherance of its principles and objectives.[123] The Consultative Parties' obligation under Article X was recalled: in the operative part, Consultative Parties 'may . . . urge such a state to make a declaration of intent to approve' effective

119. Preamble, Rec. VIII-8.
120. '. . . It is desirable for acceding States to approve existing and future Recommendations, which form an integral part of the Treaty regime.' This could be taken as similar to the US draft relating to approved recommendations which deal with matters of principle. It is more likely that 'integral part of the Treaty regime' is the equivalent of 'over-all structure of co-operation established by the Treaty' (Rec. III-VII). In any case the Preamble cannot modify the clear words of the operative clause.
121. Note of Polish Ministry of Foreign Affairs to States Parties to the Antarctic Treaty (2 March 1977). It may be stressed that this covered recommendations which had not entered into force.
122. Final Report of the Special Antarctic Treaty Consultative Meeting (July 1977).
123. Item 2, Explanatory Statement concerning Recommendation III-VII is the origin of this assertion.

recommendations, and may invite it to accept other recommendations. It has previously been suggested that the Explanatory Statement made it difficult to interpret Recommendation III-VII as allowing existing Consultative Parties to make approval of all effective recommendations a condition of Consultative status. Recommendation VIII-8 supported this view, and the July 1977 Meeting provided a final endorsement. Although Poland had accepted all recommendations, the opportunity to make this a requirement of Consultative status was not taken.

Future new entrants may therefore insist that they need only comply with the words of Article IX(2). The outcome is of considerable importance to the Antarctic system. If effective recommendations do not bind new Consultative Parties, any faint remaining hopes of arguing that recommendations could in some way affect third parties under Article X will have vanished. Nor can it be contended that Contracting Parties are bound by effective recommendations.

Contracting Parties

Throughout the discussion of the Treaty system, much has been made of the position of the Consultative Parties. Contracting Parties seem to play no role. Although they have no right to attend Meetings under the Treaty, they could well have been given observer status, as is done with SCAR. Exclusion means that they cannot influence decisions.[124] Then why accede to the Treaty at all?

The Treaty itself imposes a number of obligations on Contracting Parties, but few rights. Scientific information must be provided.[125] Article IV prevents their making new claims. Their consent is not required for amendment of the nuclear provisions.[126] Only Consultative Parties can nominate observers and carry out inspections.[127] Contracting Parties have to exert appropriate efforts to secure compliance with the principles and purposes under Article X. Their agreement is not needed for amendment of the Treaty at any time, although they are not bound by the amendment unless they have consented to it.[128] A review conference can only be called by a Consultative Party,[129] and accession by a non-member of the United Nations requires the unanimous consent of the Consultative

124. R. Lagoni, 'Antarctica's Mineral Resources in International Law' (1979), 39(1) *Zeitschrift für Ausländisches Öffentliches Recht und Völkerrecht*, 1 at 8.
125. Art. III.
126. Art. V(2).
127. Art. VII.
128. Art. XII(1)(*a*) and (*b*).
129. Art. XII(2)(*a*).

Parties.[130] The original signatories were given Consultative status permanently without having to pass any test.[131] Contracting Parties have to show substantial scientific research, and may lose status if this requirement is subsequently not complied with.[132]

Benefits are not large. In theory, scientific information is received.[133] Exchange scientists are subject to national jurisdiction only.[134] Contracting Parties are entitled to take part in a review conference.[135] It will be pointed out that a State which is a Contracting Party has the legal right, as against all the other parties, to enforce the general clauses, for example the prohibition of military measures and nuclear explosions; but these rights are not backed by any effective means of dispute resolution. The Treaty itself contains little incentive for accession unless the nation concerned intends to become a Consultative Party, and practice since 1961 has endorsed this conclusion.

SCAR

The diplomacy of Antarctica is conducted at the Consultative Meetings. Science belongs to SCAR. In September 1957 ICSU took a decision to invite the twelve nations actively engaged in Antarctic research to establish a replacement for the CSAGI.[136] SCAR preceded the Treaty and is more closely linked to the IGY than are the Consultative Meetings. Although the Committee's first session was held at The Hague in February 1958, it is not mentioned in the Treaty. Yet the Treaty draftsmen depended on SCAR to provide the machinery for cooperation in scientific research,[137] which was the sole form of activity on the continent at the time. This relationship was endorsed at the First Consultative Meeting.[138]

SCAR was the successor of the CSAGI, and represented the maintenance of the *status quo*, just as the Treaty did. Whether SCAR is properly suited to its role as the scientific arm of the Antarctic system is questionable. Whereas CSAGI was established to coordinate multi-national scientific studies extending for a year and a half, SCAR is permanent and now operates as an integral part of the

---

130. Art. XIII(1).
131. Art. IX(1).
132. Art. IX(2).
133. Art. III.
134. Art. VIII(1).
135. Art. XII(2)(*b*).
136. J. Hanessian, 'Antarctica: Current National Interests and Legal Realities' (1958), *ASIL Proc.*, 145 at 149.
137. R.D. Hayton, 'The Antarctic Settlement of 1959' (1960), 54 *AJIL*, 349 at 370.
138. Rec. I-IV.

system established under the Treaty.

The administrative arrangements of SCAR are to be found in a Constitution and Standing Resolutions which are examined at each meeting. SCAR is, in form at least, not an autonomous scientific body but a Scientific Committee of ICSU. Its purpose is to further the coordination of scientific activity in Antarctica with a view to framing a scientific programme of circumpolar scope and significance.[139] This must be read as a scientific monopoly of Antarctica parallel to the club later established by the original signatories to the Treaty.

Formal decisions are made by delegates who meet every two years,[140] and between these meetings the executive has authority to attend to all matters requiring consideration.[141] Permanent administrative headquarters with an executive secretary and modest secretariat are located at the Scott Polar Research Institute, Cambridge, England. The *SCAR Bulletin* is published as an appendix to the Institute's *Polar Record*. Most of the actual coordination of scientific research is carried out in the ten permanent Working Groups respectively on Biology, Geodesy and Cartography, Geology, Glaciology, Human Biology and Medicine, Logistics, Meteorology, Oceanography, Solid Earth Geophysics and Upper Atmosphere Physics. The pattern of membership has been that all National Committees of SCAR have one nominee;[142] in other words, there is in nearly all cases a national of each Consultative Party on a Working Group. Additional members represent other SCAR Working Groups[143] and international scientific organisations. Groups of Specialists may be established by the SCAR executive to examine multi-disciplinary issues or when a group is required to report on a specific problem direct to SCAR. Such a Group may be set up at the request of a Working Group or National Committee or in response to a request for advice from Treaty governments. Members are named individuals 'who are not necessarily representatives of national committees'.[144] A Group of Specialists will be dissolved when its purpose has been completed (an example was the Group on Ice Shelf Drilling Projects).

The Groups are of more than purely scientific interest. Membership is not as closely linked to Consultative status as is participation

---

139. SCAR Constitution, 367 *SCAR Circular* (16 December 1976).
140. Ibid., Standing Resolutions, Section 4(1).
141. Ibid., Section 4(3).
142. Ibid., Section 5.
143. So the Secretary of the Working Group on Geology represents it on the Working Group on Solid Earth Geophysics.
144. Standing Resolutions, Section 5.

in the Permanent Working Groups. There is no Belgian on any of the four Groups of Specialists,[145] but several members may come from a single nation,[146] and nationals of Contracting Parties[147] and non-members[148] take part in Groups of Specialists. Three of the four current Groups deal with issues of wider concern. The Working Group on Seals originated from the input of SCAR to the Sealing Convention, and two Groups, Environmental Impact Assessment of Mineral Resource Exploration and Exploitation in the Antarctic (EAMREA) and Living Resources of the Southern Ocean, are directly interested in the effects of resource exploitation.

SCAR requires the national organisations adhering to ICSU and seeking membership to form national committees to frame and carry out programmes designed to contribute to the scientific objectives of SCAR.[149] The major membership category is 'each country actively engaged in Antarctic research', represented by one scientific delegate.[150] SCAR's original interpretation was to demand disembarkation of a wintering party on the Antarctic continent.[151] but a leading US scientist criticised the restriction as meaningless from a scientific point of view, since a well-equipped and well-staffed oceanographic vessel which did not qualify as a base could make a substantial contribution to Antarctic research.[152] Clearly the intention was to make the requirements for Consultative status and national SCAR membership identical, as was illustrated by Poland's rejection in 1959.[153] In 1976 Poland was granted observer status in view of the details it gave of its marine research programme and indicating an intention to build a land station. SCAR then decided that the establishment of a wintering station was not a pre-requisite, and that a continuing marine science programme constituted, in principle, grounds for membership.[154] It may be noted that there had been no change in the relevant provisions of the Constitution of the Committee. There appears to be no legal impediment to the adoption of a similar construction of Article IX(2) of the Treaty.

145. Eight Permanent Working Groups have Belgian members and there is a vacant Belgian place on the Logistics Group ((1979) 61 *SCAR Bulletin*, 78–83).
146. Four US members on Late Cenozoic Studies. (ibid., at 84).
147. Denmark (ibid., at 84).
148. Canada (ibid., at 84).
149. SCAR Constitution, 367 *SCAR Circular* (16 December 1976).
150. Ibid.
151. (1959) 3 *SCAR Bulletin*, 591.
152. A.P. Crary, *The Antarctic* (1962), 1 at 7.
153. Conference participation (which would have given Consultative status) was apparently refused for the same reason (see Antarctic System/*Consultative Status*).
154. Report of the Meeting of Delegates (October 1976), XIV-SCAR-30 (Revised) in 368 *SCAR Circular* (3 December 1976).

By the time its formal application was lodged,[155] Poland had built a permanent station. The first successful request based solely on marine research was that of West Germany,[156] which made clear its intention to establish a winter base in the near future. Both nations sought SCAR membership as a prelude to Consultative status.

Although closely linked to the Consultative process, SCAR is much more flexible: acquisition of membership is one instance of this. SCAR also has a procedure for countries which cease to carry out research. Belgium closed its base in 1967, and presumably to meet this case, a resolution was passed at the 1976 meeting of SCAR that all voting rights would be withdrawn from a country that had not been active in the Antarctic or SCAR for four years. That country's National Committee should be asked whether it wished to continue membership and, if so, to state its future plans.[157]

SCAR has full provision for the granting of observer status. Interested international organisations and committees of ICSU may be invited to designate observers to attend SCAR meetings.[158] Although similar in nomenclature, the national and international observers have different functions. A national organisation adhering to ICSU may apply to send an observer to a meeting of SCAR or its executive provided that it states its intention to establish a scientific research activity in the Antarctic.[159] As the instances of Poland and West Germany indicate, an application to send a national observer is not only the means by which full membership of SCAR is obtained, but it also shows that the country concerned intends to become a Consultative Party to the Treaty. There is no need for Working Groups and Groups of Specialists to have observers because individual scientists may participate even though their countries are not members of SCAR. Working Group membership parallels Consultative status very closely, with the addition of international organisations affiliated to ICSU. Small but significant evidence of the potential for wider membership is demonstrated by the participation of a Canadian in Human Biology and Medicine and an FAO representative in Biology.[160] Groups of Specialists are more open to outsiders. A noteworthy example is the FAO member of Living Resources on the Southern Ocean.[161]

155. 386 *SCAR Circular* (15 December 1977).
156. 381 *SCAR Circular* (n.d., issued in 1977).
157. Res. XV-GEN-10 (Report of the Meeting of Delegates (October 1976), XIV-SCAR-30 (Revised) in 368 *SCAR Circular* (3 December 1976)).
158. SCAR Constitution, 367 *SCAR Circular* (16 December 1976).
159. Ibid., Standing Resolutions, Section 2(1).
160. (1979) 61 *SCAR Bulletin* 80 and 78.
161. Ibid., at p. 85. For an account of the Consultative Parties' successful opposition to the large FAO Southern Oceans research proposal see Treaty/*Third Parties*.

The purpose of SCAR is to coordinate national scientific programmes; it does not carry out research itself. In the past, SCAR has
been financed on a shoestring. Regular income is derived from
national organisations in proportion to their Antarctic activity.
There are three classes: (1) nations, maintaining at least one winter
station; (2) nations, not maintaining a winter station; (3) nations
with no current field research activity in the Antarctic. Within class
(1) there are five categories of payment:[162]

Category	Wintering Personnel	Contribution (1980) US$
1	1–10	1,000
2	11–20	4,000
3	21–50	6,000
4	51–100	8,000
5	Over 100	10,000

For 1979 the tentative expenditure of SCAR was $66,825.[163]
Various devices have been adopted to minimise costs. For example,
Working Groups conduct their work mainly by correspondence.
Two to four of these Groups are convened at each full SCAR meeting. Formal meetings may also take place at general assemblies of
other ICSU bodies, scientific symposia or SCAR executive
meetings.[164] Even Standing Resolutions may be amended by correspondence.[165] However, the real cost of running SCAR does not
appear from the budget, since time spent on SCAR business by delegates and scientists is not debited to the Committee. Participation in
meetings has largely been funded in the past by national sources.[166]
Considerable direct financial support was made available by the
National Science Foundation for EAMREA,[167] and indirect support
comes from government initiation of research on topics under study
by SCAR.

Until recently the miniscule amount of the budget was not a
serious problem: IGY had set the pattern of national scientific
research programmes, leaving to SCAR the relatively small role of

162. Standing Resolutions, Section 6. Amounts were prescribed by Res. XV-FIN 1
(Report of the Finance Committee XV-SCAR-33 (Revised) in 397 *SCAR Circular*
(3 July 1978)).
163. Ibid.
164. Procedures for Permanent Working Groups of SCAR, 367 *SCAR Circular* (16
December 1976).
165. Standing Resolutions, Section 4(6).
166. 398 *SCAR Circular* (3 July 1978).
167. 376 *SCAR Circular* (12 May 1977).

coordination. However, since 1975 SCAR has embarked upon extensive efforts which far exceed its ordinary capacity, the most significant examples being EAMREA and BIOMASS. EAMREA, a Group of Specialists, was established at the SCAR meeting in October 1976[168] in response to a recommendation drafted in June 1975 by the Consultative Parties.[169] It therefore had less than a year (until the following Consultative Meeting in September 1977) in which to assess the impact of possible mineral exploration and exploitation. The sole meeting was held in February 1977 in the absence of the members from Japan, Norway and the Soviet Union. The report itself emphasised the lack of time.[170]

In 1976 the Group of Specialists on Living Resources of the Southern Ocean formulated very comprehensive plans for Biological Investigations of Marine Antarctic Systems and Stocks (BIOMASS) covering krill, marine mammals, birds, fish, squid, benthic invertebrates, and seaweeds, and extending from 1977 to 1986. Provisional estimates suggested that this activity alone might require a budget comparable with SCAR's total current income.[171]

EAMREA arose from the Consultative Parties' concern with a regime for oil and gas. BIOMASS rather placed emphasis on krill, as the major potential food resource of Antarctic waters.[172] At the 1978 SCAR meeting it was recommended that SCAR income be at least doubled as soon as possible: the earliest date for increasing national contributions was 1980, and the scale for that year was approved accordingly. The large increase in dues was attributed to the need to make adequate provision for the new and important tasks facing SCAR, especially BIOMASS.[173]

The Consultative Parties make large demands on SCAR. For example, the 1975 Consultative Meeting asked it to review transport sources and requirements,[174] consider convening as soon as practicable a meeting on marine living resources,[175] continue its

168. Report of the Meeting of Delegates XIV-SCAR-30 (Revised) in 368 *SCAR Circular* (3 December 1976).

169. Rec. VIII-14.

170. Group of Specialists on the Environmental Impact Assessment of Mineral Resource Exploration/Exploitation in Antarctica (EAMREA), *A Preliminary Assessment of the Environmental Impact of Mineral Exploration/Exploitation in Antarctica* (August 1977), ii.

171. 398 *SCAR Circular* (3 July 1978).

172. Summary of BIOMASS prepared by SCAR/SCOR Working Group 54, ANT IX/10 (14 September 1977).

173. M. Laclavère, Chairman, Finance Committee, Final Plenary Meeting (26 May 1978), XV-SCAR-34 in 397 *SCAR Circular* (3 July 1978).

174. Rec. VIII-7.

175. Rec. VIII-10.

interest in developing scientific programmes for monitoring environmental changes,[176] and assess the environmental impact of mineral exploration and exploitation.[177] But the Consultative Parties do not finance SCAR directly, nor do they take responsibility for providing the funds necessary to carry out their requests. Much of the strain on SCAR finances is due to the need for scientific research on existing and potential resources.

Should this tendency continue, SCAR will be forced to seek additional sources of income. Increasing national contributions, after the steep rise for 1980, would meet resistance, because the national organisations are carrying out scientific research which is generally seen as a low priority in times of financial stringency. Direct and indirect national subsidies suffer from the same limitations as do contributions. Yet the additional sums needed would not be large by international standards, and are well within the capabilities of organisations such as FAO and UNEP. The Consultative Parties cannot continue to starve SCAR of funds and at the same time prevent international organisations from participating in the Antarctic system.

SCAR and the Consultative Meetings are generally taken to be complementary. However, the land area covered by SCAR is bounded by the Antarctic Convergence. The islands of Amsterdam, Crozet, Gough, Kerguelen, Macquarie, Prince Edward, St Paul and Tristan da Cunha 'may be included in SCAR's area of interest'[178] although they lie outside the Convergence. SCAR does in fact cover these islands and others north of the Convergence. The Working Group on Meteorology put forward a programme of measurements in 1978 affecting stations on the islands of the Falkland group, South Georgia, Bouvet, Marion, Amsterdam, Crozet, Gough, Kerguelen, Macquarie and Campbell.[179] In the light of this extensive concern, covering some politically sensitive islands, it is surprising that SCAR 'has not found it necessary to define limits of the oceanic area in which it is interested'.[180] The peculiar wording may well suggest legal issues.

Operational success of the Treaty depends to a very large extent on SCAR.[181] If evidence were needed it may be found in the repeated references to it in recommendations. But just as the Antarctic Treaty

176. Rec. VIII-11 and VIII-13.
177. Rec. VIII-14.
178. SCAR Constitution, 367 *SCAR Circular* (16 December 1976).
179. XV-SCAR-10 (Revised)(May 1978) in 397 *SCAR Circular* (3 July 1978).
180. 367 *SCAR Circular* (16 December 1976).
181. R.D. Hayton, 'The Nations and Antarctica' (1960), 10 *Österreichische Zeitschrift für Öffentliches Recht*, 368 at 410.

does not mention SCAR, so the SCAR Constitution and Standing Resolutions barely refer to the Treaty. There are no formal connections between Consultative Meetings and SCAR. Communications pass from SCAR to the national Antarctic committees, then to governments and finally to Consultative Meetings. The usual form in which a Consultative Meeting requests action by SCAR is: '*Recommend* to their Governments that, through their National Committees, they refer the matter to the Scientific Committee on Antarctic Research (SCAR) for further study.'[182] It is the Consultative Parties which insist on this cumbersome procedure. In 1967, SCAR suggested a more formal and direct route for conveying its resolutions, but this was not adopted by the Consultative Parties.[183] Until recently, SCAR and Consultative Meetings were held in the same year, making coordination of work difficult. As with Antarctic Treaty administration generally, the prescribed arrangements are sketchy at best. Relations with SCAR were discussed at the First Consultative Meeting, and the resulting Recommendation I-IV agreed that, without prejudice to the rights of governments to make other arrangements to further scientific cooperation under the Treaty, the free exchange of information and views among scientists participating in SCAR, and the Committee's recommendations, constitute a most valuable contribution to scientific cooperation in Antarctica. SCAR should be encouraged to continue this advisory work, since it constituted the kind of activity contemplated by Article III of the Treaty. An attempt at the Consultative Meeting to convert SCAR into an official organisation failed, because it was argued that the Committee should be free to discuss any matters it felt important for Antarctic research and able to avoid political problems; presumably it was also feared that if SCAR were given a separate identity it might develop into the Antarctic secretariat which is not acceptable to a number of Consultative Parties.[184]

A major weakness is that the communication system seems slow and bureaucratic.[185] One reason for enabling the SCAR executive to establish Groups of Specialists in response to a request for advice from the Consultative Parties[186] was to furnish preliminary consideration of a topic, regardless of the timing of SCAR or Con-

---

182. The example is from Rec. X-4 concerning the collection of geological specimens.
183. *SCAR Manual* (2nd edn, 1972), 43.
184. See previous discussion (Treaty System/*Secretariat*).
185. T. Gjelsvik, 'The Work of SCAR for Conservation of Nature in the Antarctic' in Francisco Orrego Vicuña and Augusto Salinas Araya (eds.), *El desarrollo de la Antártica* (1977), 328 at 329.
186. Standing Resolutions, Section 5.

sultative Meetings,[187] but as the case of EAMREA suggests, this procedure has not proved an unqualified success. Even with the scheduling of SCAR and Consultative Meetings in different years, there have been delays: thus there was insufficient time between the Twelfth Meeting of SCAR and the Seventh Consultative Meeting to permit adequate discussion of Man's impact on the Antarctic Environment.

Absence of any formal link between SCAR and the Consultative Meetings has resulted in the emergence of grey areas. At the First Consultative Meeting, exchange of information on logistics was recommended under the Treaty, and a symposium of experts was proposed.[188] A move to direct SCAR not to discuss logistics was blocked with the contention that the Consultative Parties should not instruct SCAR in any way. SCAR held a logistics symposium in 1962. At the 1966 Consultative Meeting it was recommended that a meeting of experts on the subject be held in 1968.[189] The SCAR Working Group on Logistics continues to function. In 1975 the Consultative Parties agreed that SCAR should examine the proposals for a cooperative air transport system.[190] Subsequently the work of the Sub-Committee on Cooperative Air Transport System for Antarctica[191] of the Working Group on Logistics received specific encouragement from the Consultative Parties.[192]

SCAR originally had a Communications Working Group, but the Consultative Parties held a first meeting of specialists on the topic in 1963,[193] in consequence of which the SCAR Group was abolished in 1966 and its functions were transferred to the Logistics Group.[194] Apparently the Consultative Parties considered that radio communications were a matter for governments and not for a scientific organisation, If this was indeed the reason, then it was equally applicable to logistics. The Treaty nations have held three meetings of telecommunications experts, the latest in 1978.[195] However the Consultative Parties recognised that SCAR had a role to play in telecommunications;[196] so SCAR was requested to prepare a handbook

187. Group of Delegates, Eleventh Meeting of SCAR (October 1970) in (1971) 37 *SCAR Bulletin* 775.
188. Rec. I-VII and Rec. II-V.
189. Rec. IV-25.
190. Rec. VIII-7.
191. CATSA.
192. Rec. IX-4.
193. Rec. I-XI and Rec. II-III.
194. H.M. Dater, 'The Antarctic Treaty in Action 1961–1971' (1971), 6(3) *Antarctic Journal*, 67 at 70.
195. 'Antarctic telecommunications' (1978), 13(4) *Antarctic Journal*, 1.
196. Rec. IX-3.

of national practices and to receive information on changes.[197] The Committee's objects of coordination of scientific research are vitally dependent on communications, and inevitably it has continued to be concerned with the topic. In 1978 a Telecommunications Sub-committee of the Logistics Working Group was established. The Working Group on Meteorology continued to express concern at the inadequacy of data available.

Additional demarcation problems may be foreseen. For example, the objectives of SCAR in relation to the marine living resources and minerals regimes will require definition. Until the boundaries are clarified, grey areas will multiply. As the example of telecommunications shows, it is not enough for the Consultative Parties to assert a monopoly of a topic unless they are also prepared to deal with it as and when the need arises.

What then is an acceptable definition of SCAR'S role? It is a received view that the Consultative Meetings deal with political and legal issues, whereas SCAR is taken to be the forum for the planning and coordination of scientific research attended only by scientists.[198] It is also seen as the advisory body of the Treaty nations, its conclusions being based on scientific considerations only.[199] Emphasis is placed on the Committee's independence.[200]

At the 1978 SCAR meeting, delegates discussed the relationship between the Committee and the Treaty governments. The issue has in fact repeatedly been canvassed by SCAR, but the Consultative Parties have shown little public interest in it, or indeed in any aspect of administration of the Antarctic system. SCAR considered that there was a clear-cut demarcation between, on the one hand, the concerns of the Treaty governments in problems of the future management of resources and, on the other, those of SCAR in its role as the authoritative source of scientific information on Antarctica. SCAR, it was said, has an important role as an independent forum where scientists and planners meet to discuss scientific programmes and to exchange ideas freely.

The Committee considered that it had a responsibility to provide scientific information which would assist governments to reach decisions about resource management, but that it should not advise governments on those issues.[201] At best it will prove difficult to make

197. Rec. X-3.
198. 'The Antarctic Treaty' (1972), 22(6) *New Zealand Foreign Affairs Review*, 19 at 29.
199. R.E. Guyer, 'The Antarctic System' (1973), 139 *Hague Recueil*, 149 at 191.
200. B. Roberts, 'International Co-operation for Antarctic Development: the Test for the Antarctic Treaty' (1978), 19(119) *Polar Record*, 107 at 118.
201. XV-SCAR-32 (Revised)(May 1978) in 397 *SCAR Circular* (3 July 1978).

such distinctions. The principle objective of BIOMASS is 'to gain a deeper understanding of the structure and dynamic functioning of the Antarctic marine ecosystem as a basis for the future management of potential living resources'.[202] Countries applying for SCAR membership must agree to comply with the principles of protection of the environment recommended by SCAR.[203] If SCAR views itself as the authoritative source of scientific advice on Antarctica, and in addition as dedicated to the safeguarding of the environment, the Committee will presumably make known its views on the inferences to be drawn from BIOMASS on vital issues such as the quantification of the standing stock of krill and the relationship between krill harvesting and the future of the whale species.

EAMREA was set up by SCAR at the request of the Consultative Parties, who invited an assessment of the possible impact on the environment of the Treaty Area and related ecosystems if mineral exploration and/or exploitation were to occur there.[204] Even at the modest level of indicating gaps in scientific knowledge and pointing out research needs, the assessment constituted advice on resource management issues. The SCAR Group of Specialists on Living Resources of the Southern Ocean is deploying an impressive array of experts on krill to plan BIOMASS.[205] No doubt the scientists will reach authoritative conclusions affecting krill management, and it may be assumed that these will be put forward by SCAR, just as the Committee has advanced conservation principles in relation to the Agreed Measures and pelagic sealing. The 1978 statement of SCAR on its relationship to the Treaty governments is unlikely to be carried out in practice.

Considerable emphasis is laid upon the independence and non-political nature of SCAR, an assertion which, although often reiterated, is somewhat surprising. All the Consultative Parties are represented by national SCAR members, and there is no national member of SCAR which is not either a Consultative Party or a Contracting Party which has announced its intention to become a Consultative Party in the near future. Both Poland and West Germany joined SCAR in order to become Consultative Parties.

The national SCAR committees set up in compliance with the Constitution of SCAR are to a considerable degree influenced by governments. Working Groups contain numerous civil servants,

202. Group of Specialists on Living Resources of the Southern Ocean, *Biological Investigations of Marine Antarctic Systems and Stocks (BIOMASS)*, Vol. I (1977), 5.
203. Standing Resolutions, Section 1(2).
204. Rec. VIII-14.
205. 409 *SCAR Circular* (22 July 1979).

whose presence is especially noteworthy in Geodesy and Cartography, Logistics and Meteorology. Generally Antarctic transport and bases are supported by governments which can veto any unwelcome SCAR proposal by refusing logistic support. Much of the scientists' direct funding is from governments.

SCAR accepts the Consultative Parties' interpretation of the Treaty, and does not obtain opinions from other sources: a clear example is the advice given at the 1975 Consultative Meeting to the President of SCAR that the Agreed Measures could be applied to offshore areas.[206] In this instance both the original narrow interpretation of Article VI and the 1975 revision had been formulated by the Consultative Parties and accepted by SCAR.

As a matter of course, SCAR responds to recommendations of Consultative Meetings addressed to it. Its meetings are held in the year following Consultative Meetings. SCAR is therefore usually taking action on recommendations which do not yet bind the Consultative Parties themselves. For example EAMREA was established in response to Recommendation VIII-14 in 1976, and made a report in August 1977 although the Recommendation was not yet effective. It is quite conceivable that SCAR might expend a considerable proportion of its scanty budget on responding to a recommendation which would then never come into force. Not only is the practice of SCAR difficult to justify in law, but it also suggests a very large measure of dependence on the Consultative Meetings. SCAR would be well within its rights to demand that the Consultative Parties take immediate action to adopt all recommendations requiring its advice.

Scientific grounds cannot however, justify the claim of SCAR to monopolise the planning of Antarctic science at the international level. For instance, UNEP has a good case for direct involvement with the Antarctic environment. Antarctic science has been isolated from the rest of the world for political reasons. The main function of SCAR is to take action at the behest of Consultative Meetings, and Treaty nations regard it as a shield against the intrusion of other international organisations such as UNEP.[207]

SCAR Consultative Party relations are very much a one-way street. Of particular concern in recent years has been the tendency for the Treaty nations to make very extensive and pressing demands on SCAR without apparent regard for the budgetary consequences.[208] To see SCAR as independent and apolitical is to

---

206. Discussed previously under Treaty/*Area*.
207. See previous discussion of Treaty/*Third Parties*.
208. F.M. Auburn, 'Offshore Oil and Gas in Antarctica' (1977), 20 *German Yearbook of International Law*, 139 at 152–3.

have regard only to the outward protestations of the interested parties. Increasing the work of SCAR dramatically over a short time-span has put the Committee in severe and continuing financial need. Although the Consultative Parties are ready to take much of the credit for SCAR's work,[209] they have not given any public indication that they are prepared to give it the resources needed for its expanded role. SCAR is a planning committee, not an international organisation.

209. For example, Item 13(vi), Final Report of the Ninth Antarctic Treaty Consultative Meeting (October 1977), 5–6.

6

JURISDICTION

Treaty Regime

Sovereignty represents the exclusive right to perform State functions over territory.[1] One of its highest forms is the exercise of jurisdiction. Today sovereignty has to be regarded no longer as a single concept but rather a bundle of different elements.[2] The distinction between multiple jurisdictional actions and sovereignty may be meaningless.

Jurisdiction is one of the major unsolved problems of the Antarctic system. At the Washington Conference, the United States, Japan, Norway and New Zealand, *inter alia*, supported jurisdiction based on nationality. Opposition from Argentina, Chile and France[3] resulted in the minimal necessary arrangements for observers and exchange scientists.[4] The sole relic of proposals for a general agreement is to be found in the listing of 'questions relating to the exercise of jurisdiction in Antarctica'[5] as a topic which may be discussed at Consultative Meetings.

Some countries, such as Norway, had seen this as a means of resolving the matter,[6] but it was not to be. At the 1962 Meeting, the United Kingdom proposed that a Committee of Experts nominated by the Consultative Parties be convened to formulate appropriate measures for submission to the next Meeting. Opposition, presumably from Argentina and Chile, led to withdrawal of the initiative. Although jurisdictional issues have continued to arise[7] they have been dealt with on an *ad hoc* basis.

The formal position of claimants is that jurisdiction is exercised in their Antarctic territories as it is elsewhere: 'If there were parking offences in such frozen wildernesses as Kaiser Wilhelm II Land or the Lars Christensen Coast they would be punished in the same way as if they were committed by a housewife in Civic Centre,

1. *Island of Palmas Case* (1928) 2 UNRIAA 829 at 838.
2. J.H.W. Verzijl, *International Law in Historical Perspective*, Vol. I (1968), 256.
3. A. Scilingo, *El Tratado Antártico* (1963), 94.
4. Art. VIII(1).
5. Art. IX(1)(e).
6. A. Scilingo, *El Tratado Antártico* (1963), 95.
7. So definition of the authority to issue permits almost deadlocked the negotiation of the Agreed Measures (T. Hanevold, 'The Antarctic Treaty Consultative Meetings-Form and Procedure' (1971), 6 *Cooperation and Conflict*, 197).

Canberra.'[8] Were matters so, the Treaty system would have rapidly been made inoperable. Claimants have not in fact enforced laws on expeditions of other nations within their Antarctic territories. Much emphasis has been placed on indirect sanctions. Military personnel can generally be dealt with by disciplinary measures and if necessary by court-martial,[9] while scientists receiving government grants for research may be placed under an obligation by their contractual conditions to observe the Treaty and recommendations. Tourist groups given access to national facilities are required to conform to the Agreed Measures,[10] and non-compliance may result in cancellation of permits.[11]

Where the necessity for enforcement is pressing, countries have made arrangements based on nationality. An interesting example is that of the Cape Royds Adélie penguin colony. This is the most southerly known penguin rookery, and is situated about 20 miles from the New Zealand and US bases on Ross Island. From 1956 numbers began to decline steeply due to a steady flow of 'congressmen, parliamentarians, journalists, diplomats, soldiers, sailors' visiting Antarctica as the guests of the two governments. In the summer of 1961 helicopter flights were recorded on almost every fine day, and each landing scattered penguins, breaking the breeding routine, exposing eggs and chicks to skua predation, and unsettling young birds seeking nest sites.[12] The situation was aggravated by the additional attraction to visitors of Shackleton's hut close to the colony.

Dr Bernard Stonehouse of the Canterbury University Antarctic Biology Unit, which had carried out the research, reported the decline and its causes to the Antarctic Division of the New Zealand Department of Scientific and Industrial Research.[13] The Division brought the matter up with the US Navy, which requested that Dr Stonehouse propose flying regulations.[14] It is noteworthy that the Division opposed 'prohibitive public notices in Antarctica' as the 'antithesis of the cooperative nature of our endeavours' and contrary to the 'spirit of the Antarctic Treaty' if issued on a unilateral

8. D. Horne, *The Next Australia* (1970), 205.
9. *Report of Operation Deep Freeze 69* (1969), 43.
10. An example is the United States which prescribed this condition before the : Measures became binding in US law.
11. Antarctic Division, DSIR, *Antarctic Operations Manual* (1975), 90.
12. B. Stonehouse, 'Counting Antarctic Animals', *New Scientist* (29 July 1965), 273 at 274.
13. B. Stonehouse, 'Penguins in High Latitudes' (1967), 15 *Tuatara*, 129.
14. B. Stonehouse, 'Animal Conservation in Antarctica' (1965), 23 (1) *NZ Science Review*, 3 at 6.

basis.[15] Restrictions on the use of helicopters were implemented by
the US Navy, and the decline in breeding pairs halted.[16] In 1969 part
of the area was turned into a visitor site under joint control of New
Zealand and the United States.[17]

Agreement on the Cape Royds rookery, like the establishment of
the McMurdo Land Management and Conservation Board,[18]
exemplifies the close cooperation between the two countries. New
Zealand, the claimant, conceded to the exercise of US jurisdiction
based on nationality. It will be pointed out that New Zealand is the
most lukewarm of the countries having a declared stake in the continent. But even the more active claimants could be deterred from
exerting jurisdiction over nationals of other Consultative Parties in
view of the possibility of the Treaty breaking down unless the matter
were to become one of national prestige. Until then the practical outcome is likely to be that the nationality principle will prevail.

Crime

Police authority is the major difficulty of jurisdiction. A resource
regime will have to provide some type of solution,[19] even if it proves
to be on an *ad hoc* basis. Its implementation would give rise to con-
frontations with countries such as the United States, which would
object to jurisdiction based on claims to sovereignty.[20] At the same
time, for the United States the question of domestic capacity to pro-
secute for Antarctic crimes has remained unresolved. In particular,
it has long been recognised that the criminal law is generally limited
to the territory of a State. Extra-territorial application is possible,
but must be clearly provided for in the statute. The legislation
extending the reach of US criminal law in a special maritime and territorial jurisdiction[21] covers the high seas, US vessels and aircraft,
US installations on land acquired for the country abroad, and guano

15. Letter from Superintendent, Antarctic Division to Commander, US Naval
    Support Force (4 October 1963).
16. R.B. Thomson, 'Effects of Human Disturbance on an Adélie Penguin Rookery
    and Measures of Control' in G.A. Llano(ed.), *Adaptations Within Antarctic
    Ecosystems* (1977), 1177 at 1179.
17. R.B. Thomson, 'United States and New Zealand Cooperation in Environmental
    Protection' (1971), 6(3) *Antarctic Journal*, 59 at 60.
18. See discussion of National Interests/*The United States*.
19. E. Hambro, 'Some Notes of the Future of the Antarctic Treaty Collaboration'
    (1974), 68 *AJIL*, 217 at 224.
20. J.H. Michel, Department of State in 'Extraterritorial Criminal Jurisdiction',
    Hearing, Subcommittee on Immigration, Citizenship and International Law,
    Committee on the Judiciary, H. Rep., 95th, Cong., 1st Sess. (21 July 1977), 66.
21. Section 7, Title 18, US Code.

islands. Apart from criminal conduct on US ships and aircraft in Antarctic waters and possibly at US stations, it would appear that the statute does not extend to cover Antarctica.[22]

In 1972 draft legislation was being prepared, but bills introduced in 1977 were not proceeded with. Despite the recognition of urgency by the State Department, the possibility of such an offence and the resulting international repercussions remained. US Navy commanders in Antarctica were well aware of the implications of criminal acts by civilians, and had there been any doubt as to the necessity for legislation, it should have been laid to rest with the *Escamilla Case*.[23]

The Naval Arctic Research Laboratory at Point Barrow, Alaska, was operated by the University of Alaska for the Office of Naval Research. Part of its work was carried out on Fletcher's Ice Island, T-3, which had an area of approximately 28 square miles at the relevant time. T-3 was 100 feet thick and consisted almost entirely of ice, probably originating from the shelf off Ellesmere Island. Less than 1 per cent of the ice island was made up of land matter. Escamilla and the other persons working on T-3 were US nationals.

On 16 July 1970 Fletcher's Ice Island was 300 miles from Greenland[24] and 200 miles off Canadian territory.[25] Apart from reading, games and films, there was little spare time activity.[26] Employees had made a practice of brewing wine from raisins and other fruit, and a dispute developed over a batch of raisin wine. Escamilla was holding a gun which discharged and killed Lightsey, the station manager. The incident took place at the height of the dispute between the United States and Canada over the latter's Arctic Waters Pollution Prevention Act, and for this reason Escamilla was taken back to the United States via the American base at Thule in Greenland. He was accused of the involuntary manslaughter of Lightsey, and was eventually acquitted.[27]

The prosecution was brought under the special maritime and territorial jurisdiction. At first instance the District Court held, after argument, that jurisdiction existed; no reasons were given and it has been asserted that the questions and comments of the judge clearly

22. R.B. Bilder, 'Control of Criminal Conduct in Antarctica' (1966), 52 *Virginia Law Review*, 231 at 254.

23. *US* v. *Escamilla* 467 F. 2d. 341 (1972).

24. Indictment, *US* v. *Escamilla*, US DC, Eastern District of Virginia, Alexandria Division, Crim. No. 210–70 – A.

25. 'Canada avoids legal wrangle in Arctic death', *Globe and Mail*, Toronto (20 August 1970).

26. C.O. Holmquist, 'The T-3 Incident' (September 1972), *US Naval Institute Proceedings*, 45 at 48.

27. D. Pharand, *The Law of the Sea of the Arctic* (1973), 200.

conveyed the uncertainties in his own mind.[28] On appeal the Court was equally divided on the issue, and therefore affirmed the holding of the District Court.[29] Sovereignty over T-3 was not directly in question, because the United States had occupied the ice island since 1952,[30] a State Department official agreeing that there was no US claim.[31] Reliance was placed on President Taft's refusal to acknowledge Peary's claim to the North Pole. Although covered by several feet of floating ice the North Pole is situated over the high seas.[32] No specific assertion had been made by Canada in respect of T-3, and the Court of Appeals described T-3 as an 'unclaimed island of ice'.[33] Canada, in a note sent on the day the District Court decided the issue, reserved its position on jurisdiction over the alleged offence. It would not object to having the drifting ice formation in question treated as a ship for the purposes of the particular legal proceedings concerned in order to facilitate the course of justice, and if it were considered necessary for the purposes of the legal proceedings, the Canadian government would waive jurisdiction.[34] This communication absolved the Court of the need to examine the international law issues between Canada and the United States.

In form the jurisdictional issue turned solely on the interpretation of the US legislation,[35] but the arguments have implications at the international level. T-3 could have been treated as a vessel, thus bringing the situation squarely within the terms of the statute. An additional advantage of this construction would have been the avoidance of any conflict with Canada. Ice islands could be seen as a new way of navigating and possibly of occupying the sea.[36] However, the prosecution specifically argued that T-3 was not a vessel,[37] the primary reason apparently being the definition of the Federal Code by which a vessel is 'every description of watercraft or other *artificial* contrivance used, or capable of being used, as a means of transportation on water'.[38] Taking into account the strict

28. A.G. Ronhovde, *Jurisdiction over Ice Island: The Escamilla Case in Retrospect* (1972), 3.
29. *US* v. *Escamilla* 467 F. 2d., 341 at 343 (1972).
30. D. Pharand, 'State Jurisdiction over Ice Island T-3: The *Escamilla* Case' (1971), 24 *Arctic*, 83 at 86.
31. Brief for Appellee, *US* v. *Escamilla*, A18-A19.
32. F.M. Auburn, *The Ross Dependency* (1972), 46.
33. *US* v. *Escamilla* 467 F. 2d. 341 at 343 (1972).
34. Note from the Canadian Embassy to the Department of State (5 May 1971).
35. E.M. Silverstein, 'United States Jurisdiction: Crimes Committed on Ice Islands' (1971), 51 *Boston University Law Review*, 77 at 81.
36. D. Pharand, 'The Legal Status of Ice Shelves and Ice Islands in the Arctic' (1969), 10 *Les Cahiers de Droit*, 463 at 474–5.
37. Brief for Appellee, *US* v. *Escamilla*, at p. 33.
38. L.W. Aubry, 'Criminal Jurisdiction over Arctic Ice Islands: *United States* v.

construction of criminal statutes[39] and the further implications of holding T-3 to be a vessel,[40] one can understand the prosecution's refusal to rely on this argument.

The special maritime jurisdiction covers vessels and the high seas. It could not therefore have been argued that T-3 was an island. Even if this contention had been open, by way of analogy with land territory, the prosecution would have had to face the problem that the United States had not claimed T-3.[41] However, it was argued that the ice island constituted high seas in frozen form.[42] There was no scientific basis for this view because T-3 was almost entirely formed from glacier ice; yet, once the vessel argument was rejected, high seas jurisdiction seemed the most likely approach. If so, the District Court heard the case on reasoning excluded by the Canadian note and contrary to that government's apparent desire to retain the option of relying on the sector theory for ice-covered areas.[43]

A variant on the high seas argument would have been to base jurisdiction on the United States nationality of all parties involved, but while nationality may be relied on under international law in unusual circumstances,[44] the statute under review in *Escamilla* did not advert to such a basis of jurisdiction. As an argument of last resort it was contended that only the United States was in a position to apprehend and punish such criminals,[45] but the facts suggest otherwise. Canadian criminal jurisdiction could have been supported[46] at least as well as that of the United States, and Canada's record of Arctic law enforcement indicates that offenders have been tried in the most difficult climatic conditions.[47] The United States took extraordinary measures to avoid the necessity of landing with Escamilla in custody at the logical refuelling stop at Alert, Ellesmere Island, solely because it wished to avoid jurisdictional controversy with Canada.[48]

Escamilla' (1975), 4 *UCLA-Alaska Law Review*, 419 at 437.

39. D. Wilkes, 'Law for Special Environments: Ice Islands and Questions raised by the T-3 Case' (1972), 16(100) *Polar Record*, 23 at 26.

40. Who would have been the owner? Would the owner be responsible if T-3 became a hazard to navigation? (F.M. Auburn, *The Ross Dependency* (1972), 55–6).

41. D.A. Cruickshank, 'Arctic Ice and International Law: The Escamilla Case' (1971), 10 *Western Ontario Law Review*, 178 at 190.

42. Brief for Appellee, *US* v. *Escamilla*, at p. 12.

43. See previous discussion of *Tootalik* (Sovereignty/*Ice*).

44. D. Wilkes, 'Law for Special Environments: Ice Islands and Questions raised by the T-3 Case' (1972); 16 (100) *Polar Record*, 23 at 24.

45. Brief for Appellee, *US* v. *Escamilla*, at p. 33.

46. D.A. Cruickshank, 'Arctic Ice and International Law: The Escamilla Case' (1971), 10 *Western Ontario Law Review*, 178 at 191–2.

47. See previous discussion of Sovereignty/*Arctic Sectors*.

48. C.O. Holmquist, 'The T-3 Incident' (September 1972), *US Naval Institute*

Escamilla is of considerable interest for Antarctic law. With the possibility of commercial oil exploration in the Antarctic, the depiction of life is relevant: 'T-3 in some ways was like the wild west. Men were brewing their own wine; there were no practical limits over consumption of alcohol on the island. There were more guns than people knew what to do with: for polar bears, but there were too many guns. They depended on the authority of the leader. The leader, on the night of the killing, was drunk himself, according to the autopsy.'[49]

Removal of Escamilla from the ice island was a unique feat involving the refuelling of a helicopter over the Arctic Ocean.[50] If a serious offence were to be committed during the Antarctic winter, particularly at a remote inland station, immediate access by plane might be possible but would be both unusual and dangerous. Even a winter landing at the coastal station of McMurdo is regarded as hazardous and justified only in a critical medical emergency.[51] To risk the lives of a plane crew for the sole purpose of law enforcement, which could in any case be carried out with the advent of summer, would be a decision which any government would be most reluctant to take. On the other hand, the prospect of restraining a possibly mentally disturbed murderer in a small and remote Antarctic base for three or four months would pose obvious problems of safety and morale for the station leader. Detention of the suspect on the spot might be questionable in law if civilians or scientists were involved.

Escamilla concerned only United States citizens. If the offender and victim had not been of the same nationality the difficulties would have been compounded. A major lesson from *Escamilla* is that governments cannot prevent serious offences in isolated regions such as the Arctic and Antarctic, nor can they rely upon the traditionally peaceful mien of scientists and research workers. Exercise of criminal jurisdiction is a direct challenge to sovereignty and could well lead to a confrontation with claimants. The death of Lightsey came at a particularly difficult juncture in Canadian-US relations. This should serve as a warning for the Antarctic.

In September 1969 the Humble Oil Co. sent the SS *Manhattan*, an oil tanker specially strengthened for ice navigation, through the

Proceedings, 45 at 50.

49. J.W. Williams, 'Legal Implications: Jurisdiction' in G.S. Schatz(ed.), *Science, Technology and Sovereignty in the Polar Regions* (1974), 55. Mr Williams appeared for the US in *Escamilla*.

50. *US* v. *Escamilla* 467 F. 2d. 341 at 345 (1972).

51. 'United States Airmen break Antarctic Winter Barrier' (1964), 3 *Antarctic*, 480 at 481.

Northwest Passage to Prudhoe Bay, Alaska.[52] Although the tanker was escorted by the Canadian Department of Transport icebreaker *John A. Macdonald*, Canadian sensitivity to US activities in the Arctic was aroused. In April 1970 two bills were introduced to the Canadian Parliament. One, an amendment to the Territorial Sea and Fishing Zone Act, enlarged the territorial sea to 12 miles, thus covering Prince of Wales Strait through which the *Manhattan* had passed. The other was the Arctic Waters Pollution Prevention Act, relating to waters adjacent to the mainland and islands of the Canadian Arctic within the areas enclosed by 60°N, 141°W and a line measured seaward from the nearest Canadian land for a 100 miles.[53] Shipping safety control zones could be prescribed and navigation in those zones prohibited unless safety conditions were complied with.[54] At the same time, a new declaration under the Statute of the International Court of Justice made a specific exception for 'disputes . . . in respect of prevention or control of pollution or contamination of the marine environment in marine areas adjacent to the coast of Canada'.

The United States countered that there was no international law basis for such a unilateral extension of jurisdiction, and particularly complained of the reservation to the Optional Clause.[55] A heated debate developed between the two countries and quickly spread to the commentators. Canada stressed the uniquely vulnerable Arctic environment[56] and the undeveloped state of international law relating to oil pollution. US views were most concerned at unilateral jurisdiction 100 miles offshore,[57] a significant setback to the American opposition to zones of extended sovereignty. Neither side had a flawless case. For example, a Canadian corporation, supported by the government, had been responsible for oil pollution incidents in the Arctic, and despite official statements, Canada's action was obviously motivated by fears for Arctic sovereignty. The United States, for its part, was on very weak ground in complaining of the Canadian reservation. On the Connally Amendment, Canada would have had little chance of bringing a case against the United States.

52. B. Keating, '*Manhattan* makes the Historic Northwest Passage' (March 1970), *National Geographic*, 374.
53. S. 3(1).
54. S. 12.
55. US Press Release (15 April 1970) in (1970) HC Deb. (Canada), 5923.
56. J.A. Beesley, 'Rights and Responsibilities of the Arctic Coastal States: The Canadian View' (1971), 3(1) *Journal of Maritime Law and Commerce*, 1 at 11.
57. L. Henkin, 'Arctic Anti-Pollution: Does Canada Make-or-Break International Law?' (1971), 65 *AJIL*, 131 at 135–6.

The Arctic Waters Pollution Prevention Act controversy has a number of lessons for Antarctica. Environmental issues were advanced in justification of extended jurisdiction with sovereignty implications. Canada and the United States generally have excellent international relations; yet this serious crisis arose from a very unlikely fear of US assertions. In the case of Antarctica the sovereignty issues would be quite clear. Development of oilfields was seen to be a vital factor in the crisis. Finally, the fortuitous and unavoidable *Escamilla Case* arose at the worst possible time for Canadian-US relations in the Arctic. Article IV of the Antarctic Treaty would be under the most severe strains in such a situation.

This dispute led Canada to press for specific measures to protect the Arctic environment at the Law of the Sea Conference. Coastal States may adopt non-discriminatory legislation to prevent, reduce or control marine pollution from vessels in ice-covered areas within the Exclusive Economic Zone (EEZ). The provision applies where particularly severe climatic conditions and the presence of ice covering such areas for most of the year create obstructions or exceptional hazards to navigation, and pollution of the marine environment could cause major harm to, or irreversible disturbance of, the ecological balance.[58] Such laws must be based on the best available scientific evidence.

Article 234 was drafted for the Arctic, but is of general application. For the Antarctic it would mean that only nations which have made claims to coastal areas could pass laws of this nature; therefore the usual method of carrying out recommendations under the Antarctic Treaty by domestic legislation of all Consultative Parties (where national implementation is required) would not be available. Nor would an international organisation established by a minerals regime come within Article 234.

Marriage

The special significance of the presence of women and children in Antarctica has already been pointed out.[59] In particular, reference was made to the celebration of a wedding at an Argentinian base. This marriage must be considered together with that performed by a Royal Canadian Mounted Police Inspector in 1973 on T-3, the bridegroom in the latter instance being a RCMP constable.[60] Both

58. Art. 234, Informal Composite Negotiating Text A. CONF. 62/WP. 10/Rev. 2 (11 April 1980).
59. See Sovereignty/*Polar Circumstances*.
60. 'Arctic Patrol includes Wedding' *Christian Science Monitor* (9 May 1973).

celebrations were specifically stated to have been carried out to support sovereignty claims. The novelty of an Antarctic wedding would seem to have motivated the celebration of nuptials in flight on a QANTAS aircraft in November 1978.[61]

The general principle for formal validity of marriage is that the law of the place of contracting governs,[62] but a question as to the legal effect of the ceremony would arise where recognition was at issue. With regard to claimant States, as with the Argentinian marriage at Esperanza Base, it would usually be accepted that the act was valid within the legal system of the country concerned. Recognition would be granted in States accepting the status of the claim, e.g. as between France and the United Kingdom, but not necessarily in other countries such as the United States.

Various solutions may be proposed. Where a marriage has been duly celebrated, a presumption in favour of validity arises.[63] Contentious proceedings would show that there had not been compliance with the rules of the place of celebration because the forum would hold the *situs* to be *res nullius*. Evidence of cohabitation as man and wife could be advanced, rebuttal of which would require cogent proof.[64] This doctrine can hardly be applied when the ceremony has clearly been carried out and a suitable certificate issued.

Perhaps the best prospect lies in the doctrine of the common law marriage.[65] It may be objected that people visiting Antarctica can quite easily marry before or after the trip. But the cases stress the impossibility of complying with local form without regard to the question whether a ceremony carried out in another jurisdiction would have been valid.[66] A modern precedent for the extension of the common law marriage doctrine to new circumstances is to be found in the Polish marriage cases.[67] Courts in a State which does not accept the validity of the relevant Antarctic claim would prefer such a solution, which avoids conflict with the foreign policy objectives of the government.

For marriages in aircraft over Antarctica the closest analogy is drawn from merchant ships on the high seas. There is wide inter-

61. J. Black (March/April 1979), 31 *Belle*.
62. *Berthiaume* v. *Dastous* [1930] AC 79 at 83. For documentation of widespread acceptance of this rule see E. Rabel, *The Conflict of Laws* (2nd edn, 1958), Vol. I, at 227–8.
63. *Jacombe* v. *Jacombe* (1961) 105 CLR 355 at 359.
64. *In re Taylor* [1961] 1 WLR 9.
65. *Wolfenden* v. *Wolfenden* [1946] P. 61.
66. *Isaac Penhas* v. *Tan Soo Eng* [1953] AC 304 (on the facts the deceased husband had travelled to England the year before the marriage and had there found a potential bride, whom he had not married due to his father's opposition).
67. *Merker* v. *Merker* [1963], P. 283.

national support for application of the law of the flag,[68] and that
legal system may then be invoked to recognise a common law marriage.[69] It has been stated that such instances are not necessarily relevant to aircraft, but this proposal was coupled with the suggestion
that the old common law form sufficed[70] and gave a similar result.

Tort

Tort law emphasises the *lex loci delicti* (law of the place where the
injury happened). England and other Commonwealth jurisdictions
demand that the act in question must not have been justifiable by the
law of the place where it was done.[71] The American Law Institute
rule for personal injury cases still gives first place to the *lex loci
delicti*.[72]

An early case suggested that an action could be maintained in England for a tort committed on the Labrador coast at a time when there
were no local courts; otherwise an injury could be done without
redress.[73] One may extend such views to decide which legal system
governs the issues (choice of law). In explanation of the origin of the
rule in *Phillips* v. *Eyre* it was pointed out that one Englishman
wrongfully injuring another in a primitive or unsettled territory
where there is no law of torts could still sue in English courts.[74]
Holmes J. would not apply the *lex loci* where a tort was committed in
a region having no sovereign,[75] an uncivilised country or in one
having no law that civilised countries would recognise as adequate.
If such were the case, a New York court would apply the substantive
law of the country which is most closely connected with the parties
and their conduct.[76] If a legal system refers a litigant to the law of an
area which has no law, there would be reason to dispose of the case
according to the internal law of the referring system.[77] On the same
lines it has been proposed that torts in 'insulated environments' such
as the Antarctic should be dealt with under the law of the place where
the members of the expedition came from.[78]

68. *Fisher* v. *Fisher* 61 ALR 1523 at 1527 (1929).
69. L. Palsson, *Marriage and Divorce in Comparative Conflict of Laws* (1974), 295.
70. A.D. McNair, *The Law of the Air* (2nd edn, 1953), 143.
71. Willes J. in *Phillips* v. *Eyre* (1870) LR 6 QB 1, at 28–9.
72. Restatement Second, *Conflict of Laws* (1971), 430.
73. Lord Mansfield in *Mostyn* v. *Fabrigas* (1774) 1 Cowp., 161 at 181.
74. Lord Pearson in *Chaplin* v. *Boys* [1971] AC 356 at 396 and 401.
75. *American Banana Co.* v. *United Fruit Co.* 53 L. Ed. 826 at 832 (1909).
76. *Walton* v. *Aramco*, 233 F. 2d., 541 at 545 (1956).
77. E.N. Griswold, 'Renvoi Revisited' (1938), 51 *HLR*, 1165 at 1193.
78. O.Kahn-Freund, 'Delictual Liability and the Conflict of Laws' (1968), 124 *Hague Recueil*, 1 at 83.

So far so good. As long as all parties to a suit are from the same law-district, there will be little difficulty in applying what appears to be a common-sense conclusion, but this view does not resolve the case of persons from different jurisdictions. Due to the extensive nature of international cooperation in the Antarctic, it is common to have various nationalities at one base. For instance scientists from Australia, France, the Soviet Union and the United States were engaged in research at Dome C in Wilkes Land in 1979.[79] In such a case the first question to be asked would be whether the tort had a substantial or predominant connection with a particular jurisdiction. The hypothetical example may be taken of a multi-national search for fossils in which logistic support is provided by the United States. If a French mechanic taking part in a French scientific team were injured while repairing US equipment, the action could involve the liability of the US mechanics alleged to have negligently maintained the machinery previously, the US contractor operating the equipment and, further, of the vendors and manufacturers in America. It could very well be argued that the balance would lie with choice of the law of one of the US states. For the most difficult situations in which the contacts with the jurisdictions are evenly distributed, it may be pointed out that the courts have faced similar issues in the ordinary run of conflict cases and resolved them by devices such as a preference for the *lex fori*.

Even in the courts of a jurisdiction which does not recognise any Antarctic claim, there is still the possibility of invoking rules relevant to the *locus delicti*. Decisions of SCAR, recommendations, final reports of Consultative Meetings and bi-national arrangements such as the McMurdo Land Management and Conservation Board[80] provide a body of rules accepted by some or all of the non-claimants, and, at the least, such material should be utilised as evidence of a reasonable standard of care in Antarctic conditions. Use could similarly be made of established practices for the safety of field camps or reports of scientific and technical committees on operations procedures.

Some examples of issues may be cited. The US Department of Health, Education and Welfare was concerned that disposal of untreated sanitary wastes offshore at McMurdo and Palmer Stations was contrary to US Pollution Control Standards. To this the National Science Foundation responded that its polar activities were in technical compliance with the law, which directed obedience to 'environmental pollution control standards of general applicability

79. 'US science projects this summer' (1979), 8(12) *Antarctic*, 413 at 415.
80. Discussed previously under National Interests/*United States*.

in the host country or jurisdiction'. For Antarctica this was Recommendation VIII-11, the rather weak Code of Conduct for Expedition and Station Activities.[81] When the McMurdo nuclear reactor was dismantled, the question arose of what should be done with the soil which contained effluent. The Treaty forbids the disposal of 'radioactive waste materials' in Antarctica,[82] so for initial guidance as to the degree of radiation which constitutes 'radioactive', the American Navy surveyed the guidelines and regulations of the Antarctic Treaty nations for a standard.[83] A body of practice has developed on the conditions for entry of tourist groups to stations.[84] But these instances are few in number, and many matters remain to be dealt with. For instance, should tourist planes on day flights to Antarctica carry polar survival suits for all on board?[85]

In the absence of proof of foreign law, it is presumed to be identical to that of the forum.[86] If no tort liability exists according to the *lex loci delicti* because that legal system is not developed, it may also be contended that the *lex fori* alone applies. In jurisdictions with a substantial connection rule for foreign torts, the fact that the place of tort is 'uncivilized' will also permit the court to disregard the possible effect which the *lex loci delicti* might otherwise have on the case.[87] The presumption of identity could be used in courts which regard Antarctica as *res nullius*.

It is common for municipal law to forbid tort claims between members of the armed forces arising out of their duties, and to extend this immunity to the government concerned.[88] Such a rule is found in US law.[89] The Treaty permits military personnel to be used for scientific research and other peaceful purposes in Antarctica,[90] and Argentina, Chile and the United States make extensive use of military logistic support. At least one instance involving this issue has been before the courts.

The widow of a former US Navy man, apparently belonging to the Cargo Handling Battalion Detachment, unsuccessfully sued the Navy and the Veterans Administration for $1,300,000, alleging that

81. *US Antarctic Program Final Environmental Impact Statement* (1980).
82. Art. V(1).
83. 'McMurdo Station reactor site released for unrestricted use' (1980), 15(1) *Antarctic Journal*, 1 at 3.
84. See Environment/*Tourism*.
85. Ibid.
86. Lord Dunedin in *Dynamit Actiengesellschaft* v. *Rio Tinto Co.* [1918] AC 260 at 295.
87. *Walton* v. *Aramco* 233 F. 2d., 541 at 545 (1956).
88. For Australia see *Parker* v. *Commonwealth* (1965) 112 CLR 295 at 302–3.
89. *Feres* v. *US* 340 US 135 (1950).
90. Art. I(2).

her husband had died in 1973 from leukaemia contracted in unloading radioactive wastes from sea-going vessels 'and the disposal thereof upon Antarctica.[91] In reliance on *Feres*, the action was dismissed on the preliminary issue. By adjudication of the Veterans Administration, the man was held to have had service-contracted leukaemia.[92]

Under Article VIII(1) of the Treaty observers, exchange scientists and accompanying staff are subject only to national jurisdiction, a privilege which apparently enures in both criminal and civil cases. New Zealand legislation specifically endorses this view,[93] and Australian law contains a total exemption from 'the laws in force in the Territory'.[94] 'Laws in force' includes 'the principles and rules of common law and equity',[95] hence the privilege extends to civil actions. United Kingdom subordinate legislation prevents courts from exercising jurisdiction over the persons protected by the Treaty. The section refers to 'jurisdiction',[96] and the following section relating to United Kingdom observers has a side-note indicating that it applies to 'criminal jurisdiction'. It may be inferred that civil cases are covered by the exemption expressed in general words.

If the argument that Article VIII(1) of the Treaty covers torts is accepted, then those countries which are bound by the Treaty and whose general law extends to the Antarctic without any form of statutory exception for observers, exchange scientists and accompanying staff must avail themselves of means to persuade courts not to assume jurisdiction over exempt persons. For civil cases a defendant would seek a stay on the basis of *forum non conveniens* or its local equivalent.[97] Courts would presumably be reluctant to assume

---

91. *Reynolds* v. *Navy*, Complaint C-2-75-427, US District Court, Southern District of Ohio, Eastern Division. The allegation of waste disposal in Antarctica is surprising. It is presumed that the handling of wastes to be shipped from McMurdo, the site of the PM-3A reactor known as 'Nukey-Poo', to the United States was intended. While the deceased was handling cargo at McMurdo, the vessel *Wyandot* was loaded. On arrival at Lyttelton, New Zealand, a much increased radiation reading was taken at one spot close to a modified bolt on a container. Three persons from the New Zealand National Radiation Laboratory took wipe and test readings, concluding that none of the containers was leaking and the Master had nothing to worry about (DF 69 Misc. Ship Reports, Wyandot, at pp. 3–4).

92. Letter from Veterans Administration to Mrs I.K. Williams (5 July 1974).

93. S. 5(1), Antarctica Act 1960 ('. . . the Courts of New Zealand shall not have any jurisdiction whether civil or criminal . . .').

94. S. 4(1), Antarctic Treaty Act 1960 (C'wlth).

95. S. 6(1), Australian Antarctic Territory Act 1954–73 (C'wlth).

96. S. 3, The Antarctic Treaty Order in Council 1962, SI 1962/401.

97. Criminal immunity is clearly intended by Art. VIII(1). Where there is no statutory provision the matter could be dealt with by the entry of a *nolle prosequi*.

jurisdiction contrary to treaty, even though the treaty itself were not incorporated into municipal law.

Immunity is granted in respect of all acts or omissions occurring while the persons concerned are in Antarctica for the purpose of exercising their function.[98] There is no requirement that there be a causal connection between the function and the cause of action. The words 'in Antarctica' have been construed to mean south of 60°S in the New Zealand, Australian and South African legislation, but the United Kingdom Order-in-Council excludes the high seas. If courts of other countries not having legislation regarding Article VIII adopt the British approach in applying law, then observers and exchange scientists will be open to civil actions in respect of acts carried out on the high seas south of 60°S. For non-claimants, the high seas may extend to the coastline of the continent.[99]

Even those countries having specific legislation do not go further than the terms of the Treaty in defining the persons covered. Observers do not constitute a problem, because they must be designated by Consultative Parties.[100] Exchange scientists may be provided by any Contracting Party;[101] it has been a common practice for Consultative Parties to have scientists from Contracting Parties in their expeditions (e.g. East Germans, in the Soviet programme).[102] The Treaty does not require designation of exchange scientists, nor does it furnish any means of deciding whether a particular national of a Contracting Party present at the station of another party to the Treaty comes within the meaning of Article III(1)(*b*). Immunity is also conferred upon 'members of the staffs accompanying' observers and exchange scientists[103] without further definition or any need for designation.

Immunity does not extend to all nationals of one Treaty party carrying out tasks or research at the facilities of another party. If a US ice-drilling project were to include say three persons from New Zealand − a biologist, a drilling specialist and the latter's assistant − the biologist would be an exchange scientist but it is not clear that the drilling specialist would so qualify. Nor could he be regarded as accompanying staff of the biologist, because the specialist would function independently of the control or presence of the biologist. The assistant would then not be entitled to immunity.

98. Art. VIII(1).
99. See the previous discussion of Treaty/*High Seas*.
100. Art. VII(1).
101. Art. III(1).
102. 'East German base planned' (1979), 8(10) *Antarctic*, 355.
103. Art. VIII(1).

Conducting a drilling programme on sea-ice[104] would raise the further issue of the high seas.

The Treaty requires that exempt persons be subject only to the jurisdiction of the Contracting State of which they are nationals. Recognition or enforcement of a judgment secured contrary to this provision of the Treaty should not be given by a party to the Treaty.

Property

For torts arising in *res nullius*, national laws offer a possible solution. One or more legal systems are available for choice. Land rights present more difficult issues. Immovables are governed by the *lex situs*, and it has been widely accepted that courts should not entertain actions to determine rights to foreign immovables.[105] Mining rights may be classified as immovables.[106].

Spitsbergen, before Norwegian sovereignty was recognised by the treaty of 1920,[107] was regarded as *res nullius*. A draft statute of 1912 prepared by Norway, Sweden and Russia contained a declaration to this effect.[108] Miners from several countries staked claims before 1920 by possession, working of tracts and notification to the governments of which they were nationals. On the basis of an examination of the correspondence concerning the Boston-based Arctic Coal Company and other miners, it has been stated that rights were acquired at international law[109] and confirmed by the treaty.[110] Recording of claims with governments was also carried out by Norway and Britain.[111]

A general argument based on the Spitsbergen precedent involves comparison of the practice of other concerned States. With regard to Britain, it was asserted that the Foreign Office showed little inclination to protect her subjects and none at all to encourage their claims.[112] There did not appear to be any effective means of resolving disputed claims which were common.[113] Each company established itself as if it were a sovereign, and followed the rules which pleased

104. Such as the McMurdo Sound Sediment and Tectonic Study ('New Zealand field work begins' (1979), 8(12) *Antarctic*, 406).
105. For England see *Hesperides Hotels* v. *Muftizade* [1978] 3 WLR 378.
106. Hodson L.J. in *Re Trepca Mines* [1960] 1 WLR 1273 at 1277.
107. Art. 1, (1924) 18 *AJIL* Supp. 199.
108. M. Ydit, *Internationalised Territories* (1961), 35.
109. L.F.E. Goldie, 'A General International Law Doctrine for Seabed Regimes' (1973), 7 *International Lawyer*, 796 at 810.
110. Ibid., at p. 811.
111. Ibid., at p. 813.
112. R.N. Rudmose Brown, *Spitsbergen* (1920), 286.
113. Ibid., at p. 229.

itself.[114] Support by States for their nationals' miners rights in Spitsbergen must be taken with the widespread acceptance by European powers in the nineteenth century that land interests of their citizens could validly be traced to transactions with native chiefs before cession.[115] This was the case even though the native law had no provision for the alienation of land.[116] Political protection of miners' interests does not necessarily connote general acceptance of miners' rights to *res nullius* at international law.

One court decision does uphold such rights. The Arctic island of Jan Mayen was declared Norwegian territory in 1929 having previously been regarded by that country as *res nullius*. In 1930 the Norwegian Supreme Court held that the prior rights of a private person to part of the island acquired by notification in 1920 and occupation in 1921 prevailed over the claim of the government to the same tract.[117] The plaintiff's argument was based on international law, and the Supreme Court invoked the effective occupation test. It is not clear how an individual's claim regarded as invalid by his government could have any effect in international law. The decision related to the competing claims of a Norwegian citizen and the government before a Norwegian court. Proclamation of sovereignty, presumably on the basis of prior occupation, would itself indicate ratification of the rights of the occupier. If this were so, then the case is akin to the nineteenth-century doctrine of miners' rights by discovery, which is to be found in a number of municipal legal systems.

The defendant's rights in this case arose from occupation by the Norwegian Meteorological Institute, a state organ. Norway informed the United States of the occupation and 'annexation' of the island by the Meteorological Institute, and assumed, although contending that Jan Mayen was *res nullius*, that no other power could annex the island.[118] The government was therefore asserting the rights of one of its own agencies to further its inchoate title at international law. In contrast to the arguments advanced regarding official support for miners' rights in Spitsbergen, the State Department advised a New York company in 1926 that general recognition of the status of Jan Mayen as *res nullius* made it impossible to

---

114. R. Waultrin, 'La Question de la Souveraineté des Terres Arctiques' (1908) 15 *Revue Général de Droit International Public* 78 at 110. A company trading in rubber on the Colombia – Peru border was held to have no rights 'except those of force' (*Re Peruvian Amazon Co.* (1913), 29 TLR 384).

115. *George Rodney Burt Claim* (1924), 18 *AJIL* 814.

116. *William Webster Claim* (1926), 20 *AJIL* 391.

117. *Jacobsen v. Norwegian Government* 1933–4 Ann. Dig. 109.

118. G.H. Hackworth, *Digest of International Law*, Vol. 1 (1940), 475.

acquire title to property there as ordinarily understood.[119]

Renewed interest in the issue arose from the filing in 1974 of a claim to exclusive mining rights over a seabed site in the North Pacific Ocean by Deepsea Ventures Inc.[120] The State Department refused to recognise the claim.[121] An opinion given to Deepsea Ventures argued that assertion of rights was consonant with the US and Norwegian diplomatic protection of their nationals' sites in Spitsbergen before 1920.[122] Rejection of the request by the State Department was apparently based upon an acceptance of the international legal regime for the deep seabed. Pending the outcome of the Law of the Sea Conference, the United States held that mining of the seabed beyond national jurisdiction could proceed as a high seas freedom.[123] In relation to the Spitsbergen precedent, it may be pointed out that the State Department refused recognition of exclusive rights and also denied diplomatic protection. Insofar as it is applicable to the general question of miners' rights in *res nullius*, the US position in 1974 contradicts the view that legal interests can be created. By 1974 there was general international consensus on the principle that the deep seabed would not be subject to national jurisdiction.

Antarctic practice has been to rely on limited expedients designed to avoid the legal issues. Tourists and non-governmental groups may only visit stations in Antarctica with the permission of the government concerned.[124] In some instances national expeditions have obtained permission to visit unoccupied bases of other countries (e.g. the Australian team which spent six days at Vostok in 1962),[125] but there have also been cases in which a request has not been made.

In 1959 the United States handed over Ellsworth Base to Argentina and Wilkes to Australia – arrangements which were to have no effect on rights or claims asserted in Antarctica.[126] US Defense Department lawyers had then to deal with the question of the transfer of real estate in *res nullius*.[127] Custody of property, defined as equipment, buildings and supplies belonging to the US

---

119. Ibid., at p. 476.
120. (1975) 14 *ILM*, 51.
121. (1975) 14 *ILM*, 66.
122. Opinion of the Law Offices of Northcutt Ely, *International Law applicable to Deepsea Mining* (14 November 1974), 42–3.
123. (1975) 14 *ILM*, 66.
124. Rec. X-8.
125. 'Half century of visits south' (1978), 8(8) *Antarctic* 260.
126. M.M. Whiteman, *Digest of International Law*, Vol. 2 (1963), 1239–40.
127. *Antarctic Journal* (Jan. – Feb. 1966), 27.

government, was given to the recipient government. The property was to be used by it without charge or liability in any respect, and except for items consumed, lost, worn out by normal use or damaged, was to be returned, upon mutual arrangement, to the custody of the United States.[128] When the Ellsworth station was closed by Argentina, it was confirmed that the buildings which were the property of the United States were generally in good condition.[129]

'Perhaps nowhere, except in Antarctica, would so simple a solution prove acceptable.'[130] This may have been the case for the countries involved in the arrangement. In essence all the property concerned was dealt with on a contractual basis as if it were movable. Such reasoning would however have provided no solution for a dispute as to title over buildings, in which case it would be necessary, if the issue arose, to decide whether the structure concerned was an immovable. It would appear that air-transportable huts used for seasonal camps would be movables, but that if the same huts should be left on the spot, utilised for a number of years, and then stocked with supplies for future use in an emergency, classification as immovables might seem appropriate. Many of the buildings used at stations are prefabricated and of unclear legal status.

The Ellsworth and Wilkes custody arrangements avoided the property problem by dealing with the issue as one of contract. As the parties were governments, any dispute would have been settled by political negotiation. But if private business ventures should utilise land or buildings in Antarctica for any length of time, they will require secure tenure. Easily accessible ice-free coastal sites with safe anchorages are at a premium in the Antarctic. From the lawyer's point of view, such an enterprise would be best advised to obtain a lease from a claimant State, because any form of contract with a non-claimant government in relation to immovables would be of doubtful validity, even in the municipal law of the grantor State. As the non-claimant would not assert or recognise any rights over the site at international law, it would have difficulty in justifying any grant of rights. There would also be a danger of violating Article IV(2) of the Treaty.

---

128. Custody Arrangement for Occupancy and Use of Certain United States Government – Navy Department Facilities at Ellsworth Station, Antarctica (2 February 1959).
129. Ellsworth (Argentina Antarctica) Scientific Station Closing Act (30 December 1962).
130. *Antarctic Journal* (Jan. – Feb. 1966), 27.

Standards

Standards of behaviour demanded by the law will require adaptation to meet the special conditions of Antarctica. Some claimants have legislated for their territories insofar as is applicable, but even without a specific statutory direction it would appear logical to require suitable changes.

One of the grounds on which the Court of Appeals ordered a new trial in *Escamilla* was that the trial judge had directed the jury that United States law was applicable in 'identically the same manner' as if the crime had been committed in North Virginia. The Court of Appeals stated that what was negligent in Virginia might not be negligent on T-3 which had no government authority and no police force, and was relatively inaccessible from the rest of the world, lacked medical facilities and facilities for securing the safety of property. If those present did not behave with self-restraint and the group leader was ineffective, the ice island became a place where no recognized means of law enforcement existed and each man had to look to himself for the immediate enforcement of his rights.[131] The defence placed considerable emphasis on this passage in the retrial.[132]

In the Canadian Arctic a series of modern cases dealing with Eskimos suggests some of the modifications needed. In one instance the wife of a hunter at a camp 200 miles from the nearest settlement became insane, tore up tents and destroyed equipment and boats. In desperation, members of the group were delegated to kill her.[133] Witnesses stated that white people in similar circumstances would have felt forced to do the same thing.[134] Although there are a number of reasons for distinguishing particular aspects of these cases, such as the different relations between men and women that prevail among the Eskimos,[135] one major factor is clearly of utility in the Antarctic, namely the isolation and harsh weather.

For criminal law it would be argued that the effect of polar circumstances should be to mitigate the usual application of rules. In tort the opposite result could be obtained for certain causes of action. Despite the apparently routine nature of current Antarctic

131. *US* v. *Escamilla* 467 F. 2d. 341 at 347 (1972).
132. 'Arctic killing suspect freed', *Washington Post* (3 November 1972).
133. D.A. Schmeiser, 'Indians, Eskimos and the Law' (1968), 33 *Saskatchewan Law Review*, 19 at 29.
134. W.G. Morrow, 'Law and the Thin Veneer of Civilization' (1971), 10 *Alberta Law Review*, 38 at 41.
135. B. Tierney, ' "Mr. Justice" in the North' (1971) 2(3) *Journal of the Canadian Bar Association*, 1 at 3.

operations, accidents are frequent and loss of life is not uncommon. Strict rules are prescribed for field operations, including the mandatory maintenance of radio schedules with the base, proper equipment, minimum numbers, and organisation of a fully prepared back-up rescue team.[136] Failure to observe such requirements could well be seen, having regard to the dangerous nature of Antarctic work, as civil negligence.

---

136. Antarctic Division, Department of Scientific and Industrial Research, *Antarctic Operations Manual* (1975), 52–3.

7
KRILL

The Resource

The Antarctic Treaty was based on the assumption that the area did not hold resources likely to be exploited in the near future. However, current exploration and research demonstrate that in krill the Southern Ocean contains the world's largest fishery stock. Antarctic krill are crustaceans with a maximum length of 6 cm. found in swarms in the upper 200 metres of the water column.[1] Although scientific investigation with a view to ultimate exploitation has been carried out for the past twenty years, it is only in the last five years that the emergence of a large-scale commercial fishery has become apparent. The Conference on the Conservation of Antarctic Marine Living Resources held at Canberra in May 1980 concluded a comprehensive treaty applicable to the whole ecosystem.

At the 1975 Consultative Meeting, there was no apparent concern for the urgent preparation of a suitable regime: the parties recommended studies which could lead to the development of effective measures for the conservation of marine living resources in the Treaty Area.[2] This leisurely approach had completely disappeared by the time the next Meeting was held in September 1977, when a detailed recommendation was agreed upon. Its most unusual feature was that a definitive regime should be concluded before the end of 1978.[3] To draft a fishing regime for a major stock within one year would be a considerable international achievement in the best of circumstances, but for the Consultative Parties to agree to take such speedy action on a highly controversial issue raising unprecedented strains on the Antarctic Treaty, the pressures must have been substantial. Furthermore, the decision to admit Poland to Consultative status and provide for future new entrants was another major innovation taken only three months previously and concluded with great haste.[4] Acceptance of Poland, whose main interest in the Antarctic lies in krill harvesting, was a necessary pre-condition to the subsequent agreement on negotiation of a living resources regime.

One impetus to speedy action came from the changing nature of

1. I. Everson, *The Living Resources of The Southern Ocean* (1977), 1.
2. Rec. VIII-10.
3. Rec. IX-2.
4. See the detailed discussion under Antarctic System/*Consultative Status*.

world fishery patterns. Traditional distant fishing stocks were declining under the pressure of expanding fleets, and a vital element in the continuing negotiations at the Third United Nations Conference on the Law of the Sea from 1973 onwards was the gradual acceptance of a 200 mile Exclusive Economic Zone. With regard to fisheries, the United States' enactment of the Fishery Conservation and Management Act in 1976, establishing a 200 mile fishery conservation zone, was a turning-point in the evolution of customary international law. Decreasing yields and partial or total exclusion from the new offshore zones forced nations with large distant fishing fleets to seek new stocks.

A second factor in the decision at the 1977 Consultative Meeting was the growing fear of action by countries and organisations outside the Treaty framework. Several nations engaged in krill research were not signatories to the Treaty, and FAO interest was demonstrated by the proposal for a ten-year research programme, halted by the Consultative Parties in 1977. Even more dangerous, from the Treaty viewpoint, was the possibility that developing countries might seek to have krill declared a common heritage resource, either within the context of the Law of the Sea negotiations or as part of the wider campaign for a New International Economic Order.[5] It was therefore no accident that the mineral recommendation of 1977 endorsed the principle that the Consultative Parties 'should not prejudice the interests of all mankind in Antarctica',[6] but the living resources recommendation[7] did not contain any such formula.

Another relevant consideration was that interest in krill accelerated in the 1976–7 season,[8] both because of an increase in research effort from nations already involved and through the entry of further countries. Particular significance should be attached to the decisions by Poland and West Germany to begin large-scale krill research, coupled with accession to Consultative status under the Antarctic Treaty. It became apparent that any of the countries engaged in exploratory fishing were capable of mounting a considerable effort and increasing the size of the fishery very quickly. Once the total catch reached a million tons (and this could be achieved by a single nation) the fishery would tend to expand rapidly to its ultimate capacity.[9] Negotiation of a treaty to regulate a substantial existing fishery would be much more difficult than the

5. Both matters were examined under Treaty/*Third Parties*.
6. Rec. IX-1.
7. Rec. IX-2.
8. Tetra Tech., *The Antarctic Krill Resource: Prospects for Commercial Exploitation* (1978), 74.
9. I. Everson, *The Living Resources of the Southern Ocean* (1977), 28.

devising of a regime before the commercial exploitation stage. Failing immediate action by the Consultative Parties, there was the serious possibility of a fundamental dispute between them. Antarctic 200 mile zones cover much of the most desirable krill-harvesting grounds, and unless claimants made some attempt to enforce their laws in the Exclusive Economic Zone, their already dubious territorial positions would be seriously weakened. This threat in turn could undermine the delicate compromise represented by Article IV of the Antarctic Treaty and put the viability of the Treaty itself in doubt.

Although discussion of an arrangement for Antarctic minerals had begun earlier, the living resources issue was far more urgent. Large-scale krill trawling is well within the capability of current technology. Due in part to the extreme variability of the density of swarms estimates of the standing stock cover a wide range. On the low side, the total population is put at 180,000,000 to 200,000,000 tons. At the other end of the scale a figure of 1,350,000,000 tons has been proposed,[10] and it is of particular interest that the latter estimate was put forward in the Soviet Union, one of the nations most heavily committed to harvesting.

With such differences in standing stock estimates it is not surprising that there were initial suggestions of extremely large annual sustainable yields of up to 150,000,000 tons.[11] Some current proposals, even taking into account the absence of information on the ecosystem, suggest that well over 10,000,000 tons could safely be taken annually.[12] The size of the permissible yearly harvest is clearly a vital issue for the Antarctic living resources regime. First, an excessive take would in due course threaten the viability of the stock itself. Secondly, krill are the main food for fish, squid, penguins, crabeater and leopard seals and fin, blue, sei, humpback and minke whales. Killer and sperm whales consume fish, seals and cephalopods. The dependence of so many predators on one prey group is a very unusual ecological situation.[13] Establishment of a major fishery at such a low level in the food chain is unprecedented, and even a regional effort with a harvest well below the lowest projected sustainable yield could have serious effects on dependent species. Apart from the unpredictable outcome of an uncontrolled harvest on the

10. K.A. Green, *Role of Krill in the Antarctic Marine Ecosystem* (1977), 17.
11. Tetra Tech. *The Antarctic Krill Resource: Prospects for Commercial Exploitation* (1978), 121.
12. Bogdanov cited in B. Mitchell and R. Sandbrook, *The Management of the Southern Ocean* (1980), 106.
13. Department of State, *Final Environmental Impact Statement for a Possible Regime for Conservation of Antarctic Living Marine Resources* (1978), 31.

ecosystem, such a fishery could easily constitute the world's largest catch and might even equal the total global haul for all species. The fleet itself would have environmental impacts.

Locations of maximum commercial interest are in the vicinity of South Georgia, the South Orkney, South Sandwich (claimed by Argentina and the United Kingdom) and South Shetland Islands (claimed by Argentina, Chile and the United Kingdom). The Polish land station was established in this sector, and the West German base is being built there. Thus a major proportion of the resource is to be found within 200 miles of islands in the most disputed portion of Antarctica.

Considerable research has been carried out on the processing and marketing of krill and its products. Whole krill has been sold in Japan on an experimental basis. Chile has test-marketed breaded krill sticks. For some years 'Ocean' krill paste was available in the Soviet Union, and krill is used in that country to enhance butter, cheese and other products and for salads, paté and pies. Soviet manufactured products include a shrimp butter, sausages and a cheese product ('*Korall*'). Krill meal and protein concentrate have been produced with the possibility of use in food aid programmes and sale in developing countries. Meal has been utilised for animal feed.[14] Commentators have pointed out the options of exploitation as a luxury food for rich nations, as fishmeal for pigs and chickens, and as food for hungry people.[15]

A number of technical difficulties have to be overcome. Once landed, krill spoil rapidly and suffer discoloration. In theory the best solution to this problem would be to hold the krill live, but this is not practical with existing catching systems.[16] Current technology therefore requires that the crustacea be frozen and undergo the first stages of processing on board ship. There have been problems with customer acceptance of krill products. Unacceptably high fluorine content means that direct human consumption is not recommended until an extraction process is perfected. Krill meal may be fed to animals at a concentration of up to 23 per cent.[17] It is widely assumed that, given the requisite effort, the technological issues can be surmounted.[18]

The remaining obstacle is economic. Vessels will have to be substantial. They will be used in large numbers and have to voyage over long distances to and from the fishing grounds. Fuel and processing

14. G.J. Grantham, *The Utilization of Krill* (1977), 34–45.
15. B. Mitchell and J. Tinker, *Antarctica and its resources* (1980), 93.
16. G.J. Grantham, *The Utilization of Krill* (1977), 20.
17. 'Fluorine in krill – a new challenge for research' (1980), 3 *BMFT Newsletter*, 24.
18. G.O. Eddie, *The Harvesting of Krill* (1977), 1.

will therefore be expensive. A high investment will be required,[19] and there will inevitably be losses of vessels and seamen in this remote and difficult environment. Provision would have to be made for the utilisation of the trawlers elsewhere during the Antarctic winter.

Profitability must depend on the end-use chosen for the product. Pastes would take a small volume at a high price, whereas meal offers the opposite choice. A recent economic analysis, assuming a free-market system, concluded that the only volume market is for meal. Existing meal sources such as fish and soya beans and new ones will set an upper limit to the price of krill meal, resulting in a return which would barely cover operating costs for 135 days at sea from a base in South America.[20] In view of the already substantial investment in harvesting, research and processing it may well be asked why countries are putting so much money into potentially unprofitable ventures. A number of explanations are possible. Among the reasons advanced, the more persuasive ones may be briefly mentioned. Current conclusions must of necessity rely on some assumptions regarding new technologies, a novel product and a market in the future. Centralised economies have to take into account factors which may not be relevant to a capitalist enterprise. General enforcement of 200 mile zones places a premium on fisheries not controlled by a coastal State. New entrants, such as the Peoples Republic of China, may harvest krill. While it is somewhat early to predict the long-term viability of a krill fishery, the concerted effort of a number of fishing nations in exploration, research, processing development and market trials suggest its strong likelihood.

The catch reported in 1977–8 was 122,000 tons and the figure for 1978–9 was presumably higher.[21] Of particular concern is the possibility that a large fishery could develop very rapidly through the redeployment of distant water fishing fleets resulting in a krill fishery of about 8 million tons 'almost overnight'.[22]

Sealing Convention

Negotiation of a resource regime by the Consultative Parties to the

19. G.J. Grantham, *The Utilization of Krill* (1977), 33.
20. S. McElroy in B. Mitchell and R. Sandbrook, *The Management of the Southern Ocean* (1980), 94.
21. B. Mitchell, 'The Politics of Antarctica' (1980), 22(1) *Environment*, 12 at 14.
22. I. Everson, 'Antarctic Fisheries' (1978), 19(120) *Polar Record*, 233 at 248. Such an effort would require the diversion of a very substantial proportion of existing distant water trawlers and this, of itself, may limit a sudden expansion (D.L. Alverson, 'Tug-of-War for the Antarctic Krill' (1980), 8(2) *Ocean Development and International Law Journal*, 171 at 180).

Antarctic Treaty had only one precedent, the Antarctic Sealing Convention, which was regarded as a model for future agreements.[23] Although pelagic seals were not subsequently exploited, this Convention was negotiated on the assumption that harvesting would occur. Reflecting the pre-1975 view of the Consultative Parties, the Agreed Measures which protect seals were taken not to apply offshore;[24] therefore the Convention applies to six seal species in the waters south of 60°S.[25] Catch limits are set for three species.[26] The Annex also contains provision for a closed season from March to August, when pelagic sealing is in any case impossible, and for protected species,[27] and specific details for the exchange of information.

Scientific advice is to be provided by SCAR.[28] Enforcement is solely a matter for the flag State.[29] There is no requirement for regular meetings of parties, but they may be held with the agreement of one-third of the parties. A meeting may establish a commission and provide for regulatory measures. However, the setting up of an effective system of control and inspection requires a two-thirds majority of the parties, including all original signatories. If commercial sealing reaches significant proportions, a two-thirds majority may set up a scientific advisory committee to assume some or all of the functions of SCAR.[30] A similar majority is needed to amend the Annex which contains detailed regulatory measures. Any party objecting to an amendment to the Annex is not bound by the new provision.[31]

Drafting of the Convention was carried out by the Consultative Parties to the Antarctic Treaty, most of whom had no intention of participating in any future harvesting. Although the actual Conference was held outside the Antarctic Treaty framework, only the Consultative Parties took part. The two features of negotiation of a separate treaty and monopolisation of drafting by the Antarctic Treaty Consultative Parties served as precedents for the living resources regime. Although quota limits were based on inadequate information,[32] at least a specific level had been set. Despite the

23. G. Knox, 'Antarctic resources' (July/August 1976), *NZ International Review*, 18 at 19.
24. This aspect of the Convention was discussed under Treaty/*Area*.
25. Art. 1.
26. The Crabeater (175,000); Leopard (12,000); Weddell (5,000) (Annex.).
27. The Ross, Southern Elephant and Fur seals.
28. Art. 5(4)(*b*).
29. Art. 2(2) and 5(5).
30. Art. 6.
31. Art. 9.
32. R. Frank in Senate Committee on Foreign Relations, *Report on the Convention*

United States' efforts, there is no international inspection procedure or regulatory body.[33] Particularly noteworthy is the veto, which may be exercised by any signatory over the establishment of an inspection system. There is no mention of national allocation of catch or effort. The seventh ratification needed to bring the Convention into force was filed six years after the adoption of the text of the treaty.

Conservation Principles

Analysis of the Convention for the Conservation of Antarctic Marine Living Resources must begin with the definition of the objective of the regime which is contained in three conservation principles:

(*a*) Prevention of decrease in the size of any harvested population to levels below those which ensure its stable recruitment. For this purpose its size should not be allowed to fall below a level close to that which ensures the greatest net annual increment.
(*b*) Maintenance of the ecological relationships between harvested, dependent and related populations of Antarctic marine living resources and the restoration of depleted populations to the levels defined in subparagraph (*a*), and
(*c*) Prevention of changes or minimization of the risk of changes in the marine ecosystem which are not potentially reversible over two or three decades, taking into account the state of available knowledge of the direct and indirect impact of harvesting, the effects of the introduction of alien species, the effects of associated activities on the marine ecosystem and of the effects of environmental changes, with the aim of making possible the sustained conservation of Antarctic marine living resources.[34]

Scientists had advocated that Article II(3)(*a*) be clarified so as to require that the harvest of prey species was not so great as to result in a serious reduction in predators. It is not enough to ensure that prey populations do not fall below levels safeguarding their own stable recruitment, because these levels may not be high enough to protect the stability of dependent species at a higher level in the food chain.[35] Fishing States strongly opposed any amendment to the principles. Australia argued that the existing text could only be construed as

---

on the Conservation of Antarctic Seals, Executive Rept. No. 94–5 (3 September 1976), 9.
33. Department of State, *Environmental Impact Statement on the Convention for the Conservation of Antarctic Seals* (1974), 17–18.
34. Art. II(3).
35. Report of the Scientific Workshop on Management of Living Resources of the Southern Ocean (1980), II-2.

already covering the scientists' proposals,[36] but this construction
depends on the drafting history of Article II,[37] which is not public
property. If the Australian interpretation is correct, the amendment
could not have injuriously affected the harvesting States, and their
opposition is difficult to explain.

Fundamental to the conservation principles is the supposition that
sufficient information will be available to the bodies set up under it
(Scientific Committee and Commission) for the stated purposes, but
this is not the case today. The Convention itself states that it is essential to increase knowledge of the Antarctic marine ecosystem so as
to be able to base harvesting decisions on sound scientific information.[38] Among the matters needing research with regard to krill
are the exact location of spawning areas, seasonal vertical migration
patterns, causes of swarming behaviour, development rates, life
span, the effect of the decline in whales on the krill population,
annual distribution variations and rates of predation.[39] Information
gaps for fish and other dependent species (apart from whales and
some species of seals) are even larger.

To meet this need the SCAR Group of Specialists on Living
Resources of the Southern Ocean, together with the Scientific Committee on Oceanic Research (SCOR), FAO and the International
Coordination Group for the Southern Ocean of the Intergovernmental Oceanographic Commission (IOC), adopted a proposal for
an international cooperative research programme. This plan, given
the title of BIOMASS (Biological Investigations of Marine Antarctic
Systems and Stocks), was accepted by SCAR. Its principal objective
is to gain a deeper understanding of the structure and dynamic functioning of the Antarctic marine ecosystem as a basis for future
management of potential living resources.[40] Krill is stressed as the
main potential Antarctic fishery and because of its vital place in the
food chain.[41] But BIOMASS is planned to study the other elements
of the Antarctic ocean ecosystem ranging from seaweeds, birds, fish
and squid to seals and whales. The programme relies on the coordi-

36. 'Antarctic marine living resources conference' (1980), *Australian Foreign Affairs Record*, 144 at 145.
37. J.N. Barnes, 'The Emerging Convention on the Conservation of Antarctic Marine Living Resources: an attempt to meet the new realities of Resource Exploitation in the Southern Ocean', MS (1980), 124.
38. Preamble.
39. Tetra Tech, *The Antarctic Krill Resource: Prospects for Commercial Exploitation* (1978), 115–17.
40. SCAR/SCOR Group of Specialists on Living Resources of the Southern Ocean, *Biological Investigations of Marine Antarctic Systems and Stocks*, Vol. 1 (1977), 5.
41. S.Z. El-Sayed, 'SCAR/SCOR conference on living resources of the southern ocean' (1977), 12 (1 & 2) *Antarctic Journal*, 3.

nation of national investigation using research vessels, krill trawlers, icebreakers, supply ships and shore stations. Two large-scale research efforts by a number of vessels in one area were planned: the first, FIBEX (First International BIOMASS Experiment), took place in 1980–1, and the second, SIBEX, is scheduled for 1984–5.

The basic assumption of BIOMASS is that current knowledge of krill and dependent species is altogether insufficient for planning an ecosystem management programme and reaching decisions on harvesting. It will culminate in a major synthesis of data at a symposium in about 1986. While the living resources regime provides for general conservation principles, all specific decisions, such as harvesting levels, are left for future resolution by the Commission established under Article VII. The SCAR/SCOR plan recognised that harvesting of krill on a commercial scale could start in the near future before firm estimates of the scientifically allowable annual yield could be made. It advocated some degree of harvesting under careful control with arrangements to ensure that the harvest could be reduced quickly if there were evidence that the quotas had been set too high. BIOMASS information on the effects of harvesting on the ecosystem relationships could then be used to develop management strategies for the whole area.[42] It has also been suggested that sufficient information should be available before extensive krill exploitation begins to permit fishing without lasting damage being done to krill or dependent species.[43]

Leaving aside the question whether unequivocal and generally accepted scientific conclusions can be translated into political decisions,[44] the view that BIOMASS results and management of the ecosystem can be synchronised would seem somewhat optimistic. Taking current krill harvesting at approximately 200,000 tons per annum, the possibility of rapid escalation cannot be discounted. Scientific research during harvesting of a species over a prolonged period is the most effective means of obtaining the necessary management data. Yet even today scientists consider themselves unable to offer advice on aspects of whaling.[45] Should BIOMASS be carried out to its fullest possible extent, one could not expect to have full scientific agreement on krill harvesting quotas, closed areas, catch effort, limited seasons and other necessary conservation measures. If this may well be the case for one species, then the postulation that all major dependent species in the Antarctic marine

42. SCAR/SCOR Group of Specialists on Living Resources of the Southern Ocean, *Biological Investigations of Marine Antarctic Systems and Stocks*, Vol. 1 (1977), 64.
43. S.Z. El-Sayed, 'BIOMASS' (1978), 43(10) *Frontiers*, 38 at 39.
44. See later discussion (Krill/*Commission and Scientific Committee*).
45. M.J. Forster, 'IWC Makes Some Progress' (1979), 5 *Environmental Policy and*

ecosystem will be sufficiently understood by 1986 to permit advice on the effect of krill trawling on fish, squid, birds, seals and whales is open to doubt.

On past experience the willingness of nations to fund an effective scientific programme for the whole ecosystem is very much in question. Like other research carried out within the Antarctic system, BIOMASS is not an international effort but rather a coordination of the work of the participant nations. Ship time is extremely expensive, and the funding of research vessels in Antarctica is to a large degree traced, directly or indirectly, to official sources. BIOMASS also stresses research to be conducted on vessels with other missions such as krill trawlers and icebreakers, which are either government ships or are reliant on government grants. Although nations have been ready to give major tasks to SCAR, they have not been prepared to allocate funds for the previous modest needs of the Committee. It has already been pointed out that SCAR was short of finance for the actual planning of BIOMASS.[46] Coordination is a minor expense compared to vessel-oriented research.

The Consultative Parties have been requested to give sympathetic consideration to BIOMASS funding.[47] Apart from their previous record of lukewarm support for SCAR programmes, there are additional obstacles to the full implementation of BIOMASS. From the open literature it is evident that plans for a commercial fishery are well advanced; this is exemplified by the extensive range of krill products already developed and by test-marketing. A substantial proportion of the information sought by BIOMASS is of potential commercial value, and nations investing millions of dollars in exploration will be understandably reluctant to publish findings of this nature. With such investments, the harvesting countries may well consider non-harvestable species as of limited research interest. On the other hand, the United States government, whose nationals are unlikely to engage in a future krill fishery, may not be prepared to expend a major proportion of its Antarctic budget on research which will be of direct commercial benefit to the Soviet Union and Poland.

BIOMASS places emphasis on the relationships between all Antarctic marine species, and the ecosystem approach is also a prominent feature of the conservation principles of the regime.[48] So the Convention applies to Antarctic living marine resources defined as 'populations of fin fish, molluscs, crustaceans, and all other species

---

Law, 170 at 174.
46. See Antarctic System/*SCAR*.
47. Rec. IX-2.
48. Art. II(3)(*b*) and (*c*).

of living organisms, including birds, found south of the Antarctic Convergence'.[49] This theme is repeatedly stressed in the Treaty. Data on dependent or related species shall be collected by the Commission, which shall facilitate research and comprehensive studies of Antarctic marine living resources and of the Antarctic marine ecosystem. Conservation measures may cover the effects of harvesting on other components of the marine ecosystem.[50] Among the tasks of the Scientific Committee are the analysis of data concerning the direct and indirect effects of harvesting on the populations of Antarctic marine living resources.[51]

This is a signal departure both from the general trend of fishery treaties and from the whaling and sealing conventions which only applied to a single species. In principle, the ecosystem provisions appear to furnish a novel and extensive degree of protection to dependent species. A vital determinant of the effects of the Convention will be the extent to which this part of the conservation principles is carried out in practice.

Definition of 'conservation' in the principles and throughout the Convention includes 'rational use'.[52] This somewhat curious use of the term may be traced to the Sealing Convention, which permits the parties to adopt measures with respect to the 'conservation, scientific study and rational and humane use of seal resources'.[53] Despite the phrasing and the liberal quotas of that agreement, one commentator who participated in its drafting considered that it had made an effective contribution towards preventing the starting of a threatened sealing industry.[54] Environmental groups proposed an interim catch of 1,000,000 to 2,000,000 tons of krill per annum, to be raised only when sufficient data had become available to apply the conservation standard of the Treaty in a scientific way.[55]

At the Ninth Consultative Meeting, the elements of the living resources treaty were decided upon. They included provision for the 'effective conservation' of the resources.[56] Harvesting nations were

49. Art. I(2).
50. Art. IX.
51. Art. XV(2)(*c*).
52. Art. II(2).
53. Art. 3(1), Convention for the Conservation of Antarctic Seals.
54. B. Roberts, 'International Co-operation for Antarctic Development: the Test for the Antarctic Treaty' (1978) 19, (119) *Polar Record*, 107 at 110. This paper was originally delivered at the International Symposium on the Development of the Antarctic in April 1977 (Francisco Orrego Vincuña and Augusto Salinas Araya (eds.), *El desarrollo de la Antártica* (1977), 336 at 340).
55. J.N. Barnes in 'Antarctic Living Marine Resources Negotiations', Hearing, National Ocean Policy Study, Committee on Commerce, Science and Transportation, Senate, 95th Cong., 2nd Sess. (14 June 1978), 33.
56. Rec. IX-2.

concerned to make it clear that conservation should not be inter-preted as prohibition.[57] To cover this problem, the Meeting's Working Group on Marine Living Resources reached an under-standing which was incorporated in the Final Report:

. . . The word 'conservation' as used in the draft Recommendation includes rational use, in the sense that harvesting would not be prohibited, but the regime would exclude catch allocation and other economic regulation of har-vesting. It was similarly the understanding of the Group that the word 'resources' was not limited to commercially exploitable species.

It has previously been suggested that the reason why this agree-ment was not made part of the recommendation itself was in order to avoid the possibility of environmental groups exerting pressure to refuse approval of the recommendation.[58] Taking into account the presumed unanimous support of the Consultative Parties for the interpretation, and the very short time (fourteen months) prescribed for finalisation of a treaty text, its practical effect was the same as that of a recommendation, without the necessity for obtaining sub-sequent government approval for entry into force. This under-standing was a vital step in the negotiation of the regime. On the one hand, a concession was made to the Consultative Parties concerned with the views of scientists and environmental groups giving rise to the ecosystem approach in the Convention, and on the other, the exploiting nations ensured that any 'economic regulation' of har-vesting would be excluded.

Sovereignty

Krill represents a major world food resource of current interest to many nations, some of which are not signatories to the Antarctic Treaty. Developing countries unable to participate in the fishery may well demand that at least a part of the harvest be devoted to feeding the hungry people of the world, few of whom are to be found in the population of the krill-harvesting nations. Hence the arro-gation of powers by the Consultative Parties to draft a living resources regime is open to justified criticism. In the case of the negotiation of the Treaty, the nations had at least carried out research on the continent during the International Geophysical Year. Some of the Consultative Parties, such as Belgium and New Zealand, have not demonstrated an intention to participate in krill harvesting; on the other hand, South Korea and Taiwan have been

57. Mr. Brewster, Department of State, in Transcript of Public Meeting on Antarctic Marine Living Resources (20 December 1977), 12.
58. See Antarctic System/*Procedure*.

involved in experimental fishing, yet were excluded from participation in the drafting of the regime.

The privileged position of the Antarctic Treaty Consultative Parties has been carried over to the Convention. For them, participation in the 1980 Conference automatically conferred membership of the Commission, whereas countries not invited to the Conference have to comply with an activity requirement[59] which Belgium and New Zealand would probably not pass. A beneficial result of this preference may well be that such nations will be prepared to give some support to the conservation aspect of the Convention, as has been the position with the recent history of the International Whaling Commission, but the outcome would be fortuitous. The purpose of drafting the Convention in this way was to perpetuate the Antarctic Treaty and the 'prime responsibilities' of the Consultative Parties for the protection and preservation of the Antarctic environment.[60]

Privilege arises from the presentation of the draft for agreement as a *fait acompli*, the issuing of invitations by the Consultative Parties, and their special position as original members of the Commission. The living resources regime was also seen as an instrument for perpetuating the Antarctic Treaty. A number of the more controversial issues of negotiation arose directly from this linkage.

It was previously pointed[61] out that the Consultative Parties were most reluctant to make recommendations covering the high seas south of 60°S, and that this view was reversed in 1975 for fear of creating a vacuum in the new era of resource interests. However, major krill concentrations occur north of 60°S, and the Consultative Parties foiled an ambitious attempt by FAO to carry out a very substantial living resources programme south of 45°S.[62] In 1977 one of the elements of the living resources regime was stated to be that it should extend north of 60°S. where that was necessary for the effective conservation of species of the Antarctic ecosystem.[63] Consultative Meetings held under Article IX of the Treaty are subject to all its provisions, including Article VI which delimits the area of

59. Art. VII (discussed under Krill/*Commission*).
60. Rec IX-2 (reiterated in the Preamble to the Convention) recalled the special responsibilities conferred on the Consultative Parties in respect of the preservation and conservation of living resources of the Antarctic by Art.IX(1)(f) of the Treaty. It may be questioned whether 'preservation and conservation' extend to 'rational use' in the context of the understanding of 1977 and the practical effect of the Convention. Negotiation of a fishery regime of the ordinary type would certainly be questionable if carried out at Consultative Meetings.
61. See Treaty/*Area*.
62. See Treaty/*Third Parties*.
63. Rec. IX-2.

application. Elaboration of a detailed and definitive regime covering vast expanses of seas north of 60°S is beyond the competence of Consultative Meetings, and can only be seen as a revision of Article VI. It is noteworthy that two major expansions of competence took place within two years under the pressures generated by a desire to retain control of Antarctic affairs.

One of the main effects of the decision to restrict drafting to the Consultative Parties was to bring about immediate and serious dispute related to sovereignty issues which came close to stalling the negotiations completely. Not one but several such questions arose.

From a scientific view point, a living resources regime is best defined by the Antarctic Convergence. Here cold surface water flowing away from the continent meets warmer nutrient-rich sub-Antarctic waters flowing southward. At this junction, which is situated at varying points between 50° and 60°S depending upon the season and the climate, conditions are ripe for developing a rich pasture of single-celled plants which are the first link in the Antarctic food chain.[64] Under the Convention it is deemed to be a fixed line[65] varying from 60°S to 45°S. For the heaviest krill concentrations the northern boundary is 50°S. At the insistence, of Argentina, part of the area within the Convergence in the Drake Passage was excluded to draw the boundary line further away from its territory,[66] presumably Argentina was concerned with the implications for the Beagle Channel and Falkland Islands. For unexplained reasons, Macquarie Island and its 200 mile zone, part of which lies within the Convergence, is excluded, although two French and one South African islands in a similar geographical position are included.

Extension of the living resources regime beyond the area of application of the Antarctic Treaty might be seen as part of the ecosystem approach. It was also a result of the assertion of prime responsibility by the Consultative Parties over activities in the seas south of 60°S, and of the impracticality of devising parallel but separate treaty systems north and south of that line. Once the decision had been made, legal difficulties emerged. Apart from the pre-existing problem of land claims, the living resources negotiations brought out the question of the 200 mile Exclusive Economic Zone in relation to disputed islands, and a subsidiary matter arose from the inclusion within the regime area of islands whose sovereignty was not in question.

64. J.F. Lovering and J.R.V. Prescott, *Last of Lands . . . Antarctica* (1979) 32–3.
65. Art. I(4).
66. J.N. Barnes, 'The Emerging Convention on the Conservation of Antarctic Marine Living Resources: an attempt to meet the new realities of Resource Exploitation in the Southern Ocean', MS. (1980), 69. .

Whether or not the proclamation of 200 mile zones south of 60°S after the Antarctic Treaty came into force contravenes Article IV is undecided.[67] For the present discussion, the legal status of all Antarctic zones of this nature, including those proclaimed before 1961, may be taken to follow that of the coastal claim. Taken with the contemporaneous preliminary negotiations for a mineral regime, the living resources issue gave rise to the first major publicised debate related to sovereignty since the Treaty came into force. Once krill had been linked to the Antarctic Treaty, any sovereignty dispute arising under the Living Resources Convention threatened to spread to the Treaty.

If claims were still insisted upon, the States concerned could hardly ignore a major fishery carried on within their Exclusive Economic or Fishery Zone in disregard of national legislation. Further complications arose from the fact that the 200 mile zone concept only began to gain general customary acceptance around 1976.[68] Argentina, Chile and France had previously ensured the application of such legislation to their Antarctic territories. Claimants which had not done so were faced with the problem of passing legislation proclaiming a 200 mile zone for their metro-politan territory and then having to decide whether to extend it to Antarctica at a time when Antarctic offshore resource jurisdiction had suddenly become a political issue. New Zealand's law pro-claiming a 12 mile territorial sea and 200 mile EEZ had the effect of excluding the Ross Dependency from the provisions creating an EEZ.[69] Australia established a 200 mile Fishery Zone applicable to the Antarctic,[70] and when the legislation was brought into force it was announced that powers to declare excepted waters to be excluded would be used against the background of Australian involvement in negotiation of the living resources regime.[71] Yet a week earlier Ambassador Brennan, head of the Australian dele-gation at the Tenth Consultative Meeting, had unequivocally stated that within 200 miles of its claim 'oil belongs to Australia'.[72]

As the ambiguity of Australian policy shows, the claimants faced unprecedented challenges. These were compounded by the prac-tical limitations on any possible attempt at enforcement action in Antarctic waters. One of the major purposes of the Convention was

67. See Treaty/*Area*.
68. See Krill/*The Resource*.
69. S. 2, Territorial Sea and Exclusive Economic Zone Act 1977.
70. Fisheries Amendment Act 1978 (C'wlth).
71. Senator Chaney, Sen. Deb. (25 September 1979), 910.
72. *International Herald Tribune* (18 September 1979). The statement relied on the EEZ concept rather than the continental shelf.

therefore to work out a formula whereby both claimants and non-claimants could agree on a system to provide for adequate conservation without compromising their legal position.[73] Not surprisingly, sovereignty was the most difficult issue at the Second Special Consultative Meeting in Canberra in February-March 1978, and caused endless arguments at the Buenos Aires session in July of that year.[74] Claimants were demanding more than an Article IV – type provision. Some required that a regime should provide them with tangible benefits.

The Convention bears the signs of this protracted battle. If Article IV of the Antarctic Treaty is obscure, then the various references to the Treaty and sovereignty in the Convention are downright confusing. In at least one instance, the text resorts to devices to placate claimants. The area of application is stated to be south of 60°S and between that latitude and the Convergence. In both cases, Antarctic marine living resources are covered, but in the latter instance there is the added proviso: 'which form part of the Antarctic marine ecosystem'. 'Antarctic marine living resource,' means all species of living organisms found south of the Convergence,[75] and indeed it is hard to conceive of such an organism between 60°S and the Convergence which is not part of the Antarctic marine ecosystem. The absence of any apparent distinction between the two areas strongly suggests that the division was inserted for purely political purposes. However, the text could be used in due course to argue that some species are within the Convention south of 60°S and outside it north of 60°S. Although such a contention would be legally weak, the record of interpretation of the Antarctic Treaty is not devoid of strained views.

The main sovereignty provision is to be found in Article IV:

1. With respect to the Antarctic Treaty area, all Contracting Parties, whether or not they are Parties to the Antarctic Treaty, are bound by Articles IV and VI of the Antarctic Treaty in their relations with each other.
2. Nothing in this Convention and no acts or activities taking place while the present Convention is in force shall
(*a*) Constitute a basis for asserting, supporting, or denying a claim to territorial sovereignty in the Antarctic Treaty area or create any rights of sovereignty in the Antarctic Treaty area.
(*b*) Be interpreted as a renunciation or diminution by any Contracting Party of, or as prejudicing, any right or claim or basis of claim to exercise coastal

---

73. R. Tucker Scully, Department of State in 'Antarctic Living Marine Resources Negotiations', Hearing, National Ocean Policy Study, Committee on Commerce, Science and Transportation, Senate, 95th Cong., 2nd Sess. (1978), 7.
74. 'Control of Marine Resources' (1978), 8(7) *Antarctic*, 237.
75. Art. I.

state jurisdiction under international law within the area to which this Convention applies,

(*c*) Be interpreted as prejudicing the position of any Contracting Party as regards its recognition or non-recognition of any such right, claim or basis of claim.

(*d*) Affect the provision of Article IV(2) of the Antarctic Treaty that no new claim, or enlargement of an existing claim, to territorial sovereignty in Antarctica shall be asserted while the Antarctic Treaty is in force.

Having provided that the parties to the Convention are bound by Article IV of the Antarctic Treaty, Articles IV(2)(*a*) and (*d*) would seem to be merely repetition, an explanation for which may be sought in the lengthy discussion of the text which took place, the contentious nature of the topic and a preparedness to add verbiage for the sole purpose of presenting claimants with apparent, if illusory, additional safeguards. Reference to Article VI of the Antarctic Treaty maintains the right of non-claimants to assert the freedom of fishing in the high seas south of 60°S. States not recognising claims will take this to cover the waters up to the coast.[76]

Article IV(2)(*b*) and (*c*) were intended to deal specifically with the EEZ issue north of 60°S. Although this approach has been termed 'bifocal'[77] and regarded as having the elements of novelty, it differs from the freezing provisions of the Antarctic Treaty only in minor respects. It had been argued that claimants can regard (*b*) and (*c*) as covering sub-Antarctic islands and the mainland, whereas non-claimants can take it to refer to the islands alone.[78] A preferable view is that (*b*) and (*c*) were intended particularly to safeguard the rights in respect of offshore areas of sub-Antarctic islands north of 60°S, the sovereignty of which is generally recognised, while at the same time avoiding prejudice to positions of claimants and non-claimants regarding zones appurtenant to disputed islands. This is borne out by 2(*a*) and (*d*), which have the same effect for the Treaty area.

France pressed for the exclusion of Kerguelen and Crozet Islands, sovereignty of which is not in question, from the regime. Had it not been for French concern on this issue and Soviet opposition to the inclusion of the European Economic Community, the 1978 timetable might have been adhered to, because the 'Washington draft' of September 1978 was ultimately adopted largely in its original form.[79]

76. See Treaty/*Area*.
77. J. Tinker, 'Antarctica: towards a new internationalism' *New Scientist* (13 September 1979), 799. For the argument that this construction applies to the Antarctic Treaty generally see Treaty/*Interpretation*.
78. B. Mitchell and J. Tinker, *Antarctica and its resources* (1980), 68.
79. J.N. Barnes, 'The Emerging Convention on the Conservation of Antarctic Marine Living Resources: an attempt to meet the new realities of Resource Exploitation in the Southern Ocean', MS. (1980), 56.

The Soviet Union carried on a considerable conventional fishery in the Kerguelen area between 1971 and 1974, and Crozet has potential crab resources. If accepted, this proposal would have weakened the ecosystem approach and put in question the inclusion of the other undisputed sub-Antarctic islands and their 200 mile zones. It would also have opened the way for deletion of South Georgia and the South Sandwich Islands which are north of 60°S, claimed by Argentina and the United Kingdom, and situated in a potential harvesting area. A statement was made by the Chairman on the Convention's application to Kerguelen and Crozet Islands and to other islands in the Convention area over which the existence of State sovereignty is recognised by all parties to the Convention. French conservation measures adopted before the entry into force of the Convention would remain effective until modified by France, and conservation measures under the Convention can only be applied to the waters adjacent to the islands with French consent. France could also adopt measures which it might deem appropriate, and would carry out national or international enforcement in those waters. The observation and inspection system may only be applied as agreed by France and in the manner so agreed. No objection was made to the statement.

The legal effect of this statement is small. It was not made by France and was therefore not a reservation. Insofar as French consent is required for a conservation measure, there is merely a restatement of the requirement of consensus and the objection procedure of the Convention;[80] coastal State jurisdiction is specifically preserved.[81] Of far greater concern are the political implications of this legally redundant and ineffective recital. France has unambiguously indicated that it is prepared to prevent Convention conservation measures applying within the EEZ of its sub-Antarctic islands, thus considerably reducing the ambit of the ecosystem approach.

Parties to the living resources regime will not engage in any activities in the Antarctic Treaty area contrary to the principles and purposes of the Treaty.[82] It has been previously argued that 'principles and purposes' in Article X of the Antarctic Treaty cannot be interpreted as meaning effective recommendations, because Contracting Parties are not covered by such recommendations and therefore third parties cannot be bound. It was also suggested that the phrase 'principles and purposes' used in recent recommendations indicates lack of certainty as to the source of a legal basis for

80. Art. IX, Convention
81. Art. IV(2)(*b*), Convention.
82. Art. III, Convention.

the measures taken.[83]. It could be contended that according to the minimal meaning of 'principles and purposes' in this context, compliance is required with the obligations contained in the text of the Antarctic Treaty. But if this is so, it is difficult to understand why there are additional undertakings to observe Articles I and V,[84] and IV and VI[85] of the Antarctic Treaty as between parties to the Convention. If the entire text of the Antarctic Treaty were binding under 'principles and purposes', the specific provisions would not be required. Furthermore, it is not easy to envisage the possibility of a party to the living resources Convention observing Articles I (peaceful purposes) and V of the Antarctic Treaty in relation to parties to the Convention, yet carrying out activities contrary to those Articles with regard to other countries. The obligations are of a general nature and not limited to their effect with respect to a particular State.

Linkage with the Antarctic Treaty is expressed in a variety of formulae. Discussion of Article IV of the Treaty has shown arguments contemplating the revival of claims and a reliance on 'continuing' State activities should the Treaty be terminated.[86] If it were to be terminated, could the Treaty be partly revived in reliance on the living resources regime? In some instances the answer is self-evident: for example, the Commission cannot cooperate with the Antarctic Treaty Consultative Parties on matters falling within their competence[87] if the Treaty giving competence is no longer in force. But where parties to the Convention undertake to observe Antarctic Treaty recommendations,[88] or the Commission is obliged to take full account of them,[89] it is arguable that termination of the Treaty would not limit the obligation to have regard to recommendations in force at the time. This duty seems to be independent of the continued existence of the Antarctic Treaty.

On the other hand, where the text specifies that parties to the Convention 'are bound by' Articles of the Antarctic Treaty,[90] it would seem logical that the duty should terminate with the demise of the Treaty. In relation to Articles I and V, parties are 'bound by the obligations contained in [the] Articles'.[91] *Prima facie* it would

83. See Treaty/*Third Parties*.
84. Art. III, Convention.
85. Art. IV, Convention.
86. See Treaty/*Claims*.
87. Art. XXIII, Convention.
88. Art. V(2), Convention.
89. Art. IX(5), Convention.
90. Art. IV(1), Convention.
91. Art. III, Convention.

appear that the content of the two Articles is thus given an existence independent of the Treaty.

Parties to the living resource regime which are not signatories of the Antarctic Treaty agree to observe within the Treaty area, as and when appropriate, the Agreed Measures and other measures recommended by the Consultative Parties in fulfilment of their responsibility to protect the Antarctic environment.[92] Invocation of the Agreed Measures and use of 'recommended' suggests that the obligation arises from the adoption of a recommendation, whether or not it has become effective under the Antarctic Treaty. A similar inference may be taken from the duty of the Commission to take full account of measures 'established or recommended' by the Consultative Parties.[93] Even the requirement placed on the Commission comports a duty. If this interpretation is correct, and it is based upon the text of the Antarctic Treaty, then recommendations which are not yet legally binding on Consultative Parties to the Antarctic Treaty — and may never become effective — would be given legal status by the living resources regime.

Commission

Unlike the Antarctic Treaty, the Convention establishes an international organisation. The Commission is to meet annually or at any other time requested by one-third of its members;[94] it is to be provided with headquarters,[95] an Executive Secretary and staff.[96] Because the Commission is the decision-making body, its constitution is a key feature of the Convention. Each State participating in the Conference is entitled to be a member of the Commission.[97] Since the Consultative Parties drafted the Convention, it was they also who issued the invitations to the Conference, and therefore decided which States would be original members of the Commission.

The significance of original membership resides in the absence of any qualificatory test. Acceding States shall be entitled to membership of the Commission during such time as they are engaged in research or harvesting activities in relation to the marine living resources to which the Convention applies.[98] Because this test clearly derived from the Antarctic Treaty, similar elements such as

92. Art. V(2).
93. Art. IX(5).
94. Art. XIII(2).
95. Art. XIII(1).
96. Art. XVII.
97. Art. VII(2)(*a*).
98. Art. VII(2)(*b*).

the time-limit[99] will not require examination. Attention will be paid to deviations from the precedent since there can be no doubt that they are intentional.

Two major differences are apparent. Unlike the Treaty, the Convention does not require that the activities be 'substantial'. Criticism has already been levelled at the large investment required to comply with the Consultative Parties' strict interpretation of this phrase,[100] but one may assume that the Convention will be construed as demanding more than a mere notional research or harvesting effort. Relying on the contrast with the Treaty, it would seem logical to suggest that a level well below the multi-million dollar investment needed for an all-year station would be appropriate, and if this is so, it can be argued that maintenance of a small krill research vessel sent to the Antarctic each summer for one or two months should suffice. By analogy of reasoning, the harvesting would not have to be on a large scale. A country taking 10,000 tons of krill a year could then satisfy the test. Alternately, such a nation could argue that its catch is for research purposes.

According to the Treaty, the research must be carried out in Antarctica, but there is no such restriction in the Convention. Could it be contended that research outside Antarctica should satisfy the test? An example might be the construction and operation of a pilot protein concentrate plant utilising krill caught by another State. It may be presumed that Commission members would not be favourably disposed to such an interpretation, despite the apparent support given by the text of the Convention when compared with the Treaty. Justification could be sought in the words 'in relation to the marine living resources' by the argument that the research must bear upon krill while they are still alive.

South Korea, although engaged in krill research, was prevented from attending the Conference due to Soviet opposition on political grounds. Could this happen in the future with regard to Commission membership? Like the Treaty, the Convention provides that a country fulfilling the test shall be 'entitled' to membership of the Commission, but as with the Treaty,[101] it is also not clear whether attainment of status is automatic or discretionary. Analysis of the 1977 Special Consultative Meeting supports the view that a discretionary approach has been adopted for the Treaty,[102] and a similar interpretation of the Convention would be a prerequisite for

99. Antarctic System/*Consultative Status.*
100. Ibid.
101. See Antarctic System/*Consultative Status.*
102. Ibid.

preventing unwanted States from obtaining membership.

Although the Convention is ambiguous on this issue, as was the decision of the 1977 Special Consultative Meeting, the living resources provisions are at least as supportive of a discretionary approach as were those of 1977. New Consultative Parties may be urged to approve effective recommendations. Candidates for Commission membership 'shall' notify willingness to accept conservation measures in force. When making a request a State is 'seeking' to participate. If existing members do not request a meeting within two months, the acceding State shall be 'deemed' to have satisfied the requirements. The Convention contains no further indication of the criteria to be considered at such a meeting, but because the decision would be on a matter of substance, consensus is required.[103] As with the Treaty, each Commission member will have a veto, and it is becoming clear that this right will be exercised on a discretionary test to exclude candidates for political reasons.[104]

Unanimity may have some justifications for a regime planned to regulate scientific research, but the same cannot be said for a resource agreement. Voting procedure was one of the major issues during the negotiations, the United States arguing for a majority vote with the support of the United Kingdom and Japan, whereas Argentina, Chile, Poland and the Soviet Union urged unanimity. The requirement of consensus is merely a restatement of the latter position in a different form.

The living resources regime sets forth its objective in the conservation principles of Article II. There are, however, no specific self-executing provisions to carry out the principles. Conservation measures must be passed by the Commission, and after adoption they become binding following the lapse of 180 days from notification to members. Within ninety days of notification, a member may inform the Commission that it is unable to accept the measures in whole or in part, whereupon they shall not bind the member to the extent stated. If this procedure is invoked, the Commission shall meet at the request of any member to review the conservation measure, and at the time of this meeting, and within thirty days following, any member shall have the right to declare that it is no longer able to accept the measure. In this case it ceases to be bound by it.[105]

---

103. Art. XII(1).
104. On a late draft text, the country seeking membership would have notified the Depositary of 'its activities'. The Convention refers to 'the basis upon which it seeks to become a member' lending additional support to the argument.
105. Art. IX(6).

A similar objection procedure is to be found in the Whaling Convention.[106] One difference is that adoption of the original measure requires a three-fourths majority in that Convention,[107] whereas the living resources regime demands consensus. From the viewpoint of conservation, it would appear that the draftsmen took one of the most criticised features of the Whaling Convention and then made attainment of the objective even more difficult by adding the Antarctic Treaty practice of unanimity. First, a harvesting State which is a member of the Commission can veto a conservation measure; then it can prevent the decision from applying to its own activities. Since no initial conservation measures have been specified, a harvesting State may never be bound by any rules under the living resources regime. A more likely outcome is that the threat of a veto by one exploiting nation or more will suffice to prevent the presentation of undesired quotas and limitations. The 1977 Working Group understanding clearly indicates the intention of the harvesting countries with regard to economic regulation.

The functions of the Commission are to give effect to the conservation principles. *Inter alia*, it shall facilitate research into the ecosystem, compile data on the population of harvested and dependent species, identify conservation needs, implement the observation and inspection system and adopt conservation measures.[108] Like the conservation principles, the execution of these functions is entirely dependent on the decision-making process of the Commission.

Conservation measures adopted by the Commission are central to the ecosystem approach and the declared objective of the regime, and particular attention should be paid to relevant headings which could have been mentioned but were not. In pursuance of the agreement of 1977 there is no heading for catch or effort allocation between participant nations. This is not a legal barrier to Commission action, because the definition of conservation measures is not exhaustive,[109] but having regard to the previously advanced interpretation of the 1977 understanding,[110] one can only conclude that national allocation will not in fact be the subject of any conservation measure. Any such proposal will be vetoed by harvesting nations or, in the final resort, made ineffective by the objection of one of the major exploiters. A single unallocated quota has been demonstrated to be futile by the experience of the Whaling

106. Art. V(3), International Convention for the Regulation of Whaling 1946.
107. Art. III(6).
108. Art. IX(1).
109. Art. IX(2).
110. See Krill/*Conservation Principles*.

Commission. When quotas are not divided between countries, the nation with the largest whaling fleet can catch the largest share, as the result of which all participants increase the size of their fleets.[111] It may also be remarked that there is no reference to the possibility of a moratorium.[112]

One advance on the Antarctic Treaty is the establishment of the rudiments of an international institution functioning on a continuing basis. Provision of an Executive Secretary and staff suggests that liaison between members will be maintained, but there is however no grant of powers to the secretariat, all decisions resting with the Commission at its annual meetings. This could well mean that matters such as archives and publications will be an improvement on the performance of the Consultative Parties, but questions of substance will raise the same problems for the living resources regime as they have posed for the Antarctic Treaty. Although conservation measures[113] and population, catch and effort statistics[114] are to be published, there is no indication that the much criticised policy of secrecy of Consultative Meetings is to be changed for the Commission.

For the first five years that the Convention is in force, each member of the Commission shall make equal contribution to the budget, after which the Commission shall determine by consensus in what proportion to apply the criteria of equal sharing and the amount harvested.[115] It has already been suggested that the living resources regime suffers from over-emphasis on linkage with the Antarctic Treaty.[116] The formula for the first period requires a Consultative Party, which becomes a member of the Commission solely to protect its sovereignty interests or to safeguard its stance on the Antarctic Treaty, to pay the same amount as the major harvesting nations. Apart from the inequity, it may be assumed that the countries which do not have krill fleets will support a low contribution level.

Discussion of the modest budgeting of SCAR has emphasised the low priority placed by the Consultative Parties on scientific research.[117] Where the results of such investigations are to be used to develop conservation measures restricting resource development, the reluctance of nations to contribute will no doubt be evident. Harvesting nations may well regard conservation measures as an

111. *Whales and Whaling*, Report of the Independent Inquiry conducted by Sir Sydney Frost, Vol. I (1978), 95.
112. Contrast Rec. IX-1 on minerals.
113. Art. IX(3).
114. Art. IX(1)(*d*).
115. Art. XIX(3).
116. See Krill/*Sovereignty*.
117. See Antarctic System/*SCAR*.

economic liability and scientific research to that end as being of no benefit to them. It is to be noted that there is no express statement that either the Scientific Committee or the Commission shall actually carry out scientific research. In effect the Scientific Committee is to encourage and promote cooperation in this field.[118] The Commission is to 'facilitate' research,[119] but from the record of the Consultative Parties, it can be regarded as quite likely that there will be no direct funding of research.[120] Financial support would then have to be given on a national basis, as is the present situation with BIOMASS. It is unfortunate that there has been no resort to a gearing of research into the growth of the industry; had this been done there would have been an automatic assurance of substantial funds. In its absence, scientists are compelled to request support on the same footing as with the Antarctic Treaty system.

A further implication of the absence of any specific statement on research support is that a natural tendency to concentrate on harvested species will gain strength, and fishing nations in particular will be much more willing to make grants carrying the implication of increased catches. Krill trawlers will provide readily available facilities to attract investigators. Together with the focus on krill, one may expect that scientific research on non-harvested species will become much less attractive. The obvious means of redressing the balance was the insertion of funding allocations in the Convention. Without such a requirement the ecosystem approach is seriously weakened in practice.

In view of the paucity of information on the Antarctic marine environment and the crucial position of krill as the basis of the food-web, special importance must be given to the work of the Scientific Committee. Conservation measures are to be based on the 'best scientific evidence available',[121] and assessment of the data is one of the Committee's main functions.[122] Governments will be able to influence the Committee. Representatives with suitable scientific qualifications will be appointed by each member of the Commission.[123] Various other methods of control exist. The Committee's budget is adopted by consensus of the Commission,[124] and the Committee shall conduct such activities as the Commission

118. Art. XV(1) and (2)(*f*).
119. Art. IX(1)(*a*).
120. In theory the Commission could support research under Art. IX(1)(*h*).
121. Art. IX(1)(*f*).
122. Art. XV(2)(*b*) and (*c*).
123. Art. XIV(2).
124. Art. XIX(1).

may direct.[125] For all practical purposes the Scientific Committee is controlled by the Commission. There is no attempt at insulation from political decisions, nor is any obligation placed upon the Commission to follow its advice.[126]

Co-operation

A number of organisations are concerned with Antarctic marine living resources, and cooperation with them will inevitably raise delimitation issues, which could well have political repercussions. Linkage with the Antarctic Treaty has already been discussed.[127] The Commission has to take full account of recommendations and (together with the Scientific Committee) shall co-operate with the Consultative Parties on matters falling within their competence.[128] A considerable degree of harmony will be ensured by the pre-dominance of Consultative Parties within the Commission and the tendency of major krill harvesters to become Consultative Parties.

Nothing in the regime shall derogate from the rights and obligations of parties to it under the Whaling and Sealing Conventions.[129] Initially it had been intended to exclude whales and pelagic seals entirely.[130] What remains is in formal congruence with the ecosystem approach because the conservation principles apply to all such species. But in effect the Living Resources Convention is subordinated to the two other treaties. Thus whale quotas may be altered without regard to the impact on krill. However the Commission is required to take into account the effect of krill harvesting on whales and seals.

The Commission and Scientific Committee shall seek to develop cooperative working relationships with the International Whaling Commission.[131] One possible example of inter-action arises from the IWC system of national inspectors and international observers. Under the living resources text principles are stated, and on that basis the Commission is to establish an observation and inspection system. Effective implementation of the system shall take into account 'existing international practice', a phrase which may be taken to require flag State consent for any such activity and which

125. Art. XV(2).
126. Compare the IWC pattern of reacting to the advice of its Scientific Committee by doing 'too little, too late' (R.M. May, 'Whaling: past, present and future' (1978), 276 *Nature*, 319 at 320).
127. See Krill/*Sovereignty*.
128. Art. XXIII(2)(*b*).
129. Art. VI.
130. Rec. IX-2.
131. Art. XXIII(3).

may also refer to IWC practice. Verification of compliance shall be carried out on board vessels engaged in scientific research or harvesting of marine living resources in the Convention area.[132] Due to the subordination provision, it would seem that whalers could not be inspected or observed under the living resources regime to check on compliance with regard to whales. Yet it could be suggested that, since whales are covered by both treaties and the vessels operate in the same area, a single system is needed.

Krill research has already raised new issues for SCAR, and the establishment of the Scientific Committee will present problems of coordination. SCAR provides scientific advice under the Sealing Convention,[133] a function which will presumably constitute a right to be preserved by the living resources regime. For other marine resources the Scientific Committee will have to pay regard to the work of SCAR[134] and seek to work together with it.[135] It has already been suggested that the relationship between the living resources Commission and the Consultative Parties should present few difficulties. But this may not necessarily be the case for SCAR and the Scientific Committee. Both bodies have jurisdiction in relation to a similar area,[136] but whereas SCAR is a non-governmental body, the Scientific Committee will consist of official representatives of countries. SCAR is oriented towards scientific research, and the Scientific Committee is concerned largely with resources. Both bodies are co-equal. The living resources text does not subordinate the Scientific Committee to SCAR.

Compliance

International dispute settlement provisions[137] are taken from Article XI of the Antarctic Treaty, but one substantive difference is the provision for an Arbitral Tribunal in an Annex. Resort to arbitration requires the consent of all parties to the dispute.[138] In practice there is no visible improvement in such a purely consensual system, the result being the same: no State is bound to submit a controversy to any form of compulsory settlement process. Discussion of the Treaty suggested that it fails to supply any useful means of deciding

132. Art. XXIV(2)(*b*).
133. Art.5, Convention for the Conservation of Antarctic Seals.
134. Art. XV(3), Convention for the Conservation of Antarctic Marine Living Resources.
135. Art. XXIII(3).
136. SCAR is not confined to the Treaty area (see Antarctic System/*SCAR*).
137. Art. XXV.
138. Art. XXV(2).

disputes, and by excluding the effect of general agreements for conflict resolution between countries,[139] may well make matters worse. Unsettled differences under the Antarctic Treaty could be seen as rather minor issues of international politics. Controversy over resource matters such as krill quotas cannot be dismissed in this way, since it could easily destroy the living resources regime and krill stocks with it.

If the Commission is of the opinion that any activity of a Contracting Party affects the implementation of the objective of the Convention or compliance by the party with its obligations under the regime, then the Commission shall draw the attention of all parties to the activity.[140] This, the only mechanism established by the Convention for dealing with infringements, cannot be seen as an effective sanction. The essential provisions requiring compliance will be the conservation measures. Yet from the express statements that members of the Commission shall implement the measures and shall be bound by them (with an objection proviso),[141] it would appear that other parties to the Convention will not be so bound. This inference is supported by the practice of the Consultative Parties under the Antarctic Treaty.[142] It is quite likely that at least one harvesting nation will be excluded from Commission membership on the discretionary interpretation of the test for admission to status.[143] In such a case it might be suggested that the activity in question affected the implementation of the objective of the Convention. A similar argument is applicable to third parties.[144]

Non-members of the Commission and third parties acting contrary to a conservation measure would not violate the Convention. Furthermore they could raise interesting legal issues. Under the Antarctic Treaty it has been assumed that any recommendation is a measure in furtherance of the principles and objectives of the Treaty, regardless of whether or not it has a basis in the Treaty text,[145] but this is not so with the Convention. Conservation measures passed by the Commission must come within its function, which is to give effect to the conservation principles contained in Article II,[146] and it is therefore open to third parties and non-members to contend that the measure in question does not constitute

139. See Treaty/*Dispute Settlement*.
140. Art. X(2).
141. Art. IX(6).
142. See Antarctic System/*Recommendations*.
143. See Krill/*Commission*.
144. Art. X(1).
145. Following the dubious practice of the Consultative Parties (see Treaty/*Third Parties*).
146. Art. IX(1).

an implementation of the objective of the Convention. The criteria set out by Article II are quantifiable, but much of the relevant scientific information is unknown, and a comprehensive understanding of the ecosystem will take many years to develop. So, for example, the establishment of a krill quota well above the minimal 1–2 million tons per year would meet opposition. Some scientists propose low initial total allowable catches,[147] and therefore a first quota of 10,000,000 tons could be held contrary to the conservation principles which form the objective of the Convention. This argument would be a considerable public embarrassment to the members of the Commission, and non-members and third parties could also avail themselves of the criticism that a decision of the Commission under Article IX(2) is a matter of substance. It is unlikely that a member of the Commission would not veto what would in effect amount to a motion of censure on its own behaviour.

Each party to the Convention shall take appropriate measures within its competence to ensure compliance.[148] Principles for the system of observation and inspection require designation of persons by Commission members, and results are to be reported to the government of which the person is a national, which in turn reports to the Commission. Effective implementation is to include procedures for flag State prosecution and sanctions on the basis of evidence from the inspections.[149] In contrast to the weak international enforcement provisions, the observation and inspection system is potentially a practical method of ensuring compliance by nationals of harvesting States, the major difficulty being that the Convention only lays down principles for the system. For it to work, there must be consensus on implementation and on the measures subject to inspection and observation.

It has been argued that parties that are not members of the Commission will not be bound by conservation measures. Implementation of the observation and inspection system by the Commission comes within Article IX(1)(g); this is distinct from conservation measures the authority for which is based on Article IX(1)(f). Much of the force of the view that conservation measures only bind members derives from their specific implementation provisions,[150] which do not apply to other decisions of the Commission. Although designation of observers and inspectors is reserved to members of the Commission, the duty to cooperate to ensure effective imple-

147. Report of the Scientific Workshop on Management of Living Resources of the Southern Ocean (1980), VIII-2.
148. Art. XXI(1).
149. Art. XXIV.
150. Art. IX(6).

mentation of the system is owned by all parties.[151]

If conservation measures do not affect non-members, it is somewhat difficult to accept that the system of compliance, including procedures for flag State prosecution, does bind them. The central feature of any national legislation must be the conservation measures. It may well be that the text uses 'Contracting Party' where the reference can only be to members of the Commission.[152] One solution is that inspection and observation are for the purpose of ensuring compliance with them. A non-member is not bound to observe such measures and is not therefore required to permit boarding and inspection. Any party to the Convention which is refused membership of the Commission despite its scientific research or harvesting activities would no doubt feel justified in taking such a stand.

One can sympathise with such an approach by a country excluded from membership for political reasons. But it would be unfortunate if this interpretation of the observation and inspection principles were to prevail. The Convention does not specify what is to be the object of the system, but to confine it to ensuring compliance with effective conservation measures ignores the wider possibilities. Formulation of conservation measures is only one of the functions of the Commission. Others, which could be the basis of decisions, include facilitation of research, compilation of data and identification of conservation needs.[153]

The system could have wider application. It has been suggested that a tendency to concentrate research on harvested species is likely, and that it would seriously weaken the ecosystem concept which is the fundamental feature of the conservation principles.[154] Effective measures contrary to the wishes of harvesting States which are members of the Commission will presumably be vetoed. However, the Convention requires all parties to take appropriate measures to the end that no one engages in any activity contrary to the objective,[155] which is conservation as defined in the conservation principles.[156] In this way the system could be used to attempt direct application of the ecosystem approach and partly to circumvent the absence of specific provisions.

151. Art. XXIV(2)(*a*).
152. As in Art. XXI with reference to conservation measures binding in accordance with Art. IX.
153. Art. IX(1)(*a*)(*b*) and (*e*).
154. See Krill/*Commission*.
155. Art. XXII.
156. Art. II.

Supporters of direct application will point out that any harvesting activities 'shall be conducted in accordance with . . . [the] principles of conservation'.[157] On the other hand, it will be contended that it is the Commission's function to give effect to the principles,[158] and that this is to be done by the adoption of conservation measures. The principles are very general and not suitable for enforcement; they are intended as guidelines in the formulation of measures. If any practical use were to be made of them in the observation and inspection system, it would require the formulation of a particular conclusion such as the upper limit of harvesting of a species. But such functions are specifically allocated to the Commission under the heading of conservation measures.

Although the balance falls against immediate reliance on the conservation principles, it cannot be said that the issue is free of doubt. In practice it will be the observers who will be concerned with direct application,[159] and provided that the system has been implemented by a decision of the Commission, an observer could acquire information relevant to the conservation principles in the course of routine operations. For some time the United States has made a practice of including representatives of environmental groups in official delegations to carry on negotiations related to the Antarctic,[160] and the participation of a duly qualified scientist proposed by such groups as one of a United States observation team would be a practical means of meeting the inevitable criticism of harvesting methods.

Ratification

The Convention enters into force thirty days after the deposit of the eighth ratification by States participating in the Conference.[161] When will the regime come into effect? The Antarctic Treaty, which has a similar provision, took effect less than two years after signature, but on the other hand the Sealing Convention, which required only seven ratifications, came into force after seven years. A particularly disturbing example is that of the Agreed Measures, which had not become effective sixteen years after their unanimous recommendation by the Consultative Parties. More important than the mere

157. Ibid.
158. Art. IX(1).
159. Presumably International Whaling Commission 'existing international practice' (Art. XXIV(2)(*a*)) will be followed in calling nationals of the State to which the scrutinised vessel belongs 'inspectors' and nationals of other States 'observers'.
160. Department of State, *Environmental Impact Statement on the Convention for the Conservation of Antarctic Seals* (1974), 45–6 (Sierra Club and Friends of the Earth, each represented at the Sealing Conference in 1972).
161. Art. XXVIII.

counting of instances of delay for Antarctic and law of the sea agreements is the question why there was a substantial time-lapse in particular cases and whether the same reasons apply to the Convention.

Entry into force of the Antarctic Treaty was seen as a prerequisite for maintenance of the *status quo* developed during the IGY. Once it became clear that the reason for negotiating the Sealing Convention — namely the advent of commercial harvesting — was not to occur in the near future, it was natural for States to lose interest in ratification. No particular urgency attached to approval of the Agreed Measures because they were implemented in practice on a voluntary basis.

From this experience it may be tentatively suggested that the possibility of relatively speedy entry into force is much higher than for the general run of international agreements. The original time-table of fourteen months for conclusion of a definitive regime[162] was surprising, yet a detailed text settling nearly all the most controversial issues was drafted in 1979. If the same factors which drove the Consultative Parties to undertake negotiations continue to apply, it will be in their interests to ensure that the Convention comes into force quickly. In particular, a continuation and increase of the already substantial research and harvesting effort will of itself put pressure on signatories to ratify.

At the same time, account must be taken of factors beyond the control of the foreign affairs departments which have negotiated the Convention. The Antarctic Treaty was essentially a written affirmation of the existing political arrangements concerning an area lacking easily exploitable resources. But as krill harvesting promises to become a major industry conducted to a large degree in areas of claimed national jurisdiction, pressure groups of various descriptions may assert that the regime relinquishes control over national resources without any visible compensation. Sovereignty sentiment has not abated in recent years. Constitutional requirements will certainly take time and may postpone ratification for States which fully support the Convention.

For this reason, the State Department proposed supplemental interim measures covering collection of data, and possibly harvesting ceilings on krill to reflect a conservative approach.[163] Interim guidelines already exist. Consultative Parties should cooperate as broadly and comprehensively as possible in the exchange of catch statistics, and the greatest possible concern and care should be shown for the harvesting of Antarctic marine living resources so that

162. Rec. IX-2.
163. Department of State, *Final Environmental Impact Statement for a Possible Regime for Conservation of Antarctic Living Marine Resources* (1978), 12.

it does not result in the depletion of stocks or jeopardise the eco-system as a whole.[164] These principles have had little effect, and at least one State, the Soviet Union, regards its statistics as con-fidential. Interim measures were suggested, but met opposition from harvesting States.[165]

Although no textual provision was made for the period before the Convention's entry into force, the matter was dealt with in a state-ment in the Final Act. Parties entitled to become members of the Commission were called upon to show the greatest possible care and concern, bearing in mind Article II, in harvesting before entry into force and examination of the status of stocks by the Scientific Committee. Research was to be intensified, and needed scientific and fisheries data was to be identified and such data compiled for distribution to Contracting Parties on entry into force of the Con-vention. It was noted that Australia would convene a meeting of parties entitled to Commission membership in 1981 to consider steps to facilitate early operation of the Convention organs. Unlike Recommendation IX-2 under the Antarctic Treaty, these interim measures are not even capable of becoming legally binding, and it would be surprising if they seriously affected the plans of harvesting States. Interim rules were needed not only until the Convention came into effect, but also until adequate conservation measures are in force.

Any State may accede to the Convention if it is 'interested in research or harvesting activities'.[166] This is a strange provision, which cannot mean that the State must be engaged in such activities, because that is the criterion for membership of the Commission.[167] If the previously advanced interpretation that 'engaged' does not demand a substantial effort[168] is accepted, then 'interested' could be read as meaning that the State need not carry on any activity at all in relation to resources, altruistic concern alone sufficing. Indeed it would be possible for a country to be interested in a moratorium on krill harvesting to comply with the accession test, as is the case with some parties to the Whaling Convention.

It will be objected that this construction deprives the test of any real content, since any nation intending to accede would *ipso facto* be 'interested'. The explanation may be that the Article is a com-promise between those wishing for a strict test involving actual

164. Rec.IX-2.
165. J.N. Barnes, 'The Emerging Antarctic Living Resources Convention' (1979), *ASIL Proc.*, 272 at 279.
166. Art. XXIX.
167. Art. VII(2).
168. See Krill/*Commission*.

research or harvesting and others supporting accession of all States. Comparison with the test for acquisition of Consultative status[169] favours the view that a nation wishing to accede to the Convention must have an 'interest' but does not have to demonstrate it by any form of activity.

Only States can accede. Taiwan could not become a party, which thus poses an immediate possibility of krill harvesting by vessels not bound by the Convention. Since the regime is based upon flag-State prosecution of nationals, parties to the Convention would have difficulty in justifying application of their own laws to Taiwanese krill trawlers. Should conservation measures impose substantial restrictions, a flag of convenience would be readily available.

Assessment

Achievement of agreement on a major resource within two years is of itself noteworthy, but all the more so when difficult issues of unresolved claims have to be dealt with. The conservation principles provide a basis for the innovative attention to an entire ecosystem, regardless of whether a particular species is of commercial interest. A regime has been drafted prior to the exploitation stage. Provision is made for an observation and inspection scheme, a form of secretariat, a Commission and a Scientific Committee with specified functions.

However, a number of dubious features of existing treaties have been incorporated into the Convention. The Antarctic system is the source of complicated freezing clauses, consensus in decision-making, absence of effective dispute settlement, lack of provision for open meetings, and a privileged position for members of the Commission. Monopolisation of negotiation of the Convention by the Consultative Parties is difficult to justify. The objection procedure for conservation measures and agreement not to consider national quota allocation come from the Whaling Convention and practice. In these important matters little seems to have been learnt from past experience.

If the Convention is to be more than a traditional fisheries regime, the central issue will be the extent to which the conservation principles can be translated into effective decisions of the Commission. Obstacles in the way of a working ecosystem approach are serious and perhaps fatal. Harvesting States will not consent to an interim arrangement which seriously limits the expansion of their com-

---

169. '. . . demonstrates its interest in Antarctica by conducting substantial . . . research activities' (Art. IX(2), Antarctic Treaty).

mercial activities. When the Convention comes into force, there are no specific directly applicable rules which can be immediately enforced, even if some parties should wish to pass appropriate national legislation. Inaction by the Commission means no standards. All decisions are subject to the veto of the exploiting members, to which must be added the objection option of each member with regard to conservation measures.

Every decision of the Commission which is thought to impede the interests of the fishing nations will involve a separate battle. Environmental groups and scientists have had considerable success in ensuring that the conservation principles are based upon concern for the entire Antarctic marine food-web south of the Convergence, but it may be seriously doubted whether this can be carried through to the Commission. Conservationists have already lost an array of issues, including the prescription of initial standards (such as quotas) in the text of the Convention, an immediately workable inspection and observation system, majority voting in the Commission, independence of the Scientific Committee, dispute settlement and interim arrangements. Of even more concern than the accumulation of defeats is the common thread linking them: opposition to the effective implementation of ecosystem standards. When these issues come before the Commission, conservation interests will be directly opposed to a large and united fishing lobby. Most governments willing to press for harvesting limitations will not themselves have a financial stake in krill, whereas harvesters, particularly from States with centralised economies, will be able to exert considerable political pressure on their governments, in a way denied to environmental groups. Any clash between harvesting interests and conservationists seeking implementation of the ecosystem principles with respect to an issue seen to be important to the fishing nations is likely to be decided in favour of the harvesters.

In theory, the ecosystem may be safeguarded, but practical application will probably not bear out the promise of conservation. If this failure affects the main resource, krill, it will be even more marked for non-harvested species. Commercial exploitation of krill on a large scale must carry with it some investment in scientific research, but the Convention provides no incentive for the outlay of funds on research into other elements of the food-chain. The Scientific Committee is composed of government representatives and has no powers of decision-making. Under the present regime it would be surprising if conservation measures seriously limiting any aspect of krill harvesting to protect non-harvested species were adopted without objection. Whales and pelagic seals are still regulated by a species approach.

Conservation of the ecosystem is the regime's objective. In practice the Convention will become a fisheries management treaty dominated by the interests of the harvesting States.

8
OIL AND GAS

Minerals

Speculation on minerals dates from the earliest period of Antarctic exploration,[1] and has continued ever since. One of the reasons for the US State Department policy study of 1939 was the continent's mineral potential.[2] Such conjecture was not confined to passing journalists or desk-bound diplomats, but was shared by Antarctic veterans like Byrd,[3] Dufek[4] and Law.[5] The natural resources issue was raised during Treaty ratification hearings. Dr Gould's remark that he would not give a nickel for all the mineral resources he knew of in Antarctica has often been quoted, but the comment was made in the context of the lack of geological knowledge of the area.[6]

Soviet interest in Antarctic minerals, both onshore and offshore, has been constantly reiterated, and Druzhnaya Station was established in the Weddell Sea sector in 1975 as the first base overtly dedicated to mineral prospecting. If land resources are to be exploited, the Soviet Union will be able to draw on its extensive Arctic experience.[7]

Even today any examination of the mineral resources of Antarctica has to be based to a large degree on analogy. It remains true that no deposits have yet been found which can be economically exploited on the basis of current prices and technology. Whether or not future developments will alter this situation will not be clear for some years.

It is widely assumed that there is little likelihood of onshore mining, even for high-value minerals such as diamonds,[8] during the remainder of the twentieth century.[9] Several factors combine to reduce the possibility of making a find and to raise the cost of

1. J.F. da Costa, *Souveraineté sur l'Antarctique* (1958), 56.
2. E.W. Cole, 'Claims of Sovereignty over the Antarctic', thesis, Judge Advocate General's Office, US Army (1958), 85.
3. R.K. McNickle, 'Antarctic Claims' (1949), 2 *Editorial Research Reports*, 781.
4. G.J. Dufek, *Operation Deepfreeze* (1957), 150.
5. P. Law, *Antarctic – 1984* (1964), 10–12.
6. 'The Antarctic Treaty', Hearings, Committee on Foreign Relations, Senate, 86th Cong., 2nd Sess. (1960), 75.
7. See National Interests/*The Soviet Union*.
8. N. Potter, *Natural Resource Potentials of the Antarctic* (1969), 27.
9. J.H. Zumberge(ed.), *Possible Environmental Effects of Mineral Exploration and Exploitation in Antarctica* (1979), 10 (Adaptation of the EAMREA Report).

mining. Ninety-eight per cent of the continent is covered by a moving ice sheet; the number of potential port sites is small; transport from an inland site to the coast on a continuous basis would be most expensive; the summer shipping season is short, and icebreaker assistance would be needed for conventional cargo carriers; and primary treatment would require energy sources and in some cases large quantities of fresh water. There is no doubt that large deposits of minerals exist in Antarctica, just as they exist in every continent,[10] but on present costing even resources of a considerable magnitude on land are considered uneconomic. Should mineral prices escalate, priority would presumably be given to the exploitation of known resources close to population centres which are not worth development at present.

However, this generally accepted view could change. Mineral exploitation has recently taken place in regions which, a few decades earlier, were considered inaccessible, an example being the North Slope of Alaska.[11] Strategic considerations may dictate a search for politically safe resources at costs above those of the world market. There is, however, one instance which demands separate discussion.

In the examination of Soviet interests, it was pointed out that one reason for the location of Druzhnaya Station was its relative proximity to the Dufek Intrusion in the Pensacola Mountains.[12] Both US and Soviet[13] commentators have placed special emphasis on this site, which was described by the US Geological Survey as of possible great economic potential. The formation covers at least 34,000 sq.km. Its interest to geologists lies in the great variety of economic minerals found in similar formations in South Africa, Montana and Ontario.[14] Both the Soviet Union and the United States have carried out research on the Intrusion, the American efforts appearing to be primarily directed to basic research with mineral appraisal as a by-product.[15] In 1979 the National Science Foundation hoped to send a small drill team to obtain some samples in due course; at that time the United States was not certain of the extent of Soviet work carried out two years previously but not published.[16]

10. N.A. Wright and P.L. Williams, *Mineral Resources of Antarctica* (1974), 18 (US Geological Survey publication).
11. M.W. Holdgate and J. Tinker, *Oil and Other Minerals in the Antarctic* (1979), 16.
12. See National Interests/*The Soviet Union*.
13. B.S. Slevich, *Basic Problems of Antarctic Exploitation* (1973), 16.
14. N.A. Wright and P.L. Williams, *Mineral Resources of Antarctica* (1974), 17.
15. 'US Science Projects this Summer' (1978), 8(8) *Antarctic*, 262.
16. Dr E.P. Todd, Director, Division of Polar Programs, National Science Foundation, in 'US Activities in Antarctica', Hearing, Committee on Energy and Natural Resources, Senate, 96th Cong., 1st Sess. (23 April 1979), 40–1.

As the Dufek Intrusion was discovered in 1957 and first studied by the US Geological Survey in 1965, it does not seem that the United States is in any hurry to carry out resource investigation in what has been described by a leading US expert as a particularly attractive target area.[17] Lack of information from the Soviet Union is not of itself remarkable, since there have been previous instances of new developments in Soviet Antarctic programmes which have been carried out secretively (e.g. the taking of seals, commercial fishing in sub-Antarctic waters, and the establishment of Leningradskaya Base). Like the United States, the Soviet Union has an announced interest in mineral resources. But the devotion of special attention to a formation discovered and subsequently examined by the United States may well have additional political implications. Apart from presenting a direct challenge to the United States, the potential for commercial exploration could be used by the Soviet Union as a bargaining counter in negotiations for a mineral regime.

Evolution

In contrast to the remoteness of exploitation on land, considerable and sometimes sensational prominence has been given to offshore oil and gas possibilities. In 1969 a study commissioned by the National Science Foundation concluded that exploitation of Antarctic continental shelf oilfields would be impractical without new and expensive technology, and might well not be worth the outlay.[18] Presumably prompted by this report, if not its conclusions, two enquiries were made to the New Zealand government in 1969.[19] Although the contents of this correspondence are not known, the government received, either on this occasion or within the next two years, applications for prospecting rights.[20] At least one application was received by the United Kingdom, as were numerous enquiries. In December 1969 a senior official of Texaco asked the State Department's views on geophysical prospecting in Antarctic coastal waters (and in the Barents Sea), and the Department discouraged the company. A request by Texas Geophysical Instruments for exclusive rights to explore the Ross and Weddell Seas made at some date before May 1975 was refused by the State Department, on the

17. J.H. Zumberge, 'Mineral Resources and Geopolitics in Antarctica' (1979), 67 *American Scientist*, 68 at 72.
18. N. Potter, *Natural Resource Potentials of the Antarctic* (1969), 29.
19. F.M. Auburn, 'Offshore Oil and Gas in Antarctica' (1977), 20 *German Yearbook of International Law*, 139 at 141–2.
20. C. Beeby, *The Antarctic Treaty* (1972), 18.

ground that there were no procedures for grants of such rights in Antarctica.[21]

A parallel development has been the expression of interest in sub-Antarctic areas exemplified by the application of the French company ERAP for a licence over the Kerguelen Plateau in 1972 and numerous requests to the British government in regard to the Falkland Islands. The incident in which the Argentinian warship *Almirante Storni* halted geophysical research by the British vessel *Shackleton* in February 1976 has been discussed previously.[22]

Apparently prompted by the enquiries, New Zealand raised the issue in 1970, but no action was taken; however, at the next Meeting in 1972, it was decided that the effects of mineral exploration be studied.[23] This oblique reaction reflected the political sensitivity of the topic and a lack of urgency. Early in 1973 the US ship *Glomar Challenger* drilled four experimental holes in the Ross Sea as part of a global geological study, the Deep Sea Drilling Project. Three holes showed small quantities of gaseous hydrocarbons. Well aware of the political impact of their research, the scientists stressed that it was extremely premature to attach any economic significance to the Ross Sea hydrocarbons 'at this time', but their presence should logically lead to a close examination of the potential, and could bring 'wishful and wild speculation' regarding reserves, leading to new negotiations within the Treaty system.[24]

The immediate effect of the *Glomar Challenger*'s drilling was to galvanise the Consultative Parties into action. A purported informal meeting of experts (in a private capacity) was convened at the Nansen Foundation in Norway in May and June 1973.[25] From the participants' identities, and the form of the report, it is clear that it was in effect a preparatory meeting,[26] called in this unusual manner because of the sensitivity of the issue. The Nansen report is therefore the sole example of a detailed official public account of the proceedings of any meeting of the Consultative Parties. On the minerals

---

21. 'US Antarctic Policy', Hearing, Subcommittee on Oceans and International Environment, Committee on Foreign Relations, Senate, 94th Cong. 1st Sess. (15 May 1975), 18.
22. See National Interests/*South America*.
23. Rec. VII-6.
24. D.E. Hayes and L.A. Frakes, 'General Synthesis' in (1975), 28 *Initial Reports of the Deep Sea Drilling Project*, 940.
25. 'Antarctic Resources' in 'US Antarctic Policy', Hearing, Subcommittee on Oceans and International Environment, Committee on Foreign Relations, Senate, 94th Cong., 1st Sess. (15 May 1975), 68.
26. F.M. Auburn, 'Offshore Oil and Gas in Antarctica' (1977), 20 *German Yearbook of International Law*, 139 at 144−5.

issue, it is of considerable interest in revealing the wide gap between the positions of these countries in 1973.

Another result of the *Glomar Challenger* holes and of the oil crisis following the Yom Kippur War in 1973 was a secret study of minerals by the US Geological Survey at the request of the Antarctic Policy Group of the National Security Council. For the Ross, Weddell and Bellingshausen Seas, estimates of 45 billion barrels of petroleum and 115 trillion cubic feet of natural gas were made.[27] Clearly such figures were only intended to be best guesses based on minimal data. The US government had not intended to publish them, and their leakage was an embarrassment. For the first time official figures for Antarctic oil and gas were available, and naturally gave rise to considerable interest. Strenuous efforts were later made to repair the damage. The US Geological Survey study published in 1974, and presumably adapted from its previous secret work, stated that there was insufficient information to estimate the petroleum potential.[28] An informal assessment prepared for internal US government use and tabled at the 1976 Paris Special Preparatory Meeting emphasised the absence of geological data; any numerical estimates would be considered as 'order of magnitude guesses'. The Antarctic shelf could contain potentially recoverable oil in the order of magnitude of tens of billions of barrels.[29] There was a growing feeling that 'there could be another Middle East in the Antarctic'.[30]

Government agencies concerned with resources began to participate in Antarctic policy decisions.[31] Druzhnaya was established in 1975. That year's Consultative Meeting decided to study the matter fully at the 1976 Paris Meeting,[32] and requested SCAR to make an environmental impact assessment. This was the origin of EAMREA. While the Consultative Parties were seeking a timely solution, States and persons were urged to refrain from commercial exploration and exploitation. Because it was contained in the Final Report, and not in a recommendation,[33] this interim moratorium could not become

27. J. Spivak, 'Frozen Assets?', *Wall Street Journal* (21 February 1974).
28. N.A. Wright and P.L. Williams, *Mineral Resources of Antarctica* (1974) 15. The EAMREA Report stated that 'there is considerable doubt that this is an official US Geological Survey estimate because it was not included' in the study (J.H. Zumberge (ed.), *Possible Environmental Effects of Mineral Exploration and Exploitation in Antarctica* (1979), 14).
29. 'Antarctic Mineral Resources', RPS-10 (1976).
30. John N. Garrett, Gulf Oil, quoted in J. Tinker, 'Cold War over Antarctic wealth', *New Scientist* (20 September 1979), 867.
31. J. Rose, 'Antarctic Condominium: Building a New Legal Order for Commercial Interests' (1976), 10 *Marine Technology Society Journal*, 19 at 23.
32. Rec. VIII-14.
33. See Antarctic System/*Procedure*.

legally binding on the Consultative Parties themselves, and *a fortiori* it could not affect Contracting Parties or countries not signatories to the Treaty.

The Paris Special Preparatory Meeting again showed the deep divisions between the Consultative Parties on minerals. Even the Final Report was not released. But by the time of the next Consultative Meeting, living resources had become the first priority. General principles were laid down, the interim moratorium became part of a recommendation, and further study was to be undertaken.[34] At the 1979 Meeting, stress was placed on laying down the general purposes of a mineral regime and assessing environmental impact.[35] Final conclusion of the Living Resources Convention in May 1980 reopened the way for concentration on minerals.

In the meantime the constant escalation of oil prices and crises in the Middle East had taken their toll. In September 1979 the Japanese Ministry of International Trade and Industry announced that it would seek a $12,000,000 appropriation for geological and geophysical surveys by the *Hakurei Maru* in the Ross, Weddell and Bellingshausen Seas from 1980 to 1982.[36] It was particularly noteworthy that the official initiative came from the powerful Ministry of International Trade and Industry (MITI). The National Institute of Polar Research of Japan had no documentation at the time other than press releases.

Location

The major geological basis for inferring that oil and gas are present off Antarctica comes from the former linking of Antarctica with India and the continents and islands of the Southern Hemisphere. The Gondwanaland super-continent began to disintegrate in the Mesozoic Era, and where they were once joined, the new continents developed continental shelves on which sedimentary rocks were deposited. Although there is still considerable dispute as to the sequence of the break-up,[37] the hypothesis has gained general acceptance among geologists. Discovery of oil and gas in areas formerly contiguous with Antarctica is therefore considered to suggest the

34. Rec. IX-1.
35. Rec. X-1.
36. 'Japan joins oil hunt', *West Australian* (7 September 1979). It can hardly have been a coincidence that the news was made public immediately before the Consultative Meeting opened on 17 September.
37. C. Craddock, 'Antarctica and Gondwanaland' in M.A. McWhinnie (ed.), *Polar Research* (1978), 63 at 84.

possible presence of resources on the Antarctic continental shelf. The Bellingshausen shelf is similar to offshore Chile, which has so far yielded natural gas. South Africa and South America have small oil and gas fields hinting at the same result for the Weddell Sea. The Ross Sea may resemble the Gippsland Basin of Australia, which contains significant amounts of oil and gas.[38] This summation represented the view of the US Geological Survey in 1974, and the internal assessment of the US government in 1976 added the basin underlying the Amery Ice Shelf and the Scotia Sea.[39] Current geological and geophysical knowledge is too limited to permit the identification of specific areas where more detailed exploration activities could be concentrated,[40] and to enlarge that knowledge is the purpose of the *Hakurei Maru* survey.

A number of factors suggest that the Ross Sea is one of the most attractive area for commercial exploration. Sea-ice is less severe there than on other parts of the Antarctic continental shelf,[41] and thick sedimentary formations are known to exist.[42] The finding of methane and ethane in three of the four holes drilled by the *Glomar Challenger* showed, at the least, that the shelf is not devoid of hydrocarbons.[43] In November 1975 the Dry Valley Drilling Project (DVDP) halted work on a hole in McMurdo Sound, having detected methane in core sediments. Although methane is not evidence of deposits, it is significant that the DVDP impact assessment had given low probability to the presence of hydrocarbons.[44] The Ross Sea sector is perhaps the most promising because it is best known. When it was part of Gondwanaland, it was proximate to the Kingfish, Barracouta, Halibut, Tuna and Cobia oilfields of the offshore Gippsland Basin of Southeast Australia.[45] The Ross Sea is the centre

38. N.A. Wright and P.L. Williams, *Mineral Resources of Antarctica* (1974), 16. The same reasoning suggests the presence of significant mineral deposits on land, such as copper in the Antarctic Peninsula.
39. 'Antarctic Mineral Resources' RPS-10 (1976).
40. J.H. Zumberge (ed.), *Possible Environmental Effects of Mineral Exploration and Exploitation in Antarctica* (1979), 12.
41. J.F. Splettstoesser, 'Offshore Development for Oil and Gas in Antarctica' in *Proceedings of the Fourth International Conference on Port and Ocean Engineering under Arctic Conditions* (1978), 811 at 813.
42. Institute of Polar Studies, Ohio State University, *A Framework for Assessing Environmental Impacts of Possible Antarctic Mineral Developments* (1977), IV-22.
43. 'Antarctic Resources' in 'US Antarctic Policy', Hearing, Subcommittee on Oceans and International Environment, Committee on Foreign Relations, Senate, 94th Cong., 1st Sess. (15 May 1975), 74.
44. R.V. Howard, B.C. Parker and R.D. Rugo, 'DVDP environmental impact assessment and monitoring' (1976), 11(3) *Antarctic Journal*, 90.
45. J.H. Zumberge, 'Mineral Resources and Geopolitics in Antarctica' (1979), 67 *American Scientist*, 68 at 73.

of activities of the United States, which has close and friendly relations with the sole announced claimant in the sector, New Zealand.
American oil companies would therefore prefer to work in the Ross
Sea rather than in the Weddell Sea, which presents the maximum of
political difficulties. Previous discussion[46] has, however, suggested
that the establishment of Leningradskaya and Russkaya Stations
should be seen as a Soviet strategy designed to forestall American
commercial and political interests.

Technology

Discussion of a regime for offshore oil and gas is made more difficult
by the lack of knowledge concerning location of possible deposits
and the manner of exploitation. It is a temptation to assume that
recent Arctic offshore developments can be transposed to
Antarctica, but while techniques invented for polar exploitation will
be of some use, it should be stressed that offshore Arctic drilling is a
recent innovation, and work has been carried out in shallow water.
Icebergs have been towed but they are small in comparison with
those to be met in the Antarctic.[47] With this note of caution, the
Arctic still presents the closest available analogy for the Antarctic.
Current Arctic technology, such as emplacement of blow-out preventers beneath the sea floor to avoid scour, icebreaking tankers and
extended exploratory drilling seasons,[48] are already relevant. Future
progress will doubtless be transferable.

One obstacle is the unusual depth of the Antarctic continental
shelf (800 metres at the seaward edge of the shelf of the Ross Sea).[49]
But from the standpoint of technical feasibility, water depth criteria
are of relatively little importance in the light of expected progress.[50]
Exploration is already taking place at such depths, and licences cover
even deeper areas. By the time Antarctic exploitation is due to begin,
it may be expected that rigs designed for other offshore areas will be
capable of drilling in the Southern Ocean.

Antarctic icebergs colliding with oil rigs would completely destroy
those structures; even placement of the drilling gear on the sea
bottom would provide no protection down to a water depth of at

46. See National Interests/*The Soviet Union*.
47. Institute of Polar Studies, Ohio State University, *A Framework for Assessing
    Environmental Impacts of Possible Antarctic Mineral Developments* (1977),
    IV-21.
48. G.R. Harrison, 'Exploratory Drilling: The Polar Challenge', Tenth World
    Petroleum Congress (1979).
49. M.W. Holdgate and J. Tinker, *Oil and Other Minerals in the Antarctic* (1979),
    18.
50. France, 'Petroleum Production in Antarctic Offshore Conditions', ANT IX/17
    (19 September 1977).

least 200 metres because icebergs would scour the sea bottom.[51] Towing is now a routine practice in the Labrador Sea and off West Greenland. However, attempts to transport icebergs of even a moderate size are only in the experimental stage. When a 292,000 ton berg was harnessed off Eastern Canada, it was mostly a case of the berg towing the ship.[52] In Antarctica weights of 100 million tons and more are encountered, and this is one of the main obstacles to proposals for extracting fresh water from large Antarctic icebergs. Efforts to destroy them with bombs, torpedoes and mines have shown little result.[53] Towing is at present impracticable when the weight exceeds 2 million tons, if the sea is rough or if the berg is unstable or inconveniently shaped.[54] It may then be assumed that production wells and pipelines would have to be buried unless the water is more than 300 metres deep.[55] Exploratory drilling would not face this problem. If timely warning has been given (ten minutes in the Arctic[56]), it is possible to extract the equipment.

Current operations work on a three-month shipping season. Even for this limited period, icebreakers are needed if regular traffic on a large scale is contemplated. Taking into account the assumption that only a very large oilfield could be economically exploited in the Antarctic, the resulting density of traffic of fully laden tankers would present additional risks. Although the construction of specially built very large crude tankers to operate all the year round in the Ross Sea has been suggested,[57] such vessels are not at present available. Also, it is not clear where the oil would be stored after extraction. Construction of pipelines would be expensive, to avoid iceberg scour in shallow water, and access to ports and land storage would involve further problems.[58] Undersea holding tanks have been built elswhere, but Antarctic structures would require substantial capacity to cope with vessel delays due to bad weather.[59] Various

51. J.H. Zumberge (ed.), *Possible Environmental Effects of Mineral Exploration and Exploitation in Antarctica* (1979), 12.
52. A.A. Bruneau, R.T. Dempster and G.R. Peters, 'Iceberg Towing for Oil Rig Avoidance' in A.A. Husseiny (ed.), *Iceberg Utilization* (1978), 379 at 384.
53. G.M. Schultz, *Icebergs and their Voyages* (1975), 67−9.
54. Report of the Working Group of Experts on Mineral Exploration and Exploitation, ANT/IX/51 (Rev I) (29 September 1977), para. 19.
55. Institute of Polar Studies, Ohio State University, *A Framework for Assessing Environmental Impacts of Possible Antarctic Mineral Developments* (1977), V-22.
56. 'Canadian offshore drilling' (1980), 8(12) *Canada Weekly*, 4.
57. M.W. Holdgate and J. Tinker, *Oil and Other Minerals in the Antarctic* (1979), 29.
58. Report of the Working Group of Experts on Mineral Exploration and Exploitation, ANT/IX/51 (Rev I) (29 September 1977), para. 35.
59. M.W. Holdgate and J. Tinker, *Oil and Other Minerals in the Antarctic* (1979), 29.

semi-submersible and submarine transport vessels have been proposed for the Arctic,[60] but none has yet been constructed.

Antarctic oil exploitation will require deep water polar experience, and even the Soviet Union has only recently embarked upon the building of mobile oil rigs for work at such depths.[61] The Consultative Parties include most of the nations with the requisite technological capacity.[62] But although this monopoly offers a temporary respite to the Antarctic system, it would be rash to assume that it can be preserved until exploitation is likely. Recent history provides numerous examples of vain predictions that specific countries could not develop advanced technologies.

From this brief review it would appear that the development of suitable techniques and equipment is not impossible, but that it will be expensive:[63] there can be no doubt that the cost will be far beyond that of conventional fields. So many unknown factors exist that any estimate can only be guesswork. However, the suggestion that a well will involve an outlay three times greater than in the Gulf of Mexico[64] is an indication of current views. The investment will be such that only exceptionally extensive finds will be worth exploiting.

If exploitation is carried out, is it possible to provide an approximate time-scale? Even the roughest estimate would be of some assistance in indicating the date by which the Consultative Parties will have to devise a regime. From the purely industrial viewpoint, available information justifies exploration now. Seismic operations by the *Hakurei-Maru*, to be shared with other nations,[65] will increase the pressure on all concerned countries to carry out their own work. There are wide differences in projections. One group of experts suggested exploratory drilling would be possible by 1987;[66] on another view such drilling will not be feasible before 1998 at the earliest.[67] Yet another source suggests two to four years for seismic surveying and five to ten years for exploratory drilling, followed by exploitation.[68]

60. J.P. Riva and J.E. Mielke, *Polar Energy Resources Potential* (1976), 88–9.
61. Congressional Research Service, *Soviet Oceans Development* (1976), 495.
62. P. Jones, 'Whose Oil Resources? – The Question of Antarctic Sovereignty' (1976), 61 *Geography*, 167 at 168.
63. J.B. Oerding, 'The Frozen Friction Point: a Geopolitical Analysis of Sovereignty in the Antarctic Peninsula', MA thesis, University of Florida (1977), 49.
64. Institute of Polar Studies, Ohio State University, *A Framework for Assessing Environmental Impacts of Possible Antarctic Mineral Developments* (1977), VI-14.
65. 'Japanese plans for oil exploration' (1979), 8(11) *Antarctic*, 389.
66. Report of the Working Group of Experts on Mineral Exploration and Exploitation, ANT/IX/51 (Rev I) (29 September 1977), para. 5.
67. M.D. Turner, 'Antarctic Mineral Resources' (1978), 43(1) *Frontiers*, 27 at 29.
68. M.W. Holdgate and J. Tinker, *Oil and Other Minerals in the Antarctic* (1979), 26 and 28.

SCAR indicated that exploitation could begin before the turn of the century.[69] It is the second step, exploratory drilling, which is vital for the time-table. Exclusive licenses will be required before it can begin. Otherwise the substantial financial investment could not be safeguarded. This stage could well be relatively close.

A number of additional factors dictate the speedy conclusion of a regime. First, by the time exploitation is envisaged, suitable equipment may already be available, whether developed in the Arctic, the North Sea or elsewhere, and secondly, oil sanctions have prompted renewed interest in energy autarchy.[70] It may not be possible to isolate Antarctica from world politics indefinitely. Exploration may be carried out in order to preserve political options. Once one country begins work, as Japan has done, there will be considerable pressure on others to follow suit.

Various political considerations will also have to be taken into account. An unexpected event could upset the apple-cart of the Consultative Parties: for instance, the discovery of a particularly attractive geological formation, a further international oil crisis or yet another sovereignty dispute. Although exploitation may still be twenty years in the future, the conclusion of a regime is now a matter of urgency for the Consultative Parties.

Environment

Concern for the environment has been a dominant feature of the public attitude at Consultative Meetings.[71] Even at the present stage of knowledge it is obvious that Antarctic oilfields will present major new problems. There is general agreement that costs will ensure that only very large deposits will be economical.[72] Combining the hazards of severe pack-ice, prolonged high-intensity storms and bottom-scouring icebergs, exploitation will face unprecedented risks. Is it possible to predict them comprehensively so far in advance of operations? The answer must be in the negative. However, it is feasible to define the main issues.

An inevitable result of exploitation is the escape of oil, of which current Antarctic work yields a number of documented examples.[73]

---

69. SCAR response to Antarctic Treaty Recommendation IX-6 (398 *SCAR Circular* (3 July 1978)).
70. R. Lagoni, 'Antarctica's Mineral Resources in International Law' (1979), 39(1) *Zeitschrift für Ausländisches Öffentliches Recht und Völkerrecht*, 1 at 6.
71. See, for example, the repeated references in Rec. IX-1, IX-6 and X-1.
72. 300,000–400,000 barrels per day production (M.W. Holdgate and J. Tinker, *Oil and Other Minerals in the Antarctic* (1979), 29).
73. e.g. G.J. Wilson, 'Oiled Penguins in Antarctica' (1979), 2(2) *NZ Antarctic*

Even carefully controlled scientific research under the Dry Valley Drilling Project involved unavoidable contamination from spills and leaks of drill fluid and fuel. On world statistics, a blow-out is taken to be rather unlikely if adequate surveys and blow-out preventers are installed.[74] This inference is based on conditions in less hazardous areas. It was made before the blow-out of the Ixtoc I well in Campeche Bay, Gulf of Mexico, in 1979 when millions of barrels of oil escaped over a period of ten months, although the site was in a very accessible area close to modern technological aid.[75] A specific weakness of statistical assumptions of this nature lies in the great severity of operating conditions in the Antarctic. Pressures on workers are peculiarly likely to lead to mistakes; and the main factor in blow-outs has been on-site operator error.[76]

Possible consequences of a blow-out were a major issue in Canadian Arctic exploratory drilling in the Beaufort Sea. Early contingency plans were criticised because several months could elapse before a relief well could be drilled.[77] Such an accident at the end of a season could lead to a year's release of oil with the possibility of a further year if the site proved difficult to reach in the following summer.[78] Intervention by the US government in February 1976[79] led to consultations and, apparently, some amendments to the conditions attached to the authorisation; but Canadian officials were unable to suggest any adequate clean-up procedure once the oil had escaped.[80] *A fortiori*, this conclusion applies to the Antarctic.

Given the scale of any Antarctic undertaking and the past record of accidents in less hazardous seas, tanker losses and serious accidents due to iceberg collision, storms or other causes would appear

Record 3. On its experimental unladen voyage through the Northwest Passage in 1969 the tanker *Manhattan* suffered two large holes in the unprotected area below the water-line. One 'would have accomodated a large truck' (R. Perrault cited in G.F. Graham, 'The Canadian Arctic Waters Pollution Prevention Act of 1970 and the Concept of Self-Protection', MA thesis, Carleton University (1974), 109).

74. J.H. Zumberge (ed.), *Possible Environmental Effects of Mineral Exploration and Exploitation in Antarctica* (1979), 34.

75. 'Lessons from the Bay of Campeche should be heeded' (1980) 16(3) *ECO* 2.

76. Fisheries and Environment Canada, *Probabilities of Blowouts in Canadian Arctic Waters* (1978), 132.

77. D.H. Pimlott, 'The Hazardous Search for Oil and Gas in Arctic Waters' (1974), 4(3) *Nature Canada*, 20 at 24.

78. P. Wadhams, 'Oil and Ice in the Beaufort Sea' (1976), 18(114) *Polar Record*, 237 at 246.

79. L.J. Carter, 'Oil Drilling in the Beaufort Sea: Leaving it to Luck and Technology' (1976), 191 *Science*, 929 at 930.

80. P. Wadhams, 'Oil and Gas in the Beaufort Sea' (1976), 18(114) *Polar Record*, 237 at 245.

inevitable, and on the assumption of a three-month shipping period, the probability is further increased. It has been argued that a single spill, even of the entire cargo of a 500,000 ton tanker, would be unlikely to affect overall krill and fish stocks significantly, but repeated large spills would present the real hazard.[81] Prediction is made most difficult because the vessels that would be used – presumably ice-strengthened tankers – have yet to be designed.

Routine accidental or deliberate discharges of ballast and bilge wastes are already a minor source of Antarctic pollution, but with the advent of frequent voyages by the world's largest cargo ships this will constitute a major proportion of the total environmental effects. Onshore facilities will be required, and one scenario envisages pipelines delivering oil to storage tanks on land, in which case extensive docks and related buildings would be needed, employing 1,000 people in the summer season.[82] Impacts would include possible pipeline or tank failure.

Antarctica has few suitable terminal sites,[83] and scientific stations have been established in the most prospective port areas, such as McMurdo Bay. Competition between science and industry will be difficult to avoid; and furthermore, onshore facilities would be attracted to existing scientific bases by the availability of ice-breakers, airfields, docks, search and rescue personnel, and other advantages.

It is argued that the vast size of the Southern Ocean and its strong circulation would disperse a single large spill at sea and it would therefore not affect the ecosystem as a whole[84] – in other words, that it would not be a total catastrophe. But impacts on a smaller scale would still have major consequences. Degradation of hydrocarbons is slower in cold regions. The simple food chain could easily be damaged. The continuing effect of contamination of krill by oil is unknown, but if krill reproduction were significantly lowered, the impact on the dependent species would be serious, quite apart from the damage to the emerging krill trawling industry. Ingestion of hydrocarbons by krill used for human consumption might give rise to a health hazard.[85] Coastal concentrations of birds and mammals

81. M.W. Holdgate and J. Tinker, *Oil and Other Minerals in the Antarctic* (1979), 30.
82. Institute of Polar Studies, Ohio State University, *A Framework for Assessing Environmental Impacts of Possible Antarctic Mineral Developments* (1977), V-26.
83. Report of the Working Group of Experts on Mineral Exploration and Exploitation, ANT/IX/51 (Rev I) (29 September 1977), para. 55.
84. National Science Foundation, *US Antarctic Program Draft Environmental Impact Statement* (1979), 4–15.
85. J.H. Zumberge (ed.), *Possible Environmental Effects of Mineral Exploration and Exploitation in Antarctica* (1979), 39.

could be seriously affected,[86] particularly when breeding. In the Arctic it has been pointed out that large-scale trapping of oil in ice could bring gradual melting of the ice-cover with drastic results.[87] A small reduction in the reflective characteristics of the surface (albedo) caused by impurities could increase the intensity of solar heating in the Antarctic by 20 per cent.[88] Although Antarctic sea-ice waxes and wanes each year by natural processes, even the small likelihood of such vast effects is cause for concern.

A common thread in scientific attempts to assess the impact of oil and gas development in the Antarctic is that lack of knowledge places serious limitations on predictions. The same point has been made in relation to the living resources regime.[89] The SCAR Group of Specialists identified some of the gaps in knowledge and outlined research requirements. These include experiments on the biodegradability of crude oil at different temperatures and on controlled oil spills in polar conditions, research on the tolerances of krill and other Antarctic animals, and surveys of environments, habitats and marine communities.[90] It was stressed that these needs should not compete for funds with current projects.[91] In accordance with an agreement reached at the Ninth Consultative Meeting,[92] a Treaty Group of Ecological, Technological and Other Related Experts on Mineral Exploration and Exploitation met in Washington in June 1979 with a view to developing scientific programmes to improve prediction of the impacts of possible technologies, and developing measures for the prevention of damage.

Their report dealt with the issues at a very generalised level and proposed to remit the matter to SCAR, drawing the Consultative Parties' attention to the costs involved.[93] The resulting recommendations[94] encouraged SCAR to define new programmes, but the terms used[95] suggested that this would be at the expense of current

86. J. Dyson, *The Hot Arctic* (1979), 104.
87. R.O. Ramseler, 'Oil on Ice' (1974), 16(4) *Environment*, 7 at 8.
88. Institute of Polar Studies, Ohio State University, *A Framework for Assessing Environmental Impacts of Possible Antarctic Mineral Developments* (1977), F – 28 – 29.
89. See Krill/*Conservation Principles*.
90. J.H. Zumberge (ed.), *Possible Environmental Effects of Mineral Exploration and Exploitation in Antarctica* (1979), 47–50.
91. Ibid., at p. 49.
92. Rec. IX-1 and IX-6.
93. Annex 6, Report of the Tenth Consultative Meeting (September-October 1979), 102 at 104.
94. Rec. X-1 and X-7.
95. 'Identifying and developing new programs that should have priority . . .' (Rec. X-1).

research. Countries were requested to support such developments through their National Committees 'insofar as feasible'.[96] There does not appear to have been any real change in the attitude of the Consultative Parties to the financial problems of SCAR,[97] despite their repeated public statements of concern at the effect of mineral developments on the environment.

The credibility of the Antarctic system will in part depend on the degree to which the Consultative Parties fulfil their assumed responsibility to evaluate the environmental impact of mineral developments.[98] In planning major operations, such an evaluation has been required of the operating organisations concerned.[99] Impact assessment for informed decision-making is one of the principles to form the basis of the regime. The Consultative Parties have gone even further by requiring that the regime should include means to determine whether mineral resource activities are acceptable.[100] Not only are there to be assessment measures, but there will also be the possibility of refusing permission for exploitation on environmental grounds. If this is to be so, then the funding of research is a vital issue.

National attempts at environmental impact assessment of treaties raise serious problems. Perhaps the most relevant examples are taken from the application by the United States of its National Environmental Policy Act to Antarctica. Shortcomings include the secrecy of international negotiations, presentation of treaty or specific principles as accomplished facts, and the short response times available to interested parties.[101] For the regime to contain effective impact assessment procedures, a number of innovations in Antarctic affairs would be necessary. Meetings of the mineral regime consultative body would have to be public; private organizations would have to be given the right of intervention; and hearings and some form of judicial process would be needed. Given the limitations of enforcement of the US legislation municipally with regard to Antarctic issues, the obstacles in the way of international assessment are daunting.

To be of any practical utility in protecting the environment, a regime would have to set standards − including shipping lanes, ice protection for tankers, protected areas, drilling equipment require-

96. Ibid.
97. See Antarctic System/*SCAR*.
98. M.W. Holdgate and J. Tinker, *Oil and Other Impacts in the Antarctic* (1979), 6.
99. Rec. VII-11, Annex.
100. Rec. X-1.
101. On this Act and impact assessment generally, see Environment/*Impact Assessment*.

ments, and operating procedures. Some form of enforcement would be essential.[102] It will not be possible to circumvent the issue of jurisdiction by flag State enforcement, as was done with the Living Resources Convention.

Treaty

Until a mineral regime comes into force and has been ratified by all nations capable of exploitation and wishing to undertake it, the Consultative Parties will have to take their rules for mineral exploitation from the Treaty. Does it apply to the extraction of minerals on a commercial scale? The only reference to resources in the text is in Article IX(1), permitting recommendations to cover the 'preservation and conservation of living resources'. There can be no doubt that participants at the Washington Conference of 1959 were well aware of the possibility of such discoveries, since minerals were a recurrent theme in private and public discussions of Antarctic policy at the time.[103] However, the matter was not raised at the meetings which preceeded the Conference,[104] and if the issue had been pursued, there would not have been a treaty.[105] The absence of any mention of economic problems from the Treaty does not mean that they cannot be discussed at Consultative Meetings,[106] but it does suggest that the specific operative provisions were not drafted with the intention of being applied to future resource exploitation.

For the initial attitude of the Consultative Parties, one may resort to the published report of the semi-official meeting at the Nansen Foundation in 1973. One approach was that Contracting Parties could engage in mining provided that they complied with the Treaty and recommendations.[107] The Articles on peaceful purposes,[108] non-

102. Both the application of national safety regulations and their policing in hazardous offshore areas have been the subject of serious criticism (W.G. Carson, 'The Other Price of Britain's Oil' (1980), 4 *Contemporary Crises*, 239 at 241.)

103. Some examples are cited in Oil and Gas/*Minerals*.

104. J. Hanessian, 'The Antarctic Treaty' (1960), 9 *ICLQ*, 436 at 452.

105. B. Roberts, 'International Co-operation for Antarctic Development: the Test for the Antarctic Treaty' (1978), 19(119) *Polar Record*, 107 at 111.

106. E. Hambro, 'Some Notes on the Future of the Antarctic Treaty Collaboration' (1974), 68 *AJIL*, 217 at 222.

107. 'Antarctic Resources' in 'US Antarctic Policy', Hearing, Subcommittee on Oceans and International Environment, Committee on Foreign Relations, Senate, 94th Cong., 1st Sess. (15 May 1975), 79. This was the view of the United States (J. Rose, 'Antarctic Condominium: Building a New Legal Order for Commercial Interests' (1976), 10 *Marine Technology Society Journal*, 19 at 24).

108. Art. I.

conflict with research,[109] information exchange,[110] inspection[111] and notice of expeditions[112] were cited. But this interpretation does little to resolve matters.[113] Oil and gas exploration is not a military purpose, nor would the freedom of scientific research as defined in the Treaty necessarily be limited by exploitation. It is far from clear that industrial secrets would come within the information exchange provisions of Article III, particularly if science is defined within the limits of application during the International Geophysical Year.[114] Apart from the question of the effect of the Treaty in the high seas south of 60°S, there are substantial grounds for limiting the inspection of ships to embarkation and disembarkation, and for contending that oil rigs at sea cannot be inspected.[115] Expeditions must be the subject of advance notice but there is no suggestion in the Treaty text that full details are to be divulged or that business secrets must be made public.

Some participants at the Nansen meeting proposed that amendment of the Treaty would be required, it being argued that commercial mining would interfere with scientific research which is one of the Treaty's principle aims.[116] This is surely too sweeping an assertion. What is required of Contracting Parties is observance of the terms of the Treaty, and provided that oil and gas ventures are in compliance, it cannot be argued that they are bound by norms outside the text. Another construction demanded the agreement of all Consultative Parties to mining, and unless such consent was forthcoming, it was suggested that the purposes and objectives of the Treaty would be violated. This argument, based on the 'peaceful purposes' clause of the Preamble and on Article X, is similar to the view that parties to the Treaty, or States which have not signed, may be bound by principles, purposes or objectives not specifically spelled out in the Treaty text, and it may be rejected on the same grounds.[117] Further, it cannot be accepted that an activity otherwise contrary to the Treaty is validated by the unanimous agreement of the Consultative Parties unless this is specifically done under the

109. Art. II.
110. Art. III.
111. Art. VII.
112. Ibid.
113. R. Lagoni, 'Antarctica's Mineral Resources in International Law' (1979), 39(1) *Zeitschrift für Ausländisches Öffentliches Recht und Völkerrecht*, 1 at 10.
114. Art. II (see Treaty/*Scientific Investigation*).
115. See Treaty/*Inspection*.
116. 'Antarctic Resources' in 'US Antarctic Policy', Hearing, Subcommittee on Oceans and International Environment, Committee on Foreign Relations, Senate, 94th Cong., 1st Sess. (15 May 1975), 79.
117. Discussed under Treaty/*Third Parties*.

amendment procedure of Article XII. No doubt the Consultative Parties would be most hesitant to invoke that Article unless absolutely necessary.[118]

More substantial difficulties would arise if recommendations were to be applied to commercial mining, as was the general view at the Nansen meeting. But this approach has its own limitations, since only effective recommendations could be enforced against mining companies. On the interpretation of the Consultative Parties themselves, it is only they who are bound by recommendations.[119] Attempts to impose restrictions would no doubt be met by a vigorous questioning of the validity of recommendations: for example, companies would examine the extent to which the measures which it was sought to enforce were consistent with the Treaty.[120] Attempts to invoke recommendations against unwilling enterprises could well backfire.

Recommendations provide the body of particular rules directly applicable to Antarctic activities. They are directed to the regime of scientific research, and have little relevance to offshore oil and gas exploration and exploitation. If commercial activities of this nature do impinge upon recommendations, the effect will be marginal unless specific provisions are made for continental shelf extractive industry. At present there does not appear to be any serious impediment to observance of the main applicable recommendations and, in particular, the system of Specially Protected Areas,[121] Sites of Special Scientific Interest[122] and the Code of Conduct for Antarctic Expeditions and Station Activities[123] the focus of which is onshore. Most recommendations do not demand obedience by individuals or companies, because they are addressed to governments and require action by them, but even when such a form is adopted, there is generally a need for national legislation. Of the nine recommendations drafted by the 1979 Consultative Meeting, only three were potentially relevant to individuals or companies. One proposed voluntary

118. An amendment requires unanimous consent plus individual ratification. Non-ratification within two years is deemed to constitute withdrawal from the Treaty (Art. XII). This is a real danger for nations with a popular concern for sovereignty. The nature of the risk, with the resultant possibility of total collapse of the Treaty regime, suggests that amendment was a political threat rather than a legal argument.
119. See Antarctic System/*Recommendations*.
120. Instances would be the effect of Art. VI and the extent to which a particular recommendation complied with the principles and objectives of the Treaty (Art. IX(1)).
121. Rec.III-8.
122. Rec.VIII-4.
123. Rec.VIII-11.

observance of a new Site of Special Scientific Interest,[124] another extended the expiry dates of current Sites,[125] and the third re-stated existing recommendations for the guidance of visitors and contained other non-mandatory suggestions such as an encouragement to commercial tour operators to carry guides with Antarctic experience.[126]

On an objective view there is little in the Treaty or currently effective recommendations to pose a hindrance to offshore oil and gas activities. One gains the impression that some Consultative Parties have sought to interpret the Treaty so as to constitute such an obstacle, without success. It is clear, however, that the Treaty is inherently unsuited for adaptation to an oil and gas regime. The difficulties of amendment have already been noted. Article IV raises considerable complications for any attempt at licensing under the Treaty, and on the precedent of the Living Resources Convention, the inference that a separate agreement on minerals is needed becomes almost inescapable. Until such a regime is concluded, offshore exploration can proceed, and the Treaty will be ineffective to regulate it.

Moratorium

One apparently attractive solution to the problem posed by exploration, and the accompanying threat to the stability of the Treaty system itself, would be to halt all activity of this nature until a mineral regime comes into effect. The view that mining required Treaty amendment or the unanimous consent of the Consultative Parties was an early form of moratorium. At the Second World Conference on National Parks in 1972 a resolution was adopted that the Antarctic Continent and surrounding seas should be established by the United Nations as the first world park; the recommendation envisaged that this should be done by negotiations carried out by the Contracting Parties to the Antarctic Treaty. Recalling this resolution, the South Pacific Conference on National Parks and Reserves of 1975 proposed to regional governments that they examine the possibility of establishing world parks in the region to protect significant marine ecosystems, and that they support this concept at the United Nations Law of the Sea Conference. Similar proposals have been made by environmental organisations such as the Sierra Club and the Friends of the Earth. In 1975 New Zealand espoused the concept of a world park free from commercial activity.[127] A common

124. Rec.X-5.
125. Rec.X-6.
126. Rec.X-8.
127. B.E. Talboys, 'New Zealand and the Antarctic Treaty' (1978), 28(3) and (4) *NZ Foreign Affairs Review*, 29 at 33.

space theory has repeatedly been advocated by private sources.[128] On the past record of the Consultative Parties, there is little doubt that any such form of moratorium involving internationalisation, in the form of United Nations or general international involvement in Antarctic decision-making, will meet the strongest opposition.[129]

On the other hand, even a country as strongly committed to free access to Antarctic resources as the United States has taken active steps to discourage its oil companies from Antarctic prospecting. When Texaco enquired regarding licensing procedures in December 1969, the State Department informed the company that there were no applicable regulations, and emphasised the prohibitions in the Antarctic Treaty. The company would have no real hope of conducting geophysical surveys in industrial secrecy because the United States would doubtless consider that the right of inspection extended to inspection of private enterprise. It has previously been argued that this right does not apply to ships on the high seas south of 60°S unless embarking or disembarking,[130] but it has also been the official US view that the high seas of Antarctica extend to the coast.[131] Texaco may well have taken the Department's attitude as a threat to invoke the supposed powers of inspection of the United States government to deter it from oil exploration. When Senator Pell asked in 1975 whether there had been any serious economic interest in Antarctic resources expressed by any US or foreign company, the State Department representatives referred to the enquiry by Texas Geophysical Instruments for a ten-year exclusive licence for the Ross and Weddell Seas which was dealt with by indicating that no licence procedures existed. The discussion with Texaco was not mentioned.[132] It would appear that other governments approached by oil and gas interests have adopted a similar attitude.[133] Several States expressed the desire during negotiations to erect a legal barrier to their own authority to issue licences under national legislation until the matter was resolved.

From the bland recommendation at the 1972 Meeting,[134] it would be impossible to guess that there had been almost two weeks of

128. E. Honnold, 'Thaw in International Law? Rights in Antarctica under the Law of Common Space' (1978), 87 *YLJ*, 804 at 853.
129. See Treaty/*Third Parties*.
130. See Treaty/*Inspection*.
131. See Treaty/*Area*.
132. 'US Antarctic Policy', Hearing, Subcommittee on Oceans and International Environment, Committee on Foreign Relations, Senate, 94th Cong., 1st Sess. (15 May 1975), 17–18.
133. B. Roberts, 'International Co-operation for Antarctic Development: the Test for the Antarctic Treaty' (1978), 19(119) *Polar Record*, 107 at 113.
134. Rec.VII-6.

debate. Chile supported an indefinite moratorium, Argentina and France wanted fifteen years, the Soviet Union ten to fifteen years, and Australia, New Zealand, Norway and the United Kingdom at least two years. It was the refusal of the United States to accept any moratorium formula that led to the referral of the mineral issue to the next meeting without a decision being reached. While the attitude of claimants such as Argentina and Chile in the closed Consultative Meeting is understandable, it does demonstrate a gap between public pronouncements on sovereignty and private negotiation. A further inconsistency appeared in the opposition of the United States to a moratorium at a time when it had taken active steps to discourage US commercial interests from exploration.

At the 1975 Meeting, the Final Report noted that all governments present urged States and persons to refrain from actions of commercial exploration and exploitation while, acting as Consultative Parties, they sought timely agreed solutions. US support for this peculiar statement[135] was based upon a policy of opposing any formal moratorium but urging interim resistance to commercial exploration.[136] In other words, having one's cake (free access to minerals) and eating it (interim moratorium).

One reason for the reluctance of the United States to back an official endorsement could have been that a moratorium under the Treaty cannot limit scientific research,[137] and insofar as the subsequently adopted moratorium purports to do so, it is contrary to the terms of Articles II and III. By the time of the 1977 Meeting, American policy had again changed, and the passage from the 1975 Final Report was incorporated into a recommendation.[138] However, the wording was now addressed to their 'nationals and other States' but not to the Consultative Parties themselves. In theory, commercial exploration by a Consultative Party was not covered by this portion of the recommendation.

But the second sentence of the paragraph stated that the Consultative Parties would endeavour to ensure that no exploration or exploitation activity would be conducted pending the timely adoption of agreed solutions. Both 'urge' and 'endeavour' fall short of a precise injunction. The second sentence applies to the Consultative Parties themselves with an effect similar to that of the first; therefore

135. Peculiar because the request was not made part of a recommendation in 1975 and could not therefore become binding.
136. 'US Antarctic Policy', Hearing, Subcommittee on Oceans and International Environment, Committee on Foreign Relations, Senate, 94th Cong., 1st Sess. (15 May 1975), 6–7.
137. See Treaty/*Scientific Investigation*.
138. Rec.IX-1.

the *Hakurei Maru* expedition is covered by the Recommendation. Japan, however, could argue that the measure has not become effective, and it might also contend, somewhat unconvincingly, that the expedition did not constitute resource exploration. A leading American scientist has recently stated that past or current geological and geophysical activities on land and sea, conducted as part of scientific programmes in Antarctica, would be classified as mineral exploration if they had been sponsored and funded by commercial companies.[139] The equation of mineral exploration with private enterprise is difficult to sustain, and is certainly not applicable to centralised economies. Recommendation IX-1 and its so-called policy of 'voluntary restraint' has not been followed by the Consultative Parties; therefore Contracting Parties and nations at large will be quite free to ignore the interim moratorium.

A moratorium is no solution to the resource issue,[140] since it is unrealistic to assume that the pressure to search for oil can be resisted indefinitely.[141] Realising this, the Consultative Parties linked the interim moratorium to the early drafting of a minerals regime. At the 1979 Meeting they were at pains to point out that progress had been made to the timely adoption of an agreement and that the importance of these advances should be noted.[142] But this optimism was not supported by the Report of the Working Group on Legal and Political Aspects, which, in its published form, revealed that informal views of individuals on a wide range of topics, including differing attitudes to sovereignty, had been canvassed and that the continuing validity of the four principles enunciated in Recommendation IX-1 had been demonstrated. The recommendation resulting from these discussions did not suggest that any detailed agreement had been reached.[143] But the interim moratorium has become a means of exerting continuing pressure on the Consultative Parties, although it was devised by them. If real advances are not publicly demonstrated in the near future, outside critics will be very ready to point out that the issue has been on the agenda of Consultative Meetings since 1972. Nearly ten years should be

---

139. Dr J.H. Zumberge, Chairman, Committee on International Polar Relations of the Polar Research Board, National Academy of Sciences, in 'US Antarctic Program', Hearings, Subcommittee on Science, Research and Technology, Committee on Science and Technology, H. Reps., 96th Cong., 1st Sess. (1979), 55.

140. E. Hambro, 'Some Notes on the Future of the Antarctic Treaty Collaboration' (1974), 68 *AJIL*, 217 at 226.

141. R. Lagoni, 'Antarctica's Mineral Resources in International Law' (1979), 39(1) *Zeitschrift für Ausländisches Offentliches Recht und Völkerrecht*, 1 at 29.

142. Rec.X-1.

143. Ibid.

sufficient time to show considerable progress towards the timely adoption of a minerals regime.

Principles

Several major decisions on the minerals regime have been made by the Consultative Parties. The topics of interim moratorium and environment have been discussed previously. At the Paris Special Preparatory Meetings four principles were adopted, and further elements were added at the 1979 Consultative Meeting. The Consultative Parties will continue to play an active and responsible part in dealing with the minerals question.[144] The precedents of the Sealing and Living Resources Conventions suggest that this can be taken to mean that all negotiations will be carried out by the Consultative Parties and in secret. On the example of the Living Resources Convention, States which are Contracting Parties to the Antarctic Treaty or have demonstrated an interest in minerals will not be admitted to a Conference to finalise the draft agreement if there is opposition from some Consultative Parties.[145]

The Antarctic Treaty must be maintained 'in its entirety' and the provisions of Article IV shall not be affected by the regime, which should ensure that the principles embodied in that Article are safeguarded in application to the Treaty area.[146] There is no possibility then of a mineral regime based on national sovereignty, and on past practice one may assume that a separate agreement will be reached. The connection between the institutions of the mineral treaty and those of the Antarctic Treaty and Living Resources Convention will presumably follow the pattern set in the Living Resources agreement for its relations with the Antarctic Treaty Consultative Meetings. If so, there will be general provisions to the effect that nothing in the minerals regime will alter the rights and duties of parties to the Antarctic Treaty and the Convention on Living Resources. The redundant reference to Article IV in the 1977 Recommendation suggests that the wording of that Article may be paraphrased in the minerals agreement, with the addition of a more specific statement on the area protected. Any organisation set up will have to coordinate its work with the Consultative Parties, the Living Resources Commission and Scientific Committee, and SCAR. Assuming that there will be no subordination of one treaty, nor any final means of

144. Rec.IX-1.
145. The Netherlands (a Contracting Party) and South Korea (which has a strong commercial interest in krill) were excluded from the 1980 Conference which concluded the Living Resources regime.
146. Rec.IX-1.

settling disagreements, problems of cooperation are likely to arise if membership of the decision-making bodies of the three regimes should differ in the future. Such a possibility is underlined by the continued support for unanimity and the giving of a veto to each participant. This consideration may militate against admission of a State to privileged status under one treaty only. Should this occur, it is not likely that the 'entry fee' under each of the agreements will be reduced, for fear of a flood of applicants. It is possible that the current Consultative Parties would decide to admit a small number of active States and then in effect close the club register to all comers. Such action would deter nations interested in resources from becoming parties to any of the three treaties.

Establishment of a third Antarctic decision-making process will complicate the inevitable clashes of interests. A primary focus of conflict may well be the use of ice-free coastal areas with easy access. Current base activity has already had serious local effects on fauna,[147] and the exploitation of resources will provide a further source of stress. The multiplication of regimes is due to a desire to preserve the Antarctic Treaty without amendment, but it cannot be justified on the grounds of efficiency or conservation.

In dealing with the question of mineral resources, the Consultative Parties should not prejudice the interests of all mankind in Antarctica.[148] No such concept was to be found in the contemporaneous recommendation on Living Resources. May it then be inferred that common heritage principles will be utilised in the minerals treaty? Past experience suggests that this will not be the case. It would certainly be surprising if the future International Seabed Authority (ISA) were to be given a say in Antarctic affairs in the light of the Consultative Parties' attitude to United Nations organs and the Law of the Sea Conference.[149]

Apart from the collective desire of the Consultative Parties to ensure that international organisations are excluded from Antarctic politics, there would be specific opposition to involvement of the ISA for to grant that Authority the equivalent of Consultative status under a minerals treaty would give grounds for the argument that the ISA could exercise its authority in part of the Treaty area as seabed beyond national jurisdiction. There would even be the possibility of its extension up to the coast of the continent. Consultative Parties asserting sovereignty could hardly accept with equanimity that such

147. See Environment/*Specially Protected Areas*.
148. Rec.IX-1.
149. See Treaty/*Third Parties* and Treaty/*Area*.

a potential competitor could have any rights in the area.

Nor would the interests of all mankind be satisfactorily dealt with by a form of royalty or tax. First, any payment as of right would involve the problem of the ISA and sovereignty canvassed previously. A general purposes grant to an international body is, however, conceivable, but leaving aside the political issues, there would be practical impediments. It could only be an expenditure from surplus income; before a payment were made, there would have to be a subtraction of funds to cover the substantial investment costs, a profit margin commensurate with the high risks involved and the costs of the regulatory mechanism established by the minerals regime. It is already clear that claimant States will demand tangible benefits in return for their agreement to such a treaty, and in this case they are hardly likely to consent to giving way to a grant for general international purposes. Scientists will also argue that any surplus should be devoted to environmental research. Any appropriation of useful amounts of Antarctic mineral revenue to the interests of all mankind would be surprising.

It would therefore seem that international concern with Antarctica is to be served, in the same manner as the parallel wording in the Preamble of the Antarctic Treaty, by the maintenance of peace and the prevention of international discord. Critics of the Antarctic system, especially representatives of the Group of 77 (the developing countries) will not be satisfied with such lip-service to outside views. But the Consultative Parties have recently had success in warding off attempts to have Antarctic issues raised in a variety of international fora. Negotiation of the Living Resources Convention, without interference from the Group of 77, showed that a serious assault on the present system is not yet contemplated by the developing countries, and it remains to be seen whether sufficient interest in the minerals regime can be generated to arouse pressure on the Consultative Parties. As the deep seabed debate indicates, predictions of large cash flows can of themselves generate international concern, although the surplus revenue could be relatively small and exploitation on a commercial scale could be fifteen or twenty years in the future. Therefore, even the public announcement of promising formations meriting exploratory drilling could serve to crystallise third world concern. Should discoveries be made it is also possible that OPEC may attempt to intervene to maintain world oil prices as was the case with land-based producers of seabed minerals.

In a minerals regime, licensing will be the central issue, and in view of the close relationship between the granting of mining rights and sovereignty, this will be a very sensitive issue, on which it may well be predicted that unanimity will be required.[150] On past experience, particularly the unsuccessful attempts to introduce qualified voting for the Living Resources Commission, consensus will probably be required for all substantive decisions. If it was thought necessary to preserve the interests of claimants under the Antarctic Treaty, then the demand for unanimity will surely be put for a regime covering valuable resources. There will be no possibility of avoiding the establishment of a permanent central body with extensive powers. Such a commission would have to be given the right to grant licenses, secure tenure over mine sites and deliver a valid title to extracted minerals. Of necessity a veto would thus apply to the issue of each licence. It is the direct application of purely political considerations to the administration of mining which could pose the most severe difficulties for a regime.

Although negotiation of the regime may take time and involve crises, the same factors leading to a living resources agreement may bring about a minerals treaty. Once more, the Consultative Parties have themselves stated that timely progress is required, even if a final date has not been set. Claimants, faced with the erosion of full sovereignty involved in the Treaty and the Living Resources Convention, will regard the minerals issue as affecting their interests to a greater extent than the two previous treaties. Demands will no doubt again be made for specific concessions to claimants, but unless a claimant state is prepared to issue licences outside the framework of an eventual international agreement, its views, however forcefully expressed, may have little practical effect. Opting out would involve not only the minerals regime, but it also could well (due to the link previously suggested) require withdrawal from the Antarctic Treaty.

Before a claimant would take such a step, or alternatively exercise the veto of a Consultative Party over the negotiations, careful calculation of the political implications would be required. If the United States discouraged requests by its own oil companies for exploration licences from other countries as early as 1969, it can well be presumed that an even more stringent attitude would be taken if that country were to ratify a mineral regime and an American company were to seek rights outside the framework of that agreement. All claimants with possible oil reserves are vulnerable to either political pressure or direct confrontation. Australia needs the protection of the Antarctic Treaty against the Soviet Union; New Zealand would hardly be in a position to engage in conflict with the United States;

150. S.J. Burton, 'New Stresses on the Antarctic Treaty' (1979), 65 *Virginia Law Review*, 421 at 487.

and Chile and Argentina would have to face the possibility of claims from the superpowers, the United Kingdom and perhaps Brazil if the Treaty collapsed. These considerations suggest that a single claimant will be very hesitant to act on its own, whatever may be the nature of public feelings and opposition to ratification of a minerals regime.

Should this be the case, those nations most concerned with sovereignty will continue to be part of a future three-treaty system, for which the price will be found in the terms of the mineral regime: firm support for Article IV and a comprehensive requirement of unanimity. On this basis, one cannot expect either a detailed or effective agreement. Environmental standards will be of a general nature, and enforcement by court procedures will be left to national tribunals. When every decision of importance has to be adopted by consensus, an inherently unstable regime will be subject to repeated dissension.

9
ENVIRONMENT

Past Practice

Protection of the environment of Antarctica has been a recurrent theme of recent Consultative Meetings. On a number of counts, practice under the Antarctic system is of an interest that goes beyond the immediate Antarctic framework. This is the only continent considered a Special Conservation Area,[1] and for thirty years the predominant activity has been scientific research directly supported by governments. Absence of industry, coupled with a tiny and transient population, have furnished a testing ground for the possibility of conservation regimes. For a number of years the Treaty powers have assumed that they have a particular responsibility to safeguard the Antarctic environment. Analysis of the exercise of this power should provide some indication of the extent to which third parties can accept the assertion of a monopoly on decision-making in conservation issues.

In examining man's current impact on the Antarctic, it is necessary to restrict discussion to that small proportion of the continent where there has been some measure of permanence and continuity of presence. Several factors have combined to locate a substantial proportion of the stations in coastal ice-free areas. There are instances in which bases of different nations have been established in close proximity, one motive for which (as with Deception Island[2]) is the desire to offset sovereignty claims of rivals. The use of another nation's support facilities was a factor in the location of Scott Base next to McMurdo. Shore stations have been set up to provide for scientific research, and have therefore been attracted to sites with easy access to fauna. While the primary intent was to facilitate study, the consequences have been to attract visitors and sometimes, as with the Cape Royds penguin rookery, seriously to affect breeding colonies.[3] Wildlife, bases and frequently historic sites situated in the same area constitute a focus for tourist ships.

There can be no doubt that Antarctic operations have had local impacts. IGY stations were set up under tight schedules and were planned to be temporary. In one instance – Hallett in 1957 – a

---

1. Preamble, Agreed Measures.
2. See Sovereignty/*Polar Circumstances*.
3. See Jurisdiction/*Treaty Regime*.

base was erected in the middle of a penguin breeding area, and Dumont d'Urville station was built within 300 yards of the rookeries of eight bird species.[4] Such examples are not confined to the early period of present activities. In 1968 the Soviet Union and Chile established bases on the Fildes Peninsula in an 'area of outstanding ecological interest'.[5] Poland's Arctowski Station opened in 1977 'precariously close'[6] to an exceptional assemblage of birds and mammals.[7] However strict environmental measures may be, it is difficult to avoid affecting flora and fauna to some extent in such circumstances, especially in summer when activities are at a high level.

One could therefore expect that station operations would have a substantial local environmental effect. Rubbish dumps have been the object of repeated criticism, and visitors to McMurdo had described the trash heap as a 'dreadful sight'.[8] One tourist remarked that it was difficult to determine which was the base and which was the dump.[9] But allowing for hyperbole there have been good grounds for criticising the waste disposal practices of most bases. A general method of dealing with the problem was to deposit garbage of various types on the ice in order that it should float off to sea, a practice followed at McMurdo (until a sewage plant and incinerator were installed) resulting in an offshore junkyard extending up to 3 miles from the coast.[10] It would appear that sewage was still being discharged into the sea at that station and at Palmer in 1979.[11] The procedure is common elsewhere. Despite repeated requests from US personnel, vessels of various nationalities have continued to dump wastes or pump bilges in Arthur Harbour where Palmer Base is situated.[12] There are even instances of environmental impacts in areas some distance from the main bases.[13]

This brief list is only to be taken as a presentation of typical examples of damage already done. Some measures have already

4. F.C. Mahncke, 'United States inspects four stations' (1971), 6(4) *Antarctic Journal*, 147, at 148.
5. Rec. IV-12 discussed under Environment/*Specially Protected Areas*.
6. B.C. Parker, 'Introduction and Historical Background' in B.C. Parker (ed.), *Environmental Impact in Antarctica* (1978), 1 at 3.
7. Rec. X-5.
8. D. Braxton, *The Abominable Snow-Women* (1969), 123.
9. J. and M. Darby, 'Tourism has come' (1978), 22 *NZ Environment*, 36 at 38.
10. R.T. Peterson, 'Render the penguins, butcher the seals' (1973), 75 *Audubon*, 90 at 103.
11. National Science Foundation, *U.S. Antarctic Program Draft Environmental Impact Statement* (1979), K-108.
12. J.H. Lipps, 'Man's Impact along the Antarctic Peninsula' in B.C. Parker (ed.), *Environmental Impact in Antarctica* (1978), 333 at 357.
13. e.g. in the Dry Valleys (see Environment/*Impact Assessment*).

been taken by the Consultative Parties to reduce this impact, and a number of nations have gone to pains to carry them out.[14] On the other hand, it is apparent that Antarctic programmes supporting science will continue to affect the very environment they seek to preserve. Have the Consultative Parties executed their self-imposed mandate of protection?

Agreed Measures

The starting-point for discussion is to be sought in the Agreed Measures for the Conservation of Antarctic Fauna and Flora of 1964, arrangements which are frequently praised as one of the most comprehensive and successful international instruments for wildlife conservation on land that have yet been negotiated.[15] Native mammals and birds may not be captured, molested, wounded or killed without a permit. Special protection is to be given to species listed in an Annex. Each participating government shall take appropriate measures to minimise harmful interference with the normal living conditions of native mammals and birds. Harmful interference is defined as allowing dogs to run free, flying aircraft and driving vehicles so as unnecessarily to disturb bird and seal concentrations, the use of explosives or the discharge of firearms close to such concentrations, and the disturbance of bird or seal colonies during the breeding season by persistent attention from persons on foot.

Specially Protected Areas of outstanding scientific interest may be declared. In addition to the general prohibitions, the driving of vehicles and collecting of native plants without a permit and forbidden. Parties may bar the entry of their nationals.[16] At the 1966 Consultative Meeting fifteen areas were designated and two seal species − Ross and Fur seals − were scheduled.

Antarctic fauna and flora are concentrated in coastal areas and dependent on the sea for food. It is therefore noteworthy that the Agreed Measures were assumed to be confined to land areas south of 60°S,[17] a view based on Article I of the Measures, which reiterates Article VI of the Treaty. However, so narrow an interpretation was

14. 'Waste not left behind at Scott Base' (1977), 8(3) *Antarctic*, 101 at 102 (New Zealand compliance with Rec. VIII-11).
15. B. Roberts, 'International Co-operation for Antarctic Development: the Test for the Antarctic Treaty' (1978), 19(119) *Polar Record*, 107 at 109. Examination of the Agreed Measures and SPA is based upon F.M. Auburn, 'The Antarctic Environment' (1981), *Year Book of World Affairs* 248 at 252 − 62.
16. Rec. VI-8.
17. B.B. Roberts, 'Conservation in the Antarctic' (1977), 279 *Phil. Trans. R. Soc. Lond. B.*, 97 at 100.

open to question. Article VI does not restrict the Treaty's ambit to land, but rather preserves high sea freedoms, and the Agreed Measures provide internal evidence that offshore areas are to be covered.[18] Repeated efforts by Chile to have marine areas covered, political realities, and the interest of scientists in applying conservation measures to the sea led to a re-interpretation by the Consultative Parties to allow consideration of marine SPAs.[19] It is suggested that the effect of Article I of the Agreed Measures is to preserve States' rights to fish and catch seals,[20] but high seas freedoms can be voluntarily curtailed. In fact the Consultative Parties declared the pelagic Ross Seal to be a Specially Protected Species in 1966,[21] thus ensuring that these seals could not be killed for commercial purposes.[22] It may be inferred that the original restrictive interpretation of the territorial ambit was not based upon legal arguments, but rather arose from political disagreement between the Consultative Parties relating to sovereignty. The expanded view of 1975 was due to the desire to preserve the monopoly of decision-making south of 60°S rather than to any review of legal issues. Because the Sealing Convention was negotiated on the assumption that the Agreed Measures did not apply to pelagic seals, its territorial ambit was expressed as covering 'the seas south of 60°S'.[23] Both the Convention and the Agreed Measures apply to seals. However, on the wider interpretation of the Agreed Measures, the provisions of the two regimes may conflict. One example is that the Measures provide that Fur Seals may be captured or killed only under a permit for a compelling scientific purpose,[24] whereas the Convention totally forbids the taking of this species,[25] with exceptions for scientific research, indispensable food and specimens.[26] Should an industry develop, such conflicts could assume some importance, particularly for species found on sea-ice close to the continent.

Jurisdiction remains one of the unsolved issues of the Antarctic regime,[27] and disagreement on its exercise under the Agreed Measures caused serious difficulties during negotiations.[28] The

18. For the textual arguments see Treaty/*Area*.
19. ANT/41 (10 June 1975) discussed under Treaty/*Area*.
20. D. Anderson, 'The Conservation of Wildlife under the Antarctic Treaty' (1968), 14(88) *Polar Record*, 25 at 26.
21. Rec. IV-17.
22. Art. VI(7)(*a*), Agreed Measures.
23. Art. 1, Sealing Convention.
24. Art. VI(1) and 7(*a*), Agreed Measures and Rec. IV-16
25. Annex.   26. Art. 4.
27. See Jurisdiction/*Treaty Regime*.
28. T. Hanevold, 'The Antarctic Treaty Consultative Meetings: Form and Procedure' (1971), 6 *Cooperation and Conflict*, 197.

dispute centred on which authority should be empowered to grant permits required for a number of purposes, including the taking or killing of native mammals or birds[29] and entrance to Specially Protected Areas.[30] 'Appropriate authority' was defined as any person authorised by a participating government to issue permits under the Measures.[31] Although not clearly stated in the text, it would appear that countries are under an obligation mutually to recognise each other's permits. References to permits in the Agreed Measures are in general terms: for example, each participating government is bound to prohibit the collection of any native plant in a SPA 'except in accordance with a permit'.[32] In pursuance of this requirement, Australian implementing legislation prevents action against any person where the act in question has been authorised by a permit of another Contracting Party.[33] United States law, applying to all that country's nationals,[34] does not provide for such recognition . It is therefore unlawful for any United States citizen to collect a native plant in a SPA,[35] if acting under a permit granted to him as an exchange scientist by another government.

Compromise on the definition of the appropriate authority did not settle the matter. The original Specially Protected Areas were established at the 1966 Consultative Meeting, prior to which Chile expressed concern that the issuance of permits by other nations with regard to its own territory would undercut sovereign rights. Nothing came of this initiative at the time, but the 1968 Meeting amended the relevant provision of the Measures to require that the functions of an authorised person be carried out within the framework of the Antarctic Treaty, exclusively in accordance with scientific principles, and should have as their sole purpose the effective protection of fauna and flora under the Measures.[36] Obviously Chile was not the only nation fearing that permits might be used to further claims interests.

If the Consultative Parties place such weight upon the preservation of the Antarctic environment, why is it that the Agreed Measures had still not become effective under Article IX of the Treaty fifteen years after being recommended? To cite the need for seeking

---

29. Art. VI, Agreed Measures.
30. Art. VIII, Agreed Measures.
31. Art. II(*d*), Agreed Measures.
32. Art. VIII(2)(*c*), Agreed Measures.
33. S.7(1), Antarctic Treaty (Environment Protection) Act 1980 (C'wth).
34. S.4, Antarctic Conservation Act 1978.
35. S.670.4(*b*), Title 45 CFR, Ch. VI, Regulations implementing Antarctic Conservation Act.
36. Rec. V-6.

approval in accord with constitutional processes[37] is hardly an explanation for so long a delay in implementing uncontroversial and internationally agreed means of environmental protection. No constitutional amendment or other complex procedure was called for. When the Antarctic Conservation legislation was presented to the US Congress in July 1977, one may assume that its introduction was due to the desire of the United States to press for safeguards for the ecosystem in the Living Resources regime to be discussed at the September 1977 Consultative Meeting. Nine Consultative Parties (including the Soviet Union and Poland) had approved the Agreed Measures but the United States had not, and had it not moved in that direction, it would hardly have been safe from criticism in taking a strong stand on krill. The long delay was due to the low priority accorded to Antarctic matters in national policy.[38] Similarly, Australian introduction of its implementing legislation on 23 April 1980 may be related to the holding of the Living Resources Conference in Canberra on 7 May 1980 and a wish to press for Hobart, Tasmania, as the headquarters of the regime.

Specially Protected Areas

Specially Protected Areas constitute a central feature of the Agreed Measures, and their effectiveness may be assessed with particular emphasis on those Areas close to bases. Because the prohibitions relating to SPAs are additional to the general duties imposed by the Measures, minimisation of harmful interference with the normal living conditions of native mammals and birds[39] is applicable to them. However harmful interference may be permitted to the minimum extent necessary for the establishment, supply and operation of stations.[40] Thus, for example, aircraft may be flown for that purpose in a manner which would unnecessarily disturb bird and seal concentrations. This saving clause for bases was inserted to prevent the Agreed Measures from unduly inhibiting the ability of governments to operate stations, but strictly it is redundant. Governments are not bound to prohibit harmful interference but only to minimise

37. E.P. Todd, National Science Foundation in 'Fishing and Wildlife Miscellaneous, Part I', Hearings, Subcommittee on Fisheries and Wildlife Conservation and the Environment, Committee on Merchant Marine and Fisheries, H. Rep., 95th Cong., 1st Sess. (1977), 293.
38. F.M. Auburn, 'US Antarctic Policy' (1978), 12(1) *Marine Technology Society Journal*, 31 at 35.
39. Art. VII, Agreed Measures.
40. Art. VII(2), Agreed Measures. This exception does not apply to permit dogs to run free or to allow the discharge of firearms close to bird and seal concentrations.

it.[41] Complex points of interpretation arise from the stations exception. Does it mean that dogs cannot be allowed to run free on bases, but that such harmful interference is minimally permitted on scientific trips?

Nothing in the Measures defines what is necessary for the establishment, supply and operation of stations, and there are no rules for choice of base sites. If a State decides to build a station in close proximity to a penguin colony, some degree of impact on the birds is inevitable; yet the Agreed Measures do not prevent the establishment of a base in this manner. The optimum result for protection of fauna would be to place stations at a considerable distance from birds and seals, but the tendency of governments has been to select areas close to animal concentrations.[42] Sovereignty, politics, logistic convenience and the facilitation of scientific research prevail over environmental considerations.

A SPA must be an area of 'outstanding scientific interest' and is assumed to have a unique natural ecological system,[43] but there are grounds for contending that some of the original designations did not come within the definition. Three seem to have been designated for similar reasons.[44] Byers and Fildes Peninsulas were selected in order to protect their fauna and flora, yet when their SPA status was terminated in 1975, both became Sites of Special Scientific Interest for the study of fossils.[45] It would appear that factors other than ecology were taken into account. Political considerations probably lay behind Chile's persistent efforts to set up Marine SPAs and SSSIs.[46] From a review of SPAs by SCAR and its concern to keep the number and size of sites to a minimum,[47] it seemed that the original Areas had been too widely defined.

One of the most interesting demonstrations of the effect of stations relates to the original Fildes Peninsula SPA. In 1966–7 the United States positioned Palmer Base on Anvers Island, Antarctic Peninsula. The re-entry of the United States to the South American sector was followed by the Soviet Union's establishment of its first station there, in the Fildes Peninsula SPA, in 1968. It is possible that the Soviet authorities were unaware of the projected application of the Agreed Measures to the area,[48] but rather unlikely in view of their

41. Art. VII(1), Agreed Measures.
42. See Environment/*Past Practice*.
43. Art. VIII(1), Agreed Measures.
44. Byers Peninsula (Rec. IV-10), Cape Shirreff (Rec. IV-11) and Coppermine Peninsula (Rec. VI-10).
45. Rec. VIII-4.
46. See Treaty/*Area*.
47. Rec. VII-2.
48. Neither the SPA designations nor Rec. IV-20 (Agreed Measures as interim

participation at all stages of drafting of the Measures and SPA proposals. In the same year, Chile announced its intention to set up a station in that SPA. The most obvious explanation for this sequence of events is that they constituted a political chain reaction in the particularly volatile northern Antarctic Peninsula.

There is no express prohibition on the erection of a base within a SPA. The requirement of permits for entry by foot was introduced in 1970.[49] However, the driving of a vehicle was not allowed,[50] and it would not be feasible to operate a base without wheeled transport. Moreover, the presence of a station would inevitably tend to destroy the unique natural ecological system[51] which is the justification of the SPA. Other Consultative Parties could not rely on a legally binding regime for the Area because the SPA Recommendation had not come into force. But in view of their assumption of responsibility for the protection of the Antarctic environment, they might have been expected to point out to the Soviet Union and Chile that the building of stations was inconsistent with the Recommendation which had been drafted with their concurrence.

Instead, at the 1968 Consultative Meeting, the SPA was reduced to a fraction of its former size[52] in order to exclude the Soviet Bellingshausen Station and the surrounding areas in which travel and disturbance were inevitable.[53] The original SPA designation was centred on the numerous small lakes which are ice-free in summer, providing a biologically diverse region.[54] In the 1968 Recommendation it was noted that there were 'several small lakes' of outstanding ecological interest, but only the most interesting one was specially protected.[55] In the result, even the reduced SPA was completely changed by the presence of the Soviet and Chilean bases[56] and terminated in 1975.[57]

There were a number of limitations to the SPA concept. The Agreed Measures only apply to fauna and flora. Non-biological sites such as the Dry Valleys could not be protected.[58] Regulation, especially the prohibition on entry, is uniform, and it has not been the practice to provide particulars for an individual SPA. So the

---

voluntary guidelines) were in force in 1968.
49. Rec. VI-8.
50. Art. VIII(2)(*a*), Agreed Measures.
51. Art. VIII(1), Agreed Measures.
52. Rec. V-5.
53. (1969) 32 *SCAR Bulletin* 751.
54. Rec. IV-12.
55. Rec. V-5.
56. ANT/20/Add. 1 (10 June 1975).
57. Rec. VIII-2.
58. Rec. VII-3.

concept of Sites of Special Scientific Interest was introduced to prevent a demonstrable risk of interference with research either being carried out or planned for the immediate future. Expiry dates, maps and management plans were required.[59]

Of the eight current SSSI areas,[60] three (Cape Crozier, and Fildes and Byers Peninsulas) were previously within a SPA and three (Cape Royds, Haswell Island and Admiralty Bay) were created to protect birds and mammals. There are two non-biological SSSIs. Arrival Heights, Ross Island, close to McMurdo and Scott Bases, was set up as a result of a study by the joint US/New Zealand McMurdo Land Management and Conservation Board,[61] and could well have been dealt with by agreement between the two countries. Although SSSIs are not within the Agreed Measures, several management plans require observance of portions of the Measures.[62] It may be inferred that the Consultative Parties were unable, presumably for political reasons, to amend the Agreed Measures in the extensive manner needed to implement the proposals of SCAR, and therefore created the SSSI as a separate category.

The SSSI, giving a much reduced form of protection, is an indication of the failure of some SPA designations and the effect of Antarctic programmes and logistics on the environment. The termination of three SPA designations and the subsequent creation of SSSIs at the same spot, even if for different purposes, constituted a virtual admission to this effect. Other sites provide evidence in the management plan: thus the Cape Royds SSSI was established to prevent a further drop in the penguin population due to visitors,[63] and Barwick Valley in Victoria Land was selected as one of the 'least contaminated' of the Dry Valleys. Even more than the SPA, the SSSI is related to the existence of nearby stations.[64]

The most recent designations in each category provide good illustrations. Litchfield Island, Arthur Harbour, was declared a SPA due to its unique position among neighbouring islands as a breeding-place for six species of native birds;[65] it is also within a mile of Palmer Base. Arctowski Station, established by Poland in 1977,[66] is within a

59. Rec. VIII-3. SCAR had put forward these proposals as part of a review of the SPA concept but they were not applied to SPAs.
60. Seven created by Rec. VIII-4 and Admiralty Bay under Rec. X-5.
61. See National Interests/*The United States*.
62. In the case of Cape Crozier, Cape Royds and Admiralty Bay.
63. See Rec. VIII-4 and Jurisdiction/*Treaty Regime*.
64. Instanced by the Haswell Island SSSI which 'needs protection in view of the close proximity of a large Antarctic station' (Mirny) (Rec. VIII-4).
65. Rec. VIII-1.
66. See Antarctic System/*Consultative Status*.

few hundred yards of the SSSI recommended in 1979, and the reason for designation in that case was that the area supports an exceptional assemblage of Antarctic birds and mammals.[67] Choice of the station site has been criticised as being too near to one of the few known three-species penguin rookeries and a large population of crabeater seals, and it has been pointed out that the base will serve as an additional tourist attraction.[68] This SSSI is a particular cause for concern, and it would seem to have been an obvious instance for proclamation of an SPA. Designation as an SSSI is for the purposes of scientific research, and expires in 1985. It could be an indication that the Consultative Parties do not wish to create any more SPAs but rather will give biological sites the much reduced and temporary protection of SSSI status. Building of a base so close to this exceptional fauna assembly, followed by the SSSI proposal, suggests that ecological considerations have been subordinated to Poland's requirement for a convenient station site.

The Agreed Measures, SPAs and SSSIs provide a useful index of the Consultative Parties' implementation of their professed responsibilities to safeguard the Antarctic environment. In form they are an ambitious experiment in conservation, but at the practical level breaches have been documented. Examples are letting dogs run free contrary to Article VII(2)(*a*) of the Agreed Measures;[69] entry of non-scientists into the Cape Royds penguin rookery;[70] and helicopter overflights of the Cape Crozier rookeries.[71] No doubt other instances would be available if the Treaty's inspection provisions were utilised with more vigour. But the primary cause for complaint is the continuing failure of the Consultative Parties to provide environmental criteria for station siting and their repeated choice of locations far too close to bird and mammal concentrations. Once a base is built, ecological damage is inevitable.

Tourism

Antarctica has long been a field of adventure, but in recent years the increasing numbers of private visitors have given rise to discussion at Consultative Meetings. Mountaineering parties have been attracted to the continent,[72] and flying to the Antarctic as part of a round-the-

67. Rec. X-5.
68. B.C. Parker, 'Introduction and Historical Background' in B.C. Parker (ed.), *Environmental Impact in Antarctica* (1978), 1 at 3.
69. See Treaty/*Inspection*.
70. M. Bradstock, 'A Strange Allure' (1978), 22 *NZ Environment*, 22.
71. National Science Foundation, *US Antarctic Program Draft Environmental Impact Statement* (1979), 4-20.
72. First Italian Expedition in the Antarctic, *Mountaineering in the Antarctic* (1976).

world trip has even resulted in a civil aeroplane crash at the South Pole.[73] Dr David Lewis is well-known for his daring voyages in Antarctic waters,[74] and other yachtsmen have sailed to the continent in recent years and have even been prepared to winter over there.[75] A three-man party of the British Transglobe Expedition planned to cross the continent from Sanae to Scott Base.[76]

The advent of tourist cruises by vessels such as the *Lindblad Explorer* and *World Discoverer*, carrying substantial numbers of passengers, has given the Consultative Parties special cause for concern. On several occasions such vessels have suffered damage. Day trips by Air New Zealand and QANTAS took nearly 3,000 tourists over the continent in the 1978−9 season,[77] one such flight by Air New Zealand in 1979 resulting in a crash in Antarctica, killing all on board.[78]

It would appear that several cruise ships, including some currently operating, are subject to the laws of countries which are not parties to the Antarctic Treaty: for example, the *World Discoverer* is registered in Singapore,[79] the *Lindblad Explorer* in Panama[80] and others.[81] Therefore the Consultative Parties have no direct control over such vessels, nor can the voyages be regulated or prohibited.[82] In practice, some tourist agencies, such as Lindblad Travel, have taken pains to ensure observance of environmental protection measures in the Antarctic.

Safety of ships raises a number of issues. There have been incidents in which cruise vessels have got into difficulties. In 1968 the *Magga Dan* ran aground on a shoal off Ross Island and had to be towed off by the US icebreaker *Westwind*,[83] and the next year the Chilean naval transport *Aquiles* landed passengers on a small island near Palmer Station, whereupon rapidly rising winds forced suspension of operations and the tourists had to be taken to the base by a United States boat.[84] The *Lindblad Explorer* grounded in Admiralty

73. 'The personal note' (1970), 5(9) *Antarctic*, 378.
74. D. Lewis, *Voyage to the Ice* (1979).
75. 'Yacht voyage to Antarctic' (1978), 8(8) *Antarctic*, 270.
76. 'Transglobe expedition' (1980), 9(1) *Antarctic*, 28.
77. 'Busy summer for ships and aircraft' (1979), 8(9) *Antarctic*, 330.
78. Office of Air Accidents Investigation, Ministry of Transport, *Aircraft Accident Report No. 79-139* (1980).
79. Advertisement in (1978) 43(1) *Frontiers* 43.
80. ANT/IX/INF 7 (23 September 1977).
81. e.g., the *Enrico G* flies the flag of a Genoa shipping line ('More "Day Trips" to Antarctic' (1978) 8(8) *Antarctic* 292).
82. C. Neider, *Edge of the World* (1974), 77.
83. 'First tourists arrive' (1968), *Antarctic*, 51 at 52.
84. 'Logistic Support Activities' (1969), 4(3) *Antarctic Journal*, 79 at 82−3.

Bay, King George Island, in 1972, and the passengers were taken to Puntas Arenas by a Chilean navy transport.[85] In 1979 the same ship grounded while under charter to a film company.[86] In these instances no one was injured, but it is possible that a tour ship could run on an uncharted rock in a gale with no assistance readily available. In emergencies national support vessels, such as icebreakers, would have to come to the aid of cruise vessels, disrupting the tight schedule of the short Antarctic summer.

Large numbers of tourists have been carried on some cruises. The relatively small Antarctic stations which are the focus of landings are incapable of handling 900 visitors at one time, and it is difficult to safeguard SPAs and ensure observance of the Agreed Measures. There have been repeated criticisms of the behaviour of some groups such as the unnamed cruise to the Antarctic Peninsula described by the Darbys.[87] United States authorities have complained of tours arriving at stations without warning, vandalism, and damage to remote sites, flora, fauna and SPAs. However a scientist has pointed out that tourists are indoctrinated by naturalists. The most frequent source of litter on beaches is from supply ships.[88] One can agree that national activities are the major source of local pollution in the Antarctic.

In response to the *Magga Dan* voyage in 1968, New Zealand and the United States formulated tourist guidelines,[89] and analysis of the conditions laid down by these and other countries suggests some common principles. No attempt is made to regulate the vessels in Antarctica. For example, the New Zealand government does not control access of ships into Antarctic waters for peaceful purposes.[90] Permission is required for visits to the bases of the country in question and various conditions are to be fulfilled for that purpose.[91] Observance of the Treaty and Agreed Measures is demanded. Tour groups must be entirely self-sufficient, safety being the responsibility of the tour organiser. Although support and assistance will be

85. 'Grounded tourist ship not seriously damaged' (1972), 6(6) *Antarctic*, 219.
86. 'Lindblad Explorer runs aground' (1980), 9(1) *Antarctic*, 35.
87. J. and M. Darby, 'Tourism has come' (1978), 22 *NZ Environment*, 36.
88. R.T. Peterson, 'Render the penguins, butcher the seals' (1973), 75(2) *Audubon*, 90 at 106.
89. R.B. Thomson, 'Effects of Human Disturbance on an Adélie Penguin Rookery and Measures of Control' in G.A. Llano (ed.), *Adaptations within Antarctic Ecosystems* (1977), 1177 at 1178.
90. Policy Statement on the Role of New Zealand in Tourist Expeditions to Antarctica in Department of Scientific and Industrial Research, *Antarctic Operations Manual* (1975), 88.
91. Conditions covering visits to the Argentine Sector of Antarctica, ANT/33 (13 June 1975).

provided in an emergency, the government concerned accepts no liability for accident or injury.[92]

Such rules are of very limited effect and are dictated by the reluctance to exercise jurisdiction. For instance, it has been suggested by Chile that tourist ships in Antarctic waters might be required to take on pilots; whatever the merits of such a proposal, it would immediately raise the need for national legislation and the associated issues of sovereignty. Even within the narrow sphere covered by the conditions for visits to stations, enforcement is problematical. Thus Argentina demands that tour organisers must make groups 'capable of survival in every respect',[93] but this could only be done effectively with the provision of extremely expensive logistic support.

Recognising the inadequacy of station entry rules, the Consultative Parties have initiated discussions on more general measures governing tourism. At the 1970 Consultative Meeting, it was recommended that governments make appropriate efforts to ensure that visitors do not engage in any activity contrary to the principles and purposes of the Treaty or Recommendations. Exhortations of this type are, however, too vague to be enforceable. Are efforts to be made only in relation to a particular country's own nationals? Would the exercise of criminal jurisdiction be appropriate, having regard to Article IV of the Treaty? Those responsible for expeditions proceeding from, organised in or calling at the territory of a Consultative Party should be informed that final station visit arrangements should be made at least twenty-four hours before arrival, and visitors must comply with conditions or restrictions on movement stipulated by the station commander for their safety or to safeguard scientific programmes at or near the station. Visitors must not enter SPAs and must respect designated historic monuments.[94] The very narrow scope of conditions to be imposed reflects the inability of the Consultative Parties to agree upon truly effective measures which would involve the exercise of jurisdiction. Little substantial progress was made at the Seventh Meeting.[95] But the 1975 Consultative Meeting marked a change in attitude. It was acknowledged that tourism is a natural development in the Treaty Area,[96] and a Statement of Accepted Practices and relevant Treaty provisions was

92. Policy Statement on the Role of New Zealand in Tourist Expeditions to Antarctica in Department of Scientific and Industrial Research, *Antarctic Operations Manual* (1975), 89.
93. Conditions covering visits to the Argentine Sector of Antarctica, ANT/33 (13 June 1975).
94. Rec. VI-7.
95. Rec. VII-4.
96. Preamble, Rec. VIII-9.

to be drawn up. Except in an emergency, organisers of tour groups would be requested to visit only those stations for which consent had been granted,[97] and permission should be contingent upon reasonable assurances of compliance with the Treaty, effective recommendations and conditions applicable to the bases to be visited.[98]

Areas of Special Tourist Interest are to be designated;[99] however, no such sites have yet been settled. Prescription of areas is intended to divert tourists from stations, SPAs and SSSIs, but it is precisely such attractions that serve as a focus of visits. The setting up of a new type of specified area at a distance from bases would raise problems of supervision and enforcement for which present Antarctic programmes are not equipped. A Statement of Accepted Principles formulated at the Tenth Meeting in 1979 placed special emphasis on observance of the Agreed Measures[100] which, the purist would point out, were still not effective at that time. Non-governmental expeditions were to be urged to carry adequate insurance cover against the risk of incurring financial charges or material losses.[101]

SCAR drew attention in 1978 to the fact that an aircraft carrying 350 passengers, which is unable to land in the Antarctic, would require extensive search and rescue facilities if any mishap occurred to it.[102] The 1979 Consultative Meeting noted that commercial overflights of Antarctica are operating in a particularly hazardous environment where aircraft operation systems normally available elsewhere in the world are at a minimum and emergencies could arise which are beyond the capacity of permanent Antarctic expeditions to respond to adequately.[103] Governments were recommended to notify commercial aircraft operators that the level of tourist overflight activity at the time exceeded the existing capacity for air traffic control, communications and search and rescue in Antarctica, that it could interfere with normal operational flights in support of ongoing scientific programmes, and that it exceeded the capacity of Antarctic operations to respond adequately to an unplanned emergency landing.[104]

Several incidents involving tourist vessels have been cited. Eight members of a British mountaineering expedition destined for the

97. Rec. VIII-9.
98. Rec. IV-27.
99. Rec. VIII-9.
100. Rec. X-8.
101. Ibid.
102. 398 *SCAR Circular* (3 July 1978). SCAR suggested that tourist flights should be regarded as 'self-supported expeditions'.
103. Preamble, Rec. X-8.
104. Rec. X-8.

2 Antarctic Law and Politics

Antarctic Peninsula were lost in 1977 when their ship, the *En Avant*, disappeared en route from Rio de Janeiro to the Falkland Islands.[105] The Air New Zealand DC10 accident on Mount Erebus in November 1979 brought the death of all the 257 crew and passengers. Its probable cause, according to the Accident Report issued by the New Zealand Ministry of Transport, was the decision of the captain to continue the flight at low altitude towards an area of poor surface and horizon definition when the crew were not certain of their position, and the subsequent inability to detect the rising terrain which intercepted the aircraft's flight path.[106]

Subsequently a Royal Commission into the accident exonerated the captain and crew of any blame and concluded that the overriding cause of the disaster was to be found in administrative errors by Air New Zealand in changing the computer flight track without informing the aircraft's captain and crew. The findings of the Royal Commission involved serious allegations against the management of the airline.[107] Air New Zealand indicated that it would carry out its own investigation,[108] and in view of the gravity of the accusations made by the Royal Commission it is clear that the airline will take action to publicise its views. The legal claims – if they are not settled out of court – should shed further light on the matter.

But some lessons can already be learnt from the disaster. It is already apparent that there are differing views on the safety measures which should be applicable to tourist flights. For example, the DC-10 did not carry polar survival equipment. Everyone in the plane died on impact, but had any not done so, the light summer clothing worn by nearly all the occupants would have made their chances of survival slender.[109] Air New Zealand had advised that the carrying of special polar suits was unwarranted: it said that an emergency situation was extremely unlikely, that such suits would only be used in the event of a landing at McMurdo airfield, and that some Arctic long-haul flights do not carry such gear.[110] QANTAS (Australian) Antarctic tourist flights carry polar survival clothing for all on board.[111]

The preferable means of settling this dispute and achieving

---

105. 'British climbing expedition believed lost at sea' (1978), 8(5) *Antarctic*, 172.
106. Office of Air Accidents Investigation, Ministry of Transport, *Aircraft Accident Report No. 79–139* (1980), 53.
107. 'Air NZ blamed for 257 deaths', *West Australian* (28 April 1981).
108. 'Air NZ disputes crash findings', *West Australian* (29 April 1981).
109. Office of Air Accidents Investigation, Ministry of Transport, *Aircraft Accident Report No. 70–139* (1980), 49.
110. Ibid., at p. 37.
111. J. Black, 31 *Belle* (March/April 1979).

uniform standards for the safety of Antarctic tourism would be a code of practice laid down by the Consultative Parties and incorporated in municipal legislation. Assumption of this responsibility should flow directly from the claim to monopolise decision-making for the continent.

Impact Assessment

Impact assessment is the acid test of the Treaty powers' protection of the Antarctic environment. Before examining the practice of Consultative Meetings, it is instructive to review United States procedures. The National Environmental Policy Act of 1969 (NEPA) is the most effective municipal system of assessment, and its application to Antarctica has resulted in a number of impact statements providing illustrations of the problems with national laws and an indication of the possibilities of an international system.

Although there has been controversy over the extra-territorial reach of the legislation and whether it binds agencies such as the Export-Import Bank, the State Department accepted that NEPA obliged the US government to file impact statements for Antarctica. This concession, made during Congressional hearings on the Sealing Convention in January 1972,[112] was adhered to subsequently by the Department and the National Science Foundation. In January 1979 an Executive Order required Federal agencies to review major federal actions significantly affecting the environment of the global commons outside the jurisdiction of any nation such as the oceans and Antarctica.[113] It is suggested that the Order will in future prevent NEPA from applying to Antarctica,[114] but for the present illustration, practice under NEPA may be utilised.

One problem was the timing of impact statements and the difficulty of preparing detailed comments before the requisite action had been taken. The Draft Statement on Living Resources was made public on 1 February 1978,[115] and on 27 February the Canberra Special Consultative Meeting began. Representatives decided to refer a single text for discussion by governments.[116] In diplomatic terms, elements of the regime having major environmental effects

112. 'Fish and Wildlife Legislation, Part 4', Hearings, Subcommittee on Fisheries and Wildlife Conservation, Committee on Merchant Marine and Fisheries, H. Rep., 92nd Cong., 2nd Sess. (1972), 21.
113. Exec. Order No. 12. 114, 44 Fed. Reg. 1957 (1979).
114. S.C. Whitney, 'Regulation of Federal Decision Making Affecting the Environment outside the United States' (1980), 3 *GMU Law Review*, 62 at 78.
115. Department of State, *Draft Environmental Impact Statement for a Possible Regime for Conservation of Antarctic Living Marine Resources* (1978), iii.
116. Interim Report of the Second Special Consultative Meeting, Canberra (1978) 5.

had already been settled at the 1977 Consultative Meeting,[117] and presumably other issues reached an advanced stage of negotiation at Canberra. For impact assessment to affect a State's attitude towards the negotiation of a treaty, the process must be carried out before international discussions begin; otherwise comments on the draft statement, however well justified, will founder on the rock of accomplished facts. A good example was the taking of action under NEPA for the purpose of enabling the United States to ratify an agreement. Once a final text had been agreed, after lengthy negotiations and concessions, the sole choice was between accepting and rejecting the whole text, since alterations at this stage were impracticable. Thus the Sealing Convention was concluded in 1972, and a Draft Environmental Impact Statement was published in August 1974, in which a number of criticisms were made, *inter alia* of the absence of any catch allocation between nations. Even comments made by US government agencies[118] were unlikely to persuade the State Department to attempt to re-open the Convention for amendment when it had not yet entered into force.

Assessment requires review of all relevant material. On Antarctic issues the general policy of secrecy of Consultative and other meetings officially debars from access to documents those not employed by governments. The United States has released some of its own papers.[119] But without a detailed analysis of the positions of other countries, the drafts submitted by them and the course of discussions, the public has only a very limited indication of the real policy options. If the US government proposes, as part of the impact assessment, to include specified points in its negotiating instructions, it is most difficult to assess the possibility of acceptance by other nations without a knowledge of their views. So the State Department advocated interim harvesting ceilings until the entry into force of the Living Resources Convention,[120] but the only means of estimating the likelihood of adoption of this position was through examination of the negotiations and views of the harvesting countries which were secret.

---

117. See the discussion of 'rational use' under Krill/*Conservation Principles*.
118. Environmental Protection Agency in Department of State, *Environmental Impact Statement on the Convention for the Conservation of Antarctic Seals* (1974).
119. 'Exploitation of Antarctic Resources', Hearing, Subcommittee on Arms Control, Oceans and International Environment, Committee on Foreign Relations, Senate, 95th Cong., 2nd Sess. (1978), 97.
120. 'Antarctic Living Marine Resources Negotiations', Hearing, National Ocean Policy Study, Committee on Commerce, Science and Transportation, Senate, 95th Cong., 2nd Sess. (1978), 5.

Impact statements exhibited a strong tendency to support the proposed course of action. Alternatives, particularly those of a drastic nature, did not receive comprehensive coverage. In at least one instance maintenance of the *status quo* was a foregone conclusion. This was when assessment of the US Antarctic Programme led to the hardly surprising conclusion that any major reduction in effort would require a change in national policy and for this reason, *inter alia*, should not be endorsed.[121] Even where local environmental effects were clearly recognised, proposals were often confined to mild suggestions of possible improvements. McMurdo Station was clearly the source of various forms of local pollution, yet discussion of its closure was disposed of briefly,[122] and alternative sites for a logistic base were not examined. This may well have been the reason for only two comments on the Program Draft being received. One, from the State Department, expressed total agreement, while another, from the Department of Health, Education and Welfare, argued that disposal of untreated wastes appeared to conflict with the intention and spirit of US requirements for Pollution Control Standards. The response of the National Science Foundation was that pollution standards were those of general applicability in the host country or its jurisdiction. For the Antarctic these took the form of recommendations, and the US programme was in compliance with Recommendation VIII-11.[123] In other words, NEPA applied to Antarctica, but other general United States laws prescribing specific environmental rules did not.

With regard to research, there was a tendency in the same direction. For example, acceptance of the scientific merit of such a proposal as the Ross Ice Shelf Project weighed heavily in assessments.[124] The difficulty of assigning values to the peculiarly fragile environments of Antarctica is well shown in the Dry Valley Drilling Project. The Dry Valleys of Victoria Land in the Ross Dependency constitute a large proportion of the ice-free area of the continent. Initially, the Valleys were a rare example of a portion of the Earth's surface which had not been substantially altered by man.[125] Features

---

121. National Science Foundation, *US Antarctic Program Draft Environmental Impact Statement* (1979), 5–7, and National Science Foundation, *US Antarctic Program Final Environmental Impact Statement* (1980).

122. National Science Foundation, *US Antarctic Program Draft Environmental Impact Statement* (1979), 5–6 to 5–7.

123. National Science Foundation, *US Antarctic Program Final Environmental Impact Statement* (1980).

124. B.C. Parker, 'Ross Ice Shelf Project Environmental Impact Statement' in B.C. Parker (ed.), *Environmental Impact in Antarctica* (1978), 7 at 32.

125. J.G. Mcpherson, *Footsteps on a Frozen Continent* (1975), 87.

include unique saline lakes, evidence of post-glacial erosion, and mummified seals.[126] To a considerable degree the scientific interest of the Valleys lay in their untouched state. Environmental appraisal of the DVDP recognised that a geological drilling programme would have an impact, but held that it would be sufficiently small not to jeopardise or lower the future scientific value of the area.[127]

Particular care was taken to ensure that proposed protective measures were actually implemented. The DVDP was the first Antarctic example of monitoring *in situ*,[128] and a detailed review of the effects of drilling is therefore available. One of the impacts was impregnation of sand with diesel fluid.[129] The guidelines were not always followed.[130] Although it was concluded that successful drilling had been carried out within stringent environmental constraints,[131] spills and leaks of drill fluids appeared to have been unavoidable. Microbial changes had possibly occurred at some sites.[132] One lesson from the DVDP was that assessment and monitoring for future Antarctic projects could be improved.[133] Yet the principle scientific importance of the Dry Valleys was their pristine ecology. Consideration of the alternative of not drilling at all was dealt with by pointing out that this would lead to the abandonment of the National Science Foundation's commitment to investigate the subsurface geology of the Antarctic.[134] At best it is extremely difficult to balance the value

126. H.G.R. King, *The Antarctic* (1969), 56–7.
127. B.C. Parker, M.G. Mudrey, R.E. Cameron, K. Cartwright and L.D. McGinnis, *Environmental Appraisal for the Dry Valley Drilling Project, Phase III (1973–1974)*, 3.
128. B.C. Parker, R.V. Howard and F.C.T. Allnutt, 'Summary of Environmental Monitoring and Impact Assessment of the DVDP' in B.C. Parker (ed.), *Environmental Impact in Antarctica* (1978), 211.
129. R.E. Cameron, F.A. Morelli, R. Donlan, J. Guilfoyle, B. Markley and R. Smith, 'DVDP environmental monitoring' (1974), 9(4) *Antarctic Journal*, 141.
130. B.C. Parker, R.V. Howard and F.C.T. Allnutt, 'Summary of Environmental Monitoring and Impact Assessment of the DVDP' in B.C. Parker (ed.), *Environmental Impact in Antarctica* (1978), 2 11 at 220.
131. B.C. Parker, M.G. Mudrey, K. Cartwright and L.D. McGinnis, *Environmental Appraisal for the Dry Valley Drilling Project, Phase IV (1974–1975)* (1974), 88.
132. R.E. Cameron, F.A. Morelli and R.C. Honour, 'Environmental Impact Monitoring of the Dry Valley Drilling Project (DVDP)' in *Dry Valley Drilling Project-Seminar 1* (1974), 18.
133. B.C. Parker, 'Environmental Impact Assessment and Monitoring of DVDP' (1976), 7 *Dry Valley Drilling Project (DVDP) Bulletin*, 117.
134. B.C. Parker, M.G. Mudrey, K. Cartwright and L.D. McGinnis, 'Environmental Appraisal for the Dry Valley Drilling Project, Phases III, IV, V (1973–74, 1974–75, 1975–76)' in B.C. Parker (ed.), *Environmental Impact in Antarctica* (1978), 37 at 122.

of a unique environment against the desire to carry out scientific research.

The past US record of impact assessment in Antarctica deserves praise, but the effectiveness of the procedures was limited by constraints not present in purely domestic action. If such sophisticated and effective legislation as NEPA proved difficult to apply to the Antarctic, it could be expected that international measures would also meet obstacles.

In 1975 the Consultative Parties formulated a Code of Conduct for Antarctic Expeditions and Station Activities, which governments are bound to observe 'to the greatest extent feasible'. *Inter alia*, the Code prescribes guidelines for Antarctic operating organisations undertaking substantial projects. In planning major operations in the Treaty Area, the organisation concerned should carry out an evaluation of the environmental impact of the proposed activity. Such an evaluation should describe the activity, assess its potential benefits and possible impact on the relevant ecosystems. Consideration should be given to alternative actions which might alter the pattern of benefits *vis-à-vis* the adverse environmental effects expected to result. Evaluations may be circulated for information through SCAR channels to all States engaged in Antarctic activities.[135]

These guidelines were adapted from a review undertaken by the SCAR Working Group on Biology,[136] but in a number of significant respects the Code is weaker than the SCAR proposals. The overriding proviso for observation to the greatest extent feasible was introduced by the Consultative Parties, and examples of the establishment of a new base for scientific research or the implementation of a major research project such as the Ross Ice Shelf Project were deleted. Also omitted were the requirements that the description of the proposed action be 'comprehensive' and that an assessment be allowed which should be 'adequate'. Circulation of evaluations would take place under the Working Group's report but is not mandatory under Recommendation VIII-11. Perhaps the most important omission was the requirement for 'a comprehensive statement of anticipated short-term and long-term effects on the environment and its intimately associated macro- and micro-biota, together with their primary, secondary, and tertiary consequences; a delineation of all probable unavoidable adverse environmental effects, with suggestions for means of minimising them.'

It may be presumed that the National Science Foundation's Envi-

135. Rec. VIII-11.
136. (1973) 43 *SCAR Bulletin* 913.

ronmental Impact Statement on the US Antarctic Program of 1980 was largely motivated by a desire to encourage other Consultative Parties to carry out evaluations. If so, there are few indications of this part of the Code being observed by other nations. Reference has already been made to the impact of the establishment of Arctowski Base by Poland in 1977.[137] Although Recommendation VIII-11 was not in force at the time, Poland adopted all recommendations as part of its move for Consultative status.[138] It does not appear that an impact evaluation was circulated. Future prospects for assessments prior to the setting-up of stations are not encouraging.

Even if the evaluation guidelines were followed, it would be a mistake to consider that the Code provides any meaningful form of impact reporting. Evaluation need only be carried out to the greatest extent feasible; there is no definition of 'major operations'; deletion of the detailed requirements suggested by SCAR deprived the procedure of any specific standards; circulation of the assessment is optional; no provision is made for comments by other nations or interested organisations such as UNEP or IUCN; nor is there any possibility of amendment by an independent body. An evaluation could well conclude that substantial local impacts were envisioned, but that reasons of national policy outweighed environmental considerations.

One examination has been carried out by SCAR. At the request of the Consultative Parties, the EAMREA Group of Specialists was established to assess the possible impact of mineral exploration and/or exploitation.[139] It has already been pointed out that EAMREA had less than a year in which to report, was only able to hold one meeting, and was not funded under the requesting Recommendation.[140] The editor of the EAMREA Report stressed that it was not an environmental impact assessment but rather a preliminary exploration of possible effects.[141] Once more much of the impetus came from the United States.[142] But the EAMREA

137. See Environment/*Specially Protected Areas*.
138. Discussed under Antarctic System/*Consultative Status*.
139. Rec. VIII-14
140. See Antarctic System/*SCAR*.
141. J.H. Zumberge (ed.), *Possible Environmental Effects of Mineral Exploration and Exploitation in Antarctica* (1979), 2–3. But note that the original version prepared for the 1977 Consultative Meeting was entitled *A Preliminary Assessment of the Environmental Impact of Mineral Exploration/Exploitation in Antarctica*. That title was taken from the wording of Rec. VIII-14.
142. The State Department had requested the Ohio State University study of the topic, the National Science Foundation defrayed some EAMREA expenses and staff work was done by an officer of the National Academy of Sciences.

Report cannot be regarded as in any sense as an equivalent of NEPA procedures, nor was it so intended.

To date the most significant action of environmental concern under the Antarctic system has been the Living Resources Convention. Although the conservation principles of the Convention would provide substantial protection for the marine ecosystem, previous analysis of the text suggests that there will be serious obstacles to any attempt to promulgate measures binding harvesting States contrary to their wishes. There is no specific funding mechanism for scientific research on krill stocks, and the Convention does not prescribe catch levels or any other form of regulation. Krill trawling countries can either veto conservation measures or individually refuse to accept them. The Scientific Committee is essentially under the direction of the Commission, which represents the political interests of States. Impact assessment in the municipal law sense is not provided for under the regime, and even if the Scientific Committee were to reach specific conclusions on, say, desirable catch levels, such findings would in no way bind the Commission.

Mineral negotiations have placed special emphasis on impact assessment for informed decision-making,[143] but the precedents suggest that it cannot be expected that the Consultative Parties will establish open objective assessment procedures with adequate funding for the minerals regime. As a body the Consultative Parties are not prepared to establish effective impact procedures, nor to provide adequate funding for the necessary scientific research, whether under the Antarctic Treaty, the Sealing Convention, the Living Resources Convention or a future minerals treaty.

143. Rec. X-1.

10
THE FUTURE

Interpretations of Antarctic affairs have been largely dominated by accepted views of the governments of the Consultative Parties. This is in part due to the geographical isolation of the continent and the control exercised by governments over the use of most forms of transport between it and the rest of the world. These received views are open to criticism. First, the accuracy of their construction of events may be questioned. Secondly, and perhaps of more importance, the true nature of national interests and involvement in Antarctica is obscured. A central assumption in these interpretations relates to the role and value of scientific research. Antarctica is seen as an 'International Laboratory for Science and Diplomacy',[1] and international cooperation and scientific advance there as of incalculably great value.[2]

What are the uses of such research? Studies of the cardiovascular response to diving of the Weddell seal may, for example, help to establish the cause of cot deaths. The Dry Valleys are a valuable testing ground and area of comparison for detecting life on other planets.[3] The continent has recently proved to be the world's most prolific source of meteorites,[4] a pointer to the development of the Solar System. But the immediate and practical value of science on the continent has not been demonstrated. Antarctic research is (with a few exceptions) fundamental.

Governments generally have not been interested in basic research, support for which is seen as the means of presenting national interests on the continent. From this it may be suggested that countries are not concerned with the abstract values of science and international cooperation in themselves. The IGY approach is not likely to survive with regard to resources, and evidence for this is already available in the refusal of certain nations to exchange information on krill.

Protection of the environment is a recurrent theme of the recom-

---

1. (1970), 26(10) *Science and Public Affairs*.
2. N. Potter, 'Economic Potential of the Antarctic' (1969), 4(3) *Antarctic Journal*, 61 at 72.
3. R.E. Cameron, R.C. Honour and F.A. Morelli, 'Environmental Impact Studies of Antarctic Sites' in G.A. Llano (ed.), *Adaptations with Antarctic Ecosystems* (1977), 1157 at 1170.
4. D. Sears, 'Rocks on the ice', *New Scientist* (22 March 1979), 961.

mendations made during the last decade. Ecological considerations could even determine whether mineral developments will be acceptable.[5] There is no doubt that many scientists support such measures. Governments have only recently taken a serious interest in the Antarctic environment, and their motives for so doing are suspect. Local pollution is caused by official expeditions. Where preservation of the environment has conflicted with the needs of government programmes, the latter have prevailed. Public statements of concern may be contrasted with the actual practice of the Consultative Parties, and it is difficult to escape the conclusion that their asserted responsibility for the protection of the environment and the wise use of the Treaty Area[6] is no more than a new justification to legitimate the claims of the club to a monopoly of Antarctic decision-making. An analogy may be drawn with the Arctic Waters Pollution Prevention Act which was used by Canada to improve its political stance in the Arctic.

Repeated invocation of reasoning which has no basis in the Treaty demonstrates that the Consultative Parties themselves have serious doubts regarding the justification for their monopoly. The arguments for the club are largely dated, and two of the original Consultative Parties would not today pass the test for new entrants. With the advent of krill exploration, scientific research is no longer the sole form of activity in the area. To contend that the Consultative Parties are specially qualified to make decisions because of their experience is hardly persuasive. No country has carried out offshore mineral exploitation in the Antarctic, and if anything is relevant to drafting a regime covering offshore hydrocarbons it would be polar development and work in difficult areas such as the North Sea.

Contracting Parties have no role in decision-making. The price of Consultative status is high because of the narrow interpretation of Article IX(2), but there is little incentive merely to accede to the Treaty unless the nation concerned intends to establish a winter station. A simple means of avoiding this difficulty would be to give Contracting Parties entry to the club as observers without a vote.

Unanimity places severe constraints on the Antarctic system, and claimants, especially the less powerful ones, have seen it as their shield against the widespread activities of the Soviet Union and the United States. But its practical use is more limited. Once a decision in principle is taken, claimants will not be in a position to demand major concessions to their particular interests as a condition of implementation, since such action would bring the Consultative

5. Rec. X-1.
6. Rec. X-9.

process to a halt. Opting out of the system is not at present a credible threat as against the non-claimants.

So there was little likelihood of Consultative Parties making realistic and substantial sovereignty demands during the living resources negotiations. Other participants could have called their bluff by continuing the discussions outside the framework of the Antarctic Treaty. On the other hand, some concessions were made, e.g. the deletion of part of the Antarctic Convergence in the Drake Passage at the request of Argentina, (possibly) the omission of Macquarie Island and its 200-mile zone to benefit Australia, and the statement on the Kerguelen and Crozet areas. In the final event, power is more significant than unanimity. When the Soviet Union refused to accept any alteration to the conservation principles at the Conference, its success was due to its leading role in trawling rather than the possibility of a veto.

The Living Resources Convention presents an even stronger form of blocking than the Antarctic Treaty. A double objection procedure for conservation principles is contained in the 1980 agreement itself. Here the interests of claimants and harvesting States converge. Despite the obvious drawbacks of consensus, there does not seem to be much hope of persuading the Consultative Parties to adopt majority voting, whether under the Antarctic Treaty or any other regime associated with it. Inaction, confusion and compromise are of minor political concern for a regime which regulates scientific research, but the same cannot be said where an important fishery stock or hydrocarbons are concern.

There is no indication that the Consultative Parties may be willing to relinquish their monopoly of Antarctic decision-making; if anything, the trend is in the opposite direction. Resource regimes have been negotiated in detail, and although the two Conferences held so far, for seals and living resources, have been outside the Treaty framework the draft articles previously prepared by the Consultative Parties have been insisted upon in all vital respects. Maintenance of control by the Antarctic Treaty countries is ensured by the narrow limits on invitations to third parties and the assertion of a veto over the admission of such nations to the equivalent of Consultative status under the new regime.

Poland, the first new Consultative nation, is mainly interested in krill; the second, West Germany, is in a similar position, as is a potential candidate, East Germany. That West Germany was prepared to pay the price of entry to the Treaty club, which is of secondary concern to it, underlines the continued strength of the Antarctic system. But despite their extensive research and exploration for krill the two Germanys were not apparently admitted to the living resources negotiations before the 1980 Conference.

West Germany has become a Consultative Party, and by becoming an observer at SCAR, East Germany has suggested that it may well follow suit. Assuming fifteen Consultative Parties, will there be any subsequent expansion of the club under the Antarctic Treaty? The People's Republic of China has recently shown considerable interest in the continent, and has held discussions with Australia, Chile and New Zealand. Two Chinese scientists have spent six weeks in Antarctica, and an observer was sent to the 1980 SCAR Meeting. Newspaper reports mention the possible eventual establishment of a permanent base.[7]

Looking towards Consultative status for China, or at least its cooperation and support for the Antarctic system, the question of an outside challenge recedes even further into the distance. Although there has been much speculation, it is notable that there has not yet been any public concerted effort by a significant bloc of countries to confront the system. Various sources of opposition have been suggested: one could be the International Seabed Authority, under pressure from the Group of 77, and alternatively the developing countries might press for the common heritage concept to be applied to the whole Antarctic Treaty area as part of the NIEO. More speculatively, OPEC could take a variety of measures should very substantial oil reserves be discovered south of 60°S. But to date the only interventions to assume the form of concrete proposals have come from international organisations such as UNEP and FAO. Even these instances were not challenges to the Antarctic system but rather unwanted offers of help.

The most credible source of difficulty at present lies within the Consultative Meetings. On the tentative assumption of a sixteen-member club including East and West Germany and China, general internal tensions will be maximised. The various interests will include claimants, potential claimants, non-claimants, resource States, superpower conflict, South American issues, the problem of South Africa and even the EEC fishery policy. Considerable emphasis has already been placed upon the almost total absence of administration under the Treaty. Its unwieldy procedure will be under continual pressure from the sheer diversity of national interests, particularly in the negotiation of a mineral regime.

Prospects of internationalisation in any of the multifarious forms suggested have not become more likely since the Treaty came into force. Recent years have seen a renewed flow of ideas for a world park, common space or common heritage, but the Consultative

7. 'China's interest in joint research' (1980), 9(2) *Antarctic*, 62.

Parties are not even prepared to put such ideas on the agenda for discussion. *De facto* internationalisation through the working of the Treaty[8] has not come about. History militates against this type of solution, with the as yet untested exception of the deep seabed.

National policies frequently lack firm guidelines. Several of the claimants appear to have bitten off more than they can chew. This is especially so in the case of Australia which has the largest claim, a concentration of Soviet bases within it, and a reluctance to increase spending to match its international assertions. Low priority for Antarctic issues is reflected in the level of funding of operations, repeated and prolonged departmental discussion of ship replacements, and lengthy delays in minor matters such as approval of the Agreed Measures.

Mistakes were common. For example, the British Letters Patent of 1908 covered a large area of Patagonia. New Zealand has not produced any evidence of the transfer of the Ross Dependency to its sovereignty since 1923. Chile's claim lacks a northern boundary. Amundsen's journey laid the basis for a Norwegian assertion, yet the official claim in effect surrendered that country's priority in the crucial South Pole area. The US reassured the South American countries that their interests would not be prejudiced, at the same time as Byrd's official expedition was laying the foundations of future claims. Argentina repeatedly stated that the eastern boundary of its claim was 68° 34' W.

These examples ante-date the Treaty. Some countries now pursue vigorous and clear-cut policies, Argentina and the Soviet Union being cases in point. The same cannot be said for nations such as the United States, Australia and New Zealand. The most obvious manifestation of individual countries' attitudes is the continued emphasis on sovereign assertions by Chile and Argentina. Insofar as claims support consists of the deliberate and reasoned attitude of a single government, it is not likely to threaten the Treaty system; Chile, for instance, has little option but to remain a Consultative Party, and termination of obligations would not improve its territorial position and could well weaken it even further. But such calculations can only be relied upon where the claims staking is essentially unilateral and the other parties involved are on the defensive and not prepared for escalation as with the *Shackleton* affair in 1976.

Once a rival is prepared to take positive counter-measures, the dispute is no longer limited by the policy needs of one country, and a potentially explosive situation arises. This is why the Brazilian plans

8. K.R. Simmonds, 'The Antarctic Treaty, 1959' (1960), 87 *Journal du Droit International*, 668 at 696.

for an expedition in 1972 and the sharp reactions of Argentina and Chile were of considerable significance. Such a situation could recur if promising hydrocarbon formations were located in the Weddell Sea or Drake Passage, and a crime of the *Escamilla* type could have this effect anywhere in the continent. Should a dispute arise, popular concern could take the matter out of the hands of ministries of foreign affairs, leading to a political confrontation on the lines of the sequel to the Beagle Channel Arbitration.

Twenty years' experience have shown that Article IV of the Treaty has not dissipated any of the intensity of patriotic fervour. The purpose of sovereignty is to allocate exclusive jurisdiction, and with all its drawbacks, the division of the globe into nation-States does at least serve to provide a means of governing. The Treaty prevents any resolution of claims even by a partial renunciation of the more extreme assertions such as that of Australia. But the maintenance of unacceptable territorial demands exposes the Antarctic system to constant stress. If some form of internationalisation were feasible or likely, the interim difficulties would be of less importance. This solution has been repeatedly rejected. Therefore one can predict the repetition of incidents like the declaration of Marambio as the temporary capital of Argentina in 1973. But in future the stakes, in the form of resources, may be much more tangible than in the past. A mineral regime relying on precedents of the Antarctic system will be particularly vulnerable to the uncontrolled escalation of sovereignty disputes. In effect the Treaty complicates issues, because a territorial argument on one part of the continent cannot be settled without affecting other claims.

Antarctica has been insulated from the wider reach of global politics. During the Afghanistan crisis of 1980, a retaliatory US measure reduced scientific cooperation with the Soviet Union, but this decision was not applied to Antarctic research. One reason for this insulation has been that there was nothing worthy of serious dispute. Where world issues have affected Consultative Meetings, their impact has been muted: examples are the objection to South Africa hosting a Consultative Meeting and EEC participation in the living resources regime. Resources, especially oil and gas, could introduce political considerations which prevail in every other portion of the globe.

The danger to the Antarctic system is that such a change does not require the discovery of exploitable minerals. Commercial exploration requiring licensing is the crucial stage. As the manganese nodule debate shows that the possibility of recovery in fifteen or twenty years may be sufficient to arouse worldwide interest in resources which cannot be exploited with current technology. Several Consultative Parties are almost entirely dependent on imported oil, and the *Hakurei Maru* announcement was presumably based on Japan's lack of domestic oil. Energy autarchy may dictate exploration due to non-economic factors. In view of the Iraq – Iran war, the search for hydrocarbons will have to take into account the reliability of an unbroken supply. This will be predicated upon the political regime of the resource area. If one adds the general forecast of rapid depletion of known reserves, it is possible that the minerals issue could become actual within a relatively short time. Whether any regime devised by the Consultative Parties could survive the stress of a large oil find in times of growing scarcity and rapid price increases may be doubted.

There is no real administration. Consultative Meetings are clumsy and inefficient. Unanimity seriously limits the capacity to reach controversial decisions, and the Treaty is inflexible because formal amendment is not practical. *De facto* revision may therefore be expected on the precedent of the changing interpretations of the Treaty area and the limitations placed upon the acquisition of Consultative status. It has been pointed out that a number of breaches, some of them of major significance, have taken place, and more would no doubt be revealed if the records of government departments and Treaty meetings were publicly available.

The Treaty has proved a success so far, but because the circumstances are changing decisively, past performance is no guarantee of continuing achievement. Looking forward to a three-treaty system,[9] one apparent threat is that the Antarctic Treaty may become a residual regime or a shell. Resource arrangements could overshadow scientific research, and if this were to happen, then the problem would not be the breakdown of the Treaty but its irrelevance to the central considerations of Antarctic policy. Dominance, and indeed total monopolisation, by the Consultative Parties has ensured that the three treaties will be inextricably linked. This was already apparent when the Sealing Convention, which affirmed Article IV of the Antarctic Treaty, was drafted by the Consultative Parties and gave each of them a veto on accession. The complicated linkage in the Living Resources Convention has been examined in detail, and a similar approach to minerals is evident in the affirmation that the regime should be based on principles requiring the maintenance of the Antarctic Treaty 'in its entirety' and the safeguarding of Article IV in particular.[10] A threat to one agreement could bring down all three.

9. Antarctic Treaty, Convention on the Conservation of Antarctic Marine Living Resources, mineral regime. One could add the Sealing Convention.
10. Rec. IX-1.

In times of change it would be rash to guess the future development of the Antarctic Treaty area. The appearance of underground mines fuelled by nuclear power stations or increasing pressure to dispose of radioactive wastes — assuming amendment of the Treaty — now appear unlikely. Iceberg utilisation is widely advocated as a solution to fresh-water shortages in several countries, but no one has yet towed a full-size berg to the nearest suggested target (Perth, Western Australia). What is clear is that the Antarctic system is undergoing stresses which will transform the regime. Backed by the major industrial powers, it may well survive. Whether it will prove adequate to cope with resource disputes raised by Consultative Parties themselves is far from clear.

THE ANTARCTIC TREATY

The Governments of Argentina, Australia, Belgium, Chile, the French Republic, Japan, New Zealand, Norway, the Union of South Africa, the Union of Soviet Socialist Republics, the United Kingdom of Great Britain and Northern Ireland, and the United States of America,

Recognizing that it is in the interest of all mankind that Antarctica shall continue forever to be used exclusively for peaceful purposes and shall not become the scene or object of international discord;

Acknowledging the substantial contributions to scientific knowledge resulting from international co-operation in scientific investigation in Antarctica;

Convinced that the establishment of a firm foundation for the continuation and development of such co-operation on the basis of freedom of scientific investigation in Antarctica as applied during the International Geophysical Year accords with the interests of science and the progress of all mankind;

Convinced also that a treaty ensuring the use of Antarctica for peaceful purposes only and the continuance of international harmony in Antarctica will further the purposes and principles embodied in the Charter of the United Nations;

Have agreed as follows:

ARTICLE I

1. Antarctica shall be used for peaceful purposes only. There shall be prohibited, *inter alia*, any measures of a military nature, such as the establishment of military bases and fortifications, the carrying out of military manoeuvres, as well as the testing of any type of weapons.

2. The present Treaty shall not prevent the use of military personnel or equipment for scientific research or for any other peaceful purpose.

ARTICLE II

Freedom of scientific investigation in Antarctica and co-operation toward that end, as applied during the International Geophysical Year, shall continue, subject to the provisions of the present Treaty.

ARTICLE III

1. In order to promote international co-operation in scientific investigation in Antarctica, as provided for in Article II of the present Treaty, the Contracting Parties agree that, to the greatest extent feasible and practicable:
(*a*) information regarding plans for scientific programs in Antarctica shall be exchanged to permit maximum economy and efficiency of operations;
(*b*) scientific personnel shall be exchanged in Antarctica between expeditions and stations;

(*c*) scientific observations and results from Antarctica shall be exchanged and made freely available.

2. In implementing this Article, every encouragement shall be given to the establishment of co-operative working relations with those Specialized Agencies of the United Nations and other international organizations having a scientific or technical interest in Antarctica.

ARTICLE IV

1. Nothing contained in the present Treaty shall be interpreted as:
(*a*) a renunciation by any Contracting Party of previously asserted rights of or claims to territorial sovereignty in Antarctica;
(*b*) a renunciation or diminution by any Contracting Party of any basis of claim to territorial sovereignty in Antarctica which it may have whether as a result of its activities or those of its nationals in Antarctica, or otherwise;
(*c*) prejudicing the position of any Contracting Party as regards its recognition or non-recognition of any other State's right of or claim or basis of claim to territorial sovereignty in Antarctica.

2. No acts or activities taking place while the present Treaty is in force shall constitute a basis for asserting, supporting or denying a claim to territorial sovereignty in Antarctica or create any rights of sovereignty in Antarctica. No new claim, or enlargement of an existing claim, to territorial sovereignty in Antarctica shall be asserted while the present Treaty is in force.

ARTICLE V

1. Any nuclear explosions in Antarctica and the disposal there of radioactive waste material shall be prohibited.

2. In the event of the conclusion of international agreements concerning the use of nuclear energy, including nuclear explosions and the disposal of radioactive waste material, to which all of the Contracting Parties whose representatives are entitled to participate in the meetings provided for under Article IX are parties, the rules established under such agreements shall apply in Antarctica.

ARTICLE VI

The provisions of the present Treaty shall apply to the area south of 60° South Latitude, including all ice shelves, but nothing in the present Treaty shall prejudice or in any way affect the rights, or the exercise of the rights, of any State under international law with regard to the high seas within that area.

ARTICLE VII

1. In order to promote the objectives and ensure the observance of the provisions of the present Treaty, each Contracting Party whose representatives are entitled to participate in the meetings referred to in Article IX of the Treaty shall have the right to designate observers to carry out any inspection provided for by the present Article. Observers shall be nationals of the

Contracting Parties which designate them. The names of observers shall be communicated to every other Contracting Party having the right to designate observers, and like notice shall be given of the termination of their appointment.

2. Each observer designated in accordance with the provisions of paragraph 1 of this Article shall have complete freedom of access at any time to any or all areas of Antarctica.

3. All areas of Antarctica, including all stations, installations and equipment within those areas, and all ships and aircraft at points of discharging or embarking cargoes or personnel in Antarctica, shall be open at all times to inspection by any observers designated in accordance with paragraph 1 of this Article.

4. Aerial observation may be carried out at any time over any or all areas of Antarctica by any of the Contracting Parties having the right to designate observers.

5. Each Contracting Party shall, at the time when the present Treaty enters into force for it, inform the other Contracting Parties, and thereafter shall give them notice in advance, of

(*a*) all expeditions to and within Antarctica, on the part of its ships or nationals, and all expeditions to Antarctica organized in or proceeding from its territory;

(*b*) all stations in Antarctica occupied by its nationals; and

(*c*) any military personnel or equipment intended to be introduced by it into Antarctica subject to the conditions prescribed in paragraph 2 of Article I of the present Treaty.

ARTICLE VIII

1. In order to facilitate the exercise of their functions under the present Treaty, and without prejudice to the respective positions of the Contracting Parties relating to jurisdiction over all other persons in Antarctica, observers designated under paragraph 1 of Article VII and scientific personnel exchanged under sub-paragraph 1 (*b*) of Article III of the Treaty, and members of the staffs accompanying any such persons, shall be subject only to the jurisdiction of the Contracting Party of which they are nationals in respect of all acts or omissions occurring while they are in Antarctica for the purpose of exercising their functions.

2. Without prejudice to the provisions of paragraph 1 of this Article, and pending the adoption of measures in pursuance of sub-paragraph 1 (*e*) of Article IX, the Contracting Parties concerned in any case of dispute with regard to the exercise of jurisdiction in Antarctica shall immediately consult together with a view to reaching a mutually acceptable solution.

ARTICLE IX

1. Representatives of the Contracting Parties named in the preamble to the present Treaty shall meet at the City of Canberra within two months after the date of entry into force of the Treaty, and thereafter at suitable intervals and

places, for the purpose of exchanging information, consulting together on matters of common interest pertaining to Antarctica, and formulating and considering, and recommending to their Governments, measures in further-ance of the principles and objectives of the Treaty, including measures regarding: −

(*a*) use of Antarctica for peaceful purposes only;

(*b*) facilitation of scientific research in Antarctica;

(*c*) facilitation of international scientific co-operation in Antarctica;

(*d*) facilitation of the exercise of the rights of inspection provided for in Article VII of the Treaty;

(*e*) questions relating to the exercise of jurisdiction Antarctica;

(*f*) preservation and conservation of living resources in Antarctica.

2. Each Contracting Party which has become a party to the present Treaty by accession under Article XIII shall be entitled to appoint representatives to participate in the meetings referred to in paragraph 1 of the present Article, during such time as that Contracting Party demonstrates its interest in Antarctica by conducting substantial scientific research activity there, such as the establishment of a scientific station or the despatch of a scientific expedition.

3. Reports from the observers referred to in Article VII of the present Treaty shall be transmitted to the representatives of the Contracting Parties partic-ipating in the meetings referred to in paragraph 1 of the present Article.

4. The measures referred to in paragraph 1 of this Article shall become effec-tive when approved by all the Contracting Parties whose representatives were entitled to participate in the meetings held to consider those measures.

5. Any or all of the rights established in the present Treaty may be exercised as from the date of entry into force of the Treaty whether or not any measures facilitating the exercise of such rights have been proposed, con-sidered or approved as provided in this Article.

Article X

Each of the Contracting Parties undertakes to exert appropriate efforts, consistent with the Charter of the United Nations, to the end that no one engages in any activity in Antarctica contrary to the principles or purposes of the present Treaty.

Article XI

1. If any dispute arises between two or more of the Contracting Parties con-cerning the interpretation or application of the present Treaty, those Contracting Parties shall consult among themselves with a view to having the dispute resolved by negotiation, inquiry, mediation, conciliation, arbitra-tion, judicial settlement or other peaceful means of their own choice.

2. Any dispute of this character not so resolved shall, with the consent, in each case, of all parties to the dispute, be referred to the International Court of Justice for settlement; but failure to reach agreement on reference to the International Court shall not absolve parties to the dispute from the

responsibility of continuing to seek to resolve it by any of the various peaceful means referred to in paragraph 1 of this Article.

ARTICLE XII

1. — (a) The present Treaty may be modified or amended at any time by unanimous agreement of the Contracting Parties whose representatives are entitled to participate in the meetings provided for under Article IX. Any such modification or amendment shall enter into force when the depositary Government has received notice from all such Contracting Parties that they have ratified it.

(b) Such modification or amendment shall thereafter enter into force as to any other Contracting Party when notice of ratification by it has been received by the depositary Government. Any such Contracting Party from which no notice of ratification is received within a period of two years from the date of entry into force of the modification or amendment in accordance with the provisions of sub-paragraph 1 (a) of this Article shall be deemed to have withdrawn from the present Treaty on the date of the expiration of such period.

2. — (a) If after the expiration of thirty years from the date of entry into force of the present Treaty, any of the Contracting Parties whose representatives are entitled to participate in the meetings provided for under Article IX so requests by a communication addressed to the depositary Government, a Conference of all the Contracting Parties shall be held as soon as practicable to review the operation of the Treaty.

(b) Any modification or amendment to the present Treaty which is approved at such a Conference by a majority of the Contracting Parties there represented, including a majority of those whose representatives are entitled to participate in the meetings provided for under Article IX, shall be communicated by the depositary Government to all the Contracting Parties immediately after the termination of the Conference and shall enter into force in accordance with the provisions of paragraph 1 of the present Article.

(c) If any such modification or amendment has not entered into force in accordance with the provisions of sub-paragraph 1 (a) of this Article within a period of two years after the date of its communication to all the Contracting Parties, any Contracting Party may at any time after the expiration of that period give notice to the depositary Government of its withdrawal from the present Treaty; and such withdrawal shall take effect two years after the receipt of the notice by the depositary Government.

ARTICLE XIII

1. The present Treaty shall be subject to ratification by the signatory States. It shall be open for accession by any State which is a Member of the United Nations, or by any other State which may be invited to accede to the Treaty with the consent of all the Contracting Parties whose representatives are entitled to participate in the meetings provided for under Article IX of the Treaty.

2. Ratification of or accession to the present Treaty shall be effected by each

State in accordance with its constitutional processes.

3. Instruments of ratification and instruments of accession shall be deposited with the Government of the United States of America, hereby designated as the depositary Government.

4. The depositary Government shall inform all signatory and acceding States of the date of each deposit of an instrument of ratification or accession, and the date of entry into force of the Treaty and of any modification or amendment thereto.

5. Upon the deposit of instruments of ratification by all the signatory States, the present Treaty shall enter into force for those States and for States which have deposited instruments of accession. Thereafter the Treaty shall enter into force for any acceding State upon the deposit of its instrument of accession.

6. The present Treaty shall be registered by the depositary Government pursuant to Article 102 of the Charter of the United Nations.

ARTICLE XIV

The present Treaty, done in the English, French, Russian and Spanish languages, each version being equally authentic, shall be deposited in the archives of the Government of the United States of America, which shall transmit duly certified copies thereof to the Governments of the signatory and acceding States.

AGREED MEASURES FOR THE CONSERVATION OF ANTARCTIC FAUNA AND FLORA

PREAMBLE

The Governments participating in the Third Consultative Meeting under Article IX of the Antarctic Treaty,

Desiring to implement the principles and purposes of the Antarctic Treaty;

Recognizing the scientific importance of the study of Antarctic fauna and flora, their adaptation to their rigorous environment, and their inter-relationship with that environment;

Considering the unique nature of these fauna and flora, their circumpolar range, and particularly their defencelessness and susceptibility to extermination;

Desiring by further international collaboration within the framework of the Antarctic Treaty to promote and achieve the objectives of protection, scientific study, and rational use of these fauna and flora; and

Having particular regard to the conservation principles developed by the Scientific Committee on Antarctic Research (SCAR) of the International Council of Scientific Unions;

Hereby consider the Treaty Area as a Special Conservation Area and have agreed on the following measures:

ARTICLE I
[Area of application]

1. These Agreed Measures shall apply to the same area to which the Antarctic Treaty is applicable (hereinafter referred to as the Treaty Area) namely the area south of 60° South Latitude, including all ice shelves.

2. However, nothing in these Agreed Measures shall prejudice or in any way affect the rights, or the exercise of the rights, of any State under international law with regard to the high seas within the Treaty Area, or restrict the implementation of the provisions of the Antarctic Treaty with respect to inspection.

3. The Annexes to these Measures shall form an integral part thereof, and all references to the Agreed Measures shall be considered to include the Annexes.

ARTICLE II
[Definitions]

For the purposes of these Agreed Measures:

(*a*) "Native mammal" means any member, at any stage of its life cycle, of any species belonging to the Class Mammalia indigenous to the Antarctic or occurring there through natural agencies of dispersal, excepting whales.

(*b*) "Native bird" means any member, at any stage of its life cycle (including eggs), of any species of the Class Aves indigenous to the Antarctic or occurring there through natural agencies of dispersal.

(*c*) "Native plant" means any kind of vegetation at any stage of its life cycle (including seeds), indigenous to the Antarctic or occurring there through natural agencies of dispersal.

(*d*) "Appropriate authority" means any person authorized by a Participating Government to issue permits under these Agreed Measures.

(*e*) "Permit" means a formal permission in writing issued by an appropriate authority.

(*f*) "Participating Government" means any Government for which these Agreed Measures have become effective in accordance with Article XIII of these Agreed Measures.

ARTICLE III
[Implementation]

Each Participating Government shall take appropriate action to carry out these Agreed Measures.

ARTICLE IV
[Publicity]

The Participating Governments shall prepare and circulate to members of expeditions and stations information to ensure understanding and observance of the provisions of these Agreed Measures, setting forth in particular prohibited activities, and providing lists of specially protected species and specially protected areas.

ARTICLE V
[Cases of extreme emergency]

The provisions of these Agreed Measures shall not apply in cases of extreme emergency involving possible loss of human life or involving the safety of ships or aircraft.

ARTICLE VI
[Protection of native fauna]

1. Each Participating Government shall prohibit within the Treaty Area the killing, wounding, capturing or molesting of any native mammal or native bird, or any attempt at any such act, except in accordance with a permit.

2. Such permits shall be drawn in terms as specific as possible and issued only for the following purposes:

(*a*) to provide indispensable food for men or dogs in the Treaty Area in limited quantities, and in conformity with the purposes and principles of these Agreed Measures;

(*b*) to provide specimens for scientific study or scientific information;

(*c*) to provide specimens for museums, zoological gardens, or other educational or cultural institutions or uses.

3. Permits for Specially Protected Areas shall be issued only in accordance with the provisions of Article VIII.

4. Participating Governments shall limit the issue of such permits so as to ensure as far as possible that:

(*a*) no more native mammals or birds are killed or taken in any year than can normally be replaced by natural reproduction in the following breeding season;
(*b*) the variety of species and the balance of the natural ecological systems existing within the Treaty Area are maintained.

5. The species of native mammals and birds listed in Annex A of these Measures shall be designated "Specially Protected Species", and shall be accorded special protection by Participating Governments.

6. A Participating Government shall not authorize an appropriate authority to issue a permit with respect to a Specially Protected Species except in accordance with paragraph 7 of this Article.

7. A permit may be issued under this Article with respect to a Specially Protected Species, provided that:
(*a*) it is issued for a compelling scientific purpose, and
(*b*) the actions permitted thereunder will not jeopardize the existing natural ecological system or the survival of that species.

ARTICLE VII
[Harmful interference]

1. Each Participating Government shall take appropriate measures to minimize harmful interference within the Treaty Area with the normal living conditions of any native mammal or bird, or any attempt at such harmful interference, except as permitted under Article VI.

2. The following acts and activities shall be considered as harmful interference:
(*a*) allowing dogs to run free,
(*b*) flying helicopters or other aircraft in a manner which would unnecessarily disturb bird and seal concentrations, or landing close to such concentrations (e.g. within 200m.),
(*c*) driving vehicles unnecessarily close to concentrations of birds and seals (e.g. within 200m.),
(*d*) use of explosives close to concentrations of birds and seals,
(*e*) discharge of firearms close to bird and seal concentrations (e.g. within 300m.).
(*f*) any disturbance of bird and seal colonies during the breeding period by persistent attention from persons on foot.
   However, the above activities, with the exception of those mentioned in (*a*) and (*e*) may be permitted to the minimum extent necessary for the establishment, supply and operation of stations.

3. Each Participating Government shall take all reasonable steps towards the alleviation of pollution of the waters adjacent to the coast and ice shelves.

ARTICLE VIII
[Specially Protected Areas]

1. The areas of outstanding scientific interest listed in Annex B shall be designated "Specially Protected Areas" and shall be accorded special

protection by the Participating Governments in order to preserve their unique natural ecological system.

2. In addition to the prohibitions and measures of protection dealt with in other Articles of these Agreed Measures, the Participating Governments shall in Specially Protected Areas further prohibit:
(*a*) the collection of any native plant, except in accordance with a permit;
(*b*) the driving of any vehicle.

3. A permit issued under Article VI shall not have effect within a Specially Protected Area except in accordance with paragraph 4 of the present Article.

4. A permit shall have effect within a Specially Protected Area provided that:
(*a*) it was issued for a compelling scientific purpose which cannot be served elsewhere; and
(*b*) the actions permitted thereunder will not jeopardise the natural ecological system existing in that Area.

ARTICLE IX
[Introduction of non-indigenous species, parasites and diseases]

1. Each Participating Government shall prohibit the bringing into the Treaty Area of any species of animal or plant not indigenous to that Area, except in accordance with a permit.

2. Permits under paragraph 1 of this Article shall be drawn in terms as specific as possible and shall be issued to allow the importation only of the animals and plants listed in Annex C. When any such animal or plant might cause harmful interference with the natural system if left unsupervised, within the Treaty Area, such permits shall require that it be kept under controlled conditions and, after it has served its purpose, it shall be removed from the Treaty Area or destroyed.

3. Nothing in paragraphs 1 and 2 of this Article shall apply to the importation of food into the Treaty Area so long as animals and plants used for this purpose are kept under controlled conditions.

4. Each Participating Government undertakes to ensure that all reasonable precautions shall be taken to prevent the accidental introduction of parasites and diseases into the Treaty Area. In particular, the precautions listed in Annex D shall be taken.

ARTICLE X
[Activities contrary to the principles and purposes of these Measures]

Each Participating Government undertakes to exert appropriate efforts, consistent with the Charter of the United Nations, to the end that no one engages in any activity in the Treaty Area contrary to the principles or purposes of these Agreed Measures.

ARTICLE XI
[Ships' crews]

Each Participating Government whose expeditions use ships sailing under flags of nationalities other than its own shall, as far as feasible, arrange with the owners of such ships that the crews of these ships observe these Agreed Measures.

ARTICLE XII
[Exchange of information]

1. The Participating Governments may make such arrangements as may be necessary for the discussion of such matters as:

(*a*) the collection and exchange of records (including records of permits) and statistics concerning the numbers of each species of native mammal and bird killed or captured annually in the Treaty Area;

(*b*) the obtaining and exchange of information as to the status of native mammals and birds in the Treaty Area, and the extent to which any species needs protection;

(*c*) the number of native mammals or birds which should be permitted to be harvested for food, scientific study, or other uses in the various regions;

(*d*) the establishment of a common form in which this information shall be submitted by Participating Governments in accordance with paragraph 2 of this Article.

2. Each Participating Government shall inform the other Governments in writing before the end of November of each year of the steps taken and information collected in the preceding period of 1st July to 30th June relating to the implementation of these Agreed Measures. Governments exchanging information under paragraph 5 of Article VII of the Antarctic Treaty may at the same time transmit the information relating to the implementation of these Agreed Measures.

ARTICLE XIII
[Formal provisions]

1. After the receipt by the Government designated in Recommendation I–XIV(5) of notification of approval by all Governments whose representatives are entitled to participate in meetings provided for under Article IX of the Antarctic Treaty, these Agreed Measures shall become effective for those Governments.

2. Thereafter any other Contracting Party to the Antarctic Treaty may, in consonance with the purposes of Recommendation III–VII, accept these agreed Measures by notifying the designated Government of its intention to apply the Agreed Measures and to be bound by them. The Agreed Measures shall become effective with regard to such Governments on the date of receipt of such notification.

3. The designated Government shall inform the Governments referred to in paragraph 1 of this Article of each notification of approval, the effective date of these Agreed Measures and of each notification of acceptance. The designated Government shall also inform any Government which has accepted these Agreed Measures of each subsequent notification of acceptance.

ARTICLE XIV
[Amendment]

1. These Agreed Measures may be amended at any time by unanimous agreement of the Governments whose Representatives are entitled to participate in meetings under Article IX of the Antarctic Treaty.

2. The Annexes, in particular, may be amended as necessary through diplomatic channels.

3. An amendment proposed through diplomatic channels shall be submitted in writing to the designated Government which shall communicate it to the Governments referred to in paragraph 1 of the present Article for approval; at the same time, it shall be communicated to the other Participating Governments.

4. Any amendment shall become effective on the date on which notifications of approval have been received by the designated Government and from all of the Governments referred to in paragraph 1 of this Article.

5. The designated Government shall notify those same Governments of the date of receipt of each approval communicated to it and the date on which the amendment will become effective for them.

6. Such amendment shall become effective on that same date for all other Participating Governments, except those which before the expiry of two months after that date notify the designated Government that they do not accept it.

ANNEXES TO THESE AGREED MEASURES

Annex A
Specially Protected Species

. . . .
. . . .
. . . .

Annex B
Specially Protected Areas

. . . .
. . . .
. . . .

Annex C
Importation of animals and plants

The following animals and plants may be imported into the Treaty Area in accordance with permits issued under Article IX(2) of these Agreed Measures:

(*a*) sledge dogs,
(*b*) domestic animals and plants,
(*c*) laboratory animals and plants.

Annex D
Precautions to prevent accidental introduction of parasites and diseases into the Treaty Area

The following precautions shall be taken:

1. *Dogs*: All dogs imported into the Treaty Area shall be inoculated against the following diseases:
(*a*) distemper;
(*b*) contagious canine hepatitis;
(*c*) rabies;
(*d*) leptospirosis (*L. canicola* and *L. icterohaemorrhagicae*).
Each dog shall be inoculated at least two months before the time of its arrival in the Treaty Area.

2. *Poultry*: Notwithstanding the provisions of Article IX (3) of these Agreed Measures, no living poultry shall be brought into the Treaty Area after 1st July, 1966.

APPENDIX 3

CONVENTION FOR THE CONSERVATION OF ANTARCTIC SEALS

THE CONTRACTING PARTIES,

RECALLING the Agreed Measures for the Conservation of Antarctic Fauna and Flora, adopted under the Antarctic Treaty signed at Washington on 1 December 1959;

RECOGNIZING the general concern about the vulnerability of Antarctic seals to commercial exploitation and the consequent need for effective conservation measures;

RECOGNIZING that the stocks of Antarctic seals are an important living resource in the marine environment which requires an international agreement for its effective conservation;

RECOGNIZING that this resource should not be depleted by over-exploitation, and hence that any harvesting should be regulated so as not to exceed the levels of the optimum sustainable yield;

RECOGNIZING that in order to improve scientific knowledge and so place exploitation on a rational basis, every effort should be made both to encourage biological and other research on Antarctic seal populations and to gain information from such research and from the statistics of future sealing operations, so that further suitable regulations may be formulated;

NOTING that the Scientific Committee on Antarctic Research of the International Council of Scientific Unions (SCAR) is willing to carry out the tasks requested of it in this Convention;

DESIRING to promote and achieve the objectives of protection, scientific study and rational use of Antarctic seals, and to maintain a satisfactory balance within the ecological system.

HAVE AGREED AS FOLLOWS:

ARTICLE 1
Scope

(1) This Convention applies to the seas south of 60° South Latitude, in respect of which the Contracting Parties affirm the provisions of Article IV of the Antarctic Treaty.

(2) This Convention may be applicable to any or all of the following species:
Southern elephant seal *Mirounga leonina*,
Leopard seal *Hydrurga leptonyx*,
Weddell seal *Leptonychotes weddelli*,
Crabeater seal *Lobodon carcinophagus*,
Ross seal *Ommatophoca rossi*,
Southern fur seals *Arctocephalus* sp.

(3) The Annex to this Convention forms an integral part thereof.

ARTICLE 2
Implementation

(1) The Contracting Parties agree that the species of seals enumerated in

311

Article 1 shall not be killed or captured within the Convention area by their nationals or vessels under their respective flags except in accordance with the provisions of this Convention.

(2) Each Contracting Party shall adopt for its nationals and for vessels under its flag such laws, regulations and other measures, including a permit system as appropriate, as may be necessary to implement this Convention.

ARTICLE 3
Annexed Measures

(1) This Convention includes an Annex specifying measures which the Contracting Parties hereby adopt. Contracting Parties may from time to time in the future adopt other measures with respect to the conservation, scientific study and rational and humane use of seal resources, prescribing *inter alia*:
(*a*) permissible catch;
(*b*) protected and unprotected species;
(*c*) open and closed seasons;
(*d*) open and closed areas, including the designation of reserves;
(*e*) the designation of special areas where there shall be no disturbance of seals;
(*f*) limits relating to sex, size, or age for each species;
(*g*) restrictions relating to time of day and duration, limitations of effort and methods of sealing;
(*h*) types and specifications of gear and apparatus and appliances which may be used;
(*i*) catch returns and other statistical and biological records;
(*j*) procedures for facilitating the review and assessment of scientific information;
(*k*) other regulatory measures including an effective system of inspection.

(2) The measures adopted under paragraph (1) of this Article shall be based upon the best scientific and technical evidence available.

(3) The Annex may from time to time be amended in accordance with the procedures provided for in Article 9.

ARTICLE 4
Special Permits

(1) Notwithstanding the provisions of this Convention, any Contracting Party may issue permits to kill or capture seals in limited quantities and in conformity with the objectives and principles of this Convention for the following purposes:
(*a*) to provide indispensable food for men or dogs;
(*b*) to provide for scientific research; or
(*c*) to provide specimens for museums, educational or cultural institutions.

(2) Each Contracting Party shall, as soon as possible, inform the other Contracting Parties and SCAR of the purpose and content of all permits issued under paragraph (1) of this Article and subsequently of the numbers of seals killed or captured under these permits.

ARTICLE 5
Exchange of Information and Scientific Advice

(1) Each Contracting Party shall provide to the other Contracting Parties and to SCAR the information specified in the Annex within the period indicated therein.

(2) Each Contracting Party shall also provide to the other Contracting Parties and to SCAR before 31 October each year information on any steps it has taken in accordance with Article 2 of this Convention during the preceding period 1 July to 30 June.

(3) Contracting Parties which have no information to report under the two preceding paragraphs shall indicate this formally before 31 October each year.

(4) SCAR is invited:
(*a*) to assess information received pursuant to this Article; encourage exchange of scientific data and information among the Contracting Parties; recommend programmes for scientific research; recommend statistical and biological data to be collected by sealing expeditions within the Convention area; and suggest amendments to the Annex; and
(*b*) to report on the basis of the statistical, biological and other evidence available when the harvest of any species of seal in the Convention area is having a significantly harmful effect on the total stocks of such species or on the ecological system in any particular locality.

(5) SCAR is invited to notify the Depositary which shall report to the Contracting Parties when SCAR estimates in any sealing season that the permissible catch limits for any species are likely to be exceeded and, in that case, to provide an estimate of the date upon which the permissible catch limits will be reached. Each Contracting Party shall then take appropriate measures to prevent its nationals and vessels under its flag from killing or capturing seals of that species after the estimated date until the Contracting Parties decide otherwise.

(6) SCAR may if necessary seek the technical assistance of the Food and Agriculture Organization of the United Nations in making its assessments.

(7) Notwithstanding the provisions of paragraph (1) of Article 1 the Contracting Parties shall, in accordance with their internal law, report to each other and to SCAR, for consideration, statistics relating to the Antarctic seals listed in paragraph (2) of Article 1 which have been killed or captured by their nationals and vessels under their respective flags in the area of floating sea ice north of 60° South Latitude.

ARTICLE 6
Consultations between Contracting Parties

(1) At any time after commercial sealing has begun a Contracting Party may propose through the Depositary that a meeting of Contracting Parties be convened with a view to:
(*a*) establishing by a two-thirds majority of the Contracting Parties,

including the concurring votes of all States signatory to this Convention present at the meeting, an effective system of control, including inspection, over the implementation of the provisions of this Convention;

(*b*) establishing a commission to perform such functions under this Convention as the Contracting Parties may deem necessary; or

(*c*) considering other proposals, including:

  (i) the provision of independent scientific advice:

  (ii) the establishment, by a two-thirds majority, of a scientific advisory committee which may be assigned some or all of the functions requested of SCAR under this Convention, if commercial sealing reaches significant proportions;

  (iii) the carrying out of scientific programmes with the participation of the Contracting Parties; and

  (iv) the provision of further regulatory measures, including moratoria.

(2) If one-third of the Contracting Parties indicate agreement the Depositary shall convene such a meeting, as soon as possible.

(3) A meeting shall be held at the request of any Contracting Party, if SCAR reports that the harvest of any species of Antarctic seal in the area to which this Convention applies is having a significantly harmful effect on the total stocks or the ecological system in any particular locality.

Article 7
Review of Operations

The Contracting Parties shall meet within five years after the entry into force of this Convention and at least every five years thereafter to review the operation of the Convention.

Article 8
Amendments to the Convention

(1) This Convention may be amended at any time. The text of any amendment proposed by a Contracting Party shall be submitted to the Depositary, which shall transmit it to all the Contracting Parties.

(2) If one-third of the Contracting Parties request a meeting to discuss the proposed amendment the Depositary shall call such a meeting.

(3) An amendment shall enter into force when the Depositary has received instruments of ratification or acceptance thereof from all the Contracting Parties.

Article 9
Amendments to the Annex

(1) Any Contracting Party may propose amendments to the Annex to this Convention. The text of any such proposed amendment shall be submitted to the Depositary which shall transmit it to all Contracting Parties.

(2) Each such proposed amendment shall become effective for all Contracting Parties six months after the date appearing on the notification from the Depositary to the Contracting Parties, if within 120 days of the notification

date, no objection has been received and two-thirds of the Contracting Parties have notified the Depositary in writing of their approval.

(3) If an objection is received from any Contracting Party within 120 days of the notification date, the matter shall be considered by the Contracting Parties at their next meeting. If unanimity on the matter is not reached at the meeting, the Contracting Parties shall notify the Depositary within 120 days from the date of closure of the meeting of their approval or rejection of the original amendment or of any new amendment proposed by the meeting. If, by the end of this period, two-thirds of the Contracting Parties have approved such amendment, it shall become effective six months from the date of the closure of the meeting for those Contracting Parties which have by then notified their approval.

(4) Any Contracting Party which has objected to a proposed amendment may at any time withdraw that objection, and the proposed amendment shall become effective with respect to such Party immediately if the amendment is already in effect, or at such time as it becomes effective under the terms of this Article.

(5) The Depositary shall notify each Contracting Party immediately upon receipt of each approval or objection, of each withdrawal of objection, and of the entry into force of any amendment.

(6) Any State which becomes a party to this Convention after an amendment to the Annex has entered into force shall be bound by the Annex as so amended. Any State which becomes a Party to this Convention during the period when a proposed amendment is pending may approve or object to such an amendment within the time limits applicable to other Contracting Parties.

ARTICLE 10
Signature

This Convention shall be open for signature at London from 1 June to 31 December 1972 by States participating in the Conference on the Conservation of Antarctic Seals held at London from 3 to 11 February 1972.

ARTICLE 11
Ratification

This Convention is subject to ratification or acceptance. Instruments of ratification or acceptance shall be deposited with the Government of the United Kingdom of Great Britain and Northern Ireland, hereby designated as the Depositary.

ARTICLE 12
Accession

This Convention shall be open for accession by any State which may be invited to accede to this Convention with the consent of the Contracting Parties.

ARTICLE 13
Entry into Force

(1) This Convention shall enter into force on the thirtieth day following the date of deposit of the seventh instrument of ratification or acceptance.

(2) Thereafter this Convention shall enter into force for each ratifying, accepting or acceding State on the thirtieth day after deposit by such State of its instrument of ratification, acceptance or accession.

ARTICLE 14
Withdrawal

Any Contracting Party may withdraw from this Convention on 30 June of any year by giving notice on or before 1 January of the same year to the Depositary, which upon receipt of such a notice shall at once communicate it to the other Contracting Parties. Any other Contracting Party may, in like manner, within one month of the receipt of a copy of such a notice from the Depositary, give notice of withdrawal, so that the Convention shall cease to be in force on 30 June of the same year with respect to the Contracting Party giving such notice.

ARTICLE 15
Notifications by the Depositary

The Depositary shall notify all signatory and acceding States of the following:

(*a*) signatures of this Convention, the deposit of instruments of ratification, acceptance or accession and notices of withdrawal;

(*b*) the date of entry into force of this Convention and of any amendments to it or its Annex.

ARTICLE 16
Certified Copies and Registration

(1) This Convention, done in the English, French, Russian and Spanish languages, each version being equally authentic, shall be deposited in the archives of the Government of the United Kingdom of Great Britain and Northern Ireland, which shall transmit duly certified copies thereof to all signatory and acceding States.

(2) This Convention shall be registered by the Depositary pursuant to Article 102 of the Charter of the United Nations.

IN WITNESS WHEREOF, the undersigned, duly authorized, have signed this Convention.

DONE at London, this 1st day of June 1972.

ANNEX

1. *Permissible Catch*

The Contracting Parties shall in any one year, which shall run from 1 July to 30 June inclusive, restrict the total number of seals of each species killed or captured to the numbers specified below. These numbers are subject to review in the light of scientific assessments:

(*a*) in the case of Crabeater seals *Lobodon carcinophágus*, 175,000;
(*b*) in the case of Leopard seals *Hydrurga leptonyx*, 12,000;
(*c*) in the case of Weddell seals *Leptonychotes weddelli*, 5,000.

2. Protected Species
(*a*) It is forbidden to kill or capture Ross seals *Ommatophoca rossi*, Southern elephant seals *Mirounga leonina*, or fur seals of the genus *Arctocephalus*.
(*b*) In order to protect the adult breeding stock during the period when it is most concentrated and vulnerable, it is forbidden to kill or capture any Weddell seal *Leptonychotes weddelli* one year old or older between 1 September and 31 January inclusive.

3. *Closed Season and Sealing Season*
The period between 1 March and 31 August inclusive is a Closed Season, during which the killing or capturing of seals is forbidden. The period 1 September to the last day in February constitutes a Sealing Season.

4. *Sealing Zones*
Each of the sealing zones listed in this paragraph shall be closed in numerical sequence to all sealing operations for the seal species listed in paragraph 1 of this Annex for the period 1 September to the last day of February inclusive. Such closures shall begin with the same zone as is closed under paragraph 2 of Annex B to Annex 1 of the Report of the Fifth Antarctic Treaty Consultative Meeting at the moment the Convention enters into force. Upon the expiration of each closed period, the affected zone shall reopen:
Zone 1—between 60° and 120° West Longitude
Zone 2—between 0° and 60° West Longitude, together with that part of the Weddell Sea lying westward of 60° West Longitude
Zone 3—between 0° and 70° East Longitude
Zone 4—between 70° and 130° East Longitude
Zone 5—between 130° East Longitude and 170° West Longitude
Zone 6—between 120° and 170° West Longitude.

5. *Seal Reserves*
It is forbidden to kill or capture seals in the following reserves, which are seal breeding areas or the site of long-term scientific research:
(*a*) The area around the South Orkney Islands between 60° 20' and 60° 56' South Latitude and 44° 05' and 46° 25' West Longitude.
(*b*) The area of the southwestern Ross Sea south of 76° South Latitude and west of 170° East Longitude.
(*c*) The area of Edisto Inlet south and west of a line drawn between Cape Hallett at 72° 19' South Latitude, 170° 18' East Longitude, and Helm Point, at 72° 11' South Latitude, 170° 00' East Longitude.

6. *Exchange of Information*
(*a*) Contracting Parties shall provide before 31 October each year to other Contracting Parties and to SCAR a summary of statistical information on all seals killed or captured by their nationals and vessels under their respective flags in the Convention area, in respect of the preceding period 1 July to 30 June. This information shall include by zones and months:
(i) The gross and nett tonnage, brake horse-power, number of crew,

and number of days' operation of vessels under the flag of the Contracting Party;

(ii) The number of adult individuals and pups of each species taken.

When specially requested, this information shall be provided in respect of each ship, together with its daily position at noon each operating day and the catch on that day.

(*b*) When an industry has started, reports of the number of seals of each species killed or captured in each zone shall be made to SCAR in the form and at the intervals (not shorter than one week) requested by that body.

(*c*) Contracting Parties shall provide to SCAR biological information, in particular:

(i) Sex
(ii) Reproductive condition
(iii) Age

SCAR may request additional information or material with the approval of the Contracting Parties.

(*d*) Contracting Parties shall provide to other Contracting Parties and to SCAR at least 30 days in advance of departure from their home ports, information on proposed sealing expeditions.

7. *Sealing Methods*

(*a*) SCAR is invited to report on methods of sealing and to make recommendations with a view to ensuring that the killing or capturing of seals is quick, painless and efficient. Contracting Parties, as appropriate, shall adopt rules for their nationals and vessels under their respective flags engaged in the killing and capturing of seals, giving due consideration to the views of SCAR.

(*b*) In the light of the available scientific and technical data, Contracting Parties agree to take appropriate steps to ensure that their nationals and vessels under their respective flags refrain from killing or capturing seals in the water, except in limited quantities to provide for scientific research in conformity with the objectives and principles of this Convention. Such research shall include studies as to the effectiveness of methods of sealing from the viewpoint of the management and humane and rational utilization of the Antarctic seal resources for conservation purposes. The undertaking and the results of any such scientific research programme shall be communicated to SCAR and the Depositary which shall transmit them to the Contracting Parties.

CONFERENCE ON THE CONSERVATION OF ANTARCTIC MARINE LIVING RESOURCES: FINAL ACT (EXTRACT)
(Canberra, 7–20 May 1980)

The Conference also decided to include in the Final Act the text of the following statement made by the Chairman on 19 May 1980 regarding the application of the Convention on the Conservation of Antarctic Marine Living Resources to the waters adjacent to Kerguelen and Crozet over which France has jurisdiction and to waters adjacent to other islands within the area to which this Convention applies over which the existence of State sovereignty is recognized by all Contracting Parties.

"1. Measures for the conservation of Antarctic marine living resources of the waters adjacent to Kerguelen and Crozet, over which France has jurisdiction, adopted by France prior to the entry into force of the Convention, would remain in force after the entry into force of the Convention until modified by France acting within the framework of the Commission or otherwise.

2. After the Convention has come into force, each time the Commission should undertake examination of the conservation needs of the marine living resources of the general area in which the waters adjacent to Kerguelen and Crozet are to be found, it would be open to France either to agree that the waters in question should be included in the area of application of any specific conservation measure under consideration or to indicate that they should be excluded. In the latter event, the Commission would not proceed to the adoption of the specific conservation measure in a form applicable to the waters in question unless France removed its objection to it. France could also adopt such national measures as it might deem appropriate for the waters in question.

3. Accordingly, when specific conservation measures are considered within the framework of the Commission and with the participation of France, then:
(a) France would be bound by any conservation measures adopted by consensus with its participation for the duration of those measures. This would not prevent France from promulgating national measures that were more strict than the Commission's measures or which dealt with other matters;
(b) In the absence of consensus, France could promulgate any national measures which it might deem appropriate.

4. Conservation measures, whether national measures or measures adopted by the Commission, in respect of the waters adjacent to Kerguelen and Crozet, would be enforced by France. The system of observation and inspec-

tion foreseen by the Convention would not be implemented in the waters adjacent to Kerguelen and Crozet except as agreed by France and in the manner so agreed.

5. The understandings, set forth in paragraphs 1–4 above, regarding the application of the Convention to waters adjacent to the Islands of Kerguelen and Crozet, also apply to waters adjacent to the islands within the area to which this Convention applies over which the existence of State sovereignty is recognized by all Contracting Parties.''

No objection to the statement was made.

II

The Conference on the Conservation of Antarctic Marine Living Resources,

Noting that a definitive regime for the conservation of Antarctic marine living resources has been elaborated, and desiring to have that regime enter into force as quickly as possible;

Recognizing that harvesting of Antarctic marine living resources is presently taking place and underlining the importance of the objectives of the Convention on the Conservation of Antarctic Marine Living Resources;

Recognizing the need to identify, emphasize and co-operate in carrying out research activities that will facilitate the effective operation of the Convention;

Desiring further to facilitate the implementation of the Convention by emphasizing and co-ordinating the collection of scientific and fisheries data needed for the Scientific Committee to be constituted under the terms of the Convention to begin effective work upon entry into force of the Convention;

Calls upon the Parties entitled to become Members of the Commission

1. To take all possible steps to bring the Convention on the Conservation of Antarctic Marine Living Resources into force as soon as possible;

2. To show the greatest possible care and concern, bearing in mind the principles and objectives of Article II of the Convention, in any harvesting of Antarctic marine living resources in the period prior to entry into force of the Convention and examination of the status of stocks by the Scientific Committee to be established by the Convention on the Conservation of Antarctic Marine Living Resources;

3. To the greatest extent practicable and feasible to co-operate broadly and comprehensively in the continued development of the scientific and fisheries data necessary for the effective operation of the Convention on the Conservation of Antarctic Marine Living Resources, and to this end:
(*a*) to intensify research related to Antarctic marine living resources;
(*b*) to identify the specific scientific and fisheries data needed and how those data should be collected and recorded to facilitate the work of the Scientific Committee to be established by the Convention; and

(*c*) to compile scientific and fisheries data identified pursuant to sub-paragraph (*b*) above in order to distribute those data to the Contracting Parties upon entry into force of the Convention on the Conservation of Antarctic Marine Living Resources.

III

The Conference on the Convention for the Conservation of Antarctic Marine Living Resources,

Having agreed on a text of a Convention which would establish a Commission and Scientific Committee for the Conservation of Antarctic Marine Living Resources and an Executive Secretariat;

Recognising the need to examine working methods for the Executive Secretary and Secretariat so that they may begin their work as soon as possible after entry into force of the Convention;

Takes note of the intention of the Depositary to convene a meeting of representatives of Parties entitled to become Members of the Commission within one year after expiration of the period during which the Convention is open for signature for the purpose of considering steps which might be taken to facilitate the early operation of the Commission, Scientific Committee and Executive Secretariat when these bodies are established.

IV

The Conference on the Conservation of Antarctic Marine living Resources resolves:

1. to express its gratitude to the Australian Government for its initiative in convening the present Conference and for its preparation;

2. to express to its Chairman, Mr J.E. Ryan, its deep appreciation for the admirable manner in which he has guided the Conference;

3. to express to the officers and staff of the Secretariat its appreciation for their untiring efforts in contributing to the attainment of the objectives of the Conference.

V

The Conference on the Conservation of Antarctic Marine Living Resources resolves:

That the Government of Australia be authorised to publish the Final Act of this Conference and the text of the Convention annexed hereto.

VI

The Conference on the Conservation of Antarctic Marine Living Resources resolves;

To express its deep appreciation to the Australian Government for its offer to provide a site for the Headquarters of the Commission to be established under the Convention.

322   *Appendix 4*

Done at Canberra, this Twentieth Day of May 1980, in a single original copy to be deposited in the archives of the Government of Australia which will transmit a certified copy thereof to all the other Participants in the Conference.

In witness whereof, the following representatives have signed this Final Act.

CONVENTION ON THE CONSERVATION OF ANTARCTIC MARINE LIVING RESOURCES

The Contracting Parties,
RECOGNISING the importance of safeguarding the environment and protecting the integrity of the ecosystem of the seas surrounding Antarctica;
NOTING the concentration of marine living resources found in Antarctic waters and the increased interest in the possibilities offered by the utilization of these resources as a source of protein;
CONSCIOUS of the urgency of ensuring the conservation of Antarctic marine living resources;
CONSIDERING that it is essential to increase knowledge of the Antarctic marine ecosystem and its components so as to be able to base decisions on harvesting on sound scientific information;
BELIEVING that the conservation of Antarctic marine living resources calls for international co-operation with due regard for the provisions of the Antarctic Treaty and with the active involvement of all States engaged in research or harvesting activities in Antarctic waters;
RECOGNISING the prime responsibilities of the Antarctic Treaty Consultative Parties for the protection and preservation of the Antarctic environment and, in particular, their responsibilities under Article IX, paragraph 1(f) of the Antarctic Treaty in respect of the preservation and conservation of living resources in Antarctica;
RECALLING the action already taken by the Antarctic Treaty Consultative Parties including in particular the Agreed Measures for the Conservation of Antarctic Fauna and Flora, as well as the provisions of the Convention for the Conservation of Antarctic Seals;
BEARING in mind the concern regarding the conservation of Antarctic marine living resources expressed by the Consultative Parties at the Ninth Consultative Meeting of the Antarctic Treaty and the importance of the provisions of Recommendation IX – 2 which led to the establishment of the present Convention;
BELIEVING that it is in the interest of all mankind to preserve the waters surrounding the Antarctic continent for peaceful purposes only and to prevent their becoming the scene or object of international discord;
RECOGNISING, in the light of the foregoing, that it is desirable to establish suitable machinery for recommending, promoting, deciding upon and co-ordinating the measures and scientific studies needed to ensure the conservation of Antarctic marine living organisms;

HAVE AGREED as follows:

ARTICLE I

1. This Convention applies to the Antarctic marine living resources of the area south of 60° South latitude and to the Antarctic marine living resources of the area between that latitude and the Antarctic Convergence which form part of the Antarctic marine ecosystem.

2. Antarctic marine living resources means the populations of fin fish, molluscs, crustaceans and all other species of living organisms, including birds, found south of the Antarctic Convergence.

3. The Antarctic marine ecosystem means the complex of relationships of Antarctic marine living resources with each other and with their physical environment.

4. The Antarctic Convergence shall be deemed to be a line joining the following points along parallels of latitude and meridians of longitude: 50°S, C°; 50°S, 30°E; 45°S, 30°E; 45°S, 80°E; 55°S, 80°E; 55°S, 150°E; 60°S, 150°E; 60°S, 50°W; 50°S, 50°W; 50°S, 0°.

ARTICLE II

1. The objective of this Convention is the conservation of Antarctic marine living resources.

2. For the purposes of this Convention, the term "conservation" includes rational use.

3. Any harvesting and associated activities in the area to which this Convention applies shall be conducted in accordance with the provisions of this Convention and with the following principles of conservation:
(a) prevention of decrease in the size of any harvested population to levels below those which ensure its stable recruitment. For this purpose its size should not be allowed to fall below a level close to that which ensures the greatest net annual increment;
(b) maintenance of the ecological relationships between harvested, dependent and related populations of Antarctic marine living resources and the restoration of depleted populations to the levels defined in sub-paragraph (a) above; and
(c) prevention of changes or minimization of the risk of changes in the marine ecosystem which are not potentially reversible over two or three decades, taking into account the state of available knowledge of the direct ·and indirect impact of harvesting, the effect of the introduction of alien species, the effects of associated activities on the marine ecosystem and of the effects of environmental changes, with the aim of making possible the sustained conservation of Antarctic marine living resources.

ARTICLE III

The Contracting Parties, whether or not they are Parties to the Antarctic Treaty, agree that they will not engage in any activities in the Antarctic

Treaty area contrary to the principles and purposes of that Treaty and that, in their relations with each other, they are bound by the obligations contained in Articles I and V of the Antarctic Treaty.

ARTICLE IV

1. With respect to the Antarctic Treaty area, all Contracting Parties, whether or not they are Parties to the Antarctic Treaty, are bound by Articles IV and VI of the Antarctic Treaty in their relations with each other.

2. Nothing in this Convention and no acts or activities taking place while the present Convention is in force shall:

(*a*) constitute a basis for asserting, supporting or denying a claim to territorial sovereignty in the Antarctic Treaty area or create any rights of sovereignty in the Antarctic Treaty area;

(*b*) be interpreted as a renunciation or diminution by any Contracting Party of, or as prejudicing, any right or claim or basis of claim to exercise coastal state jurisdiction under international law within the area to which this Convention applies;

(*c*) be interpreted as prejudicing the position of any Contracting Party as regards its recognition or non-recognition of any such right, claim or basis of claim;

(*d*) affect the provision of Article IV, paragraph 2, of the Antarctic Treaty that no new claim, or enlargement of an existing claim, to territorial sovereignty in Antarctica shall be asserted while the Antarctic Treaty is in force.

ARTICLE V

1. The Contracting Parties which are not Parties to the Antarctic Treaty acknowledge the special obligations and responsibilities of the Antarctic Treaty Consultative Parties for the protection and preservation of the environment of the Antarctic Treaty area.

2. The Contracting Parties which are not Parties to the Antarctic Treaty agree that, in their activities in the Antarctic Treaty area, they will observe as and when appropriate the Agreed Measures for the Conservation of Antarctic Fauna and Flora and such other measures as have been recommended by the Antarctic Treaty Consultative Parties in fulfilment of their responsibility for the protection of the Antarctic environment from all forms of harmful human interference.

3. For the purposes of this Convention, "Antarctic Treaty Consultative Parties" means the Contracting Parties to the Antarctic Treaty whose Representatives participate in meetings under Article IX of the Antarctic Treaty.

ARTICLE VI

Nothing in this Convention shall derogate from the rights and obligations of Contracting Parties under the International Convention for the Regulation of Whaling and the Convention for the Conservation of Antarctic Seals.

Article VII

1. The Contracting Parties hereby establish and agree to maintain the Commission for the Conservation of Antarctic Marine Living Resources (hereinafter referred to as "the Commission").

2. Membership in the Commission shall be as follows:
(*a*) each Contracting Party which participated in the meeting at which this Convention was adopted shall be a Member of the Commission;
(*b*) each State Party which has acceded to this Convention pursuant to Article XXIX shall be entitled to be a Member of the Commission during such time as that acceding party is engaged in research or harvesting activities in relation to the marine living resources to which this Convention applies;
(*c*) each regional economic integration organization which has acceded to this Convention pursuant to Article XXIX shall be entitled to be a Member of the Commission during such time as its States members are so entitled;
(*d*) a Contracting Party seeking to participate in the work of the Commission pursuant to sub-paragraphs (*b*) and (*c*) above shall notify the Depositary of the basis upon which it seeks to become a Member of the Commission and of its willingness to accept conservation measures in force. The Depositary shall communicate to each Member of the Commission such notification and accompanying information. Within two months of receipt of such communication from the Depositary, any Member of the Commission may request that a special meeting of the Commission be held to consider the matter. Upon receipt of such request, the Depositary shall call such a meeting. If there is no request for a meeting, the Contracting Party submitting the notification shall be deemed to have satisfied the requirements for Commission Membership.

3. Each Member of the Commission shall be represented by one representative who may be accompanied by alternate representatives and advisers.

Article VIII

The Commission shall have legal personality and shall enjoy in the territory of each of the States Parties such legal capacity as may be necessary to perform its function and achieve the purposes of this Convention. The privileges and immunities to be enjoyed by the Commission and its staff in the territory of a State Party shall be determined by agreement between the Commission and the State Party concerned.

Article IX

1. The function of the Commission shall be to give effect to the objective and principles set out in Article II of this Convention. To this end, it shall:
(*a*) facilitate research into and comprehensive studies of Antarctic marine living resources and of the Antarctic marine ecosystem;
(*b*) compile data on the status of and changes in population of Antarctic marine living resources and on factors affecting the distribution, abundance and productivity of harvested species and dependent or related species or populations;

(*c*) ensure the acquisition of catch and effort statistics on harvested populations;

(*d*) analyse, disseminate and publish the information referred to in sub-paragraphs (b) and (c) above and the reports of the Scientific Committee;

(*e*) identify conservation needs and analyse the effectiveness of conservation measures;

(*f*) formulate, adopt and revise conservation measures on the basis of the best scientific evidence available, subject to the provisions of paragraph 5 of this Article;

(*g*) implement the system of observation and inspection established under Article XXIV of this Convention;

(*h*) carry out such other activities as are necessary to fulfil the objective of this Convention.

2. The conservation measures referred to in paragraph 1(f) above include the following:

(*a*) the designation of the quantity of any species which may be harvested in the area to which this Convention applies;

(*b*) the designation of regions and sub-regions based on the distribution of populations of Antarctic marine living resources;

(*c*) the designation of the quantity which may be harvested from the populations of regions and sub-regions;

(*d*) the designation of protected species;

(*e*) the designation of the size, age and, as appropriate, sex of species which may be harvested;

(*f*) the designation of open and closed seasons for harvesting;

(*g*) the designation of the opening and closing of areas, regions or sub-regions for purposes of scientific study or conservation, including special areas for protection and scientific study;

(*h*) regulation of the effort employed and methods of harvesting, including fishing gear, with a view, inter alia, to avoiding undue concentration of harvesting in any region or sub-region;

(*i*) the taking of such other conservation measures as the Commission considers necessary for the fulfilment of the objective of this Convention, including measures concerning the effects of harvesting and associated activities on components of the marine ecosystem other than the harvested populations.

3. The Commission shall publish and maintain a record of all conservation measures in force.

4. In exercising its functions under paragraph 1 above, the Commission shall take full account of the recommendations and advice of the Scientific Committee.

5. The Commission shall take full account of any relevant measures or regulations established or recommended by the Consultative Meetings pursuant to Article IX of the Antarctic Treaty or by existing fisheries commissions responsible for species which may enter the area to which this Convention applies, in order that there shall be no inconsistency between the

rights and obligations of a Contracting Party under such regulations or measures and conservation measures which may be adopted by the Commission.

6. Conservation measures adopted by the Commission in accordance with this Convention shall be implemented by Members of the Commission in the following manner:

(*a*) the Commission shall notify conservation measures to all Members of the Commission;

(*b*) conservation measures shall become binding upon all Members of the Commission 180 days after such notification, except as provided in sub-paragraphs (*c*) and (*d*) below;

(*c*) if a Member of the Commission, within ninety days following the notification specified in sub-paragraph (*a*), notifies the Commission that it is unable to accept the conservation measure, in whole or in part, the measure shall not, to the extent stated, be binding upon that Member of the Commission;

(*d*) in the event that any Member of the Commission invokes the procedure set forth in sub-paragraph (*c*) above, the Commission shall meet at the request of any Member of the Commission to review the conservation measure. At the time of such meeting and within thirty days following the meeting, any Member of the Commission shall have the right to declare that it is no longer able to accept the conservation measure, in which case the Member shall no longer be bound by such measure.

ARTICLE X

1. The Commission shall draw the attention of any State which is not a Party to this Convention to any activity undertaken by its nationals or vessels which, in the opinion of the Commission, affects the implementation of the objective of this Convention.

2. The Commission shall draw the attention of all Contracting Parties to any activity which, in the opinion of the Commission, affects the implementation by a Contracting Party of the objective of this Convention or the compliance by that Contracting Party with its obligations under this Convention.

ARTICLE XI

The Commission shall seek to cooperate with Contracting Parties which may exercise jurisdiction in marine areas adjacent to the area to which this Convention applies in respect of the conservation of any stock or stocks of associated species which occur both within those areas and the area to which this Convention applies, with a view to harmonizing the conservation measures adopted in respect of such stocks.

ARTICLE XII

1. Decisions of the Commission on matters of substance shall be taken by consensus. The question of whether a matter is one of substance shall be treated as a matter of substance.

2. Decisions on matters other than those referred to in paragraph 1 above

shall be taken by a simple majority of the Members of the Commission present and voting.

3. In Commission consideration of any item requiring a decision, it shall be made clear whether a regional economic integration organization will participate in the taking of the decision and, if so, whether any of its member States will also participate. The number of Contracting Parties so participating shall not exceed the number of member States of the regional economic integration organization which are Members of the Commission.

4. In the taking of decisions pursuant to this Article, a regional economic integration organization shall have only one vote.

ARTICLE XIII

1. The headquarters of the Commission shall be established at Hobart, Tasmania, Australia.

2. The Commission shall hold a regular annual meeting. Other meetings shall also be held at the request of one-third of its members and as otherwise provided in this Convention. The first meeting of the Commission shall be held within three months of the entry into force of this Convention, provided that among the Contracting Parties there are at least two States conducting harvesting activities within the area to which this Convention applies. The first meeting shall, in any event, be held within one year of the entry into force of this Convention. The Depositary shall consult with the signatory States regarding the first Commission meeting, taking into account that a broad representation of such States is necessary for the effective operation of the Commission.

3. The Depositary shall convene the first meeting of the Commission at the headquarters of the Commission. Thereafter, meetings of the Commission shall be held at its headquarters, unless it decides otherwise.

4. The Commission shall elect from among its members a Chairman and Vice-Chairman, each of whom shall serve for a term of two years and shall be eligible for re-election for one additional term. The first Chairman shall, however, be elected for an initial term of three years. The Chairman and Vice-Chairman shall not be representatives of the same Contracting Party.

5. The Commission shall adopt and amend as necessary the rules of procedure for the conduct of its meetings, except with respect to the matters dealt with in Article XII of this Convention.

6. The Commission may establish such subsidiary bodies as are necessary for the performance of its functions.

ARTICLE XIV

1. The Contracting Parties hereby establish the Scientific Committee for the Conservation of Antarctic Marine Living Resources (hereinafter referred to as "the Scientific Committee") which shall be a consultative body to the Commission. The Scientific Committee shall normally meet at the

headquarters of the Commission unless the Scientific Committee decides otherwise.

2. Each Member of the Commission shall be a member of the Scientific Committee and shall appoint a representative with suitable scientific qualifications who may be accompanied by other experts and advisers.

3. The Scientific Committee may seek the advice of other scientists and experts as may be required on an ad hoc basis.

ARTICLE XV

1. The Scientific Committee shall provide a forum for consultation and cooperation concerning the collection, study and exchange of information with respect to the marine living resources to which this Convention applies. It shall encourage and promote cooperation in the field of scientific research in order to extend knowledge of the marine living resources of the Antarctic marine ecosystem.

2. The Scientific Committee shall conduct such activities as the Commission may direct in pursuance of the objective of this Convention and shall:
(*a*) establish criteria and methods to be used for determinations concerning the conservation measures referred to in Article IX of this Convention;
(*b*) regularly assess the status and trends of the populations of Antarctic marine living resources;
(*c*) analyse data concerning the direct and indirect effects of harvesting on the populations of Antarctic marine living resources;
(*d*) assess the effects of proposed changes in the methods or levels of harvesting and proposed conservation measures;
(*e*) transmit assessments, analyses, reports and recommendations to the Commission as requested or on its own initiative regarding measures and research to implement the objective of this Convention;
(*f*) formulate proposals for the conduct of international and national programs of research into Antarctic marine living resources.

3. In carrying out its functions, the Scientific Committee shall have regard to the work of other relevant technical and scientific organizations and to the scientific activities conducted within the framework of the Antarctic Treaty.

ARTICLE XVI

1. The first meeting of the Scientific Committee shall be held within three months of the first meeting of the Commission. The Scientific Committee shall meet thereafter as often as may be necessary to fulfil its functions.

2. The Scientific Committee shall adopt and amend as necessary its rules of procedure. The rules and any amendments thereto shall be approved by the Commission. The rules shall include procedures for the presentation of minority reports.

3. The Scientific Committee may establish, with the approval of the Commission, such subsidiary bodies as are necessary for the performance of its functions.

ARTICLE XVII

1. The Commission shall appoint an Executive Secretary to serve the Commission and Scientific Committee according to such procedures and on such terms and conditions as the Commission may determine. His term of office shall be for four years and he shall be eligible for re-appointment.

2. The Commission shall authorize such staff establishment for the Secretariat as may be necessary and the Executive Secretary shall appoint, direct and supervise such staff according to such rules and procedures and on such terms and conditions as the Commission may determine.

3. The Executive Secretary and Secretariat shall perform the functions entrusted to them by the Commission.

ARTICLE XVIII

The official languages of the Commission and of the Scientific Committee shall be English, French, Russian and Spanish.

ARTICLE XIX

1. At each annual meeting, the Commission shall adopt by consensus its budget and the budget of the Scientific Committee.

2. A draft budget for the Commission and the Scientific Committee and any subsidiary bodies shall be prepared by the Executive Secretary and submitted to the Members of the Commission at least sixty days before the annual meeting of the Commission.

3. Each Member of the Commission shall contribute to the budget. Until the expiration of five years after the entry into force of this Convention, the contribution of each Member of the Commission shall be equal. Thereafter the contribution shall be determined in accordance with two criteria: the amount harvested and an equal sharing among all Members of the Commission. The Commission shall determine by consensus the proportion in which these two criteria shall apply.

4. The financial activities of the Commission and Scientific Committee shall be conducted in accordance with financial regulations adopted by the Commission and shall be subject to an annual audit by external auditors selected by the Commission.

5. Each Member of the Commission shall meet its own expenses arising from attendance at meetings of the Commission and of the Scientific Committee.

6. A Member of the Commission that fails to pay its contributions for two consecutive years shall not, during the period of its default, have the right to participate in the taking of decisions in the Commission.

ARTICLE XX

1. The Members of the Commission shall, to the greatest extent possible, provide annually to the Commission and to the Scientific Committee such statistical, biological and other data and information as the Commission and

Scientific Committee may require in the exercise of their functions.

2. The Members of the Commission shall provide, in the manner and at such intervals as may be prescribed, information about their harvesting activities, including fishing areas and vessels, so as to enable reliable catch and effort statistics to be compiled.

3. The Members of the Commission shall provide to the Commission at such intervals as may be prescribed information on steps taken to implement the conservation measures adopted by the Commission.

4. The Members of the Commission agree that in any of their harvesting activities, advantage shall be taken of opportunities to collect data needed to assess the impact of harvesting.

ARTICLE XXI

1. Each Contracting Party shall take appropriate measures within its competence to ensure compliance with the provisions of this Convention and with conservation measures adopted by the Commission to which the Party is bound in accordance with Article IX of this Convention.

2. Each Contracting Party shall transmit to the Commission information on measures taken pursuant to paragraph 1 above, including the imposition of sanctions for any violation.

ARTICLE XXII

1. Each Contracting Party undertakes to exert appropriate efforts, consistent with the Charter of the United Nations, to the end that no one engages in any activity contrary to the objective of this Convention.

2. Each Contracting Party shall notify the Commission of any such activity which comes to its attention.

ARTICLE XXIII

1. The Commission and the Scientific Committee shall co-operate with the Antarctic Treaty Consultative Parties on matters falling within the competence of the latter.

2. The Commission and the Scientific Committee shall co-operate, as appropriate, with the Food and Agriculture Organisation of the United Nations and with other Specialised Agencies.

3. The Commission and the Scientific Committee shall seek to develop co-operative working relationships, as appropriate, with inter-governmental and non-governmental organizations which could contribute to their work, including the Scientific Committee on Antarctic Research, the Scientific Committee on Oceanic Research and the International Whaling Commission.

4. The Commission may enter into agreements with the organizations referred to in this Article and with other organizations as may be appropriate. The Commission and the Scientific Committee may invite such

organizations to send observers to their meetings and to meetings of their subsidiary bodies.

ARTICLE XXIV

1. In order to promote the objective and ensure observance of the provisions of this Convention, the Contracting Parties agree that a system of observation and inspection shall be established.

2. The system of observation and inspection shall be elaborated by the Commission on the basis of the following principles:
(*a*) Contracting Parties shall cooperate with each other to ensure the effective implementation of the system of observation and inspection, taking account of the existing international practice. This system shall include, inter alia, procedures for boarding and inspection by observers and inspectors designated by the Members of the Commission and procedures for flag state prosecution and sanctions on the basis of evidence resulting from such boarding and inspections. A report of such prosecutions and sanctions imposed shall be included in the information referred to in Article XXI of this Convention;
(*b*) in order to verify compliance with measures adopted under this Convention, observation and inspection shall be carried out on board vessels engaged in scientific research or harvesting of marine living resources in the area to which this Convention applies, through observers and inspectors designated by the Members of the Commission and operating under terms and conditions to be established by the Commission;

(*c*) designated observers and inspectors shall remain subject to the jurisdiction of the Contracting Party of which they are nationals. They shall report to the Member of the Commission by which they have been designated which in turn shall report to the Commission.

3. Pending the establishment of the system of observation and inspection, the Members of the Commission shall seek to establish interim arrangements to designate observers and inspectors and such designated observers and inspectors shall be entitled to carry out inspections in accordance with the principles set out in paragraph 2 above.

ARTICLE XXV

1. If any dispute arises between two or more of the Contracting Parties concerning the interpretation or application of this Convention, those Contracting Parties shall consult among themselves with a view to having the dispute resolved by negotiation, inquiry, mediation, conciliation, arbitration, judicial settlement or other peaceful means of their own choice.

2. Any dispute of this character not so resolved shall, with the consent in each case of all Parties to the dispute, be referred for settlement to the International Court of Justice or to arbitration; but failure to reach agreement on reference to the International Court or to arbitration shall not absolve Parties to the dispute from the responsibility of continuing to seek to resolve it by any of the various peaceful means referred to in paragraph 1 above.

3. In cases where the dispute is referred to arbitration, the arbitral tribunal shall be constituted as provided in the Annex to this Convention.

ARTICLE XXVI

1. This Convention shall be open for signature at Canberra from 1 August to 31 December 1980 by the States participating in the Conference on the Conservation of Antarctic Marine Living Resources held at Canberra from 7 to 20 May 1980.

2. The States which so sign will be the original signatory States of the Convention.

ARTICLE XXVII

1. This Convention is subject to ratification, acceptance or approval by signatory States.

2. Instruments of ratification, acceptance or approval shall be deposited with the Government of Australia, hereby designated as the Depositary.

ARTICLE XXVIII

1. This Convention shall enter into force on the thirtieth day following the date of deposit of the eighth instrument of ratification, acceptance or approval by States referred to in paragraph 1 of Article XXVI of this Convention.

2. With respect to each State or regional economic integration organization which subsequent to the date of entry into force of this Convention deposits an instrument of ratification, acceptance, approval or accession, the Convention shall enter into force on the thirtieth day following such deposit.

ARTICLE XXIX

1. This Convention shall be open for accession by any State interested in research or harvesting activities in relation to the marine living resources to which this Convention applies.

2. This Convention shall be open for accession by regional economic integration organizations constituted by sovereign States which include among their members one or more States Members of the Commission and to which the States members of the organization have transferred, in whole or in part, competences with regard to the matters covered by this Convention. The accession of such regional economic integration organizations shall be the subject of consultations among Members of the Commission.

ARTICLE XXX

1. This Convention may be amended at any time.

2. If one-third of the Members of the Commission request a meeting to discuss a proposed amendment the Depositary shall call such a meeting.

3. An amendment shall enter into force when the Depositary has received instruments of ratification, acceptance or approval thereof from all the Members of the Commission.

4. Such amendment shall thereafter enter into force as to any other Contracting Party when notice of ratification, acceptance or approval by it has been received by the Depositary. Any such Contracting Party from which no such notice has been received within a period of one year from the date of entry into force of the amendment in accordance with paragraph 3 above shall be deemed to have withdrawn from this Convention.

ARTICLE XXXI

1. Any Contracting Party may withdraw from this Convention on 30 June of any year, by giving written notice not later than 1 January of the same year to the Depositary, which, upon receipt of such a notice, shall communicate it forthwith to the other Contracting Parties.

2. Any other Contracting Party may, within sixty days of the receipt of a copy of such a notice from the Depositary, give written notice of withdrawal to the Depositary in which case the Convention shall cease to be in force on 30 June of the same year with respect to the Contracting Party giving such notice.

3. Withdrawal from this Convention by any Member of the Commission shall not affect its financial obligations under this Convention.

ARTICLE XXXII

The Depositary shall notify all Contracting Parties of the following:
(*a*) signatures of this Convention and the deposit of instruments of ratification, acceptance, approval or accession;
(*b*) the date of entry into force of this Convention and of any amendment thereto.

ARTICLE XXXIII

1. This Convention, of which the English, French, Russian and Spanish texts are equally authentic, shall be deposited with the Government of Australia which shall transmit duly certified copies thereof to all signatory and acceding Parties.

2. This Convention shall be registered by the Depositary pursuant to Article 102 of the Charter of the United Nations.

ANNEX FOR AN ARBITRAL TRIBUNAL

The arbitral tribunal referred to in paragraph 3 of Article XXV shall be composed of three arbitrators who shall be appointed as follows:
The Party commencing proceedings shall communicate the name of an arbitrator to the other Party which, in turn, within a period of forty days following such notification, shall communicate the name of the second arbitrator. The Parties shall, within a period of sixty days following the appointment of the second arbitrator, appoint the third arbitrator, who shall not be a national of either Party and shall not be of the same nationality as either of the first two arbitrators. The third arbitrator shall preside over the tribunal.

If the second arbitrator has not been appointed within the prescribed period, or if the Parties have not reached agreement within the prescribed period on the appointment of the third arbitrator, that arbitrator shall be appointed, at the request of either Party, by the Secretary-General of the Permanent Court of Arbitration, from among persons of international standing not having the nationality of a State which is a Party to this Convention.

The arbitral tribunal shall decide where its headquarters will be located and shall adopt its own rules of procedure.

The award of the arbitral tribunal shall be made by a majority of its members, who may not abstain from voting.

Any Contracting Party which is not a Party to the dispute may intervene in the proceedings with the consent of the arbitral tribunal.

The award of the arbitral tribunal shall be final and binding on all Parties to the dispute and on any Party which intervenes in the proceedings and shall be complied with without delay. The arbitral tribunal shall interpret the award at the request of one of the Parties to the dispute or of any intervening Party.

Unless the arbitral tribunal determines otherwise because of the particular circumstances of the case, the expenses of the tribunal, including the remuneration of its members, shall be borne by the Parties to the dispute in equal shares.

APPENDIX V

RECOMMENDATION III – VII

Acceptance of approved Recommendations

Since the Recommendations approved by the Contracting Parties entitled to participate in meetings held in accordance with Article IX of the Antarctic Treaty are so much a part of the overall structure of co-operation established by the Treaty, the Representatives recommend to their governments that any new Contracting Party entitled to participate in such meetings should be urged to accept these recommendations and to inform other Contracting Parties of its intention to apply and be bound by them.

The Representatives recommend further that their governments agree that existing Contracting Parties and any new Contracting Parties other than those entitled to participate in meetings held in accordance with Article IX of the Treaty be invited to consider accepting these recommendations and to inform other Contracting Parties of their intention to apply and be bound by them.

Explanatory Statement concerning Recommendation III – VII
(Final Report of the Fourth Antarctic Treaty
Consultative Meeting)

During their discussion of Recommendation III – VII, under which Parties by accession would be urged or invited to accept Approved Recommendations, Representatives to the Fourth Consultative Meeting agreed that the following considerations are pertinent to the application of Recommendation III – VII:
1. In becoming Parties to the Antarctic Treaty, States bind themselves to carry out its provisions and to uphold its purposes and principles;
2. Recommendations which become effective in accordance with Article IX of the Treaty are, in terms of that Article, 'measures in furtherance of the principles and objectives of the Treaty';
3. Approved Recommendations are an essential part of the overall structure of co-operation established by the Treaty;
4. In pursuance of the principles and objectives of the Treaty there should be uniformity of practice in the activity of all Parties active in Antarctica; and
5. Approved Recommendations are to be viewed in the light of the obligations assumed by Contracting Parties under the Treaty and in particular Article X.

BIBLIOGRAPHY

Books and Pamphlets

L.M. Alexander (ed.), *The Law of the Sea*, Kingston, Rhode I. 1967.

Carlos Aramayo Alzerreca, *Historia de la Antártida*, Buenos Aires 1949.

T. Armstrong, G. Rogers and G. Rowley, *The Circumpolar North*, London 1978.

F.M. Auburn, *The Ross Dependency*, The Hague 1972.

G. Battaglini, *I Diritti degli Stati nelle Zone Polari*, Turin 1974.

_____, *La Condizione dell'Antartide nel Diritto Internazionale*, Padua 1971.

Bechtel Inc., *U.S. Antarctic Research Program Scientific Support Study*, Vol. I, Washington 1972.

C. Beeby, *The Antarctic Treaty*, Wellington 1972.

K.J. Bertrand, *Americans in Antarctica 1715 – 1948*, New York 1971.

R.N. Bing, 'The Role of the Developed States in the Formulation of International Controls for Unoccupied Regions, Outer Space, the Ocean Floor and Antarctica', Ph.D. dissertation, Tufts University 1972.

L.P. Bloomfield (ed.), *Outer Space*, New York 1968.

W.N. Bonner, *The Fur Seal of South Georgia*, Cambridge (UK) 1968.

M. Booker, *Last Quarter*, Melbourne 1978.

D. Braxton, *The Abominable Snow-Women*, Wellington 1969.

P. Briggs, *Laboratory at the Bottom of the World*, New York 1970.

N. Brown, *Antarctic Housewife*, Melbourne 1971.

R.N. Rudmose Brown, *The Voyage of the Scotia*, Edinburgh 1906; reprinted London 1977.

_____, *Spitsbergen*, London 1920.

W. Buedeler, *The International Geophysical Year*, Paris, 1957.

W.E. Butler, *The Law of Soviet Territorial Waters*, New York 1967.

_____, *Northeast Arctic Passage*, Alphen aan den Rijn 1978.

S. Chapman, *I.G.Y.: Year of Discovery*, Ann Arbor, Michigan 1959.

E. Chipman, *Australians in the Frozen South*, Melbourne 1978.

E.W. Cole, 'Claims of Sovereignty over the Antarctic', thesis, Judge Advocate General's School, U.S. Army 1958.

J.D. Craig, *Canada's Arctic Islands*, Toronto 1927.

A.P. Crary, *The Antarctic*, San Francisco, 1962.

L. Crawford, *Uruguay Atlanticense y los Derechos a la Antartida*, Montevideo 1974.

J.–F. da Costa, 'Le problème de le souveraineté sur les régions antarctiques', thesis, University of Paris 1948.

_____, *Souveraineté sur l'Antarctique*, Paris 1958.

G.J. Dufek, *Operation Deepfreeze*, New York 1957.

J. Dyson, *The Hot Arctic*, London 1979.

Earthscan Press Briefing Document No. 5, London 1977.

Economist Intelligence Unit, *Economic Survey of the Falkland Islands*, London 1976.

G.O. Eddie, *The Harvesting of Krill*, Rome 1977.

Opinion of the Law Offices of Northcutt Ely, *International Law applicable to Deepsea Mining*, Washington DC 14 November 1974.

C. Embleton and C.A.M. King, *Glacial Geomorphology*, Vol. I (2nd edn), London 1975.

I. Everson, *The Living Resources of the Southern Ocean*, Rome 1977.

G. Fahl, *Internationales Recht der Rustungbeschrankungen*, Berlin 1975.

J.E.S. Fawcett, *International Law and the Uses of Outer Space*, Manchester 1968.

First Italian Expedition in the Antarctic, *Mountaineering in the Antarctic*, Milan 1976.

G. Fisher and D. Vignes, *L'Inspection Internationale*, Brussels 1976.

W. Flume, H.J. Hahn, G. Kegel and K.R. Simmonds (eds.), *International Law and Economic Order*, Munich 1977.

J.A. Fraga, *Introducción a la Geopolítica Antártica*, Buenos Aires 1978.

J. Goebel, *The Struggle for the Falkland Islands*, New Haven, Conn. 1927.

L.M. Gould, *The Polar Regions in their relation to Human Affairs*, New York 1958.

G.F. Graham, 'The Canadian Arctic Waters Pollution Prevention Act of 1970 and the Concept of Self-Protection', M.A. thesis, Carleton University 1974.

G.J. Grantham, *The Utilization of Krill*, Rome 1977.

C. Hartley Grattan, *The Southwest Pacific since 1900*, Ann Arbor, Michigan 1963.

K.A. Green, *Role of Krill in the Antarctic Marine Ecosystem*, Washington DC 1977.

G.H. Hackworth, *Digest of International Law*, Vol. I (1940); Vol. V (1943), Washington DC.

H. Harisse, *The Diplomatic History of America*, Dubuque 1897.

T. Hatherton (ed.), *Antarctica*, London 1965.

A. Hayter, *The Year of the Quiet Sun*, London 1968.

A.S. Helm and J.H. Miller, *Antarctica*, Wellington 1964.

W. Herbert, *A World of Men*, New York 1968.

_____, *Across the Top of the World*, New York 1969.

N. Hill, *Claims to Territory in International Law and Relations*, London 1945.

M.W. Holdgate and J. Tinker, *Oil and Other Minerals in the Antarctic*, London 1979.

D. Horne, *The Next Australia*, Sydney 1970.

E.P. Hoyt, *The Last Explorer*, New York 1968.

E.W. Hunter Christie, *The Antarctic Problem*, London 1951.

A.A. Husseiny (ed.), *Iceberg Utilization*, New York 1978.

C.C. Hyde, *International Law*, Vol. I, Boston, Mass. 1947.

Institute of Polar Studies, Ohio State University, *A Framework for Assessing Environmental Impacts of Possible Antarctic Mineral Developments*, Columbus, Ohio 1977.

G. Ireland, *Boundaries, Possessions and Conflicts in South America*, New York 1971.

R.Y. Jennings, *The Acquisition of Territory in International Law*, Manchester 1963.

R.J. Jensen, *The Alaska Purchase and Russian-American Relations*, Seattle 1975.

A.S.Keller, O.J. Lissitzyn and F.J. Mann, *Creation of Rights of Sovereignty through Symbolic Acts 1400 – 1800*, New York 1938.

H.G.R. King, *The Antarctic*, London 1969.

J. Kish, *The Law of International Spaces*, Leiden 1973.

A.C. Kiss, *Répertoire de la pratique française en matière de Droit International Public*, Vol. II, Paris 1966.

H.I. Kushner, *Conflict on the Northwest Coast*, Westport, Conn. 1975.

Oscar Vila Labra, *Chilenos en la Antártica*, Santiago 1947.

La Documentation Française, *L'Antarctide et les problèmes soulevés par son occupation*, Paris 28 March 1949.

J. Langone, *Life at the Bottom*, Boston, Mass. 1977.

P. Law, *Antarctic – 1984*, Hobart 1964.

D. Lewis, *Voyage to the Ice*, Sydney 1979.

M.F. Lindley, *The Acquisition and Government of Backward Territory in International Law*, London 1926.

G.A. Llano, *The Terrestrial Life of the Antarctic*, San Francisco 1962.

_____ (ed.), *Adaptations within Antarctic Ecosystems*, Washington DC 1977.

J.F. Lovering and J.R.V. Prescott, *Last of Lands . . . Antarctica*, Melbourne 1979.

W.H. McConnell, 'Canadian Sovereignty over the Arctic Archipelago' LL.M. thesis, University of Saskatchewan 1970.

R. St.J. Macdonald (ed.), *The Arctic Frontier*, Toronto 1966.

J.G. McPherson, *Footsteps on a Frozen Continent*, Sydney 1975.

M.A. McWhinnie (ed.), *Polar Research*, Boulder, Colorado 1978.

A.D. McNair, *The Law of the Air* (2nd ed.), London 1953.

J. Machowski, *Sytuacja Antarktyki w Świetle prava Miedzynarodowego*, Warsaw 1968.

K.K. Markov, V.I. Bardin, V.L. Lebedev, A.I. Orlov, I.A. Suetova, *The Geography of Antarctica*, Jerusalem 1970.

F.A. Milia *et al.*, *La Atlantártida*, Buenos Aires 1978.

B. Mitchell and J. Tinker, *Antarctica and its Resources*, London 1980.

B. Mitchell and R. Sandbrook, *The Management of the Southern Ocean*, London 1980.

Jose Manuel Moneta, *Nos Devolvéran las Malvinas?*, Buenos Aires 1972.

Juan Carlos Moneta, *La Recuperación de las Malvinas*, Buenos Aires 1973.

J.B. Moore, *International Arbitrations*, Vols. I and V, Washington DC 1898.

_____, *Digest of International Law*, Vol. I, Washington DC 1906.

C. Neider, *Edge of the World*, New York 1974.

R.K. Nelson, *Hunters of the Northern Ice*, Chicago 1969.

D.P. O'Connell and A. Riordan (eds.), *Opinions on Imperial Constitutional Law*, Sydney 1971.

J.B. Oerding, 'The Frozen Friction Point: A Geopolitical Analysis of

Sovereignty in the Antarctic Peninsula', M.A. thesis, University of Florida, 1977.

L. Palsson, *Marriage and Divorce in Comparative Conflict of Laws*, Leiden 1974.

B.C. Parker, M.G. Mudrey, R.E. Cameron, K. Cartwright and L.D. McGinnis, 'Environmental Appraisal for the Dry Valley Drilling Project, Phase III (1973 – 1974)', MS.

B.C. Parker M.G. Mudrey, K. Cartwright and L.D. McGinnis, Environmental Appraisal for the Dry Valley Drilling Project, Phase IV (1974 – 1975), MS 1974.

B.C. Parker (ed.), *Environmental Impact in Antarctica*, Blacksburg, Va. 1978.

Ezequiel Federico Pereyra, *Las Islas Malvinas*, Buenos Aires 1968.

D. Pharand, *The Law of the Sea of the Arctic*, Ottawa 1973.

R.A.J. Phillips, *Canada's North*, Toronto 1967.

O. Pinochet de la Barra, *La Antártica Chilena* (1st ed.), Santiago 1948.

R. Platzöder, *Politische Konzeptionen zur Neuordnung des Meeresvölkerrechts*, Ebenhausen, 1976.

B.M. Plott, 'The Development of United States Antarctic Policy', Ph.D. thesis, Fletcher School of Law and Diplomacy, Tufts University (1969).

L. Ponte, *The Cooling*, Englewood Cliffs, NJ 1976.

N. Potter, *Natural Resource Potentials of the Antarctic* (1969) Burlington.

M.M. Prebble, '*New Zealand's Antarctic Field Programme 1957-1965*', MA thesis, Victoria University, Wellington 1965.

Press Office of the Expedition, *First Italian Expedition to Antarctica*, Milan n.d.

A.G. Price, *The Winning of Australian Antarctica, Mawson's BANZARE Voyages 1929 – 1931*, London 1962.

J.C. Puig, *La Antàrtida Argentina ante el Derecho*, Buenos Aires 1960.

L.B. Quartermain, *South from New Zealand*, Wellington 1964.

_____, *South to the Pole*, Wellington 1967.

_____, *New Zealand and the Antarctic*, Wellington 1971.

E. Rabel, *The Conflict of Laws* (2nd ed.), Vol. I, Ann Arbor, Michigan 1958.

Restatement Second, *Conflict of Laws*, St. Paul, Minn. 1971.

G. de Q. Robin, *The Ice of the Antarctic*, San Francisco 1962.

J.P. Riva and J.E. Mielke, *Polar Energy Resources Potential*, Washington DC 1976.

A.G. Roche, *The Minquiers and Ecrehos Case*, Paris 1959.

A.G. Ronhovde, *Jurisdiction over Ice Islands: The Escamilla Case in Retrospect*, Washington DC 1972.

F. Ronne, *Antarctic Command*, New York 1961.

Primavera Acuña de Mones Ruiz, *Antàrtida Argentina, Isolas Océanicos, Mar Argentina*, Buenos Aires 1949.

Report of the Scientific Workshop on Management of Living Resources of the Southern Ocean, Washington DC (1980), MS.

G.S. Schatz (ed.), *Science, Technology and Sovereignty in the Polar Regions*, Lexington 1974.

D. Schenk, *Kontiguität als Erwerbstitel im Völkerrecht*, Ebelsbach 1978.

G.M. Schultz, *Icebergs and their Voyages*, New York 1975.

A. Scilingo, *El Tratado Antártico*, Buenos Aires 1963.

J. Sissons, *Judge of the Far North*, Toronto 1968.

M.J. Sites and G.F. Stuart, *An Electromagnetic Interference Survey of the Hut Point Peninsula and Adjacent Regions*, Stanford, Calif. 1971.

P.D.G. Skegg, 'Some Aspects of Constitutional Law relating to the Cook Islands 1888 – 1901', LL.B. Hons. thesis, University of Auckland 1968.

S.B. Slevich, *The Antarctic Must Become an Area of Peace*, Leningrad 1960 (transl. 1967).

_____, *Basic Problems of Antarctic Exploitation*, Leningrad 1973 (transl. 1974).

G. Smedal, *Acquisition of Sovereignty over Polar Regions*, Oslo 1931.

D.L. Soden, *A Political and Legal Analysis "The Antarctic Treaty"*, Institute for Marine and Coastal Studies, University of Southern California, 1978.

F. Sollie (ed.), *New Territories in International Politics*, Oslo 1974.

W. Sullivan, *Quest for a Continent*, New York 1957.

_____, *Assault on the Unknown*, New York 1961.

E.M. Suzymov, *A Life Given to the Antarctic*, Adelaide 1968.

O. Svarlien, *The Eastern Greenland Case in Historical Perspective*, Gainesville 1964.

R.A. Swan, *Australia in the Antarctic*, Melbourne 1961.

T.A. Taracouzio, *Soviets in the Arctic*, New York 1938.

Tetra Tech, *The Antarctic Krill Resource: Prospects for Commercial Exploitation*, Arlington 1978.

T. Twiss, *The Oregon Question Examined*, London 1846.

J.H.W. Verzijl, *International Law in Historical Perspective*, Vol. I, Leiden 1968.

P.W. van der Veur, *Search for New Guinea's Boundaries*, Canberra 1966.

Francisco Orrego Vicuña and Augusto Salinas Araya (eds.), *El desarrollo de la Antártica*, Santiago 1977.

D.W. Wainhouse, *International Peace Observation*, Baltimore, 1965.

W.F. Weeks and M. Mellor, *Some Elements of Iceberg Technology*, Hanover, NH 1978.

M.M. Whiteman, *Digest of International Law*, Vol. 2, Washington DC 1963.

O. Wilkes, *Protest*, Wellington 1973.

N.A. Wright and P.L. Williams, *Mineral Resources of Antarctica*, Reston, Va. 1974.

M. Ydit, *Internationalised Territories*, Leiden 1961.

M. Zaslow, *The Opening of the Canadian North 1870 – 1914*, Toronto 1971.

Articles

(*Note*. The listing begins with those articles of which the authorship is not stated.)

'Aboard Flight 902: "We Survived!" ', *Time* 8 May 1978.

'Addition to French Crew' (1979), 8 (10) *Antarctic*, 362.

'Airlift to new station in West Antarctica' (1979), 8 (9) *Antarctic*, 312.

'*Almirante Irizar* – most powerful ice-breaker in the South' (1979), *Shipbuilding and Marine Engineering International*, 194.

'Antarctic telecommunications' (1978), 13 (4) *Antarctic Journal*, 1.

'Antarctic Anniversaries' (1977), 8 (1) *Antarctic*, 9.

'Antarctic marine living resources conference' (1980), *Australian Foreign Affairs Record*, 144.

'The Antarctic Treaty' (1972), 22 (6), *NZ Foreign Affairs Review*, 19.

'Antarctica: A Continent of Harmony?' (1980), *Australian Foreign Affairs Record*, 4.

'Antarctica's first baby warmly welcomed' (1978), 8 (5) *Antarctic*, 169.

'Arctic and Antarctic Annexation' (1912), 37 *Law Magazine and Review*, 326.

'Arctic killing suspect freed', *Washington Post* 3 November 1972.

'Arctic Patrol includes Wedding', *Christian Science Monitor* 9 May 1973.

'Argentina en la Antartida', *El Mercurio* 10 August 1973.

'Argentine proposals for polar air route' (1979), 8 (10) *Antarctic*, 367.

'Base Marambio: Capital Accidental de la República' (1974), *Antartida*, 19.

'Belgium associated with European research plan' (1974), 7 (3) *Antarctic*, 89.

'Brazil may send expedition' (1973), 6 (12) *Antarctic*, 436.

'British climbing expedition believed lost at sea' (1978), 8 (5) *Antarctic*, 172.

'Busy summer for ships and aircraft' (1979), 8 (9) *Antarctic*, 330.

'Canada avoids legal wrangle in Arctic death', *Globe and Mail* 20 August 1970.

'Canadian Offshore drilling' (1980), 8 (12) *Canada Weekly*, 4.

'China's interest in joint research' (1980), 9 (2) *Antarctic*, 62.

'Contractor gains expanded role' (1974), 9 (1) *Antarctic Journal*, 31.

'Control of Marine Resources' (1978), 8 (7) *Antarctic*, 237.

'Deception Island Eruption' (1969), 4 (3) *Antarctic Journal*, 87.

'East German base planned' (1979), 8 (10) *Antarctic*, 355.

'Filchner ice shelf station major project this summer' (1975), 7 (7) *Antarctic*, 211.

'First tourists arrive' (1968), *Antarctic*, 51.

'Fluorine in krill – a new challenge for research' (1980), 3 *BMFT Newsletter*, 24.

'Grounded tourist ship not seriously damaged' (1972), 6 (6) *Antarctic*, 219.

'Half century of visits south' (1978), 8 (8) *Antarctic*, 260.

'Informal Consultation on Antarctic Krill' (1975) 153 *FAO Fisheries Reports*, 3.

'Japan joins oil hunt' *West Australian* 7 September 1979.

'Lessons from the Bay of Campeche should be heeded' (1980), 16 (3) *ECO*, 2.

'Lindblad Explorer runs aground' (1980), 9 (1) *Antarctic*, 35.

'Logistic Support Activities' (1969), 4 (3) *Antarctic Journal*, 79.

'Major traverse to Dome C and Dumont d'Urville' (1976), 7 (10) *Antarctic*, 326.

'McMurdo Station reactor site released for unrestricted use' (1980), 15 (1) *Antarctic Journal*, 1.

'More "Day Trips" to Antarctic' (1978), 8 (8) *Antarctic*, 292.

'Navy Lab Concludes the Vela Saw a Bomb' (1980), 209 *Science*, 996.

'New Soviet Station on Icebound Hobbs Coast' (1972), 6 (7) *Antarctic*, 238.

'New Zealand field work begins' (1979), 8 (12) *Antarctic*, 406.

'Norwegian Sovereignty in the Antarctic' (1940), 34 *AJIL*, 83.

'NZ programme cut about one-third' (1975), 7 (8) *Antarctic* 232.

'The Personal Note' (1970), 5 (9) *Antarctic*, 378.

'Polar storm victim dies', *West Australian* 8 August 1979.

'Possible change in plan for Russkaya' (1979), 8 (11) *Antarctic*, 395.

'Return of Sun to Ross Island' (1978), 8 (7) *Antarctic*, 233.

'Ring of Ice' (1973), 75 *Audubon*, 10.

'Russkaya established by cargo ship *Gizhiga*' (1980), 9 (3) *Antarctic*, 95.

'Russkaya Station not yet manned' (1976), 7 (10) *Antarctic*, 327.

'Second Norwegian expedition' (1978), 8 (5) *Antarctic*, 170.

'The Shackleton incident could profit international law' (1976), 259 *Nature*, 435.

'Soviet plans for another winter station' (1980), 9 (2) *Antarctic*, 56.

'Transglobe expedition' (1980), 9 (1) *Antarctic*, 28.

'265 men wintering at six permanent stations' (1978), 8 (6) *Antarctic*, 189.

'United States Airmen break Antarctic Winter Barrier' (1964), 3 *Antarctic*, 480.

'U.S. Antarctic Research Program 1978–79' (1978), 13 (3) *Antarctic Journal*, 1.

'U.S. Science Projects this Summer' (1978), 8 (8) *Antarctic*, 262.

'U.S. Science Projects this Summer' (1979), 8 (12) *Antarctic*, 413.

'U.S. Support Force reduces spending in New Zealand' (1973), 6 (10) *Antarctic*, 351.

'Voluntary restraints planned for Antarctic krill catch,' *Financial Times* 29 September 1977.

'Warm weather aids Onyx River flow' (1980), 9 (2) *Antarctic*, 49.

'Waste not left behind at Scott Base' (1977), 8 (3) *Antarctic*, 101.

'West German design for first base' (1979), 8 (10) *Antarctic*, 350.

'Will nuclear giant replace Antarctic men?' (1970), 5 (10) *Antarctic*, 434.

'Yacht voyage to Antarctic' (1978), 8 (8) *Antarctic*, 270.

F.C. Alexander, 'A Recommended Approach to the Antarctic Resource Problem' (1978), 33 *University of Miami Law Review*, 371.

D.L. Alverson, 'Tug-of-War for the Antarctic Krill' (1980), 8 (2) *Ocean Development and International Law Journal*, 171.

T. Armstrong, 'Bellingshausen and the Discovery of Antarctica' (1971), 15 (99) *Polar Record*, 887.

D. Anderson, 'The Conservation of Wildlife under the Antarctic Treaty' (1968), 14 (88) *Polar Record*, 25.

L.W. Aubry, 'Criminal Jurisdiction over Arctic Ice Islands: *United States* v. *Escamilla*' (1975), 4 *UCLA – Alaska Law Review*, 419.

F.M. Auburn, 'International Law-Sea-Ice-Jurisdiction' (1970), 48 *CBR*, 776.

_____, 'The Case of the Leningradskaya Nunatak' (1970) 5 (8) *Recent Law*, 215.

_____, 'A Sometime World of Men: Legal Rights in the Ross Dependency' (1971), 65 *AJIL*, 578.

_____, 'Offshore Oil and Gas in Antarctica' (1977), 20 *German Yearbook of International Law*, 139.

_____, 'United States Antarctic Policy' (1978), 12 (1) *Marine Technology Society Journal*, 31.

_____, 'Consultative Status under the Antarctic Treaty' (1979), 28 *ICLQ*, 514.

A.L. Aufranc, 'Antecedentes históricos y estado actual del litigio con Chile', *La Nación* 24 December 1978.

J.C. Ausland, 'Spitsbergen: Who's in Control?' (Nov. 1978), *U.S. Naval Institute Proceedings*, 63.

R.W. Bagshawe and J. Goldup, 'The Postal History of the Antarctic, 1904–1949' (1951), 6 *Polar Record*, 45.

T.W. Balch, 'The Arctic and Antarctic Regions and the Law of Nations' (1910), 4 *AJIL*, 265.

G.B. Baldwin, 'The Dependence of Science on Law and Government – the International Geophysical Year – A Case Study' (1964), *Wisconsin Law Review*, 78.

D. Ballantyne, 'When Hardy Souls go South', *Auckland Star* 18 December 1967.

J.N. Barnes, 'The Emerging Antarctic Living Resources Convention' (1979), *ASIL Proc.*, 272.

_____, 'The Emerging Convention on the Conservation of Antarctic Marine Living Resources: An attempt to meet the new realities of Resource Exploitation in the Southern Ocean' (1980), MS.

J.A. Beesley, 'Rights and Responsibilities of the Arctic Coastal States: The Canadian View' (1971), 3 (1) *Journal of Maritime Law and Commerce*, 1.

J.P.A. Bernhardt, 'Sovereignty in Antarctica' (1975), 5 *California Western International Law Journal*, 297.

G.A. Bertrand, 'Antarctica' (1978), 43 (1) *Frontiers*, 9.

R.B. Bilder, 'Control of Criminal Conduct in Antarctica' (1966), 52 *Virginia Law Review*, 231.

H. Bogen, 'Main Events in the History of Antarctic Exploration' (1957), *Norsk Hvalfangst Tidende*, 218.

S.W. Boggs, 'Delimitation of Seaward Areas under National Jurisdiction' (1951), 45 *AJIL*, 240.

M. Bradstock, 'A Strange Allure' (1978), 22 *NZ Environment*, 22.

E.K. Braybrooke, 'The Future of Antarctica' (1956), 10 *Landfall*, 330.

L. Breitfuss, 'Territorial Division of the Arctic' (1929), 8 *Dalhousie Review*, 456.

S.J. Burton, 'New Stresses on the Antarctic Treaty' (1979), 65 *Virginia Law Review*, 421.

S.O. Butler, 'Owning Antarctica' (1977), 31 (1) *Journal of International*

Affairs, 35.

P. Cahier, 'Le Problème des Effets des Traités a l'égard des États Tiers' (1974), 143 *Hague Recueil*, 489.

R.E. Cameron, F.A. Morelli, R. Donlon, J. Guilfoyle, B. Markley and R. Smith, 'DVDP environmental monitoring' (1974), 9 (4) *Antarctic Journal*, 141.

B.M. Carl, 'Claims to Sovereignty – Antarctica' (1955), 28 *Southern California Law Review*, 386.

L.J. Carter, 'Oil Drilling in the Beaufort Sea: Leaving it to Luck and Technology' (1976), 191 *Science*, 929.

W.G. Carson, 'The Other Price of Britain's Oil' (1980), 4 *Contemporary Crises*, 239.

A.H. Charteris, 'Australasian Claims in Antarctica' (1929), 3 (11) *Jo. Comp. Leg.*, 226.

T.-P. Chen, 'International Law – Arctic Sovereignty – Northwest Territories Act R.S.C. 1906, c.62 R.v. Tootalik' (1970), 8 *Alberta Law Review*, 456.

T. Cheng, 'The Sino-Japanese Dispute over the Tiao-yu-tai (Senkaku) Islands and the Law of Territorial Acquisition' (1974), 14 *Virginia Journal of International Law*, 221.

J.W. Clough and B. Lyle Hansen, 'The Ross Ice Shelf Project' (1979), 203 *Science*, 433.

J. Crawford, 'The Criteria for Statehood in International Law' (1976–7), 48 *BYBIL*, 93.

W.J. Cromie, 'The Navy's Stake in Antarctica' (October 1968) *US Naval Institute Proceedings*, 37.

D.A. Cruickshank, 'Arctic Ice and International Law: The Escamilla Case' (1971), 10 *Western Ontario Law Review*, 178.

J.-F. da Costa, 'A teoria dos setores polares' (1951), 13–14 *Boletim da Sociedade Brasileira de Direito Internacional*, 87.

_____, 'Antártida: O Problema Político' (1961), 4 (15) *Revista Brasileira de Política Internacional*, 85.

J. Daniel, 'Conflict of Sovereignties in the Antarctic' (1949), 3 *YBWA*, 241.

P.C. Daniels, 'The Antarctic Treaty' (1970), 26 (10) *Science and Public Affairs*, 11.

J. and M. Darby, 'Tourism has come' (1978), 22 *NZ Environment*, 36.

H.M. Dater, 'The Antarctic Treaty in Action 1961-1971' (1971), 6 (3) *Antarctic Journal*, 67.

_____, 'Byrd Station; the first 2 years (1956–1958)' (1975), 10 (3) *Antarctic Journal*, 96.

G. de Gerlache de Gomery, 'A proposed European Antarctic Expedition' (1973), 8 (1) *Antarctic Journal*, 15.

Department of State Press Release (1964), 58 *AJIL*, 166.

R. Dollot, 'Le droit international des espaces polaires' (1949), 75 (2) *Hague Recueil*, 114.

R.-J. Dupuy, 'Le statut de l'Antarctique' (1958), *AFDI*, 196.

_____, 'Le Traité sur l'Antarctique' (1960), *AFDI*, 111.

C.P. Economides, 'Le Statut International de l'Antarctique résultant du

346   *Bibliography*

Traité du 1 Décembre 1959' (1962), 15 *Revue Hellénique de Droit International*, 76.

S.Z. El-Sayed, 'SCAR/SCOR conference on living resources of the Southern Ocean' (1977), 12 (1 & 2) *Antarctic Journal* 3.

_____, 'BIOMASS' (1978), 43 (10) *Frontiers*, 38.

L. Ellsworth, 'My Four Antarctic Expeditions' (1939), 76 (1) *National Geographic*, 129.

I. Everson, 'Antarctic Fisheries' (1978), 19 (120) *Polar Record*, 233.

R.L. Fahrney, 'Status of an Island's Continental Shelf Jurisdiction: A Case Study of the Falkland Islands' (1979), 10 (4) *Journal of Maritime Law and Commerce*, 539.

Y.K. Fedorov, 'Antarctica: Experimental Proving Ground for Peaceful Coexistence and International Collaboration' (1970), 26 (10) *Science and Public Affairs*, 22.

G.G. Fitzmaurice, 'The Law and Procedure of the International Court of Justice 1951 – 1954' (1954) 30 *BYBIL*, 1.

_____, 'The Law and Procedure of the International Court of Justice 1951 – 1954' (1957), 32 *BYBIL*, 20.

M.J. Forster, 'IWC Makes Some Progress' (1979), 5 *Environmental Policy and Law*, 170.

T.M. Franck, 'Word made law: The Decision of the I.C.J. in the Nuclear Test Cases' (1975), 69 *AJIL*, 612.

S. Fur, 'Les Affaires des Essais Nucléaires' (1975), 59 *R.G.D.I.P.*, 972.

L.F.E. Goldie, 'International Relations in Antarctica' (March 1958), 30 *The Australian Quarterly*, 7.

_____, 'The Critical Date' (1963), 12 *ICLQ*, 1251.

_____, 'A General International Law Doctrine for Seabed Regimes' (1973), 7 *International Lawyer*, 796.

J. Goldblat, 'The Arms-Control Experiment in the Antarctic' (1973), *SIPRI Yearbook*, 477.

J.N. Goodsell, 'South American Nations again take Interest in Antarctica's Future', *Otago Daily Times* 2 November 1973.

R. Gott, 'Imperial Sunset over the Falklands', *Guardian Weekly* 5 December 1968.

E.N. Griswold, 'Renvoi Revisited' (1938), 51 *HLR*, 1165.

R.E. Guyer, 'The Antarctic System' (1973), 139 *Hague Recueil*, 149.

E. Hambro, 'Some Notes on the Future of the Antarctic Treaty Collaboration' (1974), 68 *AJIL*, 217.

J. Hanessian, 'Antarctica: Current National Interests and Legal Realities' (1958), *ASIL Proc.*, 145.

_____, 'The Antarctic Treaty (1959)' (1960), 9 *ICLQ*, 436.

_____, 'Der Antarktis-Vertrag vom Dezember 1959' (1960), 12 *Europa-Archiv*, 371.

T. Hanevold, 'Inspections in Antarctic' (1971), 6 *Cooperation and Conflict*, 103.

_____, 'The Antarctic Treaty Consultative Meetings – Form and Procedure' (1971), 6 *Cooperation and Conflict*, 197.

G.R. Harrison, 'Exploratory Drilling: The Polar Challenge' (1979), Tenth

World Petroleum Congress, Bucharest.

D.E. Hayes and L.A. Frakes, 'General Synthesis' in (1975) 28 *Initial Reports of the Deep Sea Drilling Project*, La Jolla, California, 940.

R.D. Hayton, 'Chile, Argentina and Great Britain in the Antarctic' (1955–7) *Anuario Juridico Interamericano*, 119.

_____, 'The 'American' Antarctic' (1956), 50 *AJIL*, 583.

_____, 'Polar Problems and International Law' (1958), 52 *AJIL*, 746.

_____, 'The Antarctic Settlement of 1959' (1960), 54 *AJIL*, 349.

_____, 'The Nations and Antarctica' (1960), 10 *Österreichische Zeitschrift für Öffentliches Recht*, 368.

I.L. Head, 'Canadian Claims to Territorial Sovereignty in the Arctic Region' (1963), 9 *McGill LJ*, 200.

L. Henkin, 'Arctic Anti-Pollution: Does Canada Make-or-Break-International Law?' (1971), 65 *AJIL*, 131.

D.M. Himmelreich, 'The Beagle Channel Affair' (1979), 12 *Vanderbilt Journal of Transnational Law*, 971.

C.O. Holmquist, 'The T-3 Incident' (September 1972), *U.S. Naval Institute Proceedings*, 45.

E. Honnold, 'Draft Provisions of a new International Convention on Antarctica' (1977), 4 *Yale Studies in World Public Order*, 123.

_____, 'Thaw in International Law? Rights in Antarctica under the Law of Common Spaces' (1978), 87 *YLJ*, 804.

R.V. Howard, B.C. Parker and R.D. Rugo, 'DVDP environmental impact assessment and monitoring' (1976), 11 (3) *Antarctic Journal*, 90.

R.F. Huáscar, 'Un análisis a fondo de la cuestión de limites con Chile en la zona austral', *Clarin* 21 August 1977.

T. Hughes, 'Is the West Antarctic Ice Sheet Disintegrating?' (1973), 78 *Journal of Geophysical Research*, 7884.

C.C. Hyde, 'Acquisition of Sovereignty over Polar Areas' (1934), 19 *Iowa LR*, 286.

S.C. Jain, 'Antarctica: Geopolitics and International Law' (1974), 17 *Indian Year Book of International Affairs*, 249.

D.H.N. Johnson, 'Consolidation as a Root of Title in International Law' (1955), *CLJ*, 215.

E.W. Johnson, 'Quick, before it melts: Toward a Resolution of the Jurisdictional Morass in Antarctica' (1976), 10 *Cornell International Law Journal*, 173.

G.C. Jonathan, 'Les Îles Falkland (Malouines)' (1972), 18 *AFDI*, 235.

H.S. Jones, 'The Inception and Development of the International Geophysical Year' (1959), 1 *Annals of the IGY*, 393.

T.O. Jones, 'Developing the US Antarctic Research Programme' (1970), 26 (10) *Science and Public Affairs*, 81.

P. Jones, 'Whose Oil Resources? The Question of Antarctic Sovereignty' (1976), 61 *Geography*, 167.

O. Kahn-Freund, 'Delictual Liability and the Conflict of Laws' (1968), 124 *Hague Recueil*, 1.

B. Keating, 'North for Oil', (March 1970) *National Geographic*, 374.

G. Knox, 'Antarctic resources' (July/August 1976), *NZ International*

Review, 18.

G. Kojanec, 'La situazione giuridica dell'Antartide' (1960), 15 *La Comunità Internazionale*, 21.

W.W. Kulski, 'Soviet Comments on International Law' (1951), 45 *AJIL*, 762.

R. Lagoni, 'Antarctica's Mineral Resources in International Law' (1979), 39 (1) *Zeitschrift fur Ausländisches Öffentliches Recht und Völkerrecht*, 1.

W. Lakhtine, 'Rights over the Arctic' (1930), 24 *AJIL*, 703.

H. Lauterpacht, 'Sovereignty over Submarine Areas' (1950), 27 *BYBIL*, 376.

R.M. Laws, 'Seals and Birds Killed and Captured in the Antarctic Treaty Area, 1964–1969' (1972), 41 *SCAR Bulletin*, 847.

_____ and E.C. Christie, 'Seals and Birds Killed or Captured in the Antarctic Treaty Area' (1980), 65 *SCAR Bulletin*, 21.

R. Lewis, 'Antarctic Dilemma' (February 1963), *Bulletin of the Atomic Scientists*, 37.

J.H. Lipps, 'The United States 'East Base' Antarctic Peninsula' (1976), 11 (4) *Antarctic Journal*, 211.

_____, 'East Base, Stonington Island, Antarctic Peninsula' (1978), 13 (4) *Antarctic Journal*, 231.

E. Paul McClain, 'Eleven Years Chronicle of one of the World's most gigantic Icebergs' (1978), 22 (5) *Mariner's Weather Log*, 328.

R.K. McNickle, 'Antarctic Claims' (1949), 2 *Editorial Research Reports*, 781.

F.C. Mahncke, 'United States inspects four stations' (1971), 6 (4) *Antarctic Journal*, 147.

J.M. Marcoux, 'Natural Resource Jurisdiction on the Antarctic Continental Margin' (1971), *Virginia Journal of International Law*, 374.

R.M. May, 'Whaling: past, present and future' (1978), 276 *Nature*, 319.

P.K. Menon, 'International Boundaries – a Case Study of the Guyana-Surinam Boundary' (1978), 27 *ICLQ*, 738.

J.H. Mercer, 'West Antarctic ice sheet and CO_2 greenhouse effect; a threat of disaster' (1978), 271 *Nature*, 321.

D.J. Millard, 'Heard and Macdonald Islands Act 1953' (1955), 1 *Sydney Law Review*, 374.

B. Mitchell, 'Antarctica: a special case?', *New Scientist* 13 January 1977, 64.

_____, 'Resources in Antarctica' (April 1977), *Marine Policy*, 91.

_____, 'Attention on Antarctica' *New Scientist* 22 September 1977, 714.

_____, 'The Politics of Antarctica' (1980), 22 (1) *Environment*, 12.

C.J. Moneta, 'Antártida Argentina: Los problemas de 1975–1990' (1975), 1 *Estrategia*, 5.

J.-Y. Morin, 'Le progrès technique, la pollution et l'évolution récente du droit de la mer au Canada, particulièrement à l'égard de l'Arctique' (1970), 8 *CYBIL*, 158.

W.G. Morrow, 'Law and the Thin Veneer of Civilization' (1971), 10 *Alberta LR*, 38.

M.W. Mouton, 'The International Regime of the Polar Regions' (1962), 107

Hague Recueil, 175.

A.L.W. Munkman, 'Adjudication and Adjustment – International Judicial Decision and the Settlement of Territorial and Boundary Disputes' (1972–3), 46 *BYBIL*, 1.

Naval War College (1948–9), 46 *International Law Documents*, 239.

M. Nicolet, 'The ICY Meetings' (1958), 2A *Annals of the IGY*, 176.

D.P. O'Connell 'The Condominium of the New Hebrides' (1968–9), 43 *BYBIL*, 71.

_____, 'Bays, Historic Waters and the Implications of *A. Raptis & Son* v. *South Australia*' (1978), 52 *ALJ*, 64.

B. Orent and P. Reinsch, 'Sovereignty over Islands in the Pacific' (1941), 35 *AJIL*, 443.

B.H. Oxman, 'The Antarctic Regime: An Introduction' (1978), 33 *University of Miami Law Review*, 285.

V. Palermo, 'Espacio Continental y Espacio Antártico' (1978), 21 *Revista Escuela de Defensa Nacional*, 81.

_____, 'Una Argentina bicontinental y biocéanica' (1978), 82 *Discusión*, 50.

_____, 'El Espacio Antártico en la formacion de la Conciencia geopolitica Argentina' (1979), MS.

F. Pallone, 'Resources Exploitation: The Threat to the Legal Regime of Antarctica' (1978), 8 *Manitoba Law Journal*, 597.

B.C. Parker, 'Environmental Impact Assessment and Monitoring of DVDP' (1976), 7 *Dry Valley Drilling Project (DVDP) Bulletin*, 117.

J. Pedrero, 'América, las Malvinas y el Derecho Internacional' (1954), 270 *Argentina Austral*, 2.

R.T. Peterson, 'Render the penguins, butcher the seals' (1973), 75 *Audubon*, 90.

V.N. Petrov, 'Soviet Participation in the International Geophysical Year' (1957), 4 *Bulletin of the Institute for the Study of the USSR*, 3.

O.J. Pettingill, 'People and Penguins of the Faraway Falklands' (1956), *National Geographic*, 387.

D. Pharand, 'Soviet Union Warns United States Against Use of Northeast Passage' (1968), 62 AJIL, 927.

_____, 'The Legal Status of Ice Shelves and Ice Islands in the Arctic' (1969), 10 *Les Cahiers de Droit*, 463.

_____, 'State Jurisdiction over Ice Island T-3; The *Escamilla* Case' (1971), 24 *Arctic*, 83.

D.H. Pimlott, 'The Hazardous Search for Oil and Gas in Arctic Waters' (1974), 4 (3) *Nature Canada*, 20.

N. Potter, 'Economic Potential of the Antarctic' (1969), 4 (3) Antarctic Journal, 61.

E. Pruck, 'Die Sowjets in der Antarktis' (1958), 8 *Osteuropa*, 658.

S. Rakusa-Suszczewski, 'Preliminary Report from the first Polish Marine Research Antarctic Expedition on the R/V *Professor Siedlecki* and the M/S *Tazar*' (August 1976), International Conference on Living Resources of the Southern Ocean, Woods Hole.

R.O. Ramseier, 'Oil on Ice' (1974), 16 (4) *Environment*, 7.

J.S. Reeves, 'Antarctic Sectors' (1939) 33 AJIL, 519.

I.L.M. Richardson, 'New Zealand's Claims in the Antarctic' (1957), *NZLJ*, 38.

F.V. Rigler, 'Navy's continuing commitment in Antarctica' (June 1975), *U.S. Naval Institute Proceedings*, 101.

B. Roberts, 'Chronological list of Antarctic Expeditions' (1958), 9 (59) *Polar Record*, 97.

_____, 'Conservation in the Antarctic' (1977), 279 *Phil. Trans. R. Lond. B.*, 97.

_____, 'International Co-operation for Antarctic Development: the Test for the Antarctic Treaty' (1978), 19 (119) *Polar Record*, 107.

I.M. Roggen, 'La position juridique des Belges en Antarctique' (1960), 11 *Aile et Roue*, 9.

D.A. Schmeiser, 'Indians, Eskimos and the Law' (1968) 33 *Saskatchewan Law Review*, 19.

J.B. Scott, 'Arctic Exploration and International Law' (1909) 3, *AJIL*, 928.

_____, 'The Swiss Decision in the Boundary Dispute between Colombia and Venezuela' (1922), 16 *AJIL*, 428.

D. Sears, 'Rocks on the Ice' (22 March 1979), *New Scientist,* 961.

D. Shapley, 'Antarctic Problems: Tiny Krill to Usher in New Resource Era' (1977), *Science*, 503.

E.M. Silverstein, 'United States Jurisdiction: Crimes Committed on Ice Islands' (1971), 51 *Boston University Law Review*, 77.

K.R. Simmonds, 'The Antarctic Treaty, 1959' (1960), 7 *Journal du Droit International* 668.

J. Simsarian, 'The Acquisition of Legal Title to Terra Nullius' (1938), 53 *Political Science Quarterly*, 111.

_____, 'Inspection Experience under the Antarctic Treaty and the International Atomic Energy Agency' (1966), 60 *AJIL*, 502.

G. Skagestad, 'The Frozen Frontier-Models for International Co-operation' (1975), 10 *Co-operation and Conflict*, 167.

F. Sollie, 'The Political Experiment in Antarctica' (1970), 26 (10) *Science and Public Affairs*, 16.

_____, 'The Legal Status of the Antarctic' (1976), MS, 12.

J. Spivak, 'Frozen Assets?' *Wall Street Journal* 21 February 1974.

J.F. Splettstoesser, 'The Ross Shelf Project' (1977) *Nebraska Blue Print*, 10.

_____, 'Offshore Development for Oil and Gas in Antarctica' (1978), in *Proceedings of the Fourth International Conference on Port and Ocean Engineering under Arctic Conditions*, 811.

B. Stonehouse, 'Animal Conservation in Antarctica' (1965), 23 (1) *NZ Science Review*, 3.

_____, 'Counting Antarctic Animals', (29 July 1965) *New Scientist*, 273.

_____, 'Penguins in High Latitudes' (1967), 15 *Tuatara*, 129.

G.F. Stuart and M.J. Sites, 'A radio noise survey of the McMurdo Area' (1973), 8 (1) *Antarctic Journal*, 1.

W. Sullivan, 'The International Geophysical Year' (1959), 521 *International Conciliation*, 324.

O. Svarlien, 'The Sector Principle in Law and Practice' (1960–1), 10 *Polar Record*, 248.

K. Taijudo, 'Japan and the Problems of Sovereignty over the Polar Regions' (1959), 3 *Japanese Annual of International Law*, 12.

B.E. Talboys, 'New Zealand and the Antarctic Treaty' (1978), 28 (3) and (4) *NZ Foreign Affairs Review*, 29.

H.J. Taubenfeld, 'A Treaty for Antarctica' (Jan. 1961), 531 *International Conciliation*, 245.

_____, 'The Antarctic Treaty of 1959' (1964), 2 (2) *Disarmament and Arms Control*, 136.

R.B. Thomson, 'United States and New Zealand Cooperation in Environmental Protection' (1971), 6 (3) *Antarctic Journal*, 59.

B. Tierney, ' "Mr. Justice" in the North' (1971), 2 (3) *Journal of the Canadian Bar Association*, 1.

J. Tinker, 'Antarctica: towards a new internationalism' (13 September 1979), *New Scientist*, 799.

_____, 'Cold War over Antarctic wealth' (20 September 1979) *New Scientist*, 867.

Y. Tolstikov, 'Drifting over the Arctic' (1968), *Geographical Journal*, 1058.

P.A. Toma, 'Soviet Attitude toward the Acquisition of Territorial Sovereignty in the Antarctic' (1956), 50 *AJIL*, 611.

M.D. Turner, 'Antarctic Mineral Resources' (1978), 43 (1) *Frontiers*, 27.

T.M. Tynan, 'Canadian-American relations in the Arctic' (1979), *The Review of Politics*, 402.

C. Vallaux, 'Droits et prétentions politiques sur les régions polaires' (1932), 2 *Affaires Étrangères*, 14.

A. van der Essen, 'Le problème politico-juridique de l'Antarctique' (1960), 20 *Annales de Droit et de Sciences Politiques*, 227.

_____, 'L'Antarctique et le Droit de la Mer' (1975–6), 5–6 *Iranian Review of International Affairs*, 89.

G. Vane, 'Soviet Antarctic Research, 1972–1973' (1973), 8 (6) *Antarctic Journal*, 325.

J.E. Greño Velasco, 'La Adhesion de Brasil al Tratado Antartico' (1976), *Revista de Politica Internacional*, 71.

J.L. Verner, 'Legal Claims to Newly Emerged Islands' (1978), 15 *San Diego Law Review*, 525.

Enrique Gajardo Villarroel, 'Brasil y la Antártida Sudamericana', *El Mercurio*, 1 March 1973.

_____, 'Apuntes para un libro sobre la Historia Diplomática del Tratado Antártico y de la participación chilena en su elaboración' (1977), 10 *Revista de difusión INACH*, 40.

I. von Münch, 'Völkerrechtsfragen der Antarktis' (1958), 7 *Archiv des Völkerrechts*, 225.

F.A. Wade, 'Geological Survey of Ruppert-Hobbs Coasts sector, Marie Byrd Land' (1978), 13 (4) *Antarctic Journal*, 4.

P. Wadhams, 'Oil and Ice in the Beaufort Sea' (1976), 18 (114) *Polar Record*, 237.

C.H.M. Waldock, 'Disputed Sovereignty in the Falkland Islands Dependencies' (1948), 25 *BYBIL*, 311.

R. Waultrin, 'La Question de la Souveraineté des Terres Arctiques' (1908),

15 *Revue Général de Droit International Public*, 78.

J.H. Weir, 'New Zealand in the Antarctic' (1964), 5 (8) *Bulletin of the US Antarctic Projects Officer*, 6.

I.M. Whillans, 'Radio-echo layers and the recent stability of the West Antarctic ice sheet' (1976), 264 *Nature*, 153.

S.C. Whitney, 'Regulation of Federal Decision Making Affecting the Environment outside the United States' (1980), 3 *GMU Law Review*, 62.

D. Wilkes, 'Law for Special Environments: Ice Islands and Questions raised by the T-3 Case' (1972), 16 (100) *Polar Record*, 23.

O. Wilkes, 'Antarctica: The New Frontier' (1974) 20 *Canta*, n.p.

_____, and R. Mann, 'The story of Nukey Poo' (October 1978), *Science and Public Affairs*, 32.

G.J. Wilson, 'Oiled Penguins in Antarctica' (1979), 2 (2) *NZ Antarctic Record*, 3.

G.P. Wilson, 'Antarctica, the Southern Ocean and the Law of the Sea' (1978), 30 *JAG Journal*, 47.

R.E. Wilson, 'National Interests and Claims in the Antarctic' (1964), 17 (1) *Arctic*, 15.

S. Wolk, 'The Basis of Soviet Claims in the Antarctic' (1958), 5 *Bulletin of the Institute for the Study of the USSR*, 43.

R.D. Yoder, 'United States inspects four Peninsula stations' (1975), 10 (3) *Antarctic Journal*, 92.

F. Zegers, 'El Sistema Antártico y la Utilización de los Recursos' (1978), 33 *University of Miami Law Rev.*, 426.

W.J. Zinsmeister, 'Effect of formation of the west antarctic ice sheet on shallow water marine faunas of Chile' (1978), 13 (4) *Antarctic Journal*, 25.

J.H. Zumberge, 'Mineral Resources and Geopolitics in Antarctica' (1979), 67 *American Scientist*, 68.

Official Publications

1. *Antarctic Treaty Consultative Meetings*
ANT/4 (19th October 1970).
ANT/41 (10 June 1975).
ANT/INF/4 (10 June 1975).
ANT/INF/22 (19 June 1975).
ANT/IX/42 (26 September 1977).
ANT/IX/INF 13 (28 September 1977).
ANT/IX/75 (29 September 1977).
ANT/IX/84 (7 October 1977).
'Antarctic Mineral Resources' RPS – 10 (1976).
Conditions Governing Visits to the Argentine Sector of Antarctica, ANT/33 (13 June 1975).
Final Report of the Sixth Antarctic Treaty Consultative Meeting (1970).
Final Report of the Seventh Antarctic Treaty Consultative Meeting (1972).
Final Report of the Eighth Antarctic Treaty Consultative Meeting (1975).
Final Report of the Special Antarctic Treaty Consultative Meeting (July 1977).
Final Report of the Ninth Antarctic Treaty Consultative Meeting (1977).
Final Report of the Tenth Antarctic Treaty Consultative Meeting (1979).
France, 'Petroleum Production in Antarctic Offshore Conditions' ANT/IX/17 (19 September 1977).
Interim Report of the Second Special Consultative Meeting, Canberra (1978).
Report of the Working Group of Experts on Mineral Exploration and Exploitation, ANT/IX/51 (Rev I) (29 September 1977).

2. *SCAR*
Group of Specialists on Living Resources of the Southern Ocean, *Biological Investigations of Marine Antarctic Systems and Stocks (BIOMASS)*, Vol. I (1977).
Group of Specialists on the Environmental Impact Assessment of Mineral Resource Exploration/Exploitation in Antarctica (EAMREA), *A Preliminary Assessment of the Environmental Impact of Mineral Exploration/Exploitation in Antarctica* (1977).
Group of Delegates, Eleventh Meeting of SCAR (October 1970) in (1971). 37 SCAR Bulletin, 775.
SCAR Manual (1972) (2nd ed.) Cambridge.
SCAR Working Group on Biology, Report of Thirteenth Meeting of SCAR (1975) 49 SCAR Bulletin 69.
Report of the Meeting of Delegates (October 1976), XIV – SCAR – 30 (Revised) in 368 SCAR Circular (3 December 1976).
SCAR Constitution, 367 SCAR Circular (16 December 1976).
376 SCAR Circular (12 May 1977).
381 SCAR Circular (n.d. issued in 1977).
Summary of BIOMASS Prepared by SCAR/SCOR Working Group 54,

ANT IX/10 (14 September 1977).
386 SCAR Circular (15 December 1977).
XV – SCAR – 10 (Revised) (May 1978) in 397 SCAR Circular (3 July 1978).
XV – SCAR – 32 (Revised) (May 1978) in 397 SCAR Circular (3 July 1978).
398 SCAR Circular (3 July 1978).
409 SCAR Circular (22 July 1979).
J.H. Zumberge (ed.), *Possible Environmental Effects of Mineral Exploration and Exploitation in Antarctica* (1979).

3. *United Nations*

Note by the Secretary-General, 'Natural Resources Information and Documentation: General Issues,' U.N. Doc. E/C.7/5 (25 Jan 1971).
Summary Records of the Committee on Natural Resources, U.N. Doc. E/C. 7/SR. 12 – 29 (2 March 1971).
U.N. Doc. A/8368 (27 August 1971).
U.N. Doc. A/AC. 109/482 (28 March 1975).
U.N. Doc. A/10023/Add 8 (Part III) (31 October 1975).
U.N. Doc. A/31/55 (24 February 1976).
U.N. Doc. A/AC.109/520 (7 May 1976).
Informal Composite Negotiating Text U.N. Doc. A/Conf. 62/WP.10/ Rev. 2 (11 April 1980).

4. *U.S. Congressional Hearings*

'Antarctic Living Marine Resources Negotiations', Hearing, National Ocean Policy Study, Committee on Commerce, Science and Transportation, Senate, 95th Cong., 2nd Sess. (1978).
'Antarctica Legislation – 1961' Hearings, Subcommittee on Territorial and Insular Affairs, Committee on Interior and Insular Affairs, H. Rep. 87th Cong., 1st Sess. (1962).
'Antarctic Report – 1965' Hearings, Subcommittee on Territorial and Insular Affairs, H. Rep. 89th Cong., 1st Sess. (1965).
'Exploitation of Antarctic Resources', Hearing, Subcommittee on Arms Control, Oceans and International Environment, Committee on Foreign Relations, Senate, 95th Cong., 2nd Sess. (1978).
'Extraterritorial Criminal Jurisdiction', Hearing, Subcommittee on Immigration, Citizenship and International Law, Committee on the Judiciary, H. Rep., 95th Cong., 1st Sess. (1977).
'Fish and Wildlife Legislation, Part 4', Hearings, Subcommittee on Fisheries and Wildlife Conservation, Committee on Merchant Marine and Fisheries, H. Rep., 92nd Cong., 2nd Sess. (1972).
'Fish and Wildlife Miscellaneous, Part I', Hearings, Subcommittee on Fisheries and Wildlife Conservation and the Environment, Committee on Merchant Marine and Fisheries, H. Rep., 95th Cong., 1st Sess. (1977).
'The Antarctic Treaty' Hearings, Committee on Foreign Relations, Senate, 86th Cong., 2nd Sess. (1960).
'U.S. Activities in Antarctica' Hearing, Committee on Energy and Natural Resources, Senate, 96th Cong., 1st Sess. (1979).

'U.S. Antarctic Policy', Hearing, Subcommittee on Oceans and International Environment, Committee on Foreign Relations, Senate, 94th Cong., 1st Sess. (1975).
'U.S. Antarctic Program', Hearings, Subcommittee on Science, Research and Technology, Committee on Science and Technology, H. Reps., 96th Cong., 1st Sess. (1979).

5. *Other U.S. Government documents*

Area Development Plan, Hut Point Peninsula (July 1965).
Arms Control and Disarmament Agency and Department of State, *Report of the 1971 Antarctic Inspection* (1971).
H. Bullis, *The Political Legacy of the International Geophysical Year* (1973).
Central Intelligence Agency, *Polar Regions Atlas* (1979).
Commander, Naval Support Force, Antarctica, Instruction 11010.2A (22 December 1975).
Congressional Quarterly (12 May 1979) 902.
Congressional Record (8 August 1960) 15981.
Congressional Research Service, *Soviet Oceans Development* (1976).
Custody Arrangement for Occupance and Use of Certain United States Government – Navy Department Facilities at Ellsworth Station, Antarctica (2 February 1959).
Department of State Press Release (28 August 1948).
Department of State, *Conference on Antarctica* (1960).
Department of State, *Environmental Impact Statement on the Convention for the Conservation of Antarctic Seals* (1974).
Department of State, *Draft Environmental Impact Statement for a Possible Regime for Conservation of Antarctic Living Marine Resources* (1978).
Department of State, *Final Environmental Impact Statement for a Possible Regime for Conservation of Antarctic Living Marine Resources* (1978).
Historical Studies Division, Department of State, *United States Antarctic Policy and International Cooperation in Antarctica* (1964).
Minutes of McMurdo Land Management and Conservation Board Meeting (21 January 1976).
Minutes of McMurdo Land Management and Conservation Board Meeting (8 February 1979).
National Academy of Sciences, *Antarctic Glaciology* (1974).
National Academy of Sciences, *Upper-Atmosphere Physics Research in the Antarctic* (1974).
National Research Council, *Antarctic Geology and Solid-Earth Geophysics* (1974).
National Science Foundation. *U.S. Antarctic Program Draft Environmental Impact Statement* (1979).
National Science Foundation, *U.S. Antarctic Program Final Environmental Impact Statement* (1980).
Report of Operation Deep Freeze (1965).
Report of Operation Deep Freeze (1969).
Report of Operation Deep Freeze (1976).
Senate Committee on Foreign Relations, *Report on the Convention on the*

Conservation of Antarctic Seals, Executive Rept. No.94–35 (3 September 1976).

U.S. Arms Control and Disarmament Agency, *Report of the 1975 United States Antarctic Inspection* (1975).

U.S. Naval Construction Battalion Reconnaissance Unit, *Applied Construction Feasibility Study, Marble Point, Antarctica* (1958).

U.S. Naval Support Force, Antarctica, *Introduction to Antarctica* (1967).

U.S. Naval Support Force, Antarctica, *Support for Science: Antarctica* (1968).

6. *Various*

J. Bernier *Report on the Dominion of Canada Government Expedition to the Arctic Islands and Hudson Strait* (1910).

J. Capelle, Explanatory Memorandum, Consultative Assembly, Council of Europe, Doc. 3257 (29 January 1973).

Central Office of Information, 'The Falkland Islands and Dependencies' (September 1968).

Central Office of Information, *The Antarctic* (1966).

Debates, House of Lords (18 February 1960), 182.

Department of Foreign Affairs (Australia), *Documents relating to Antarctica* (1976).

Department of Scientific and Industrial Research (N.Z.), *Antarctic Operations Manual* (1975).

Fisheries and Environment Canada, *Probabilities of Blowouts in Canadian Arctic Waters* (1978).

House of Representatives Debates (Australia) (28 September 1960), 1435.

Joint Committee on Foreign Affairs, Interim Report, *Australia, Antarctica and the Law of the Sea* (1978).

W.F. King, *Report Upon the Title of Canada to the Islands North of the Mainland of Canada* (1905).

New Zealand's Gateway to the South, The Ross Dependency (1962).

Note of Polish Ministry of Foreign Affairs to States Parties to the Antarctic Treaty (2 March 1977).

Note from the Canadian Embassy to the Department of State (5 May 1971).

N.Z. Antarctic Research Programme, *Antarctic Field Manual* (1978).

Office of Air Accidents Investigation, Ministry of Transport, *Aircraft Accident Report No. 79–139* (1980).

Parliamentary Assembly, Council of Europe, 'Report on the Exercise in Scientific Cooperation: Situation and Prospects', Doc. 3840 (15 September 1976).

R.C.M.P. *Canadian Sovereignty in the Arctic* (n.d.).

Report of the Advisory Committee on Antarctic Programs (Australia), Vol. III *Automatic Stations: Past Experience and Future Applications* (1974).

Senate Debates, (Australia) (25 September 1979), 910.

Senate Debates (Canada) (20 February 1907), 271.

Whales and Whaling, Report of the Independent Inquiry conducted by Sir Sydney Frost, Vol. I (1978).

INDEX